Essays in Panel Data Econometrics

This volume collects seven of Marc Nerlove's previously published, classic essays on panel data econometrics written over the past thirty-five years, together with a cogent new essay on the history of the subject, which began with George Biddell Airey's monograph published in 1861. Since Professor Nerlove's 1966 *Econometrica* paper with Pietro Balestra, panel data and methods of econometric analysis appropriate to such data have become increasingly important in the discipline. The principal factors in the research environment affecting the future course of panel data econometrics are the phenomenal growth in the computational power available to the individual researcher at his or her desktop and the ready availability of data sets, both large and small, via the Internet. The best way to formulate statistical models for inference is motivated and shaped by substantive problems and our understanding of the processes generating the data at hand to resolve them. The essays illustrate both the role of the substantive context in shaping appropriate methods of inference and the increasing importance of computer-intensive methods.

Marc Nerlove is Professor of Agricultural and Resource Economics at the University of Maryland, College Park. After receiving his doctorate from Johns Hopkins University, he began his teaching career at the University of Minnesota and subsequently served as a professor at Stanford, Harvard, and Yale universities, the University of Chicago, Northwestern University, and the University of Pennsylvania. The winner in 1969 of the John Bates Clark Medal of the American Economic Association, awarded to the most outstanding economist in the United States under age 40, Professor Nerlove is a Fellow of the American Academy of Arts and Sciences and the American Statistical Association, a member of the National Academy of Sciences, and a Fellow of the Econometric Society, serving as the Society's president in 1981. He is the author or coauthor of more than two hundred articles in leading journals and six other books and is working on a monograph on *Likelihood Inference in Econometrics*. Professor Nerlove has twice held Guggenheim and Fulbright Fellowships and has received honorary doctorates from the Universities of Geneva and Mannheim.

Further Praise for *Essays in Panel Data Econometrics*

"Marc Nerlove has been a pioneer in many important econometric models, especially the panel data models discussed in this book. His seminal paper with Balestra and the two follow-up papers have had a great impact on the econometricians and led to a rapid growth of the analysis of panel data. Nerlove's research is characterized by the thorough analysis and the keen insight that cut through apparently impregnable problems and has been singularly successful in the analysis of panel data, which presents a host of complicated statistical issues. Everyone interested in panel data will welcome this volume, in which Nerlove has newly written a characteristically thorough survey of the area and put together his previously published articles, some of which are not so easily accessible."

– Takeshi Amemiya, *Stanford University*

"Marc Nerlove's history of panel data econometrics is a welcome contribution to narrowing the gap between econometric theory and empirical practice. His thought-provoking account of the early developments in fixed nd random effects models masterfully brings together economic and statical considerations. It will certainly not leave readers indifferent. This 'ume also brings together Nerlove's pioneering articles on dynamic ran-ı effects models, and his more recent reflections on empirical country th analysis, likelihood inference, and panel data methodology. The parts together become a valuable reference source and give us a ehensive picture of the working of a very influential mind in the of the field of panel data econometrics."

– Manuel Arellano, *CEMFI, Spain*

Essays in Panel Data Econometrics

MARC NERLOVE

University of Maryland, College Park

CAMBRIDGE UNIVERSITY PRESS
Cambridge, New York, Melbourne, Madrid, Cape Town, Singapore, São Paulo

Cambridge University Press
The Edinburgh Building, Cambridge CB2 2RU, UK

Published in the United States of America by Cambridge University Press, New York

www.cambridge.org
Information on this title: www.cambridge.org/9780521815345

First published 2002
This digitally printed first paperback version 2005

A catalogue record for this publication is available from the British Library

ISBN-13 978-0-521-81534-5 hardback
ISBN-10 0-521-81534-7 hardback

ISBN-13 978-0-521-02246-0 paperback
ISBN-10 0-521-02246-0 paperback

For Anke Sofia Meyer

Contents

Preface to the Book

The econometrics of longitudinal or panel data sets and of cross sections over time, even if not strictly longitudinal, has become a "growth industry" in the broader econometric context, in terms of both development of new econometric tools and methods and numerous applied studies.

Observations on many individual economic units (firms, households, geographical areas, and the like) over a period of time are said to be a "panel data set." For example, in Balestra and Nerlove (1966, reprinted in this volume), data on thirty-six states over a thirteen-year period were used in the analysis. Panel data may be contrasted with pure *cross-section data*, observations on individual units at a point in time, and with pure time-series data, observations, usually of an aggregate nature, over time without any "longitudinal" dimension. For some purposes, it may be useful to view a cross section as a panel with time dimension 1. Panel data are sometimes treated as "cross sections over time" or "pooled" cross section time-series data, but this terminology leaves open the question of whether the cross sections over time refer to identical individuals or not.[1]

Panel data offer several important advantages over data sets with only a temporal or a longitudinal dimension. First, more observations are generally available than with conventional time-series data, although cross-section data sets are often very large.

Second, because panel data are not so highly aggregated as typical time series and because, in the best of circumstances, we observe the same individual units through time, more complicated dynamic and behavioral hypotheses can be tested than those that can be tested using unidimensional data. In the preface to Chapter 1, I argue that economic behavior is inherently dynamic so

---

[1] Verbeek (1996) gives a useful survey of methods used to treat repeated cross sections, not necessarily involving the same individuals. Although this is clearly a part of panel data econometrics, none of the essays in this volume deal with such methods.

that most econometrically interesting relationships are explicitly or implicitly dynamic.[2]

Finally, the use of panel data may also provide a means for analyzing more fully the nature of the latent, or unobserved, disturbance terms in the econometric relationships. These disturbances are supposed to measure the effects of all sorts of left-out factors and, as such, may frequently be subject to the objection that some of them are correlated with the included explanatory variables. Not only do panel data frequently provide the opportunity for introducing many more explanatory variables and more complicated dynamics, but they also permit us to model more explicitly the latent disturbances themselves as components common to all individuals at a point in time and as time-persistent components.

Panel data need not be restricted to two dimensions, one of which is time: for example, many types of cross-sectional survey data are obtained through "cluster" sampling. Certain geographical units are first selected (e.g., villages), then individuals are sampled within each village. Thus, the village from which an individual observation comes may be thought of as one dimension of the data just as in a traditional panel the time period associated with an observation on an individual is a dimension of the data. It follows that panel data methods are of special importance in research in developing countries, which may not have a long tradition of statistical data collection and for which, therefore, it is generally necessary to obtain original survey data to answer many significant and important questions. But it undoubtedly remains true that the most important use of panel data and methods is in the analysis of dynamic models of behavior over time. The analysis of such models is a great deal more complicated than of static models and, for this reason, the essays in this book are devoted primarily to the study of likelihood inference for dynamic panel models.

While it is impossible to do full justice to the now vast literature on panel data econometrics, there are several sources that may be consulted: Maddala (1993) is a compendium of classic and recent (up to 1992) papers on panel data econometrics. Hsiao (1986) surveys models and methods up to 1985 and contains much original material. Baltagi (1995) is not only a text devoted solely to panel data econometrics, but also a fine survey with many original contributions. An important and comprehensive compendium of original papers, now in its second edition, is Mátyás and Sevestre (1996). It comes as close to an encyclopedic treatment as may be possible at this time.

---

[2] The dynamic component is not always obvious. For example, any relationship that involves a stock or a flow based on a stock, which is, in turn, a result of the past decisions we are trying to explain or related to them, will constitute a dynamic element of greater or lesser importance than the behavior modeled. A particularly insidious example is family size and composition in cross-section studies of farm households, in which past fertility decisions and decisions to invest in the health and nutrition of children partly determine demographic variation across families at a given time.

The essays contained in this volume represent my work on panel data econometrics, beginning with a long historical essay on the development of methods for the analysis of panel data from their inception in the 1861 work of George Biddell Airy down to and including the Paris Conference of 1997 on panel data econometrics (Sevestre, 1999). This essay is published here for the first time. Several nonhistorical, substantive appendixes are included to make the historical presentation of the text more comprehensible. In them, I deal with the decomposition of panel data observations, alternative formulations of the concentrated likelihood function, the derivation of the likelihood function for the three-component random-effects nondynamic model with serially correlated period-specific effects, and the likelihood function for stationary panel data-generating processes. I have also included as an appendix, with permission of the publisher, an edited version of my introduction to the proceedings of the 1977 Paris Conference, which marked the beginning of a period of intense research on panel data econometrics. This appendix gives a detailed summary of the papers presented there, many of which were seminal.

The remaining essays, all previously published, appear in chronological order of their writing, which does not correspond exactly to their dates of publication. I begin with the 1966 paper by Balestra and me and continue with two follow-up Monte Carlo studies of the curious results we encountered in the 1966 paper. A paper on the decomposition of panel data observations written at that time follows. Although the 1977 introduction to the proceedings of the 1977 Paris Conference was written in the intervening years, the remaining three papers, written in the 1990s, deal with the elaboration of the likelihood function for the case of dynamic stationary models and the application of likelihood techniques to the study of growth convergence and related problems using cross-country panels.

I am especially indebted to Patrick Sevestre for his encouragement to return to the study of the methods of panel data econometrics and to pursue this often difficult topic. His input and that of Alain Trognon were essential to this work. Of course, I owe a special debt to Pietro Balestra who started me off on this intellectual odyssey and with whom I had more recently a great deal of interchange on the topic of panel data econometrics, beginning with our introductions to the first and second editions of the Mátyás-Sevestre volume. I acknowledge with thanks the helpful comments of my colleagues Bob Chambers and Bruce Gardner. Finally, I gratefully acknowledge the financial support of the Maryland Agricultural Experiment Station in the preparation of this volume and in the writing of the first essay. Acknowledgments to those who have contributed to the various essays reprinted are given in each. Here I want to thank especially Anke Sofia Meyer for her help and encouragement throughout my work on many of the essays presented here and the book as a whole.

References

Balestra, P., and M. Nerlove (1966), "Pooling Cross-Section and Time-Series Data in the Estimation of a Dynamic Model: The Demand for Natural Gas," *Econometrica, 34*: pp. 585–612.

Baltagi, B. H. (1995), *Econometric Analysis of Panel Data*, New York: Wiley.

Hsiao, C. (1986), *Analysis of Panel Data*, Cambridge, UK: Cambridge University Press.

Maddala, G. S., ed. (1993), *The Econometrics of Panel Data*, Aldershot: Edward Elgar Publishing.

Mátyás, L., and P. Sevestre, Eds. (1996), *The Econometrics of Panel Data, 2nd Ed.*, Dortrecht: Kluwer Academic Publishers.

Sevestre, P., ed. (1999), Special Issue on Panel Data Econometrics, *Annales dÉconomie et de la Statistique*, pp. 55–56.

Verbeek, M. (1996), "Pseudo Panel Data," in Mátyás and Sevestre, pp. 280–292.

ONE

The History of Panel Data Econometrics, 1861–1997

Preface

In his famous and influential monograph, *The Probability Approach in Econometrics*, Haavelmo (1944) laid the foundations for the formulation of *stochastic* econometric models and an approach that has dominated our discipline to this day. He wrote:

> ... *we shall find that two individuals, or the same individual in two different time periods, may be confronted with exactly the same set of specified influencing factors [and, hence, they have the same y*, ...], and still the two individuals may have different quantities y, neither of which may be equal to y. We may try to remove such discrepancies by introducing more "explaining" factors, x. But, usually, we shall soon exhaust the number of factors which could be considered as common to all individuals, and which, at the same time, were not merely of negligible influence upon y. The discrepancies y – y* for each individual may depend upon a great variety of factors, these factors may be different from one individual to another, and they may vary with time for each individual.* (Haavelmo, 1944, p. 50).

And further that:

> ... *the class of populations we are dealing with does not consist of an infinity of different individuals, it consists of an infinity of possible decisions which might be taken with respect to the value of y.*
>
> ... *we find justification for applying them [stochastic approximations] to economic phenomena also in the fact we usually deal only with – and are interested only in – total or average effects of many individual decisions, which are partly guided by common factors, partly by individual specific factors* ... (Haavelmo, 1944, pp. 51 and 56).

Marschak (1950) and (1953) further amplified Haavelmo's themes in his introduction to Cowles Commission Monographs 10 and 14, observing that: The numerous causes that determine the error incurred ... are not listed separately; instead their joint effect is represented by the probability distribution of the error, a random variable (1950, p. 18) [, which] ... is called 'disturbance' or 'shock,' and can be regarded as the joint effect of numerous separately insignificant variables that we are unable or unwilling to specify but presume to be independent of observable exogenous variables. (1953, p. 12).

Since the early work of Mundlak (1961) and Balestra and Nerlove (1966), panel or longitudinal data have become increasingly important in econometrics, and methods for the analysis of such data have generated a vast literature, the history of which is selectively recounted in the essay that follows. A recurrent theme in this historical essay is the interpretation of what is not observed; that is, the disturbances in the relationships about which we wish to draw inferences and the proper interpretation of these disturbances. In the beginning, Sir George Biddell Airy's 1861 monograph on astronomical observations made essentially the same point.

The stochastic elements in the analysis, which are reflected in the unobserved variables characterizing individual heterogeneity and heterogeneity of individual decisions, lie at the heart of econometric analysis. Some conclusions that may be drawn from the historical overview presented in this essay are as follows:

(a) One of the main reasons for being interested in panel data is the unique possibility of uncovering disaggregate dynamic relationships using such data sets.
(b) In a dynamic context, one of the primary reasons for heterogeneity among individuals is the different history that each has.
(c) If the relevant "population" is, following Haavelmo, the space of possible decisions, different past histories take the form of individual specific random variables that are generally correlated with all of the variables taken as explanatory, not just the lagged values of the endogenous variable. The former, therefore, cannot be conditioned upon in the usual way.

History is important, not only because

> "Whereof what's past is prologue, what's to come, . . ."
> *The Tempest, II, i,* 247

but also because

> "Those who cannot remember the past are condemned to repeat it."
> George Santayana, *The Life of Reason, Vol. 1*, 1905.

References

Airy, G. B. (1861), *On the Algebraical and Numerical Theory of Errors of Observations and the Combination of Observations*, Cambridge: Macmillan.

Balestra, P., and M. Nerlove (1966), "Pooling Cross-Section and Time-Series Data in the Estimation of a Dynamic Economic Model: The Demand for Natural Gas," *Econometrica*, 34: pp. 585–612.

Haavelmo, T. (1944), "The Probability Approach in Econometrics," *Supplement to Econometrica*, 12.

Marschak, J. (1950), "Statistical Inference in Economics: An Introduction," in *Statistical Inference in Dynamic Economic Models*, T. C. Koopmans (Ed.), New York: John Wiley, pp. 1–50.

Marschak, J. (1953), "Economic Measurements for Policy and Prediction," pp. 1–26 in *Studies in Econometric Method*, W. C. Hood and T. P. Koopmans, Eds., New York: John Wiley.

Mundlak, Y. (1961), "Empirical Production Functions Free of Management Bias," *Journal of Farm Economics, 43*: pp. 44–56.

The History of Panel Data Econometrics, 1861–1997[1]

Whereof what's past is prologue, what's to come, ...
The Tempest, II, i, 247

1. INTRODUCTION

I was asked a while ago to discuss the future of panel data econometrics. Being rather bad at forecasting, I took my cue from Prospero's line in *The Tempest,* quoted above, and reviewed instead the history of panel data econometrics from Hildreth (1950) down to Mátyás and Sevestre's monumental handbook (1996) and the Paris Conference of 1997. This essay is the fruit of that endeavor. Alain Trognon (2000) discusses much more fully more recent developments emphasizing more than me the internal methodological momentum of the subject. Our conclusions regarding the future, such as they are, are not greatly at variance. The future of panel data econometrics I hope for is much like its past, viewed in a long-term perspective. Our concern has been, and I hope will continue to be, with the best way to formulate statistical models for inference

[1] An earlier version of this essay was presented at the Ninth International Conference on Panel Data, June 22–23, 2000, Geneva, Switzerland, at the session on "The Future of Panel Data Econometrics." The research on which it is based was supported by the Maryland Agricultural Experiment Station.

The essay is dedicated to the memory of Zvi Griliches (1930–1999) and G. S. Maddala (1933–1999), who both contributed greatly to the development of panel data econometrics. It also marks the fiftieth anniversary of the first paper ever in panel data econometrics (Hildreth 1950), regrettably unpublished to this day.

A portion of the present survey is freely adapted from Nerlove (Chapter 19, "Analysis of Panel Data," 1999a). I am indebted to John Aldrich, Ramon Lopez, and Patrick Sevestre for helpful comments on earlier partial drafts. Anke Meyer read and commented on several earlier drafts, as well as the present one. Appendix D is based on an unpublished paper by Karlsson and Skoglund and on the work of Pietro Balestra contained in a personal communication to me.

4

motivated and shaped by substantive problems and our understanding of the processes generating the data at hand to resolve them. If the present trend toward increasing internalization pointed out by Trognon continues, however, these hopes may be unrealized. The principal factors in the research environment affecting the future course of panel data econometrics, in contrast to its past, are the phenomenal growth in the computational power available to the individual researcher at his or her desktop and the ready availability of data sets, both large and small, via the Internet. Whether these factors will lead to increasing proliferation of "special" methods applied to a few "illustrative" data sets or to a broader, more comprehensive analytical framework and the analysis of a greater variety of data, I cannot say. I also hope that increased understanding of panel data econometrics will lead to more sophisticated design of surveys for the collection of panel data, and thus to a greater variety of data appropriate for the analysis of important and relevant policy issues, although by no means a certain outcome given the present academic climate in which we work.

Observations on many individual economic units (firms, households, geographical areas, and the like) over a period of time are said to be a "panel data set." For example, in Balestra and Nerlove (1966), data on thirty-six U.S. states over a thirteen-year period were used in the analysis. Panel data may be contrasted with pure *cross-section data*, observations on individual units at a point in time, and with pure time-series data, observations, usually of an aggregate nature, over time without any "longitudinal" dimension. For some purposes, it may be useful to view a cross section as a panel with time dimension 1. Panel data are sometimes treated as "cross sections over time" or "pooled" cross-section time-series data, but this terminology leaves open the question of whether or not the cross sections over time refer to identical individuals.[2]

Panel data offer several important advantages over data sets with only a temporal or a longitudinal dimension. First, more observations are generally available than with conventional time-series data, although cross-section data sets are often very large.

Second, because panel data are not so highly aggregated as typical time-series and because, in the best of circumstances, we observe the same individual units through time, more complicated dynamic and behavioral hypotheses can be tested than those that can be tested using unidimensional data. In the next section, I argue that economic behavior is inherently dynamic so that most econometrically interesting relationships are explicitly or implicitly dynamic.[3]

---

[2] Verbeek (1996) gives a useful survey of methods used to treat repeated cross sections, not necessarily involving the same individuals, which is apropos in this context.

[3] The dynamic component is not always obvious. For example, any relationship that involves a stock or a flow based on a stock, which is, in turn, a result of the past decisions we are trying to explain or related to them, will constitute a dynamic element of greater or lesser importance to the behavior modeled. A particularly insidious example is family size and composition

Finally, the use of panel data may also provide a means for analyzing more fully the nature of the latent, or unobserved, disturbance terms in the econometric relationships. These disturbances are supposed to measure the effects of all sorts of left-out factors and, as such, may frequently be subject to the objection that some of them are correlated with the included explanatory variables. Not only do panel data frequently provide the opportunity for introducing many more explanatory variables and more complicated dynamics, but they also permit us to model more explicitly the latent disturbances themselves as components common to all individuals at a point in time and as time-persistent components. The problem of latent individual heterogeneity is the central problem in panel data econometrics.

Panel data need not be restricted to two dimensions, one of which is time: for example, many types of cross-sectional survey data are obtained through "cluster" sampling. Certain geographical units are first selected (e.g., villages), then individuals are sampled within each village. Thus, the village from which an individual observation comes may be thought of as one dimension of the data, just as in a traditional panel the time period associated with an observation on an individual is a dimension of the data. Thus, panel data methods are of special importance in research in developing countries, which may not have a long tradition of statistical data collection and for which, therefore, it is generally necessary to obtain original survey data to answer many significant and important questions. But it undoubtedly remains true that the most important use of panel data and methods is in the analysis of dynamic models of behavior over time.

In the following section, I discuss the early development of panel data statistical methods from their introduction by Airy in 1861 for the analysis of astronomical data, through the work on human heredity of Galton and Fisher, development of fixed-effects ANOVA by Fisher and his disciples, down to recent work on variance-components or random-effects models in the analysis of animal breeding experiments. In Section 3, I take up the thread in econometrics, focusing on the earliest work of Hildreth, Hoch, Mundlak, and Balestra and Nerlove, culminating in the First Paris Conference on Panel Data Econometrics of 1977. In Section 4, I continue the story more selectively dealing with the work on specification tests, dynamic models, and estimation of limited dependent panel data models during the period leading up to the twentieth anniversary conference held in Paris in 1997. Finally, I draw a somewhat pessimistic conclusion about the future of panel data econometrics based on my reading of its past history.

in cross-section studies of farm households, in which past fertility decisions and decisions to invest in the health and nutrition of children partly determine demographic variation across families at a given time.

2. IN THE BEGINNING: ASTRONOMY, AGRONOMY, AND STATISTICS

"Those who cannot remember the past are condemned to repeat it."
George Santayana, *The Life of Reason, Vol. 1*, 1905.

a. Fixed- versus Random-Effects Models

Both so-called fixed-effects models and random-effects models have a long history in statistics.[4] It is a theme that runs through the history of the subject that I emphasize in this essay.

The origins of least squares in the astronomical work of Gauss (1809) and Legendre (1805) are well known.[5] And the relation of least squares to the analysis of variance as developed by R. A. Fisher (1918, 1925) is widely appreciated. In the Gauss-Legendre formulation, the independent or explanatory variables are treated as fixed and the dependent variable as subject to error. The conventional interpretation of Fisher's formulation of the analysis of variance is as an extension of least-squares theory, but, as Eisenhart (1947) points out, this was not the only interpretation Fisher placed on his analysis. In (1925, Chapter 7, especially Section 40), Fisher interprets the *intraclass correlation* in analysis of variance terms and, in this discussion, implies a random-effects formulation. Eisenhart (1947, pp. 3–5) is the classic locus of the distinction. He writes:

... analysis of variance can be, and is, used to provide solutions to problems of two fundamentally different types. These two distinct classes of problems are:
Class I: Detection and Estimation of Fixed (Constant) Relations Among Means of Sub-Sets of the Universe of Objects Concerned. This class includes all of the usual problems of estimating and testing to determine whether to infer the existence of, true differences among "treatment" means, among "variety" means, and, under certain conditions, among "place" means. Included in this class are all the problems of univariate and multivariate regression and of harmonic analysis. With respect to problems of estimation belonging to this class, analysis of variance is simply a form of the method of least squares....
Class II: Detection and Estimation of Components of (Random) Variation Associated with a Composite Population. This class includes all problems of estimating, and testing to determine whether to infer the existence of components of variance ascribable to random deviation of the characteristics of individuals of a particular generic type from the mean values of these characteristics in the 'population' of all individuals of that generic type, etc. In this sense, *this is the true analysis of variance*, and the estimation of the respective components of the overall variance of a single observation requires further steps beyond the evaluations of the entries of

---

[4] Accounts are given, *inter alios*, by Scheffé (1956); Anderson (1978); and Searle, Casella, and McCulloch (Chapter 2, 1992).

[5] In Nerlove (Chapter 1, *The Likelihood Principle*, 1999), I retell the story emphasizing the relation of least squares to likelihood methods for the optimal combination of observations.

the analysis-of-variance table itself. Problems of this class have received considerably less attention in the literature of the analysis of variance than have problems of Class I....

...the mathematical models appropriate to problems of Class I differ from the mathematical models appropriate to problems of Class II and, consequently, so do the questions to be answered by the data.

The typical problem addressed by models of Class I is the analysis of experimental data such as occur in agronomic investigations, while the typical problem addressed by models of Class II is the analysis of nonexperimental, observational data such as are the norm in astronomical or economic investigations. Scheffé (1956) calls Class I "Model I" or the fixed-effects model, and Class II "Model II" or the "random-effects model." Often, if the effects are assumed to be independent of one another and random, Model II is the basis for an analysis of *variance components*. In the random-effects model, all effects are assumed to have zero mean, which can be enforced by assuming some fixed effects such as an overall mean. And, as usual in regression formulations, any mean may be regarded as a function of observed variables with unknown parameters. Moreover, even in a purely fixed-effects model, there is always at least one random effect called the error. In an experimental context, randomness of this error and independence from any fixed effects included is often enforced by randomizing aspects of the experiment reflecting uncontrolled variation. But in any model, some effects are always assumed random and others fixed. Scheffé (1956, pp. 254–255) writes: "We see that in formulating a model one must ask for each factor whether one is interested individually in the particular levels occurring in the experiment or primarily in a population from which the levels in an experiment can be regarded as a sample: the main effects are accordingly treated as fixed or as random. (It is conceivable that for two different purposes the same data might be analyzed according to two different models in which the same main effects are regarded as fixed or as random effects.) Interactions between several factors are naturally treated as fixed if all these factors have fixed effects and as random if one or more of these factors have random effects." It is clear that Scheffé is thinking primarily in terms of data generated by experimentation. To make the distinction between fixed and random effects clear, however, it is useful to consider two extreme examples in which the contrast between experimental and nonexperimental data is made clear.

b. An Example in Which Mostly Fixed Effects Are Appropriate

Suppose we are evaluating two varieties of high-yielding rice. We want to know how each variety responds to fertilizer application and to water availability, so we design an experiment in which each variety is planted several times over and is subjected to various determined and accurately measured levels of fertilizer and water application. At the end of the day, we measure the yield of each variety on each plot and for each combination of fertilizer and water application. If we have designed the experiment well, varieties are allocated to plots and treatments in a random manner. Clearly, there are a great many unobserved factors affecting the yields of each variety observed besides water availability and level of fertilizer application, most of which have to do with the particular plot. Suppose that we distinguish three levels of fertilizer application: low, medium, and high; and three levels of water application: low, medium, and high. The standard fixed-effects ANOVA model consists of an overall mean, a main effect for each of the factors: variety, fertilizer, and water, represented respectively by one, two, and two parameters; three bivariate interaction effects; and one trivariate interaction.[6] The treatment levels and varieties can be represented by dummy variables with appropriate restrictions, so that this ANOVA problem can be treated as a regression problem in which rice yield is the dependent variable and the observed independent variables are the dummies and various products thereof, the disturbance is assumed to be a random variable, independent of variety and treatment levels, which represents all the left-out variables associated with plot. This is the kind of problem Fisher (1925) considered in detail. The important thing to note is that variety and fertilizer and water treatment levels are fixed by the experimenter; there is no thought that they might have been selected from a larger, possibly unknown, population of varieties or levels. On the other hand, the plot effects can be considered random draws from an unknown population of unobserved plot-specific factors. In an experimental context, these effects are "controlled" by randomization.[7]

c. An Example in Which Mostly Random Effects Are Appropriate; Airy's Problem

For my next example, I turn to a quintessentially nonexperimental science, astronomy (at least it used to be so!). It is perhaps no accident that much of the early work of Gauss, Legendre, Laplace, and others of those who founded statistics was done in an astronomical context. As remarked, fixed-effect

---

[6] If there are Q variables, there are, in general, $\binom{Q}{k}$, $k = 1, \ldots, Q$ main and interaction effects. If all of them are present, the model is called saturated. If each variable is categorical, as is the case in the example, it does not require the number of parameters equal to the product of the number of categories for each variable included in an interaction to represent that effect, but a considerably lesser number since the ANOVA restrictions imply that the unconstrained parameter values sum to zero over any index. In the case discussed, for example, there are only two parameters required for each main effect, but four for each bivariate interaction, and eight for the single trivariate interaction. See Nerlove and Press (1978, 1986).

[7] This was not always so. Fisher's battles with the experimental establishment to introduce randomization into experimental design, which had been heretofore systematic, are described in detail in Box (1978, pp. 140–166).

models have their origin in the work on least squares of Gauss and Legendre, who were concerned with the optimal combination of astronomical observations, but the random-effects or variance-components models also originated in the attempts of nineteenth-century astronomers to make sense of their observations. In a monograph published in 1861, George Biddell Airy makes explicit use of a variance-component model for the analysis of astronomical panel data.[8] Here is how (1861, p. 92) Airy puts the problem (note that what Airy calls a *Constant Error*, we would call a random day effect):

When successive series of observations are made, day after day, of the same measurable quantity, which is either invariable ... or admits of being reduced by calculation to an invariable quantity ...; and when every known instrumental correction has been applied (as for zero, for effect of temperature upon the scale, etc.); still it will sometimes be found that the result obtained on one day differs from the result obtained on another day by a larger quantity than could have been anticipated, the idea then presents itself, that possibly there has been on some one day or on every day, some cause, special to the day, which has produced a *Constant Error* in the measures of that day. It is our business now to consider the evidence for, and the treatment of, such constant error.

Continuing (pp. 93–94), Airy writes:

First, it ought, in general, to be established that there is possibility of error, constant on one day but varying from day to day.... suppose ... that we have measured the apparent diameter of Jupiter. It is evident that both atmospheric and personal circumstances may sensibly alter the measure; and here we may admit the possibility of the error.... Now let us take the observations of each day separately, and ... investigate from each separate day the probable error of a single measure. We may expect to find different values (the mere paucity of observations will sufficiently explain the difference); but as the different observations on the different days either are equally good, or (as well as we can judge) have such a difference in merit that we can approximately assign the proportion of their probable errors, we can define the value of error for observations of the standard quality as determined from the observations of each day; and combining these with greater weight for the deductions from the more numerous observations, we shall have the final value of the probable error of each observation not containing the effects of the Constant Error.

[8] Reference to and a brief discussion of Airy's work (1861) are found in Scheffé (1956), who credits Churchill Eisenhart for the reference. George Biddell Airy was born July 27, 1801, at Alnwick, Northumberland, England, and died six months short of his ninety-first birthday at Greenwich, England, on January 2, 1892. He went down to Cambridge to study mathematics, becoming successively Senior Wrangler in 1823, Fellow of Trinity College in 1824, and Lucasian Professor of Mathematics in 1826, a professorship once held by Isaac Newton. He was appointed Astronomer Royal of England and Director of the Royal Observatory at Greenwich in 1835, a post he held until 1881. He was knighted by Queen Victoria in 1872. Although the Greenwich meridian, Longitude 0°, had been used by seafarers since 1767 as a reference point for time and longitude (Sobel, 1995, p. 166), it was Airy's precise measurement of the location of the meridian by means of an instrument he invented that made it the universal standard.

Airy goes on, on subsequent pages, to develop verbally the following model: Let us observe the phenomenon, say the apparent diameter of Jupiter, on I nights, with J_i observations being made the ith night. Let the measurement be y_{ij}; then

$$y_{ij} = \mu + \delta_i + \varepsilon_{ij}, \quad j = 1, \ldots, J_i, \quad i = 1, \ldots, I, \tag{1}$$

where μ is the "true" value, and $\{\delta_i\}$ and $\{\varepsilon_{ij}\}$ are random effects with the following interpretation: δ_i is what Airy calls the Constant Error associated with day i, what we would call the "day effect"; that is, the atmospheric and personal circumstances peculiar to the ith night, and ε_{ij} is all the rest, or the errors about the conditional mean, $\mu + \delta_i$, on the ith night. He assumes that the ε_{ij} and δ_i are each independently and identically distributed and independent of each other and have zero means. Let the variances of δ and of ε be σ_δ^2 and σ_ε^2, respectively, and suppose, for simplicity, J equals numbers of observations each night (a balanced panel). To make his point, Airy wants to reject the hypothesis that $\sigma_\delta^2 = 0$. He computes an estimate of the "within" variance for each night i as

$$\hat{\sigma}_{\varepsilon,i}^2 = \frac{1}{J-1} \sum_{j=1}^{J} (y_{ij} - \bar{y}_{i.})^2,$$

and then takes the arithmetic mean of the square roots to estimate the root of σ_ε^2:

$$\hat{\sigma}_\varepsilon^2 = \left(\frac{1}{I} \sum_{i=1}^{I} \sqrt{\hat{\sigma}_{\varepsilon,i}^2} \right)^2.$$

To estimate σ_δ^2 Airy uses not the between-nights sum of squares, but rather the corresponding mean absolute deviation:

$$d = \frac{1}{I} \sum_{i=1}^{I} |\bar{y}_{i.} - \bar{y}_{..}|.$$

He then calculates an approximate probable error for d from a standardized normal by replacing σ_ε^2 by $\hat{\sigma}_\varepsilon^2$ and μ by $\bar{y}$... The calculated value of d being larger than this value, Airy rejects the hypothesis of no night effect. If the details of Airy's analysis seem a bit clumsy from a modern point of view, the spirit of his model and calculations are surprisingly up-to-date.

Only a few years later, William Chauvenet (1863) published the first edition of his two-volume text in spherical astronomy, which became the standard reference work until the end of the century.[9] His calculations of the probable

---

[9] William Chauvenet (1820–1870) was professor of mathematics at the U.S. Naval Academy in Annapolis from its founding in 1845 until his departure for Washington University in St. Louis in 1859, where he ultimately became Chancellor of the University. His book, *A Manual of*

error of transit observations (1863; fifth edition, 1889, pp. 194–200) uses the estimate

$$\text{Var}(\bar{y}..) = \frac{1}{I}\left(\hat{\sigma}_\delta^2 + \frac{1}{J}\hat{\sigma}_\varepsilon^2\right).$$

Clearly the random-effects model for the analysis of panel data was well established long before Fisher wrote about the *intraclass* correlation in 1925. Indeed, Francis Galton (1889) introduced the concept, although under another name, and used a variance-components model in his work on human inheritance and his anthropometric investigations. See Stigler (1999, p. 182).[10]

d. Fisher

The terms *variance* and *Analysis of Variance* were both introduced by R. A. Fisher in his famous and seminal papers on quantitative genetics (1918a) and (1918b).[11] The concepts and methods of both fixed-effects and random-effects models were elaborated greatly in Fisher (1925), especially in Chapters 7 and 8, "Intraclass Correlations and the Analysis of Variance" and "Further Applications of the Analysis of Variance." But Fisher was never clear on the distinction between the fixed-effects model and the random-effects model. In Sec. 40, Chapter 7 (page references are to the 1970 reprint of the 14th edition), Fisher (1925, reprinted 1970, p. 234) writes the usual ANOVA table for assessing the significance of the variation of the heights of brothers from the same family across families (i.e., the table appropriate for the question can the family "effect" account for a significant part of the total variation in heights). He then goes on to interpret the problem in terms of the proportion of variance attributable to the "family effect," with a clear "random-effect" flavor (pp. 225–226):

Let a quantity be made up of two parts, each normally and independently distributed; let the variance of the first part be A, and that of the second part B; then it is easy to see that the variance of the total quantity is $A + B$. Consider a sample of n' values of the first part, and to each of these add a sample of k values of the second part, taking a fresh sample of k in each case. We then have n' families of values with k in each family. *In the infinite population from which these are drawn* [italics supplied] the correlation between pairs of members of the same family will be

$$\rho = \frac{A}{A+B}.$$

Theoretical and Practical Astronomy, went through many editions, the fifth and last, to which I have had access, being published in 1889.

[10] Hald (1988, p. 675) mentions two additional precursors of Fisher: Edgeworth (1885) and Thiele (1903).

[11] See also Moran and Smith (1966). Fisher (1918b) was the paper submitted first to *Biometrika* that Pearson rejected as editor. Relations between the two men were never the same after that!

From such a set of kn' values we make estimates of the values of A and B, or in other words we may analyse the variance into the proportions contributed by the two causes; the intraclass correlation will be merely the fraction of the total variance due to *the cause which observations in the same family have in common* [italics supplied]. The value of B may be estimated directly, for the variation due to this cause alone, consequently [note that Fisher uses S where we would use Σ and doesn't bother with expectation operators],

$$\overset{kn'}{\underset{1}{S}} (x - \bar{x}_v)^2 = n'(k-1)B.$$

The mean of the observations in any family is made up of two parts, the first part with variance A, and a second part, which is the mean of k values of the second parts of the individual values, and therefore a variance B/k; consequently from the observed variation of the means of the families, we have

$$k\overset{kn'}{\underset{1}{S}} (\bar{x}_v - \bar{x})^2 = (n'-1)(kA + B).$$

Although Fisher may have been perfectly clear in his own mind what the distinction between fixed effects and random effects was, by eschewing the use of the expectation operator and working from a standard AVOVA table but giving it a population interpretation appropriate to a random-effects model, he greatly muddied the waters for those that followed.[12]

e. Daniels and Eisenhart

The distinction between random effects and fixed effects, and its importance for the analysis of nonexperimental versus experimental data was not clarified until Churchill Eisenhart's "survey" in 1947. Although Daniels (1939) had it substantially right, his paper was largely overlooked until much later.

Daniels (1939, p. 190) puts the matter as follows: "The requirements of the particular problem decide whether the systematic or random interpretation is relevant. From the machine-makers point of view, for instance, the k units might be more properly thought of as a sample taken at random from all possible units. But when the aim is to measure and reduce variation in the output of a given plant, the systematic interpretation appears to be the correct one. Cases may, of course, arise where a combination of the two types of factor is operating, ..."

Eisenhart (1947, pp. 19–20) is much clearer but less succinct; he writes, "In practical work a question that often arises is: which model is appropriate to

---

[12] Scheffé (1956), Anderson (1978), and Searle, Casella and McCulloch (Chapter 2, 1992), cited earlier, give more details on the development of analysis of variance in the years following Fisher (1925).

the present instance – Model I [fixed effects] or model II [random effects]? Basically, of course, the answer is clear as soon as a decision is reached on whether the parameters of interest specify *fixed relations* or *components of random variation*. The answer depends in part, however, on how the observations were obtained; on the extent to which the experimental procedure employed sampled the respective variables at random. This generally provides the clue. For instance, when an experimenter selects two or more treatments, or two or more varieties, for testing, he rarely, if ever, draws them at random from a population of possible treatments or varieties; he selects those that he believes are most promising. Accordingly, Model I is generally appropriate where treatment, or variety comparisons are involved. On the other hand, when an experimenter selects a sample of animals from a herd or a species, for the study of the effects of various treatments, he can insure that they are random.... But he may consider such a sample to be a random sample from the species, only by making the assumption that the herd itself is a random sample from the species. In such a case, if several herds (from the same species) are involved, Model II would clearly be appropriate with respect to variation among the animals from each of the respective herds, and might be appropriate with respect to the variation of the herds from one another.

"The most difficult decisions are usually associated with *places* and *times*: Are the *fields* on which the tests were conducted a random sample of the county, or of the state, etc.? Are the *years* in which the tests were conducted a random sample of years?"[13]

f. Further Development of the Statistical Literature

The ANOVA table, which is the heart of the analysis of variance method proposed by Fisher (1925), is simply a way of arranging a series of calculations involving the partitioning of sums of squares of observations. What one does next depends, as suggested in the preceding discussion, on the context. For the greater part of agricultural and industrial research, which involves the statistical analysis of experimental data, the fixed-effects model is appropriate. Moreover, the fixed-effects interpretation lends itself to an analysis by linear

---

[13] Eisenhart is raising here a rather deep problem in the theory of probability. Whether or not a particular variable can be considered a random draw from some population or not is, in principle decidable by applying the principle of "exchangeability" introduced by de Finetti (1930); see also de Finetti (1970; trans. 1990, Vol. 2, pp. 211–224) and Lindley and Novick (1981). In a nutshell, the idea, very Bayesian in flavor, is to ask whether we can exchange two elements in a sample and still maintain the same subjective distribution: Thus, in a panel study of households are any two households in the sample exchangeable without affecting the distribution from which we imagine household effects to be drawn? In a panel of state data, are California and Maryland exchangeable without affecting the subjective distribution of the state effects? It's a dicey question – sometimes.

methods and to estimation and hypothesis testing by least-squares methods.[14] Although a random-effects interpretation is appropriate for many types of agricultural research, as suggested by Eisenhart's examples of animal-breeding experiments and Fisher's own genetic research, it is principally adapted to the analysis of nonexperimental, observational data such as are common in astronomy and the social sciences. Moreover, the easy treatment by linear least-squares methods is not possible. Generally speaking, likelihood methods, or related approximate methods, are required. And these were, before the advent of high-speed electronic computers, very computationally demanding. This is especially true for models in which the variable or variables of interest are also latent.[15] Snedecor's influential texts (1934; 1937–1980) make no mention of random-effects or variance-components models and deal almost exclusively with fixed-effects models in which the only random effect is the overall disturbance. In 1952, two important books appeared, Rao (1952) and Anderson and Bancroft (1952), which set the agenda for the work of the generation that followed, although they contain some discussion of variance-components models, emphasized fixed-effects models and the relation of ANOVA to least squares.[16] Scheffé (1956), following Eisenhart (1947), gave a balanced discussion of the two types of models, but emphasized (Sec. 3, pp. 257–264) the difficulties associated with the analysis of random-effects models. In his definitive 1959 book, Scheffé (1959) describes his goal as "a unified presentation of the basic theory of the analysis of variance – including its geometrical aspects." But in the preface (p. vii) he writes: "The theory . . . for fixed-effects models with independent observations of equal variance, I judge to be jelled into a fairly permanent form, but the theory of . . . other models [random-effects and mixed models], I expect will undergo considerable extension and revision. Perhaps this presentation will help stimulate the needed growth. What I feel most apologetic about is the little I have to offer on the unbalanced cases of the random-effects models and mixed models. These cannot generally be avoided in planning biological experiments, especially in genetics. . . . This gap in the theory I have not been able to fill." Indeed, Scheffé devotes only forty pages in a 477-page book to random-effects models. In the next section of this paper,

---

[14] See especially Rao (1946). Rao (1971a, b) works out details of the MINQUE alternative to maximum likelihood.

[15] As, for example, in the ANOVA interpretation of loglinear probability models for the analysis of categorical data (Nerlove and Press, 1978, 1986).

[16] Anderson and Bancroft (1952, pp. 313–377) have five chapters (22–25) on variance-components models and a thorough discussion of method-of-moments estimation of such models. C. R. Rao's book (1952) is restricted to linear models and doesn't mention variance-components models, although he later published a number of papers dealing with minimum variance quadratic unbiased estimation (MINQUE) of variance-components models (1970, 1971a–b, 1972, 1979). See P. S. R. Rao (1997, Chaps. 7–8) for a discussion of this and related methods.

I suggest that this emphasis on fixed effects in the more general ANOVA literature has carried over into the econometrics literature on panel data analysis, despite the greater similarity of the problems there addressed to the animal breeding or genetic analyses described by Eisenhart (1947) and Fisher (1918) or to the analysis of astronomical observations described by Airy (1861).[17]

Of course, the work of statisticians on random-effects, mixed, and variance-components models did not cease despite the formidable computational problems encountered. The history of the development of the subject is well summarized by Searle (1992, Chap. 2) and Anderson (1978); Rao (1997) gives a more technical account emphasizing developments since 1950. Here are some highlights: Henderson (1953), who worked primarily on animal breeding, developed method-of-moments methods for handling random-effects and mixed models. Hartley and J. N. K. Rao (1967) dealt broadly with the then-thorny question of maximum-likelihood methods for variance-components models. They give a completely general ML solution to the n independent random-effects case with unknown overall mean depending linearly on some observed conditioning variables and an overall disturbance independent of the random-effects. (See also Harville, 1977, and the discussion between him and J. N. K. Rao that follows.) Searle (1979) carried out a detailed analysis of maximum-likelihood and related methods of estimating variance-components models. Searle, Casella, and McCullough (1992) contains nearly all of this material in revised form in one place or another in a long book. Nerlove (1971) works out the appropriate transformation of the observed variables required for the diagonalization of the variance-covariance matrix of the three-component random-effects model with unknown overall mean depending on strictly exogenous variables (but discussion of this and related matters more properly belongs in succeeding sections on development of panel data models in the econometrics literature). Back to back, in the same issue of *Econometrica*, Henderson (1971) complains that he solved the problem of finding the inverse

---

[17] At least part of the responsibility for the dominance of the fixed-effects model must be laid at the door of Fisher himself. See Aldrich (1999). Joan Fisher Box reports in her biography of her father (1978, p. 117) that in a 1922 paper, Fisher showed that "... the significance of the coefficients of regression formulae – linear or curvilinear, simple or multiple – could be treated exactly by Student's test. Though in May, Gosset had seemed convinced by Fisher's argument to this effect, when he read this paper again after visiting Fisher, he became bothered about it; even as he was setting about the calculation of the new t- table, he was putting the problem to Fisher with a pertinacity that refused to be quieted, until he could be convinced that this use of his table was, in fact, correct. Gosset's difficulty was one that has troubled other statisticians in other contexts.... In making the regression of y on x and estimating the significance of deviations about the regression line, Fisher had proved that the distribution of the ratio of a regression coefficient b to its standard error followed the t-distribution. It was not obvious to Gosset that the resulting test was legitimate, because the sampling distribution of the x's themselves was not taken into account. Fisher, however, argued that it was only the distribution of ys relative to the fixed sample of values of x actually obtained, not to the population of the xs, that had relevance."

of the variance-covariance matrix, which is essential to ML estimation, much earlier in (Henderson, 1953). But this is not the same thing as finding the transformation that diagonalizes this matrix; a method for transforming the original observations in order to diagonalize the variance-covariance matrix, it seems to me, is essential for applying maximum-likelihood methods to panels with a large cross-section dimension. This is done for the three-component model in Nerlove (1971) and much more generally in Searle and Henderson (1979), whose results are also reported in Searle, Casella, and McCullough (1992, pp. 144–146).[18]

For more details on the statistical literature on random-effects and mixed models, see the survey by Khuri and Sahai (1985) and the bibliographies of Sahai (1979), containing two thousand citations, and Sahai, Khuri, and Kapadai (1985), containing an additional seven hundred citations.

3. ECONOMETRIC DEVELOPMENT, THE EARLY YEARS: FROM CHICAGO TO THE PARIS CONFERENCE OF 1977

a. Hildreth

In a remarkable but unfortunately virtually inaccessible paper, Clifford Hildreth (1950), then at the Cowles Commission at the University of Chicago, set out a three-component model for the latent disturbances in a simultaneous-equations model and considered estimation when these components might be considered random effects or when two of them, period effects and individual effects, might be considered fixed effects and thus parameters to be estimated.[19] The case Hildreth considers". . . is that in which the investigator has observations on each of a group of economic units for a number of time periods." Using the old Cowles terminolgy but a somewhat altered notation, Hildreth's model is as follows: Let y_{it} be a vector of the current values of the ith economic unit in the tth time period and let z_{it} be a vector of values of predetermined variables. μ is an overall constant. Then

$$By_{it} + \Gamma z_{it} + \mu = u_{it}, \quad i = 1, \ldots, N, \quad t = 1, \ldots, T. \qquad (2)$$

Hildreth then goes on to say that some of the variables, both endogenous and predetermined may not vary across individuals at a point in time or may remain fixed for a given individual over time. He then says some of these may be

---

[18] See also Hemmerle and Hartley (1973).

[19] In the 1950 paper, Hildreth refers to a still earlier paper, Hildreth (1949). In it, Hildreth discusses a disaggregated system of behavioral relations and points out that what might be considered as predetermined in a time-series context might not be in a cross section. It is possible that this observation led him to the error-component formulation of the disturbances in the 1950 paper. I am indebted to Peter Phillips for retrieving the 1949 paper from the Cowles archives for me.

unobserved or latent: "It may be believed that there are unobserved individual characteristics which cause individuals to act differently and which are persistent over time. There may be unobserved influences that affect individuals in pretty much the same way but change over time." To take account of these, Hilderth then introduces vectors of constants interpreted as fixed variables, μ_{i*} and μ_{*i}, and rewrites (2) as

$$By_{it} + \Gamma z_{it} + \mu + \mu_{i*} + \mu_{*t} = u_{it}, \quad i = 1, \ldots, N, \quad t = 1, \ldots, T. \quad (3)$$

But he adds – significantly – "I find it difficult to choose between the alternatives of allowing for these variations peculiar to individuals and variations peculiar to time through fixed parameters [as in (3)] or through random parameters." In this case, Hildreth writes

$$By_{it} + \Gamma z_{it} + \mu = \omega_i + \lambda_t + \varepsilon_{it}, \quad i = 1, \ldots, N, \quad t = 1, \ldots, T, \quad (4)$$

where ω_i, λ_t and ε_{it} are, respectively, "part of the disturbance in all equations relating to the ith individual," "part of the disturbance for each individual in the tth time period," and all the rest. Hildreth goes on to consider the special case of one equation in one endogenous variable in detail. He goes on to write down a likelihood function for the parameters in a single equation:

$$y_{it} + \gamma z_{it} + \mu = \omega_i + \lambda_t + \varepsilon_{it}, \quad i = 1, \ldots, N, \quad t = 1, \ldots, T, \quad (5)$$

assuming ω_i, λ_t and ε_{it} to be jointly normal with constant variances and uncorrelated. But then he adds: "Maximum likelihood did not work at all well in this case. The estimation equations are difficult to derive and appear to be highly nonlinear in the unknown parameters." But derive them he does and thus his story ends, but not his influence.

b. Management Bias and the Estimation of Production Functions: Hoch and Mundlak

In 1944, Marschak and Andrews (1944) published their famous article, "Random Simultaneous Equations and the Theory of Production."[20] The basic problem raised by Marschak and Andrews is that in a model which involves profit maximizing or cost minimizing firms, the choices of input levels and, in the case of profit maximization, output levels as well, are endogenous. Imperfections in profit maximization, differing knowledge of technology, and unobserved variations in other variables such as weather, fixed factors of production, and

---

[20] For extended "variations on the theme" of Marschak and Andrews, see Nerlove (1965). The Marschak-Andrews paper gave rise to a considerable literature on the estimation of production functions in the context of models involving the kind of unobserved variations among firms detailed in the text. See, for example, Mundlak and Hoch (1965) and Zellner, Kmenta, and Dreze (1966).

heterogeneity of inputs, all give rise to disturbances in the relation among inputs and outputs and factor and product prices. Even if the latter are exogenously determined, in a cross section of firms, the relation between output(s) and inputs is what is termed a *confluent* relationship, that is, the relationship reflects the unobserved differences among firms and variations in the prices they face.

In the mid-1950s, Irving Hoch, then a graduate student at the University of Chicago, tackled this problem. His Ph.D. dissertation completed in 1957, written under the direction of a committee chaired by D. Gale Johnson, which also had earlier included Hildreth, dealt with the problem of how to combine cross section and time series data for a panel of firms in order to resolve or partially resolve the identification and estimation issues posed by Marschak and Andrews (1944). The bulk of his research was published in two papers in *Econometrica* (Hoch, 1958, 1962), but a preliminary report of his inquiry was presented to the meeting of the Econometric Society in Montreal in September, 1954, and reported in Hoch (1955).[21] In the research reported in 1954, Hoch used a panel of 63 Minnesota farms over the six-year period, 1946–1951 to estimate a Cobb-Douglas production function relating the dollar value of output to the value of inputs in four categories of inputs, all in logs. He introduced fixed effects for both year and farm, the logarithmic part being regarded as the overall mean in what was then, and now, called Analysis of Covariance in the general statistical literature, as suggested in Hildreth (1950).[22] Hoch (1962) interpreted his results in terms of left-out factors, particularly the firm effects in terms of differential managerial ability, or *technical efficiency* as he called it. Mundlak (1961) builds on this idea in his famous article, "Empirical Production Functions Free of Management Bias."

Suppose there is an unobserved factor of production called management. Mundlak (1961, p. 44) writes: "... we shall assume that whatever management is, it does not change considerably over time; and for short periods, say a few years, it can be assumed to remain constant." Mundlak then asks what the usual OLS regression of the log of output on the logs of the input levels means, interprets the result in terms of the "intrafirm" function as distinguished from

---

[21] His dissertation title was "Estimation of Agricultural Resource Productivities Combining Time Series and Cross Section Data," University of Chicago, March, 1957.

[22] In his more detailed summary, Hoch (1962) cites both Hildreth (1950) as his source for the idea of using the Analysis of Covariance and Wilks (1943) for its implementation. In Wilks (1943, pp. 195–199), the Analysis of Covariance is explained as standard fixed-effects ANOVA in which the overall mean is a linear function of some continuously measured variables which are uncorrelated with the disturbance. It is interesting to note that variance components or random effects are nowhere mentioned in Wilks (1943), but in the greatly augmented second edition, Wilks (1962, pp. 308–313) devotes five pages to the subject and cites Eisenhart (1947). Presumably on the basis of his earlier derivation of the likelihood equations for the random-effects model, Hildreth advised Hoch to adopt a fixed-effects framework, which by then dominated the statistical literature as well.

the "interfirm" function (Bronfenbrenner, 1943), and argues that along the lines suggested by Hoch (1955), a panel of firms for which the management factor can be assumed to be approximately fixed over time for each firm can be used to obtain unbiased estimates of the intrafirm production function. The technique he suggests is covariance analysis and cites Scheffé (1959) as his statistical authority. Mundlak treats the firm fixed effects as proportional to a latent variable measuring "management" and is thus able to measure "management bias" by comparing the fixed firm effect regression with the OLS regression without firm effects. He suggests introducing a year effect as well. He implements these suggestions in a panel study of 66 family farms in Israel for the period 1954–1958. Several more papers followed along similar lines (Mundlak, 1963; Mundlak, 1964; Mundlak and Hoch, 1965) and, in Mundlak (1978a,b), he mounted a spirited defense of the fix-effects approach.

Mundlak (1978a) bases his defense of fixed-effects models on two counts: First, "Without loss of generality, it can be assumed from the outset that the effects are random and view the [fixed-effects] inference as a conditional inference, that is conditional on the effects that are in the sample." And, second, "The whole literature which has been based on the imaginary difference between the two estimators... is based on an incorrect specification which ignores the correlation between the effects and the explanatory variables." (1978a, p. 70). The issue of conditional versus unconditional inference is not so trivial as Mundlak appears to suggest; it lies at the heart of the debate between Fisher and his critics described by Aldrich (1999) who further points out that the question lies behind the simultaneous-equations debate stemming from Haavelmo (1944) and much discussion that preceded his work. One can condition on what one pleases, but then one cannot generally interpret the result as structural.[23] This is the same point made by Eisenhart (1947). What of the correlation between the effects and the observed explanatory variables? As Mundlak and others have been at pains to point out, fixed effects are equivalent to considering only deviations from individual means and ignoring the cross-sectional variation of the means themselves. Using this information is equivalent to attributing some of the explanatory effect of an observed variable to the relation between it and an effect. A good thing in my view, not a bad thing as Mundlak would have us believe. Another way of saying the same thing is to say that fixed-effects methods throw away important and useful information about the relation between the explanatory and the explained variables in a panel.[24] Because this point is widely misunderstood among econometric

---

[23] Consider a simple supply and demand model. Condition on price. Can one interpret the regression of quantity on price as the supply curve or as the demand curve? What is the appropriate interpretation?

[24] The absurdity of the contention that possible correlation between some of the observed explanatory variables and the individual-specific component of the disturbance is a ground for using fixed effects should be clear from the following example: Consider a panel of

practitioners and the reason cited by Mundlak is frequently used to justify the choice of a fixed-effects model notwithstanding its inappropriateness for getting at structural relations in a nonexperimental context, I include a short appendix to this essay describing the information content of a single panel data variable (Appendix A).

c. Balestra and Nerlove: Error Components and Dynamic Panel Models

It is often said that "Ignorance is bliss." But one should also remember Santayana: "Those who cannot remember the past are condemned to repeat it." Because I was a participant in the development of what used to be called Balestra-Nerlove models, I will tell the story of Balestra and Nerlove (1966) in some detail. It is less a story of bliss than of repetition of the past.

Balestra arrived in Stanford in 1959, having spent the previous two years at the University of Kansas acquiring a Master's degree in Economics and teaching French and Italian to keep body and soul together. I arrived in 1960. We did not immediately meet. In 1963, Balestra completed a second Master's degree (in Statistics) and went to work for the Stanford Research Institute (SRI) in Menlo Park as an economist and econometrician. In the summer of 1963, he came in with a proposed thesis topic using the data on natural gas consumption by individual U.S. states over a period of years, which he had collected for an SRI project. His idea was to treat the demand for gas as a derived demand from the demand for residential space heating and so, in the manner of Fisher and Kaysen (1962), to include the stock of gas using durables in the equation to be estimated. Such a derived-demand model is presented in our joint paper (Balestra and Nerlove, 1966, pp. 585–589) and results in a dynamic demand model, which is of the familiar geometrically distributed lag

households with data on consumption and income. We are trying to estimate a consumption function. Income varies across households and over time. The variation across households is related to ability of the main earner and other household specific factors that vary little over time, that is to say, reflect mainly differences in permanent income. Such permanent differences in income are widely believed to be the source of most differences in consumption both cross sectionally and over time, whereas, variations of income over time are likely to be mostly transitory and unrelated to consumption in most categories. Yet, fixed-effects regressions are equivalent to using only this variation and discarding the information on the consumption-income relationship contained in the cross-section variation among the household means.

Mundlak (1978, pp. 71–72) also makes the seemly contrary argument that if the individual-specific effects are linear functions of the individual-specific means of the observed explanatory variables plus an uncorrelated error, GLS estimation with error components collapses to fixed effects in the nondynamic case. This is the basis for Chamberlain's "Π-matrix" approach (Chamberlain, 1980, 1984); see also Crépon and Mairesse (1996). As Maddala (1987, p. 305) points out, however, this is no longer true if only *some* of the individual-specific means enter. It is also not true if the relationship to be estimated is dynamic or if the error includes a period-specific effect.

form including a lagged value of gas consumption, when the unobserved stock is eliminated by substitution from the appropriate stock-flow relationship. The importance of this derivation lay in the particular interpretation it implied of the coefficient of lagged gas consumption in the relationship to be estimated: It could be interpreted in terms of the annual depreciation rate for the durable gas-using input used together with gas to yield space heat (1 minus that rate, in fact). The data collected by Balestra for thirty-six states over the period 1950–1962 comprised gas consumption normalized by degree days, average price per Btu deflated by the CPI, population, and per capita personal income in 1961 dollars. Because of the presumption of structural change about the middle of the period, attention was restricted to the data for the thirty-six states over the six-year period, 1957–1962. Within a couple of weeks, Balestra, always a fast worker, reappeared with a set of OLS regressions, involving various restrictions, using the pooled sample and also one regression including fixed effects for the individual states. The correlations were all uniformly high ($\sim$0.99) but, in view of the interpretation afforded by the theoretical model of the coefficient of lagged gas consumption, the estimates of this parameter were bizarre: all greater than one implying *negative depreciation* of gas space-heating equipment for the regressions based on the pooled sample, and an implausibly low value (0.68) for the regression that included state-specific fixed effects, implying extremely rapid depreciation (32 percent per annum). We now understand why such results were obtained, but in 1963 about all we understood was the inadequacy (bias) of the regressions based on the pooled sample.[25]

I recall rather pedantically explaining that the disturbances represented numerous, individually insignificant variables affecting the gas consumption in a particular state in a particular year, some of which were peculiar to the state (i.e., state-specific), and didn't change much or at all over time. I must have sounded much like Sir George Biddell Airy 102 years before explaining the day-specific effects in the measurements taken in the course of a single night of the angular diameter of Jupiter! Being quite unaware of Airy, Fisher, or Eisenhart, and even of Scheffé, we proceeded to formulate a simple two-component random-effects model, although we do mention the possibility of a separate-year effect.[26] We also had some doubts about the independence of state-specific time-invariant effects, one from another, because of the

---

[25] Throughout I use bias to refer to inconsistency of an estimate, with no possibility of confusion in the present context. As discussed later, I succeeded in reproducing these results of bias in Monte Carlo studies published in 1967 and 1971 (Nerlove, 1967; 1971a). It was not until much later, however, that the bias in the coefficient of the lagged dependent variable in the fixed-effects regression was understood (Nickell, 1981). The comparative properties of alternative estimators in dynamic panel models are summarized and illustrated in Nerlove (1999b).

[26] In Balestra and Nerlove (1966), we cite Kuh (1959) as our authority. Kuh, in turn, cites nobody but, interestingly enough, mentions the possibility that the effects of capital stock (equivalent to a lagged dependent variable) in an investment equation may be biased downwards by inclusion of fixed-firm effects.

arbitrariness of the geographical boundaries with respect to the economic behavior analyzed. Our formulation then leads to the familiar block-diagonal
residual variance-covariance matrix, dependent on two unknown parameters:

$$u_{it} = \mu_i + \varepsilon_{it}, \quad i = 1, \ldots, N, \quad t = 1, \ldots, T, \text{ where}$$

(i) $E(\mu_i) = E(\varepsilon_{it}) = 0$, all i and t,

(ii) $E(\mu_i \varepsilon_{jt}) = 0$, all i, j and t,

(iii) $E(\mu_i \mu_j) = \begin{cases} \sigma_\mu^2 & i = j \\ 0 & i \neq j, \end{cases}$

(iv) $E(\varepsilon_{it} \varepsilon_{js}) = \begin{cases} \sigma_\varepsilon^2 & t = s, i = j \\ 0 & otherwise \end{cases}$. (6)

Both μ_i and ε_{it} are assumed to be uncorrelated with x_{it} for all i and t. Stacking
the us

$$Euu' = \sigma^2 \Omega = \sigma^2 \begin{pmatrix} A & \ldots & 0 \\ \vdots & \ddots & \vdots \\ 0 & \ldots & A \end{pmatrix}, \text{ where } A \text{ is a } T \times T \text{ matrix}$$

$$A = \begin{pmatrix} 1 & \ldots & \rho \\ \vdots & \ddots & \vdots \\ \rho & \ldots & 1 \end{pmatrix} \text{ and}$$

$$\sigma^2 = \sigma_\mu^2 + \sigma_\varepsilon^2 \quad \text{and} \quad \rho = \frac{\sigma_\mu^2}{\sigma^2}. \tag{7}$$

ρ was called the *intraclass correlation* by Fisher (1918a, 1925). In our case,
$T = 6$ and $N = 36$, so the matrix Ω was 216×216. Inverting such a large
matrix, even were ρ known, would have been a problem for us at that time.
Wallace and Hussain (1969) and Henderson (1971) were yet to come. However,
the matrix Ω has a rather simple structure despite its large size. Balestra was
then, as he has ever been, a wiz with matrices; it took him about a week to find
the characteristic roots of Ω and the orthogonal transformation, which would
reduce Ω to diagonal form.[27] The roots of Ω are

$\xi = 1 - \rho + T\rho$ with multiplicity T and $\eta = 1 - \rho$ with multiplicity $N(T-1)$.

The orthogonalizing transformation effectively weights the deviations of each
observation from its individual specific mean and the individual specific means

---

[27] After we had prepared a draft of a report on the investigation, William Madow of SRI called
our attention to Halperin (1951). Halperin uses the same orthogonal transformation and
considers only the case in which no lagged value of the dependent variable is included as
explanatory. Even in this case, however, Halperin remarks (p. 574) that: "The maximum
likelihood equations for the estimation of the parameters ... are of such a formidable character that an explicit solution does not appear possible." Later, Hartley and Rao (1967) were
independently to use the same transformation.

themselves by the reciprocals of the square roots of the characteristic roots. Thus, if z_{it} is a typical observation (either on the dependent variable or on one of the dependent variables), the transformed observations are

$$z_{it}^* = \xi^{-1/2}\bar{z}_{i.} + \eta^{-1/2}(z_{it} - \bar{z}_{i.}), \quad i = 1, \ldots, N, \quad t = 1, \ldots, T.$$

If T is very large, the importance of the individual-specific means in the transformed observations becomes negligible and we are left with transformed observations which are simply the deviations from these means. The analysis is then equivalent to one which includes individual-specific fixed effects. But if T is small, cross section variation plays a greater role.

Of course, ρ is unknown. Although a great deal of Balestra's 1965 dissertation (published as Balestra, 1967) and of the paper we ultimately published together (Balestra and Nerlove, 1966) deals with various alternative methods of estimation, I recall that in late 1963 we headed straight for maximum likelihood as the preferred method for estimating ρ simultaneously with the other parameters. It was only because this method seemed to fail that we turned to other alternatives later.[28] At the time, however, we didn't realize, as Bhargava and Sargan (1983) were to show us twenty years later, that the presence of a lagged value of the dependent variable as one of the explanatory variables, i.e., the autoregressive nature of the relationship to be estimated from the panel data, makes all the difference in the formulation of the variable as predetermined, that is, as fixed just like one of the xs.[29] In terms of ξ and η, the

[28] I was then, as now, a great fan of likelihood methods. Although I had acquired and almost certainly had read Hildreth (1950) ten years earlier when I was research assistant to Tjalling Koopmans and Jacob Marschak at the Cowles Commission then at the University of Chicago, the part I internalized was his characterization of the appropriate formulation of the disturbances in a panel context and not, fortunately as it turned out, his warning that the method of maximum likelihood was too difficult to be of use and that fixed effects would have to suffice.

[29] Hildreth (1949) would have told us this, but we were unaware of this paper at the time. Consider

$$y_{it} = \alpha + \beta x_{it} + \gamma y_{it-1} + \mu_i + \varepsilon_{it}, \quad i = 1, \ldots N, \quad t = 1, \ldots T. \qquad (*)$$

Taking deviations from overall means eliminates the constant α. The usual assumptions are made about the properties of the μ_i and the ε_{it}. Assume that, possibly after some differencing, both the y_{it} and the x_{it} are stationary. In this case, the initial observations are determined by

$$y_{i0} = \sum_{j=0}^{\infty} \gamma^j \beta x_{i,-j} + \frac{1}{1-\gamma}\mu_i + v_{i0}, \text{ where } v_{it} = \gamma v_{it-1} + \varepsilon_{it}. \qquad (**)$$

The joint distribution of $y_{iT}, \ldots, y_{i1}, y_{i0}$ depends on the distribution of μ_i, ε_{it}, and x_{it}. If y_{i0} is literally taken as fixed, which is to deny the plausible assumption that it is generated by the same process as generates the y_{it} that are observed, the conditional likelihood function for the model (*) with $u_{it} = \mu_i + \varepsilon_{it} \sim N(0, \sigma^2\Omega)$ is derived in the usual way from the product of the densities of y_{it} conditional on x_{it} and y_{it-1}. Our formulation in 1963 treated y_{i0} exactly as if it were fixed just as one of the xs. This is again the problem of fixed X regression (Aldrich, 1999); clearly not legitimate in this case.

characteristic roots of Ω, this leads to the likelihood function:

$$\log L\big(\beta, \gamma, \sigma_\mu^2, \sigma_\varepsilon^2 \,\big|\, y_{11}, \ldots, y_{NT}; x_{11}, \ldots x_{NT}; y_{10}, \ldots, y_{N0}\big)$$

$$= -\frac{NT}{2}\log 2\pi - \frac{NT}{2}\log \sigma^2 - \frac{N}{2}\log \xi - \frac{N(T-1)}{2}\log \eta$$

$$- \frac{1}{2\sigma^2}\sum_{i=1}^{N}\sum_{t=1}^{T}(y_{it}^* - \beta x_{it}^* - \gamma y_{it-1}^*)^2, \tag{8}$$

where y^*, x^*, and y_{-1}^* are the transformed variables and the overall constant has been eliminated by expressing all observations as deviations from their overall means.

Fresh from the study of Koopmans and Hood (1953, esp. pp. 156–158), I suggested concentrating $\log L$ in (8) with respect to σ^2, β, and γ, resulting in

$$\log L^*(\rho \,|\, x, y, y_0)$$

$$= -\frac{NT}{2}\{\log 2\pi + 1\} - \frac{NT}{2}\log \frac{\mathrm{RSS}(\rho)}{NT} - \frac{N}{2}\log \xi - \frac{N(T-1)}{2}\log \eta, \tag{9}$$

where

$$\mathrm{RSS}(\rho) = \min_{\beta,\,\gamma}\left\{\sum_{i=1}^{N}\sum_{t=1}^{T}(y_{it}^* - \beta x_{it}^* - \gamma y_{it-1}^*)^2\right\}.$$

It was, we thought, a simple enough matter to find the maximum of $\log L^*$ with respect to ρ. Within a week, Balestra was back with the disconcerting news that $\log L^*$ didn't have a maximum within the open interval $(0, 1)$; indeed the maximum of the concentrated log likelihood function occurred for $\rho = 0$, which implied that the OLS estimates of β and γ from the pooled sample were best, but this we knew led to estimates of depreciation that were negative and therefore unacceptable.[30]

What to do? Being youthful, and therefore somewhat unwise from my present perspective, we rejected the likelihood approach. Instead, we turned to a two-stage procedure. Balestra suggested using instrumental variables in the manner of 2SLS to obtain consistent estimates of γ and then a method of calculating an estimate of ρ from the residuals from the first-stage instrumental variables regression in such a way that the estimate would have to lie in the interval $(0, 1)$.[31] The second stage then consisted of GLS applied to the original

---

[30] I was later able to reproduce such boundary solutions in the Monte Carlo results reported in Nerlove (1971a) but not in those reported for estimation in the case of a pure autoregression reported in Nerlove (1967). This was all later explained by Trognon at the first Paris conference in 1977 (Trognon, 1978).

[31] The formula was later adapted in Nerlove (1967) to calculate the first-stage estimate of ρ from the fixed-effects regression. Unfortunately, the method of ensuring the first-stage estimate is non-negative has not been followed in many subsequent expositions and computer programs for doing panel data analysis with the result that the random-effects model is frequently rejected in favor of the fixed-effects model. When a lagged value of the dependent variable

data (equivalent to OLS applied to the data transformed using the first-stage estimate of ρ). The instruments chosen were simply the lagged values of the exogenous explanatory variables (the xs). This resulted in a positive annual depreciation rate of about 4.5 percent, which we both regarded as plausible. A Technical Report of the Stanford Institute for Mathematical Studies in the Social Sciences appeared in late 1964, Balestra's dissertation was completed in 1965, a joint paper was published in 1966, and Balestra's dissertation was published as a book in 1967. I think the important thing about this investigation was the way in which our economic theory of the determination of the demand for natural gas informed and guided the estimation of the relationship. Many investigators would have stopped with an R^2 of 0.99, but it was the odd result of negative depreciation that prevented us from doing so. Nonetheless, there were lots of loose ends that remained to be tied up.

In a subsequent Monte Carlo study (Nerlove, 1971a), I succeeded in reproducing the main estimation results of Balestra and Nerlove (1966): (1) upward bias in the coefficient of the lagged dependent variable in the pooled OLS regression; (2) downward bias in this coefficient in the fixed-effects regression; (3) the occurrence of an unacceptable number of boundary solutions at $\rho = 0$ for maximum-likelihood estimates based on the likelihood function (8); and (4) improved estimates based on feasible GLS using an estimate of ρ derived from a first-stage instrumental variables regression. I also demonstrated the greater stability (reduced variance of feasible GLS) using a first-stage fixed-effects regression as compared with the instrumental variables approach used in Balestra and Nerlove (1966). In Nerlove (1971b) I worked out the details of the three-component model including the transformation required to reduce its more complicated variance-covariance matrix to diagonality.

d. Highlights of the Ten Years Preceding the First Paris Conference, 1967–1976

In this subsection, I briefly summarize a number of important contributions to the method and application of panel data econometrics that were made in the decade following publication of Balestra's dissertation, which preceded the first Paris Conference on Panel Data Econometrics of 1977.

One of the most widely cited papers of the decade is Wallace and Hussain (1969). In this paper, the authors consider a model of fixed X regression in which the disturbances follow a three-component error formulation. They find, by trial and error, the inverse of the variance-covariance matrix of the disturbances for known error-component variances.[32] Using this result, they

---

is included among the explanatory variables, the most common method of estimating ρ from a first-stage regression is almost bound to give a negative estimate (Nerlove, 1999b, pp. 146–147).

[32] The main difference between this and Nerlove (1971b), which it precedes, is that in the latter I explicitly give the transformation of the data that reduces the disturbance variance-covariance matrix to the scalar matrix, which makes much clearer the relation between

establish the greater efficiency of the GLS estimates and the asymptotic equivalence of the two estimators when observations on the independent variables remain nonstochastic but increase nonrepetitively in number. A two-stage estimation procedure is suggested in which the error-component variances are estimated from a first-stage OLS regression. Of course, it is crucial in establishing their results that the explanatory regressors are assumed to be nonstochastic and, in particular, that no lagged value of the dependent variable is included among them. Other notable papers written in this period are Amemiya (1971) and Fuller and Battese (1974). These treat the relation between the use of analysis of covariance methods (fixed effects) and GLS and ML methods for the estimation of panel regression models with error components (called linear crossed-error models), but they do not confront the dynamic issues peculiar to econometric application. These papers are principally concerned with the loss of efficiency in the application of fixed-effects methods. Maddala (1971a) is concerned with efficiency too, although he also confronts the problem of estimating a dynamic panel model.

Early on in the development of panel data econometrics, it was widely recognized that dynamic panel models are of key importance and, indeed, it is the need to estimate dynamic models that differentiates the econometric problems from those generally discussed in the general statistical literature on variance components and on the analysis of covariance. Elsewhere, Balestra and I (Nerlove and Balestra, 1996) have argued that all models of economic behavior are basically dynamic, whether or not the dynamics is explicit or not.[33] The appropriate dynamics may be modeled by formulating the relation to be estimated as a difference equation or by modeling stocks and flows explicitly with multiple-equation models or by admitting the possibility that the errors may themselves be correlated over time or both. When both state dependence and serially correlated errors are present, interesting identification issues arise. In surveying the subsequent development of the econometric literature, it is helpful to bear in mind the centrality of the dynamic issues. Balestra and Nerlove (1966) and the two follow-on papers (Nerlove, 1971a–b) were explicitly concerned with the problems of analyzing dynamic panel models.

the GLS and fixed-effects estimates and, under appropriate assumptions concerning the independent variables as N and T increase, the asymptotic equivalence. Of course, we were both preceded by the much earlier work of Henderson (1953). Maddala (1971), to be discussed later, also contains, *inter alia*, an alternative derivation of a slightly different formulation of these results.

[33] Current behavior is almost always dependent on the state of system describing it, and this state in turn often depends on how it got to where it is. In the simplest cases, state dependence may be expressed as a distributed lag or by inclusion of lagged values of the endogenous behavioral variables, but sometimes the dynamics is implicit as when current investment expenditures are assumed to depend on the capital stock. The arbitrary nature of calendar time in relation to the relevant date or period over which behavior is measured is also a source of dependence over time among observations.

Maddala (1971a) considers both two-component and three-component random-effects models. He derives the results for the moments presented in Appendix A to this paper on the moments for the within-group, between-group, within-period, between-period, etc., variation, and, in somewhat different form than Nerlove (1971b), the properties of GLS in weighting these various moments inversely to the variances of the errors associated with them. In the nondynamic two-component case (no lagged values of the dependent variable included as explanatory and no period effects), Maddala analyzes the behavior of the maximum-likelihood estimates in terms of a reparametrization of the likelihood function in terms of the ratio of the characteristic roots of the variance-covariance matrix of the disturbances:

$\xi = 1 - \rho + T\rho$ with multiplicity T and $\eta = 1 - \rho$ with multiplicity $N(T - 1)$,

from (7). Maddala introduces $\theta = \frac{\eta}{\xi} = \frac{1-\rho}{1-\rho+T\rho}$ and notes that, as ρ increases from 0 to 1, θ decreases from 1 to 0.[34] In terms of the notation of the Appendix A, write the moments:

$$W_{xx} = \text{within-group SS, around the group means: } \sum_{1}^{N}\sum_{1}^{T}(x_{it} - \bar{x}_i)^2$$

$$= x'\left[I_{NT} - \left(I_N \otimes \frac{J_T}{T}\right)\right]x$$

$$W_{yx} = y'\left[I_{NT} - \left(I_N \otimes \frac{J_T}{T}\right)\right]x$$

(10)

$$B_{xx} = \text{within-period SS, around period means: } \sum_{1}^{N}\sum_{1}^{T}(x_{it} - \bar{x}_i)^2$$

$$= x'\left[I_{NT} - \left(\frac{J_N}{N} \otimes I_T\right)\right]x$$

$$B_{yx} = y'\left[I_{NT} - \left(\frac{J_N}{N} \otimes I_T\right)\right]x$$

Then the GLS estimate of β is

$$\hat{\beta} = [W_{xx} + \theta B_{xx}]^{-1}[W_{yx} + \theta B_{yx}].$$

(11)

As remarked earlier, GLS weights the within and between moments in relation to the error variances of the components of the disturbance; if ρ is large (i.e.,

---

[34] He does so primarily for the sake of mathematical convenience in deriving the results he presents, some of which I describe later. While the two formulations are *mathematically* equivalent, they may not be equivalent from the standpoint of *numerical* calculation. In Appendix B to this paper, I present an example for the two different parameterizations and formulations of the same likelihood function which, in fact, yield the same *numerical* results despite the highly nonlinar relationship between the two.

if the unobserved variation of the individual-specific effects is large relative to the total unobserved variation), θ, the weight given to the between-group moments, is small. It is interesting to note, as Maddala does, that variations in ρ produce relatively larger variations in θ when ρ is small than when ρ is large.[35] In terms of θ and the moments, the estimated variance of the residual variance, σ_ε^2 in my earlier notation, is

$$\hat\sigma_\varepsilon^2 = \frac{1}{NT}[W_{yy} + \theta B_{yy} - (W_{yx} + \theta B_{yx})(W_{xx} + \theta B_{xx})^{-1}(W_{xy} + \theta B_{xy})].$$

The concentrated likelihood function, written as (9) above in terms of ρ, can then be written in terms of θ as

$$-2\log L = \mathrm{const} + NT\log\hat\sigma_\varepsilon^2 - N\log\theta. \tag{12}$$

Maddala notes that

$$\frac{\partial(NT\hat\sigma_\varepsilon^2)}{\partial\theta} = [1 \quad \lambda']\begin{bmatrix} B_{yy} & B_{yx} \\ B_{xy} & B_{xx} \end{bmatrix}\begin{bmatrix} 1 \\ \lambda \end{bmatrix} > 0,$$

where

$$\lambda = (W_{xx} + \theta B_{xx})^{-1}(W_{xy} + \theta B_{xy}),$$

since

$$\begin{bmatrix} B_{yy} & B_{yx} \\ B_{xy} & B_{xx} \end{bmatrix}$$

is positive definite. Since

$$\frac{\partial\lambda}{\partial\theta} = -[W_{xx} + \theta B_{xx}]^{-1}[B_{xx}\lambda - B_{xy}],$$

$$\frac{\partial^2(NT\hat\sigma_\varepsilon^2)}{\partial\theta^2} = -2(\lambda'B_{xx} - B_{yx})[W_{xx} + \theta B_{xx}]^{-1}(B_{xx}\lambda - B_{xy}) < 0,$$

for $\theta > 0$. Thus, apart from the constant, the first term of the concentrated likelihood function is increasing in θ at a decreasing rate and so is $N\log\theta$; thus, the concentrated likelihood is maximized when the difference between the two terms is minimum. The latter is fixed, given T and N, but the former depends on the data and its position may vary. Following Maddala (1971a, p. 346), these curves, which are obtained from the numerical example presented in Appendix B, are plotted in Figure 1:

---

[35] See the preceding footnote. This means, in effect, that for certain ranges of ρ, the results of calculations based on the parameterization θ may differ substantially from those based on the parameterization ρ. In Appendix B, I present an example in which the maximum of the concentrated likelihood function shows that the problem does not arise for the difference between the parameterization based on characteristic roots and the Maddala formulation. However, the technique actually employed by Balestra and Nerlove was to transform the observations and work with these in the concentrated likelihood function. I now believe that this procedure is subject to greater problems of numerical accuracy.

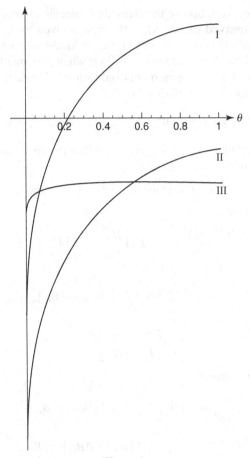

Figure 1.

Curve I plots $NT \log \hat{\sigma}_\varepsilon^2(\theta)$. Curve II plots $\log \theta$; the position of this curve is fixed. The position of Curve I may vary. Curve III shows Curve I in another position (i.e., for different values of the within and between SS and cross-products). The value of θ, which maximizes the concentrated log likelihood, is that for which the distance between Curves I and II is a minimum: it is smaller for Curve III than for Curve I. Maddala draws the following conclusions from Figure 1 and the results on the curvature and slopes of these pieces of the concentrated log likelihood function: (a) The maximum cannot occur at a boundary value where $\theta = 0$ or $\rho = 1$ (but, of course, it can occur where $\theta = 1$ or $\rho = 0$). (b) Since both parts of the log LF are increasing at a decreasing rate and Curve II is fixed, there could be multiple maxima, but only two. (c) Finally, there exists a possibility of a boundary solution at $\theta = 1$; thus, $\rho = 0$, if β and the sums of squares and cross-products bear a certain relation to one another, which Maddala suggests is a possibility even in the case in which no lagged value of the dependent variable is included.[36,37] But he considers the possibility of boundary solutions more likely than in the case of purely exogenous variables.

In a paper written in 1975 but not published until 1994, Maddala (1975) attacked the problem of estimating dynamic panel models. He argued that taking proper account of initial conditions was the key to avoiding boundary solutions to the maximum likelihood problem, foreshadowing Anderson and Hsiao (1981, 1982). He repeated the Monte Carlo experiments run in Nerlove (1971a) but with a twist. In Nerlove (1971a), I ran the processs, starting with random initial conditions for ten periods before starting the estimation in which the tenth value of the dependent variable was take as given or fixed for the sample estimation beginning with the eleventh observation. What Maddala did, in contrast, was to base likelihood inference on a likelihood function formed from the distribution of the last ten observations conditional on the first ten rather than only the tenth. Although Maddala did not obtain any boundary solutions in his Monte Carlo, his procedure does not really resolve the problem since the initial values at the beginning of the presample period are not generated by the same process as that which generates the remaining observations. Boundary solutions may still be obtained with positive probability although Maddala did not happen to encounter any. The issue of taking proper account of the initial conditions in a dynamic panel model will be discussed in the next section, but I think that the question of boundary solutions is still open.

In two papers published shortly after Maddala (1971a), Maddala (1971b) dealt with a Bayesian approach to the estimation of variance-components models with purely exogenous regressors and reported additional Monte Carlo results for this case (Maddala and Mount, 1973).

In the decade preceding the first Paris conference, methodogical research emphasized alternatives to maximum-likelihood estimation: Mundlak (1978), already noted, was circulating widely in preliminary from prior to its publication. Also notable were Amemiya (1971), C. R. Rao (1972), and Fuller and Battese (1974). But a number of remarkable empirical applications appeared in the course of the decade. (Although several were not published until after

---

[36] Trognon (1978) later showed that such boundary solutions will occur with a positive probability when the parameters of the process generating the data fall in certain quite plausible ranges, thus confirming the Monte Carlo findings reported in Nerlove (1971). See below.

[37] Breusch (1987) later followed through on Maddala's results, showing in the course of a paper on iterated GLS applied to the nondynamic random-effects model that the estimated values of Maddala's parameter θ, the ratio of the characteristic roots of the variance-covariance matrix of the disturbances in a two-component model, form a monotonic sequence. He argued that this property could be used to check for the possibility of multiple maxima, which Maddala had noted, and for the existence of a local maximum of the likelihood satisfying the non-negativity condition.

1977, the year of the watershed Paris conference, I include them here since working paper versions were in wide circulation.)[38]

Disturbances in the structual equations are the best-known example of latent or unobserved or latent variables in econometrics: "An unobservable variable is one that is measured with error. Sometimes, the error is due to inaccurate measurement in the narrow sense. More broadly, it arises whenever measurable quantities differ from their theoretical counterparts." (Goldberger, 1974, p. 193.) Beginning with Griliches and Mason (1972), Griliches (1974, 1977) and Chamberlain and Griliches (1975) undertook a series of investigations on the relation among income, ability, and schooling. Here is a typical example from Griliches and Mason (1972): Let y_{kij} be the kth indicator of success (earnings, occupational status, etc.) of an individual j belonging to a family i; X_{kij} are some exogenous observed factors affecting the individual or the family into which he was born; S_{ij} is schooling received; A_{ij} is an unobserved variable reflecting "ability"; u_{kij} is the usual econometric disturbance reflecting left out factors (see Haavelmo, 1944), and is assumed to be independent of the disturbance for any other indicator of success and of X_{kij}, S_{ij}, and A_{ij}. A and X are also assumed to be independent. The relations we want to estimate are

$$y_{kij} = X_{kij}\alpha_k + S_{ij}\beta_k + A_{ij}\gamma_k + u_{kij},$$

one for each k. The parameter of interest is β, the effect of schooling on earnings in particular, for the adjustment of labor input in the measurement of total factor productivity. The problem is, of course, that we don't observe A_{ij}. We can assume that it is highly correlated with schooling so that just leaving it out would bias the measured effects of schooling upwards. Assume

$$S_{ij} = Z_{ij}\delta + A_{ij}\theta + w_{ij},$$

where Z_{ij} are some exogenous variables, possibly among those included in X, and w_{ij} is a disturbance independent of u_{kij}. Although we cannot observe A_{ij}, we have what Goldberger refers to as multiple indicators of it, namely schooling *and* all the success measures, which, however, also depend on schooling. We might have other indicators of ability not depending also on the amount of schooling received, such as IQ test scores or scores on the Armed Services Qualification test. Such "multiple indicators," as Goldberger (1974) refers to them, help to identify the coefficients in the earnings/schooling relationship despite the unobservability of the latent ability variable.[39] Because of the

[38] Mention should also be made of two Harvard Ph.D. dissertations done under Zvi Griliches's supervision: Mazodier (1971), partially published as Mazodier (1972), and Chamberlain (1975). Mazodier organized the watershed Paris conference of 1977.

[39] Alternatively, multiple causes are also distinguished by Goldberger (1974, pp. 200–204); e.g., the same unobservable, permanent income, affects various categories of expenditures. This too aids identification.

obvious dependence of economic success on unobserved factors related to the family into which an individual is born, as well as to his or her genetic inheritance, the problem cries out for a panel data analysis.

In subsequent papers published in the decade, Griliches (1974, 1977) and Chamberlain and Griliches (1975) further refined these methods relating them to the notion of individual-specific unobserved effects due to left-out variables. The contribution of Chamberlain and Griliches (1975) is specifically to take into account the information afforded by more than one relationship involving the *same latent variable*; that is, to confront the problem of simultaneous-equations bias head on. They write (pp. 422–423):

> The usual response to the availability of data with a group structure, e.g., families and family members, firms and time, is to estimate the relationships of interest from the within-group data. In the context of estimating income and schooling relationships, such calculations would "take care" of parental background differences, even though inefficiently (they ignore the between families information in the sample), but would not correct for possible bias from the individual (within family) genetic differences which may be correlated with achieved schooling levels later on. To take this explicitly into account would require the availability of direct measures of such ability, which were not available in the particular data set we were interested in analyzing. But even in their absence, if the missing variable (such as ability) affects more than one *dependent* variable, a bootstrap operation [not in the sense used today] may be possible. The basic idea for the new approach comes from the realization that such a left-out variable must cause similar biases (proportional to each other) in different equations and that taking advantage of that fact may allow one to achieve identification of most of the coefficients of interest.

Because their model and analysis are so relevant to current discussions of panel data econometrics, I will summarize here the gist of the problem and model posed in Chamberlain and Griliches (1975), hereinafter CG: Let X_1 and X_2 be matrices of k_1 and k_2 indicators that may be all or in part the same, and which are taken to be exogenous, such as age. Any discrepancies among the simultaneous equations in the exogenous variables can be handled by zero restrictions, so we can formulate the problem in terms of a common X matrix. In general, truly exogenous variables are hard to come by and difficult to exclude from any particular equation, and this problem is no exception. Let y_1 be the dependent endogenous variable in which we are interested, such as earnings, occupation, test scores, and so forth. There may be several of interest simultaneously, but for this discussion I will restrict the formulation to one plus one more, y_2, such as schooling. Let a be an unobserved (latent) variable reflecting innate ability. Suppose that we have observations on $i = 1, \ldots, I$ families and $j = 1, \ldots, J_i$ individuals within each family, and suppose a_{ij} consists of two components: a family effect and all the rest. Thus,

$$a_{ij} = f_i + g_{ij}, \quad i = 1, \ldots, I, \quad j = 1, \ldots, J_i.$$

CG assume the following structure, where the subscripts i and j have been suppressed:

$$y_1 = X\alpha_1 + \beta y_2 + \gamma_1 a + u_1$$
$$y_2 = X\alpha_2 + \gamma_2 a + u_2.$$

Solving for y_1 and y_2 yields

$$y_1 = X(\alpha_1 + \beta\alpha_2) + w_1$$
$$y_2 = X\alpha_2 + w_2,$$

where

$$w_1 = (\gamma_1 + \beta\gamma_2)(f + g) + u_1 + \beta u_2 \quad \text{and}$$
$$w_2 = \gamma_2(f + g) + u_2.$$

Stacking first with respect to equation, then with respect to family, and finally with respect to family member, the variance-covariance matrix of the ws can be obtained. It has a more complicated structure than the usual error-components model. The assumption that u_1 and u_2 are uncorrelated is one that might be difficult to justify, but under it and the assumption of no correlation between f and g and between each and the us, CG are able to show that the parameters α_1, α_2, and β are identified (exactly so if there is only one exogenous variable), and that γ_1 and γ_2 are identified up to a multiplicative scale factor (reasonable since the units of a are arbitrary). In principle, then, one can form the likelihood for a set of observations on X, y_1, and y_2. Dynamics, such as we might expect in a model of firm behavior, will still further complicate the likelihood formulation (see the discussion of dynamic panel models in the next section), but the principles are clear. Griliches amplified these ideas in his Henry Schultz Memorial Lecture and in his Presidential Address to the Econometric Society (Griliches, 1974, 1977). While structural models involving latent variables were common in the psychometric literature earlier, and CG (1975) represents a return to the 1920s tradition of Sewell Wright in genetics and a major departure in the econometric literature.[40]

During the decade, due in part to the availability of panel data from the University of Michigan Panel Study of Income Dynamics, several papers appeared that used panel data to study the determination of earnings profiles: Hause (1977), Lillard and Willis (1978), and Lillard and Weiss (1979). These are basically dynamic panel models and the problems encountered underscore the difficulties apparent in retrospect in the Balestra-Nerlove (1966) investigation. But at that time, these difficulties were still poorly understood. The stimulus to methodological development in this period afforded by interesting and readily available data sets cannot be overemphasized.

---

[40] See Goldberger (1971, 1972, 1974) and Goldberger and Duncan (1973), especially the introductory chapter by Goldberger. Wright (1921) is the seminal paper.

e. The First Paris Conference, 1977

In August 1977, Pascal Mazodier organized the first conference on panel data econometrics (Colloque International du CNRS, 1978). He had written his thesis (1971) on panel data econometrics at Harvard under Griliches's supervision and was at that time Director of the Unité de Recherche of the Institut National de la Statistique et des Etudes Economiques (INSEE), of which Edmond Malinvaud was then Director General. The influence of this conference on the subsequent course of research was enormous. Over the subsequent two decades, the burbling stream, respectable though it was, became a raging torrent. A major factor was the increased availability of panel data sets. Another factor was the recognition that quantitative investigations were essential to the formulation of good policies for economic development; for the majority of developing countries in which a statistical tradition had not existed for very long, the only recourse to relevant data was to generate cross-section data by survey or, better, if one needed to get at dynamic aspects of behavior, panel surveys, perforce short. But the conference itself set the major directions for subsequent research and brought together many of those who had done, or were to do, research in the field. Rather than summarize the papers presented at the 1977 conference here, I have appended my introduction to the published proceedings (Colloque, 1978) as Appendix C. Note that I refer to panel data as longitudinal data, the older terminology still prevalent in the survey literature.

4. ECONOMETRIC DEVELOPMENT, THE LATER YEARS: FROM PARIS TO PARIS

The twenty years between the first Paris Conference on Panel Data Econometrics of 1977 and the conference held in Paris in 1997, VII Conference on Panel Data Econometrics (CPDE), witnessed a vast amount of both methodological and applied research in the area. Beginning in 1987, when the second conference was held at the University of Paris-XII at Val de Marne, conferences were held every two years in 1989, 1991, 1993, 1995 and, on the twentieth anniversary of the first Paris Conference in 1997, at the Sorbonne. In 1998, the VIII CPDE continued the series in Göteborg, Sweden, with a switch to even-numbered years, and followed by the IX CPDE in Geneva, Switzerland, in 2000. Proceedings were not generally published except partially for the 1997 conference in 1999, but many of the papers were published elsewhere in revised or modified form. The IV CPDE in Budapest in 1991 resulted in the first edition of Mátyás and Sevestre (1991), of which a greatly enlarged second edition was published in 1996. In these years, Gary Chamberlain's (1984) survey for the *Handbook of Econometrics*, Heckman and Singer's (1985) more substantively oriented volume, Cheng Hsiao's (1986) monograph, and Badi Baltagi's (1995) advanced text were also published. My coverage of this twenty-year period must of necessity be highly selective, and being so, somewhat idiosyncratic, representing a personal view and interests. I discuss research primarily of a methodological nature on four topics: (a) problems of testing specification: fixed versus random effects; serially correlated effects; (b) dynamics: properties of alternative estimators and the problem of initial conditions; (c) discrete and qualitative panel data; and (d) very briefly, hazard and duration models.

a. Problems of Testing Specification: Fixed versus Random Effects; Serially Correlated Effects

(1) Hausman Tests. Hausman (1978) proposed a very general test for specification of an econometric model and applied it to test for random versus fixed effects. Hausman and Taylor (1981), in a subsequent paper, generalize the Hausman test and use it to develop an asymptotically ($N \to \infty$, sometimes called *semi-asymptotics*) efficient instrumental variables procedure.[41] Briefly, a Hausman test of a null specification (e.g., the assumption of zero correlation between observed explanatory variables and the individual-specific random effects in a two-component panel model) is based on the existence of an alternative estimator that is consistent under both the null and alternative specifications. "By comparing the estimates from this estimator with the efficient estimator ... [under the assumption that the included explanatory are indeed uncorrelated with the disturbances or any part thereof] and noting that their difference is uncorrelated with the efficient estimator when the null hypothesis is true, easily used tests may be devised from the regression

$$y = X\beta + \tilde{X}\alpha + v,$$

where $\tilde{X}$ is a suitably transformed version of X. The specification tests are performed by constructing a test of the null hypothesis $H_0; \alpha = 0$" (Hausman, 1978, p. 1252). How does this idea play out in the case of the simplest nondynamic panel model? Hausman (1978, pp. 1261–1264) offers the following answer: Consider the simplest case of a panel model, suitably stacked,

$$y = X\beta + u,$$

where, in terms of the notation introduced in Appendix A,

$$u = \begin{bmatrix} \mu_1 \ell_T \\ \vdots \\ \mu_N \ell_T \end{bmatrix} + \begin{bmatrix} \varepsilon_{11} \\ \vdots \\ \varepsilon_{1T} \\ \vdots \\ \varepsilon_{N1} \\ \vdots \\ \varepsilon_{NT} \end{bmatrix} = \mu \otimes \ell_T + \varepsilon,$$

---

[41] Clearly N-asymptotics doesn't make much sense if the individual-effects in the panel model are considered to be fixed. Indeed, the problem is worse than that: the individual effects are then *incidental parameters* in the sense of Kiefer and Wolfowitz (1956) and wreak havoc all around. See also Neyman and Scott (1948), discussed later.

where ℓ_T is a column vector of T ones and $\mu = (\mu_1 \cdots \mu_N)'$. Treating the μs as fixed effects and assuming $\varepsilon \sim N(0, \sigma_\varepsilon^2 I_{NT})$ leads to the within-group estimate of the slope coefficients β as the OLS estimates in the transformed regression:

$$W_N y = W_N X\beta + W_N \varepsilon \quad \text{or } \tilde{y} = \tilde{X}\beta + \tilde{\varepsilon},$$

say, $b_{\text{FE}} = (\tilde{X}'\tilde{X})^{-1}\tilde{X}'\tilde{y} = W_{xx}^{-1}W_{xy}$, in the notation of Appendix B. On the other hand, consider the random-effects specification, equations (6) and (7). If we knew ρ, we could obtain the GLS estimates of β, which in this nondynamic case would be consistent and efficient.[42]

$$b_{\text{GLS}} = \left[\frac{W_{xx}}{\eta} + \frac{B_{xx}}{\xi} \right]^{-1} \left(\frac{W_{xy}}{\eta} + \frac{B_{xy}}{\xi} \right),$$

where $\xi = 1 - \rho + T\rho$ and $\eta = 1 - \rho$. Alternatively in the formulation of Maddala (1971):

$$b_{\text{GLS}} = [W_{xx} + \theta B_{xx}]^{-1} (W_{xy} + \theta B_{xy}), \quad \text{where } \theta = \frac{\eta}{\xi}.$$

While it's not difficult to obtain the ML estimate of ρ or θ, as the case may be (as is done in Appendix B), this method was not considered by Hausman. But in the nondynamic case, any consistent estimate of ρ will do. Suppose that the null hypothesis is taken to be the random-effects specification; in this case, the fixed-effects estimator is unbiased and consistent but not efficient. On the other hand, feasible GLS using a consistent estimate of ρ or θ is efficient. Suppose we have some estimate of ρ or θ, we can define a feasible GLS estimate, b_{FGLS} to be the estimate b_{GLS} above evaluated for such an estimate. If the random-effects specification is correct, the two estimates should be close for large samples (I think Hausman means large T; as $T \to \infty$, the between moments terms drop out of b_{GLS}). Of course, the problem is that we usually don't have large samples, especially large T. Hence, Hausman suggests basing a test on the difference $q = b_{\text{FGLS}} - b_{\text{GLS}}$. If this difference is large, it would suggest, in Hausman's view, a misspecification of the random-effects model; that is, a high degree of correlation between the explanatory variables and the random individual-specific effects. However, if one believes that one ought to expect some correlation between the explanatory variables and the individual-specific effects in a random-effects model if the cross-section variation of the explanatory variables is significant relative to the unexplained cross-sectional differences, as explained in the previous section, a large difference only underscores the importance of the cross-sectional variation in the individual means, which is discarded in the fix-effects formulation.[43] In a Lemma and Corollary, Hausman (1978) shows that the

---

[42] But are neither in the dynamic case. See the following discussion.

[43] Of course, if the correlation is due to a common latent factor affecting both the unobserved individual-specific random effect and one or more of the explanatory variables, this would bias the coefficients of the explanatory variables in the relationship being estimated. But this is a simultaneous-equations problem, as explained in the previous section, and ought to be treated as such.

variance-covariance matrix of the difference $V(q) = V(b_{FE}) - V(b_{GLS})$ and is positive definite. Since $\hat{q} = b_{FE} - b_{FGLS}$, where b_{FGLS} is any feasible GLS estimate using any consistent estimate of ρ or θ, is shown by Hausman to be asymptotically normally distributed, this suggests basing a test of misspecification on

$$ h = \hat{q}'[V(b_{FE}) - V(b_{GLS})]\hat{q}, $$

which, under the circumstances, is χ^2 with as many degrees of freedom as parameters in q, under the null hypothesis of a random-effects model. In view of the orthogonality of X^* and $\tilde{X}$, this is equivalent to testing $\alpha = 0$ in the regression:

$$ y^* = X^*\beta + \tilde{X}\alpha + v. $$

Alternatively, in a likelihood framework, the test is equivalent to testing H_0: $\theta = 0$, but this, of course, maintains the random-effects model.[44] Indeed, this a general problem with the test proposed by Hausman. In the present context, it means that, if the test rejects the null, random effects assuming no correlation of effects and independent explanatory variables is rejected, but it doesn't mean that fixed effects are true. The Hausman test is merely a test for the exogeneity of the explanatory variables included in the model.[45]

Hausman and Taylor (1981), hereinafter HT, again within a random-effects framework, develop a test for individual-specific, time-invariant latent effects, which may be correlated with observed explanatory variables. They discuss conditions for identification when some time-invariant observed variables are treated as explanatory and the conditions under which asymptotically efficient instrumental variables estimates differ from fixed-effects estimates. (Asymptotics are semi-asymptotics with $N \to \infty$.) The model considered is more general than in Hausman (1978) in that time-invariant, observed explanatory variables are included, but it remains nondynamic. The Hausman-Taylor model is

$$ y_{it} = X_{it}\beta + Z_{it}\gamma + \mu_i + \varepsilon_{it}, \quad i = 1, \ldots, N, \quad t = 1, \ldots, T, $$

[44] For the example reported in Appendix B, the estimate b_{FE} is $(0.110, 0.310)'$ and $b_{FGLS} = (0.110, 0.308)'$ (i.e., extremely close) for the ML estimate of $\theta = 0.4179$. In this case, $h = 5.65 \times 10^{-15}$, which is extremely small. It would have been better to have chosen a different example to illustrate my point.

In the dynamic case, for example, if a lagged value of the dependent variable is included as one of the explanatory variables, this explanatory variable, at least, *must* be correlated with the individual-specific effects. This is noted by Hausman (1978, p. 1263, Footnote 18) with the briefest of suggestions concerning the revision of the test required.

[45] This point was made by Holly (1982), who suggested an alternative test of a fixed-effects null based on eliminating the nuisance parameters represented by the fixed effects by concentrating the likelihood function with respect to these parameters and using the likelihood function now only a function of the parameters of primary interest to construct a Lagrange multiplier test of this more relevant null. See also Godfrey (1988, pp. 30–34).

with the assumptions made previously about μ_i and ε_{it}. HT remark that it may be difficult to find appropriate instruments for those columns of X and Z that are potentially correlated with the individual-specific effects and so base a method of obtaining consistent estimates on additional assumptions that some of the variables included are indeed uncorrelated with the latent individual-specific effects, as well as providing under certain circumstances tests for these identifying restrictions. But instruments are required in order to relax some of the zero-correlation assumptions; HT make ingenious use of the time-varying variables to serve as instruments for the observed time-invariant variables, as well as to estimate their own coefficients (means and deviations from means for individuals). Amemiya and MaCurdy (1986) and Breusch, Mizon, and Schmidt (1989) further extend the HT results in the direction of developing more asymptotically efficient estimators.

(2) Serially Correlated Remainder Effects. In the standard two-component random-effects model, serial correlation among the disturbances is assumed to be represented by the individual-specific effects, which induce a strong form of serial correlation for a particular individual across all the time periods for which that individual is observed. But more complicated forms are possible and the three-component model introduces the empirically relevant and plausible possibility of serially correlated period effects.

In Lillard and Willis (1978), an AR(1) process is assumed for the remainder effects, ε_{it}, in a panel study of life-cycle earnings and mobility among discrete earnings classes. Data from the University of Michigan Panel Study of Income Dynamics, 1967–1973, for 1,041 white and 103 black male heads of households are used to estimate an earnings function with permanent and serially correlated transitory components due to both measured and unmeasured variables. The object of this analysis is to develop statements for the probability that an individual's earnings will fall into a particular sequence of income states and to contrast these results with those yielded by Markov chain models of income mobility. In the standard two-component model, this represents an extension of the error term u_{it} to

$$u_{it} = \mu_i + \varepsilon_{it}, \quad i = 1, \ldots, N, \quad t = 1, \ldots, T, \text{ where}$$
$$\varepsilon_{it} = \varphi\varepsilon_{i,t-1} + v_{it}, \quad |\varphi| < 1,$$
$$\mu_i \sim IID\left(0, \sigma_\mu^2\right), \qquad v_{it} \sim IID\left(0, \sigma_v^2\right),$$
$$E(\mu_i v_{jt}) = 0, \quad \text{all } i, j, \text{ and } t, \text{ and}$$
$$\mu_i \text{ and } v_{it} \text{ uncorrelated with } x_{it} \text{ for all } i \text{ and } t. \tag{13}$$

Lillard and Willis (1978) estimate both the variance components and the AR(1) parameter φ from the calculated OLS residuals from the pooled sample, which, if no lagged endogenous variables are included as explanatory in the earnings function, is a consistent way to go. They then make the standard transformation for first-order serially correlated disturbances and re-estimate.[46] Lillard and Weiss (1979) use a model in which both serially correlated remainder effects and stochastic linear trends are introduced to study the earnings of American scientists over the period 1960–1970.[47] Their model

[46] This involves transforming the observations for each of the N individuals by premultiplying by

$$
C = \begin{bmatrix}
\sqrt{1 - \varphi^2} & 0 & \cdots & 0 \\
-\varphi & 1 & \cdots & 0 \\
\vdots & \vdots & & \vdots \\
0 & \cdots & -\varphi & 1
\end{bmatrix}.
$$

As Baltagi and Li (1991a) show, the transformed stacked vector of disturbances is

$$
u^* = (I_N \otimes C)u = (I_N \otimes C)\mu + (I_N \otimes C)\varepsilon = (1 - \varphi)(I_N \otimes \ell_T^{\vartheta})\mu + (I_N \otimes C)\varepsilon,
$$

where

$$
\ell_T^{\vartheta} = (\vartheta, \ell'_{T-1})' \quad \text{and} \quad \vartheta = \sqrt{\frac{1 + \vartheta}{1 - \vartheta}}.
$$

Hence, the variance-covariance matrix of the stacked disturbances is

$$
\Omega^* = E(u^* u^{*\prime}) = \sigma_\mu^2 (1 - \varphi^2)(I_N \otimes \ell_T^{\vartheta} \ell_T^{\vartheta\prime}) + \sigma_v^2 (I_N \otimes I_T),
$$

since

$$
(I_N \otimes C) E(\varepsilon \varepsilon')(I_N \otimes C') = \sigma_v^2 (I_N \otimes I_T).
$$

Let

$$
\ell_T^{\vartheta\prime} \ell_T^{\vartheta} = \dfrac{\bar{J}_T^{\vartheta} = \ell_T^{\vartheta} \ell_T^{\vartheta\prime}}{\dfrac{\ell_T^{\vartheta} \ell_T^{\vartheta\prime}}{(1 - \varphi^2) + (T - 1)}} ;
$$

then Baltagi and Li (1991a) show the spectral decomposition of Ω^* can be written

$$
\Omega^* = ((1 - \varphi^2) + (T - 1))(1 - \varphi)^2 \sigma_\mu^2 (I_N \otimes \bar{J}_T^{\vartheta}) + \sigma_v^2 (I_N \otimes (I_T - \bar{J}_T^{\vartheta})).
$$

Thus, the observations may be transformed by premultiplying by

$$
\sqrt{\sigma_v^2} \Omega^{*-\frac{1}{2}} = (I_N \otimes I_T) - \theta(I_N \otimes \bar{J}_T^{\vartheta}), \quad \text{where}
$$

$$
\theta = 1 - \sqrt{\dfrac{\sigma_v^2}{((1 - \varphi^2) + (T - 1))(1 - \varphi)^2 \sigma_\mu^2}},
$$

has the same form as the Maddala (1971) transformation. The likelihood function is now easily constructed and can be concentrated with respect to φ and $\sigma_\varepsilon^2 = \sigma_v^2/(1 - \varphi^2)$. A likelihood ratio test may be constructed for hypotheses jointly referring to φ and σ_μ^2 (Baltagi and Li, 1991b).

[47] A model with stochastic linear trends alone was used to study growth rates and convergence for a panel of countries in Nerlove (1999c). The problem with stochastic linear trends is that the resulting model is nonstationary, a problem that is addressed in Nerlove (1999c) by differencing but does not seem to have occurred to Lillard and Weiss (1979). See also Moon and Phillips (1999) for a discussion of the fixed-effects case.

for the panel disturbance is

$$u_{it} = \mu_i + \xi_i t + \varepsilon_{it}, \quad i = 1, \ldots, N, \quad t = 1, \ldots, T, \text{ where}$$

$$\varepsilon_{it} = \varphi \varepsilon_{i,t-1} + v_{it}, \quad |\varphi| < 1,$$

$$\mu_i \sim IID(0, \sigma_\mu^2), \qquad v_{it} \sim IID(0, \sigma_v^2),$$

$$E(\mu_i v_{jt}) = 0, \quad \text{all } i, j \text{ and } t,$$

$$E\mu_i \xi_{i'} = \begin{cases} \sigma_{\mu\xi}, & i = i' \\ 0, & \text{otherwise} \end{cases} \tag{14}$$

and

$$\mu_i \text{ and } v_{it} \text{ uncorrelated with } x_{it} \text{ for all } i \text{ and } t.[48]$$

The problem of testing for serial correlation using modified Durbin-Watson statistics in fixed-effects models for panel data is addressed by Bharghava, Franzini, and Narendranathan (1982).

(3) Serially Correlated Period Effects. The time periods over which economic phenomena are measured are to a large extent arbitrary, at least with respect to the decisions underlying the data-generating processes we seek to understand. In a panel analysis, it is plausible both that some factors affect all individuals observed in the same period and that these factors tend to persist over time during several of the periods for which the data are collected. For example, in his dissertation, Grunfeld (1958) studied the investment decisions of major U.S. corporations using a panel of ten firms over twenty years, 1935–1954. He collected data for each of the firms on real gross investment, I_{it}, on the real value of shares in the firm outstanding (his major innovation at the time), F_{it}, and on the real value of the capital stock (cumulated depreciated past investments), C_{it}. He fit relationships of the form:

$$I_{it} = \alpha + \beta_1 F_{it} + \beta_2 C_{it}, \quad i = 1, \ldots, 10, \quad t = 1, \ldots, 20.$$

His data covered a period that included both recovery from the depression of the 1930s (and a brief further sharp recession in 1937) and World War II and its aftermath. Not only were many of the same things happening to the ten firms analyzed in any particular year, but surely these effects, both observed and unobserved, were not confined to any particular year but tended to be spread over several years. An appropriate model for the panel disturbance in

[48] First differencing each individual's observations over time would leave $\Delta u_{it} = \xi_i + \eta_{it}$, where η_{it} is generated by the ARMA(1, 1) model: $\eta_{it} - \varphi \eta_{i,t-1} = \varepsilon_{it} - \varepsilon_{i,t-1}$; that is, a two-component random-effects model with ARMA(1, 1) remainder effect. AR(2), AR(4), and MA(q) processes in the remainder component have been discussed in the literature (summarized in Baltagi, 1995, pp. 81–88).

this case would be

$$u_{it} = \mu_i + \lambda_t + \varepsilon_{it}$$

with

   (i) $E(\mu_i) = E(\lambda_t) = E(\varepsilon_{it}) = 0,$ all i and t,

   (ii) $E(\mu_i \varepsilon_{jt}) = E(\mu_i \lambda_t) = E(\lambda_t \varepsilon_{it}) = 0,$ all i, j, and t,

   (iii) $E(\mu_i \mu_j) = \begin{cases} \sigma_\mu^2 & i = j \\ 0 & i \neq j, \end{cases}$

   (iv) $\lambda_t = \varphi \lambda_{t-1} + \psi_t,$ $E(\psi_t \psi_{t'}) = \begin{cases} \sigma_\psi^2, & t = t' \\ 0, & t \neq t' \end{cases},$

   (v) $E(\varepsilon_{it} \varepsilon_{js}) = \begin{cases} \sigma_\varepsilon^2 & t = s, i = j \\ 0 & \text{otherwise} \end{cases}.$ (15)

   Revankar (1979) suggested a two-step transformation procedure to which GLS or feasible GLS might be applied in order to estimate a nondynamic panel model with disturbances of the form (15). His transformation makes use of the transformation suggested by Pesaran (1973), and independently by Balestra (1980), for the diagonalization of the variance-covariance matrix of the first-order moving-average process. While Revankar's transformation can be used to formulate the joint likelihood function for the three-component model, it is unfortunately the case that the initial observations are correlated with the transformed observations so that the variance-covariance matrix of the stacked transformed residuals cannot be reduced to diagonal form in the usual way by weighting deviations from individual and period means and the means themselves appropriately. Moreover, because of individual-specific effects, a partial likelihood function of the sort suggested by Cox (1975) based on only the T-1 transformed observations of the data cannot be shown to have the optimal asymptotic properties he describes for other models. Revankar (1979) does not go all the way to the likelihood function for this reason, but suggests instead a feasible GLS approach. A more straightforward approach to the likelihood function, which is not subject to these difficulties, has been suggested by Balestra (unpublished correspondence, March 27, April 3, and April 17, 2000) and is reported in Appendix D. An essentially equivalent reformulation has been proposed by Karlsson and Skoglund (2000) in a paper presented at the IX CPDE in June 2000. The Karlsson-Skoglund formulation also includes the case in which the process generating the time-specific effects is MA(1) as well as AR(1) and is, at least in principle, easily generalized to general ARMA processes. It is useful to see how the Revankar approach to the problem goes as evidence of the kinds of difficulties that led researchers at the time to seek nonlikelihood methods for panel model estimation.[49]

Here's how Revankar (1979) proceeded: Suppose we want to estimate

$$y_{it} = \alpha + \beta x_{it} + u_{it}, \quad i = 1, \dots N, \quad t = 1, \dots, T, \tag{16}$$

with disturbances given by (15). Transform

$$y_i = (y_{i1}, \dots, y_{it}), x_i = (x_{i1}, \dots, x_{iT}), \quad \text{and} \quad u_i = (u_{i1}, \dots, u_{iT})$$

to

$$\tilde{y}_i = R y_i, \tilde{x}_i = R x_i, \tilde{u}_i = R u_i,$$

where

$$R = \begin{bmatrix} \sqrt{1 - \varphi^2} & 0 & \dots & 0 \\ -\varphi & 1 & \dots & 0 \\ \dots & \dots & \dots & 0 \\ 0 & \dots & \dots & 1 \end{bmatrix}.$$

$$\tilde{u}_{i1} = \sqrt{1 - \varphi^2} u_{i1}$$
$$\tilde{u}_{it} = u_{it} - \varphi u_{it-1}$$
$$= \mu_i(1 - \varphi) + \psi_t + \varepsilon_{it} - \varphi \varepsilon_{it-1}, \quad t = 2, \dots, T.$$

Stacking for individual i, we obtain

$$\tilde{y}_i = \tilde{\alpha} + \beta \tilde{x}_i + \tilde{u}_i, \tag{17}$$

where

$$\tilde{\alpha} = \alpha(1 - \varphi),$$

$$\tilde{u}_i = \begin{bmatrix} \tilde{u}_{i1} \\ \tilde{u}_{i2} \end{bmatrix} = R u_i = \begin{bmatrix} \sqrt{1 - \varphi^2} u_{i1} \\ u_{i2} - \varphi u_{i1} \\ \vdots \\ u_{iT} - \varphi u_{iT-1} \end{bmatrix}$$

$$= \begin{bmatrix} \sqrt{1 - \varphi^2} \mu_i + \sqrt{1 - \varphi^2} \lambda_1 + \sqrt{1 - \varphi^2} \varepsilon_{i1} \\ (1 - \varphi)\mu_i + \psi_2 + \varepsilon_{i2} - \varphi \varepsilon_{i1} \\ \vdots \\ (1 - \varphi)\mu_i + \psi_T + \varepsilon_{iT} - \varphi \varepsilon_{iT-1} \end{bmatrix}.$$

Note that for $\varphi = 0$, this reduces to the standard three-component model. The final term in the disturbances for $2, \dots, T, \varepsilon_{it} - \varphi \varepsilon_{it-1}$, is a first-order moving

---

[49] I am indebted to Patrick Sevestre for some corrections to my original exposition of the Revankar formulation.

average with variance-covariance matrix

$$\Omega = \begin{bmatrix} 1+\varphi^2 & -\varphi & 0 & \cdots & 0 \\ -\varphi & 1+\varphi^2 & -\varphi & \cdots & 0 \\ \cdots & \cdots & \cdots & \cdots & \cdots \\ 0 & 0 & \cdots & -\varphi & 1+\varphi^2 \end{bmatrix}.$$

Ω is a $T-1 \times T-1$ tridiagonal matrix.

Following Pesaran (1973) and Shaman (1969), a further transformation can be made to reduce Ω to diagonal form: The characteristic vectors of Ω are

$$P_{t+1} = \sqrt{\frac{2}{T+1}}\left(\sin\frac{t\pi}{T+1}, \sin\frac{2t\pi}{T+1}, \ldots, \sin\frac{Tt\pi}{T+1}\right), \qquad t = 1, \ldots, T-1,$$

(18)

with corresponding characteristic roots

$$\gamma_{t+1} = (1+\varphi^2) - 2\varphi\cos\frac{t\pi}{T+1}, \qquad t = 1, \ldots, T-1.$$

(19)

The matrix

$$P = \begin{bmatrix} P_2 \\ \vdots \\ P_T \end{bmatrix} \text{ transforms } \Omega \text{ to } \Gamma, \qquad \text{where } \Gamma = \begin{pmatrix} \gamma_2 & \cdots & 0 \\ \vdots & \ddots & \vdots \\ 0 & \cdots & \gamma_T \end{pmatrix},$$

$$P\Omega P' = \Gamma.$$

(20)

It is useful to normalize the characteristic vectors by multiplying P by the inverse of the square root of PP', $(PP')^{-\frac{1}{2}}$, since this results in a matrix, as noted by Balestra (1980), that does not depend on φ.

Further transform $\tilde{u}_i$ by premultiplying by the $T \times T$ matrix

$$\tilde{P} = \begin{bmatrix} 1 & 0 \\ 0 & P \end{bmatrix}.$$

Thus,

$$\tilde{u}_i^* = \tilde{P}\tilde{u}_i = \tilde{P}\begin{bmatrix} \tilde{u}_{i1} \\ \tilde{u}_{i2} \end{bmatrix} = \tilde{P}Ru = \begin{bmatrix} \sqrt{1-\varphi^2}\mu_i + \sqrt{1-\varphi^2}\lambda_1 + \sqrt{1-\varphi^2}\varepsilon_{i1} \\ P\begin{bmatrix} (1-\varphi)\mu_i + \psi_2 + \varepsilon_{i2} - \varphi\varepsilon_{i1} \\ \vdots \\ (1-\varphi)\mu_i + \psi_T + \varepsilon_{iT} - \varphi\varepsilon_{iT-1} \end{bmatrix} \end{bmatrix},$$

$$= \begin{bmatrix} \sqrt{1-\varphi^2}\mu_i + \sqrt{1-\varphi^2}\lambda_1 + \sqrt{1-\varphi^2}\varepsilon_{i1} \\ (1-\varphi)\mu_i(P\ell_{T-1}) + P\psi + P\tilde{\varepsilon}_i \end{bmatrix},$$

where $\psi = (\psi_2, \ldots \psi_T)'$ and $\tilde{\varepsilon}_i = (\varepsilon_{i2} - \varphi\varepsilon_{i1}, \ldots, \varepsilon_{iT} - \varphi\varepsilon_{iT-1})'$.

(21)

Because μ_i, ψ_t, and ε_{it} are assumed to be mutually uncorrelated and uncorrelated for different i's and t's and since $\sigma_\lambda^2 = \sigma_\psi^2/(1 - \varphi^2)$ and $PP' = I$:

$$E\tilde{u}_i^* \tilde{u}_{i'}^{*\prime} = \begin{bmatrix} (1 - \varphi^2)\sigma_\lambda^2 & 0 \\ 0 & PE\psi\psi'P' \end{bmatrix} = \sigma_\psi^2 I_T, \quad i \neq i'. \tag{22}$$

When $\varphi = 0$, $\sigma_\psi^2 = \sigma_\lambda^2$. But for $i = i'$, we have a much more complicated form than for the standard three-component model with serially uncorrelated period effects:

$$E\tilde{u}_i^* \tilde{u}_i^{*\prime} = \begin{bmatrix} \sigma_{11} & \sigma_{12} \\ \sigma_{21} & \Sigma_{22} \end{bmatrix},$$

$$\sigma_{11} = (1 - \varphi^2) \left\{ \sigma_\mu^2 + \frac{\sigma_\psi^2}{(1 - \varphi^2)} + \sigma_\varepsilon^2 \right\}, \tag{23}$$

where

$$\sigma_{21} = \sigma_{12}' = \sqrt{1 - \varphi^2}(1 - \varphi)\sigma_\mu^2 P\ell_{T-1} + 0 + 0$$

$$\Sigma_{22} = (1 - \varphi^2)\sigma_\mu^2 Q + \sigma_\psi^2 I_{T-1} + \sigma_\varepsilon^2 \Gamma, \quad Q = P\ell_{T-1}\ell_{T-1}'P'.$$

Note that when $\varphi = 0$,

$$\Gamma = I_{T-1}, \quad P = \begin{bmatrix} 0 & \cdots & 0 & 1 \\ 0 & \cdots & 1 & 0 \\ \cdots & \cdots & \cdots & \cdots \\ 1 & 0 & \cdots & 0 \end{bmatrix}, \quad P\ell_{T-1} = \ell_{T-1}, \quad \text{and} \quad Q = \ell_{T-1}\ell_{T-1}'.$$

So,

$$\Sigma = \begin{bmatrix} \sigma_\mu^2 + \sigma_\lambda^2 + \sigma_\varepsilon^2 & \sigma_\mu^2 & \cdots & \sigma_\mu^2 \\ \sigma_\mu^2 & \sigma_\mu^2 + \sigma_\lambda^2 + \sigma_\varepsilon^2 & \cdots & \sigma_\mu^2 + \sigma_\lambda^2 + \sigma_\varepsilon^2 \\ \cdots & \cdots & \cdots & \cdots \\ \sigma_\mu^2 & \sigma_\mu^2 + \sigma_\lambda^2 + \sigma_\varepsilon^2 & \cdots & \sigma_\mu^2 + \sigma_\lambda^2 + \sigma_\varepsilon^2 \end{bmatrix}. \tag{24}$$

Thus, when there is no serial correlation of period effects, $\varphi = 0$, the model reduces to the standard three-component model, which assumes serially independent effects–as it should.

Stacking, we obtain the variance-covariance matrix for the panel:

$$\Omega = \Sigma \otimes I_N + \sigma_\psi^2 (I_T \otimes (J_N - I_N)). \tag{25}$$

Ω is an NT × NT positive definite matrix in terms of which the likelihood of the transformed observations $\tilde{P}Ry$ and $\tilde{P}Rx$ can be expressed. Unfortunately, because of the way in which Σ depends on the initial observations, the easy determination of Ω^{-1} and det Ω in terms of its characteristic roots and the within and between variation of the observations no longer seems possible.

However, since both the transformation of the observations and Ω depend on the parameter φ, the likelihood function can be concentrated in the usual way by holding that parameter fixed and doing GLS on the transformed observations, substituting the results in the likelihood function for the given value of φ. Although sparse, the matrix Ω can be rather large and difficult to invert numerically. Since both Ω^{-1} and det Ω must be evaluated repeatedly for triples of values

$$\varphi, \rho = \frac{\sigma_\mu^2}{\sigma_\mu^2 + \sigma_\lambda^2 + \sigma_\varepsilon^2}, \quad \omega = \frac{\sigma_\lambda^2}{\sigma_\mu^2 + \sigma_\lambda^2 + \sigma_\varepsilon^2},$$

the need to obtain the inverse and the determinant in the nondiagonal form makes computation for large panels highly problematic. An alternative to the Revankar approach is given in Appendix D, in which the observations are not transformed, thus avoiding the initial value problem.

b. Dynamics: Comparative Properties of Alternative Estimators and the Problem of Initial Conditions

Estimation of dynamic panel data models is a great deal more difficult than the estimation of nondynamic models. Not only do the properties of various estimators differ substantially in the static and dynamic cases, but a formulation of the appropriate likelihood function for the data is complicated and depends not only on whether one assumes that the effects are random or fixed, but also on what one assumes about the data-generating process prior to the time individuals begin to be observed. If one believes, as I do, that all interesting economic behavior is inherently dynamic, dynamic panel models are the only relevant models; what might superficially appear to be a static model only conceals underlying dynamics, since any state variable presumed to influence present behavior is likely to depend in some way on past behavior; and cross-section data are only panels with time dimension 1, for which we may effectively be precluded from studying the dynamics, but in which the dynamics affects what is observed.[50]

In Balestra and Nerlove (1966), the dynamic aspects of behavior, which were central to the theoretical development and used to assess the adequacy of the statistical results, were handled inappropriately in the formulation of the likelihood function. (What's past is not predetermined in cross-section or panel data, especially when individual-specific effects are important.) But this

---

[50] Ridder and Wansbeek (1990) give a derivation of most of the results of this section assuming that the initial observations on the dependent variable have been generated by the same data-generating process in the pre-sample as in the sample period. This section surveys the historical development of knowledge about the comparative properties of alternative methods of estimation.

paper uncovered a number of interesting anomalies in otherwise plausible estimates: (1) OLS for the pooled sample, ignoring the panel nature of the data, led to unreasonably high ("biased") estimates of the coefficient of the lagged dependent variable; (2) the incorporation of individual state dummies, what we would now call fixed effects, led to unreasonably low estimates for the coefficient of the lagged dependent variable; and, finally, (3) treatment of both exogenous variables and the lagged value of the dependent variable as if it were fixed in repeated samples led to maximum likelihood estimates of the intraclass correlation in a random-effects model on the boundary of the permissible region; in fact, zero, thus giving back the pooled OLS regression estimate of the coefficient of the lagged dependent variable. All of these anomalies were verified in the Monte Carlo study of Nerlove (1971a). Nerlove (1967) verified the first two anomalies but not the presence of boundary solutions. For simplicity, I restrict attention in this section to the simple model containing one exogenous variable x_{it} and one lagged value of the dependent variable y_{it-1} as explanatory. The lagged value of the dependent variable should be considered as a "stand-in" for a general state variable (i.e., a variable that reflects the state of a dynamic system at each point in time). Extension to the case in which more than one exogenous explanatory variable is included presents no serious difficulty. More complicated forms of state dependence are not considered. The relationship to be estimated is

$$y_{it} = \alpha + \beta x_{it} + \gamma y_{it-1} + \mu_i + \varepsilon_{it}, \quad i = 1, \dots N, \quad t = 1, \dots T. \quad (26)$$

Taking deviations from overall means eliminates the constant α. The disturbances are assumed to follow the customary two-component random-effects model. The usual assumptions, as laid out in equation (6), are made about the properties of the μ_i and the ε_{it}.

Both μ_i and ε_{it} are assumed to be uncorrelated with x_{it} for all i and t. While this assumption is far from innocuous, for example, if the independent variable x_{it} is not independent of the dependent variable y_{it} or unobserved factors that affect it (see for example the discussion of Chamberlain and Griliches, 1975), it is the one typically made in this period. Clearly, however, y_{it-1} cannot be assumed to be uncorrelated with μ_i. This is the heart of the difference between dynamic and nondynamic panel models, and this was recognized already in Balestra and Nerlove (1966).

Because y_{it-1} cannot be assumed to be uncorrelated with μ_i, it is clear that OLS applied to (1) ignoring the component nature of the disturbances $u_{it} = \mu_i + \varepsilon_{it}$, which I call the *pooled regression*, will yield inconsistent estimates; in particular, if $\gamma > 0$, γ_{pooled} is "biased" upwards. So, just as in the case of ordinary serial correlation, β_{pooled} is also "biased" and the OLS residuals understate the amount of serial correlation, which in this case is measured by the intraclass correlation coefficient ρ. This parameter measures the extent of unobserved or latent time-invariant, individual-specific, variation relative to the total unobserved variation in the sample, $\rho = \sigma_\mu^2/(\sigma_\mu^2 + \sigma_\varepsilon^2)$. It is extremely important in understanding the nature of the variation, both observed and unobserved, in the panel.

(1) Inconsistency of the Pooled-Sample OLS Estimates of the Dynamic Error-Components Model. Since the panel has two dimensions, it is possible to consider asymptotic behavior as $N \to \infty$, $T \to \infty$, or both. Generally speaking, it is easier to imagine increasing the cross-section dimension of a panel, so the most relevant asymptotics are as $N \to \infty$. This is called *semi-asymptotics* in the panel data literature generally. It is not necessary to assume $|\gamma| < 1$ as long as T is fixed, but the way in which the initial values of the dependent variable, y_{i0}, are assumed to be generated is crucial. To see why, write (26), with (6), as

$$y_{it} = \gamma^t y_{i0} + \sum_{j=0}^{t-1} \gamma^j \beta x_{it-j} + \frac{1 - \gamma^t}{1 - \gamma} \mu_i + v_{it}, \quad \text{where } v_{it} = \sum_{j=0}^{t-1} \gamma^j \varepsilon_{it-j}.$$

(27)

Equation (27) expresses y_{it} as the sum of four terms: the first, $\gamma^t y_{i0}$, depends on the initial values; the second on lagged values of the exogenous variable; the third on the individual, time-invariant, component of residual variance; and the fourth on lagged values of the remaining component. This last term is an autoregressive process with initial values $v_{i0} = 0$ and $v_{it} = \gamma v_{it-1} + \varepsilon_{it}$.[51] It need not be assumed to be stationary as long as T is fixed. It does not make sense in this context to assume that the y_{i0} are uncorrelated with either the μ_i or the lagged values of the x_{it}'s. On the other hand, ε_{i0} is a random variable with mean 0 and variance σ_ε^2 independently and identically distributed for all i. Thus, the initial observation can be written as a function of lagged x's, the μ_i and ε_{i0}:

$$y_{i0} = f(x_{i0}, x_{i-1}, \ldots, \mu_i, \varepsilon_{i0}).$$

(28)

Clearly, if the individual effects μ_i are assumed to be fixed and the lagged x's to be given, the y_{i0} are also fixed and uncorrelated with the disturbances in (27), $v_{it}, t = 1, \ldots, T$. But, if the individual effects are considered random, the

---

[51] See Ridder and Wansbeek (1990, p. 559). RW go on to ask what the estimate of δ would be in a simple nondynamic cross-sectional relationship for fixed t, $y_{it} = \delta x_{it} + u_{it}, i = 1, \ldots, N$, if the process that generates the exogenous variable is covariance stationary and identical for all i, $E(x_{it}x_{i,t-k}) = \sigma_x^2 r_k$. If d_t is the OLS estimate, $E(d_t) = (1 - \gamma)\beta \sum_{k=0}^{\infty} \gamma^k r_k$, certainly nothing like many authors at the time described as "the long-run relationship" between x and y. Moreover, if the exogenous variable is not autocorrelated, $E(d_t)$ is the impact multiplier, $(1 - \gamma)\beta$, whereas if x_{it} is constant or follows a deterministic trend, the OLS estimator in a cross section is an unbiased estimate of β. For panel data, the OLS estimator is simply a weighted average of the cross-section estimates with weights that depend on the moments of the exogenous variable (suppressing a subscript i denotes an $N \times 1$ column vector): $d = \sum_{t=1}^{T} w_t d_t$, where $w_t = \frac{x_t' x_t}{\sum_{t=1}^{T} x_t' x_t}$, so that $E(d) = E(d_t)$.

initial observations are not exogenous since they are correlated with them, as they are part of the disturbance term, namely the third and fourth terms of (27). The assumption that the initial conditions are fixed is inconsistent with the assumption of a random-effects model for the disturbance. Nonetheless, fixed initial conditions were the basis for almost all methods of estimation up to the papers by Anderson and Hsiao (1981, 1982), including maximum likelihood.

It is common in the literature on random-effects panel data models beginning in the 1980s (Hsiao, 1986, Chapter 4, pp. 71–96) to assume that the y_{i0} are i.i.d. random variables that are characterized by their second moments and correlations with the individual effects and not necessarily generated by the same process that generates the rest of the y_{it}s. The properties of various estimators depend on the process generating them. One possibility is to try to model and estimate this process together with the dynamic panel model (1).[52] Popular method-of-moments estimators (see, for example, Chamberlain, 1984) are, generally speaking, unaffected by initial conditions. But I would argue that, since these conditions contain information about how the process has operated in the past before the panel observations were obtained, they ought to be highly relevant and thus their effects should not be minimized.

(2) Inconsistency of the OLS Estimators of the Dummy Variable, or Fixed-Effects, Model. A second finding in Balestra and Nerlove (1966), verified in the Monte Carlo results reported in Nerlove (1971a), was that the fixed-effects estimates of the coefficient of the lagged dependent variable appear to be biased downward. Nickell (1981) demonstrates analytically that this should be the case: The ordinary least-squares estimates of both the coefficient of the lagged dependent variable and the exogenous variable are inconsistent in the fixed-effects model. As is well known, the fixed-effects model is equivalent to taking deviations from individual/group means and then estimating an ordinary OLS regression:

$$y_{it} - \bar{y}_{i.} = \beta(x_{it} - \bar{x}_{i.}) + \gamma(y_{i,t-1} - \bar{y}_{i,-1}) + v_{it}, \text{ where}$$

$$v_{it} = \varepsilon_{it} - \bar{\varepsilon}_{i.}. \tag{29}$$

Although $\sigma_{x\varepsilon} = 0$,

$$\sigma^2_{y(-1)\varepsilon} = N \xrightarrow[]{p \lim} \infty \frac{1}{T} \sum_t (y_{i,t-1} - \bar{y}_{i,-1})(\varepsilon_{it} - \bar{\varepsilon}_{i-1})$$

$$= -\frac{1}{T^2} \frac{T - 1 - T\gamma + \gamma^T}{(1 - \gamma)^2} \sigma^2_\varepsilon \neq 0. \tag{30}$$

---

[52] Besides Hsiao (1986), the following deal with this problem: Anderson and Hsiao (1981, 1982), Lee (1981), Bhargava and Sargan (1983), Ridder and Wansbeek (1990), Blundell and Smith (1991), Hahn (1999), Nerlove (1999c), and Arellano and Honoré (2001).

Thus, the OLS estimates of both β and γ in the fixed-effects model are inconsistent, although at $T \to \infty$, the inconsistency disappears. But for finite,
typically small T, it remains (Nickell, 1981, p. 1424).[53] For $T = 10$ and $\gamma = 0.5$,
for example, the "bias" of the OLS estimate of γ, say c, is proportional to
-0.16, the factor of proportionality being the OLS estimate of the variance of
c from the within regression. It is always negative, implying that the bias of the
OLS estimate of β, say b, is therefore upward. This conclusion holds regardless
of whether one assumes the true model is fixed- or random-effects.[54]

(3) Generalized Least Squares and Feasible GLS. The means-, or between-
regression, and the fixed-effects regression both contain information about the
parameters of the model: the means regression reflects purely cross-sectional
variation; whereas the fixed-effects regression reflects the individual variation
over time. GLS combines these two types of information with weights that depend on the characteristic roots of $Euu' = \sigma^2 \Omega$. The individual means themselves are weighted by the reciprocal of the square root of $\xi = 1 - \rho + T\rho$,
while the deviations from these means are weighted by the reciprocal of the
square root of $\eta = 1 - \rho$. A representative transformed observation is

$$y_{it}^* = \xi^{-1/2}\bar{y}_{i.} + \eta^{-1/2}(y_{it} - \bar{y}_{i.}), \quad i = 1, \ldots, N, \quad t = 1, \ldots, T.$$

Thus, y_{it}^* is a *weighted* combination (weighted by the reciprocals of the square
roots of the characteristic roots of Ω) of individual means of the original observations $\bar{y}_{i.}$ and deviations from individual means ($y_{it} - \bar{y}_{i.}$). The other variables
are similarly transformed to X_{it}^* and $y_{it}^*(-1)$. GLS amounts to running the OLS
regression:

$$y_{it}^* = \alpha^* + \beta X_{it}^* + \gamma y_{it-1}^* + v_{it}. \tag{31}$$

v_{it} is the transformed disturbance. Note that the constant has a different interpretation.

As discussed in the previous section, Maddala (1971a) gave an analysis
of the case in which the between and the within moments were weighted in
proportion to the ratio of the characteristic roots ξ and η of the variance-
covariance matrix of the panel disturbances. These GLS estimates are both
consistent and efficient in the static case but, remarkably, are neither in the
dynamic case. This case was first analyzed for the estimation of an AR(1)

---

[53] Beggs and Nerlove (1988) also derive a nonasymptotic approximation to the bias using the
result of Kendall (1954).

[54] Ridder and Wansbeek (1990, pp. 561–563) also deal with the first-difference model designed,
as is the fixed-effects model, to eliminate the individual-specific effects. The same analysis as
outlined in Footnote 48 applies, except the expected value of the least-squares estimate of
the slope in a cross-section nondynamic regression is $E(d_{\Delta t}) = (1 - \gamma)\beta \sum_{k=0}^{\infty} \gamma^k \bar{r}_k$, where
$\bar{r}_k$ is the kth autocorrelation of the first differenced series. So only if x_{it} is integrated of order
1 is d_Δ an unbiased estimate of β. In general, the bias of various estimators of β in a cross
section with dynamic adjustment depends on the correlations of the successive values of
whatever transforms of x are employed.

model from panel data by Sevestre and Trognon (1985), who showed that the asymptotic behavior of the GLS and FGLS estimators for T fixed and $N \to \infty$ depends on Ey_{i0}^2 and $Ey_{i0}\mu_i$.[55] It was in this paper that Sevestre and Trognon first proved the famed Sevestre-Trognon Inequality, equation (32) in Maddala's parametrization.

Maddala (1971a) pointed out that the GLS estimates with $\lambda = \frac{\xi}{\eta}$ can be considered members of a more general class of estimators obtained through different choices of λ. Let $\hat{\lambda}(\lambda)$ be the estimator of γ obtained by solving the GLS normal equations for an arbitrary value of λ. Sevestre and Trognon (1985, 1996, pp. 130–133) show that for the case in which $\beta = 0$, the purely autoregressive case, the following inequality holds:

$$p \lim \hat{\gamma}(0) < \gamma < p \lim \hat{\gamma}(\lambda) < p \lim \hat{\gamma}(1) < p \lim \hat{\gamma}(\infty)$$

$$\text{within} \qquad\qquad \text{GLS} \qquad \text{OLS pooled} \qquad \text{between} \tag{32}$$

Remarkably, the GLS estimate is inconsistent even when a consistent estimate of ρ is used to compute FGLS estimates. The problem is that the lagged dependent variable is correlated even with the transformed disturbance. (See Ridder and Wansbeek, 1990, pp. 566–571, who also derive (32) under the assumption that the process generating the initial observations is the same as for the within-sample observations.)

Since $p \lim \hat{\gamma}(\lambda)$ is a continuous function of λ, there exists a value λ^* in the interval $[0, \xi/\eta]$ for which $p \lim \hat{\gamma}(\lambda) = \gamma$. Sevestre and Trognon (1983) show that this value is

$$\lambda^* = K(1 - \rho) \bigg/ \left\{ \frac{(1 - \gamma^T)E(y_{i0}\mu_i)}{(1 - \gamma)\sigma^2} + K\xi \right\}, \tag{33}$$

where

$$K = \frac{T - 1 - T\gamma + \gamma^T}{T(1 - \gamma)^2}, \tag{34}$$

and ρ, ξ, and σ^2 are as before.

---

[55] Sevestre and Trognon (1985) make the following alternative assumptions: (1) $y_{i0}, i = 1, \ldots, N$, are fixed constants (of course, then $Ey_{i0}\mu_i = 0$, all i); (2) $y_{i0}, i = 1, \ldots, N$, are drawn independently from a population with mean c and variance σ_μ^2 (if μ_i and ε_{it} are also independent, this implies $Ey_{i0}^2 = c^2 + \sigma_\mu^2$ and $Ey_{i0}\mu_i = 0$); (3) $y_{i0}, i = 1, \ldots, N$, are drawn randomly so that they are correlated with the individual specific effects: $y_{i0} = c + k_1\mu_i + k_2\varepsilon_{i0}$ so that $Ey_{i0}^2 = c^2 + k_1^2\sigma_\mu^2 + k_2^2\sigma_\varepsilon^2$, $Ey_{i0}\mu_i = k_1\sigma_\mu^2$. This formulation was first used independently by Beggs (1980) and Sevestre (1983) in two unpublished dissertations (see also Beggs and Nerlove, 1988). It includes as special cases, Anderson and Hsiao (1980), with $k_1 = 1$, and $k_2 = 0$, or $c = 0$ and $k_1 = 1/(1 - \gamma)$, and Nerlove (1967, 1971a) with $c = 0$ and

$$k_1 = \frac{1}{1 - \gamma}, \qquad k_2 = \sqrt{\frac{1}{1 - \gamma^2}}.$$

Ridder and Wansbeek (1990, pp. 566–571) give a somewhat simpler derivation assuming that the process generating the ys is stationary and has been in operation long enough to render the effect of $y_{i, -\infty}$ negligible. They extend the analysis to the case in which a stationary exogenous variable is included among the explanatory variables.

They also show that when $\beta \neq 0$, the estimate $\hat{\gamma}(\lambda)$ behaves almost the same as in the purely autoregressive case. This is also proved by Ridder and Wansbeek (1990) when the exogenous variable follows an independent stationary process. Since the λ^* estimate is consistent when there are no exogenous variables, it remains so when there are. The trick is to obtain a consistent estimate of λ^*, which can be accomplished by finding an appropriate instrumental variable for y_{-1}. Such an instrument may be difficult to find, however, and, even in this case, the results depend heavily on the distribution of the estimate of λ^*.

In the dynamic error-components model, not only are the OLS pooled-regression estimates, the fixed-effect or within estimates, and the between estimates inconsistent, but so are the GLS estimates using the true value of ρ. However, the method of instrumental variables may be used to obtain a feasible member of the λ-class of estimates, which is consistent. (See Sevestre and Trognon, 1996.) An instrumental-variable estimator often removes the dependence of the consistency on the initial observations. Unfortunately, this estimate may have a very large variance, as demonstrated in Nerlove (1971a). I would also argue that the initial observations themselves contain a great deal of information on how the data-generating process (DGP) operated before we began to observe it (Nerlove, 1999c).

The problem of the dependence on the initial observations, however, may be more fully discussed in connection with the maximum-likelihood estimates, to which GLS and FGLS are often considered an approximation more easily computed or more robust to specification error.

(4) Maximum Likelihood and the Problem of Initial Observations. Maddala (1975) underscored the importance of the initial observations in panel data maximum likelihood when he replicated the Monte Carlo experiments reported in Nerlove (1971a) using the distribution of the initial values implied by the design of the Monte Carlo itself rather than treating them, as had Nerlove (1971a), as fixed at the values observed. He did not obtain the boundary solutions obtained in a significant number of cases in the earlier Monte Carlo. He was later to write (Maddala, 1987a, p. 316): "... the assumption made about y_{i0} is important but the most reasonable assumption to make is that the distribution of y_{i0} is implied by the model itself." This idea was later carried forward in Ridder and Wansbeek (1990) and in Nerlove (1999c), but there's a lot of history to come before that.

The developments of the 1980s were foreshadowed in a remarkable paper by Trognon (1978). What Trognon shows is that, when the exogenous variable x is generated by a first-order autoregression with white noise input, $w \sim wn(0, \sigma_w^2\, I)$, also assumed in the Monte Carlo experiments reported in Nerlove (1971a),

$$x = \delta x_{-1} + w.$$

Then maximization of the likelihood function (8), which treats the initial values

y_{i0} as fixed, yields boundary solutions $\hat{\rho} = 0$, which, unlike interior maximum likelihood solutions, are inconsistent, for a considerable and indeed likely range of parameter values. In particular, there is a value of γ,

$$\gamma^* = \frac{(T-3)^2 - 8}{(T+1)^2},$$

such that when $\gamma < \gamma^*$, there exists an interior maximum of the concentrated likelihood function (9), which yields consistent ML estimates, but that when $\gamma \geq \gamma^*$, there are values of ρ for which the conditional likelihood function (8) is maximized at the boundary $\rho = 0$ (i.e., for the OLS estimates of the pooled regression, which we know to be inconsistent). The problem is that, when T is small, the permissible range of γ, the coefficient of the lagged dependent variable, is implausible (e.g., negative or very small). For example, for $T = 5$, $\gamma^* = -0.11$, while for $T = 10$, $\gamma^* = 0.34$. When $\gamma \geq \gamma^*$, whether or not an interior maximum with consistent ML estimates occurs depends on the value of ρ: For $\rho < \rho^*$ boundary maxima occur where

$$\rho^* = \left(\frac{T-1}{T+1}\right)^2 \frac{\beta^2 \sigma_w^2}{\sigma^2} \frac{1-\gamma}{(\gamma - \gamma^*)(1 - \gamma\delta)^2}.$$

For example, when $T = 5$, $\beta = 1.0$, $\gamma = 0.75$, $\delta = 0.5$, and $\frac{\sigma_w^2}{\sigma^2} = 1.0$, $\gamma^* = -0.11$ and the critical value of ρ is $\rho^* = 0.31$. That means that any true value of the intraclass correlation less than 0.31 is liable to produce a boundary solution to (9) $\rho = 0$ and inconsistent estimates of all the parameters. Using these results, Trognon (1978) is able to replicate the Monte Carlo results reported in Nerlove (1971a) theoretically.

The next major developments in understanding the role of initial conditions were two papers by Anderson and Hsiao (1981, 1982), followed by a thesis by Sevestre (1983) and a paper by Sevestre and Trognon (1985).

Anderson and Hsiao (1981), hereinafter AH81, studied the maximum-likelihood estimation of an AR(1) with no additional exogenous explanatory variables under a variety of assumptions concerning the initial conditions. They considered

$$y_{it} = \gamma y_{i,t-1} + \mu_i + \varepsilon_{it}, \quad i = 1, \ldots, N, \ t = 1, \ldots, T, \ |\gamma| < 1. \quad (35)$$

AH81 consider four different cases based on what assumptions are made about the initial values, y_{i0}, and two different estimates for each case. The two estimates are: (1) What AH81 call the "covariance estimator," but what I would call the fixed-effects estimator (FE), based on transforming the observations by premultiplying by $I_T - \frac{J_T}{T}$, in the notation of Appendix B, to

$$y_{it}^* = \left(I_T - \frac{J_T}{T}\right) y_{it}, \quad i = 1, \ldots N, \ t = 1, \ldots T$$

and estimating $y_{it}^* = \gamma y_{i,t-1}^* + \varepsilon_{it}^*$, $i = 1, \ldots, N, t = 1, \ldots, T$ by OLS; and (2) assuming μ_i, ε_{it} normally and independently distributed, maximum-likelihood estimates (ML). The four cases for the initial values, y_{i0}, considered are:

CASE I: FIXED INITIAL OBSERVATIONS. The initial values, y_{i0}, are fixed constants and observable, such that

$$\lim_{N\to\infty} \frac{1}{N} \sum_{i=1}^{N} y_{i0}^2 < \infty.$$

CASE II: RANDOM INITIAL OBSERVATIONS, INDEPENDENT OF μ_i, ε_{it}, WITH A COMMON MEAN AND VARIANCE. Let the common mean be c and the common variance be σ_0^2. Then the joint likelihood for the ith individual is derived from the joint probability of the sample and the initial values:

$$f_i(y_{iT}, \ldots, y_{i1}, y_{i0}) = f_i(y_{iT}, \ldots, y_{i1} \mid y_{i0}) f_i(y_{i0}).$$

The values c and σ_0^2 are to be estimated jointly with γ and σ_μ^2 and σ_ε^2 in the case of the ML estimators. The initial values are considered unknown constants in the case of the FE estimators.

CASE III: RANDOM INITIAL OBSERVATIONS, INDEPENDENT OF μ_i, ε_{it}, WITH DIFFERENT MEANS AND A COMMON VARIANCE.

CASE IV: RANDOM INITIAL OBSERVATIONS WITH A STATIONARY DISTRIBUTION. This is the case considered by Ridder and Wansbeek (1990). In the case of a pure autoregression, the case considered in AH81, the joint density of $y_{iT}, \ldots, y_{i1}, y_{i0}$ is

$$f_i(y_{iT}, \ldots, y_{i1}, y_{i0}) = \left(\frac{1}{2\pi}\right)^{\frac{T+1}{2}} \left(\frac{1}{\rho\sigma^2}\right)^{\frac{T+1}{2}} |\Omega|^{-\frac{1}{2}} \tag{36}$$

$$\times \exp\left\{-\frac{1}{\rho\sigma^2}(y_{i0}, y_{i1}, -\gamma y_{i0}, \ldots, y_{iT} - \gamma y_{i,T-1})'\Omega^{-1}\right.$$

$$\left. \times (y_{i0}, y_{i1} - \gamma y_{i0}, \ldots, y_{iT} - \gamma y_{i,T-1})\right\},$$

where

$$\Omega = \frac{1-\rho}{\rho}\begin{pmatrix} \frac{1}{1-\gamma^2} & 0' \\ 0 & I_T \end{pmatrix} + \begin{pmatrix} \frac{1}{1-\gamma} \\ \ell_T \end{pmatrix}\begin{pmatrix} \frac{1}{1-\gamma} & \ell_T' \end{pmatrix},$$

so that

$$\Omega^{-1} = \frac{\rho}{1-\rho}\left\{\begin{pmatrix} 1-\gamma^2 & 0' \\ 0 & I_T \end{pmatrix} - \left(\frac{1-\rho}{\rho} + T + \frac{1+\gamma}{1-\gamma}\right)^{-1}\begin{pmatrix} 1+\gamma \\ \ell_T \end{pmatrix}(1+\gamma \, \ell_T')\right\},$$

and

$$|\Omega| = \frac{\left(\frac{1-\rho}{\rho}\right)^T}{1-\gamma^2}\left(\frac{1-\rho}{\rho} + T + \frac{1+\gamma}{1-\gamma}\right).$$

Table 1. *Fixed-Effects versus Maximum-Likelihood Estimates of an AR(1) Model from Panel Data; Various Assumptions Regarding the Initial Values,* y_{i0}

Assumption on y_{i0}	Maximum-Likelihood Estimator		Fixed-Effects Estimator	
	$T \to \infty$, N fixed	T fixed, $N \to \infty$	$T \to \infty$, N fixed	T fixed, $N \to \infty$
Case I: Fixed Initial Observations	Consistent	Consistent	Consistent	Inconsistent
Case II: Random Initial Observations, Common Mean and Variance	Consistent	Consistent	Consistent	Inconsistent
Case III: Random Initial Observations, Different Means, Common Variance	Consistent	Inconsistent	Consistent	Inconsistent
Case IV: Random Initial Observations with a Stationary Distribution	Consistent	Consistent	Consistent	Inconsistent

Source: Anderson and Hsiao (1981).

The results obtained in AH81 for a purely AR(1) model are summarized in the above table; the reader is referred to their original paper for detailed derivations.

Anderson and Hsiao (1982), hereinafter AH82, extend the analysis of AH81 to relationships containing exogenous regressors but do not, as noted by Ridder and Wansbeek (1990), make use of the considerable simplification afforded by the twin assumptions that both the dependent variable and the exogenous regressors are generated by stationary DGPs observed in stochastic equilibrium.[56] Indeed, AH82 make a great variety of assumptions about the initial values and whether or not the relationship to be estimated contains time-varying exogenous variables, or time-invariant exogenous variables, or both. Their paper, as a consequence, is quite difficult to follow. Let me, therefore, single out one salient case: the relationship to be estimated contains only time-varying exogenous variables. Building on the path-breaking paper of Heckman (1978a) published in the proceedings of the first Paris conference, AH82 distinguish between what is called the *serial correlation model* and the *state space model*. It is worth making the distinction clear.

---

[56] I have derived the likelihood function in Appendix E, following Ridder and Wansbeek's development, for what I consider to be the most empirically relevant case. When, as seems likely in many empirically relevant situations, the process considered is not stationary because the dependent and exogenous regressors are cointegrated, some adjustments in the formulation are required. These are detailed in Nerlove (1999a, 1999c).

It is possible to write (26) with (6) in two nearly equivalent forms:
Serial Correlation Model:

$$w_{it} = \gamma w_{i,t-1} + \varepsilon_{it}, \quad i = 1, \dots, N, \quad t = 1, \dots, T,$$
$$y_{it} = w_{it} + \beta x_{it} + \mu_i, \quad i = 0, 1, \dots, N, \quad t = 1, \dots, T, \tag{37}$$

which implies

$$y_{it} = \gamma y_{i,t-1} + \beta x_{it} - \beta \gamma x_{i,t-1} + \mu_i + \varepsilon_{it}. \tag{36'}$$

Or alternatively as
State Dependence Model:

$$w_{it} = \gamma w_{i,t-1} + \beta x_{it}, + \varepsilon_{it}, \quad i = 1, \dots, N, \quad t = 1, \dots, T,$$
$$y_{it} = w_{it} + \mu_i, \quad i = 0, 1, \dots, N, \quad t = 1, \dots, T, \tag{37}$$

which implies

$$y_{it} = \gamma y_{i,t-1} + \beta x_{it} + \mu_i + \varepsilon_{it}.^{57} \tag{37'}$$

In the serial correlation model y_{it} is only affected by x_{it}, not by $x_{i,t-1}, \dots$. In the state dependence model y_{it} is affected not merely by x_{it}, but by $x_{i,t-1}, \dots$ through $y_{i,t-1}$; the unobservable w_{it} carry the effected [sic] x and can be called a state inclusion of the time-invariant individual affect [sic]. . .implies the aggregate effect of unobservable variables. . .are serially correlated in another way. . . .The key distinction between these two models is whether there is a dynamic response to changes in the observed variables (AH82, p. 61).[58]

In contrast to the case in which time-varying exogenous variables are included, when the only exogenous variables are time-invariant, the two models cannot be distinguished; when time-varying exogenous variables are included, the distinction hinges on the differential effects of current and lagged xs, a weak reed on which to lean at best if the xs are serially correlated. AH82 consider the following cases and subcases:

Case I: y_{i0} fixed. The initial level is unaffected by the individual specific time-invariant effect μ_i, which, however, affects all subsequent ys.

---

[57] I find it interesting, although perhaps no one else does, to note that the difference between (36) and (37) is exactly the difference between a combined partial adjustment and adaptive expectations model of agricultural supply response and a model that assumes either one or the other but not both. Nerlove (1958, p. 240)

[58] Heckman (1978, p. 228) puts the matter better:" Is it possible to explain the frequently noted empirical regularity that individuals who experience an event in the past are more likely to experience the event in the future? There are two distinct explanations for this regularity. One explanation is that individuals who experience the event are altered by their experience. A second explanation is that individuals may differ in their propensity to experience the event. If individual differences are stable over time, individuals who experience the event in the past are likely to experience the event in the future, even though the actual experience of the event has not modified individual behavior."

Case II: y_{i0} *random.* $y_{i0} \sim n(\mu_{y_0}, \sigma^2_{y_0})$ with two subcases:

   Case IIa: y_{i0} independent of μ_i.

   Case IIb: y_{i0} correlated with μ_i. Denote the correlation by $r\sigma^2_{y_0}$.

Case III: w_{i0} *fixed.* The unobserved individual process $\{w_{it}\}$ is independent of the individual effect, μ_i.

Case IV: w_{i0} *random.* The unobserved individual process $\{w_t\}$ is independent of the individual effect, μ_i. The initial state is:

$$\text{Case IVa: } w_{i0} \sim n\left(\mu_w, \frac{\sigma^2_\varepsilon}{1 - \gamma^2}\right).$$

$$\text{Case IVb: } w_{i0} \sim n\left(\mu_w, \sigma^2_{w_0}\right).$$

$$\text{Case IVc: } w_{i0} \sim n\left(\mu_{iw}, \frac{\sigma^2_\varepsilon}{1 - \gamma^2}\right).$$

$$\text{Case IVd: } w_{i0} \sim n\left(\mu_{iw}, \sigma^2_{w_0}\right).$$

There are altogether eight cases and subcases. The likelihood function is worked out for some of these and the properties of the ML and fixed-effects estimates. But not all the cases are likely to be equally relevant empirically. Moreover, in the case of state dependence, the likelihood of the sample depends on past values of the xs and, thus, some assumption about how they were generated in the presample period is needed. This matter is not addressed in AH82 except in the case *IVc* where it is assumed that "... the process $\{w_{it}\}$ [is assumed to have been] generated from the infinite past and [to have] achieved stationarity after conditioning on the exogenous variable." (AH82, p. 63). This is essentially the case considered by Bhargava and Sargan (1983), by Ridder and Wansbeek (1990), and in Appendix E.

Central to the approach of Bhargava and Sargan (1983), hereinafter BS83, is the assumption that the initial observations are generated by the same DGP as that which generates the observed panel data. But their formulation goes much beyond this by treating the problem as a simultaneous equations problem with cross-equation restrictions. A panel of N individuals and T periods (plus an initial observation) is regarded as a simultaneous system with $T + 1$ structural equations and N observations available for each of the equations. They consider a panel model in which some of the explanatory variables are correlated with the disturbances and some not, but, more importantly, a lagged value of the dependent variable is included as explanatory. In simplified form, the BS83 model is just (26) plus (6); their innovation is to add an equation for y_{i0}. For $i = 1, \ldots, N$ this is taken to be a linear function of the xs, as it turns out, just those observed in the sample. This relationship is derived as a reduced form of the system for y_{i0} by observing that each y_{i0} is determined by a sequence of equations exactly like (26). Working backwards, BS83 observe that each y_{i0} is determined by an equation of the form (27), which reduces to

(28) on the assumption of stationarity. They then take the rather heroic step of assuming that each initial value is the optimal predictor of y_{i0} from (28). BS83 then consider the estimation by maximum likelihood of the "system" consisting of the N structural equations (26) plus the equation derived from (28) subject to the appropriate restrictions. Although it's a little difficult to sort out the details, their approach comes to much the same result as that outlined in Appendix E and by Ridder and Wansbeek (1990, Case I, pp. 580–582) but, of course, BS83 were there first.

c. Estimation of Limited Dependent, Discrete, and Qualitative Panel Data Models

Panel data, or longitudinal data, as they are often called in the social science literature more generally, have long been of interest. But the more general social science data sets rarely fit neatly into a linear framework so beloved by econometricians. Measurements are often qualitative, discrete, or limited by truncation or censoring. Moreover, the dimensions of panels in other contexts are not always what we econometricians might expect.[59] The models that arise in these contexts are typically highly nonlinear. Easy transformations and decompositions of sums of squares, common simplifications for linear models or those that can be transformed to linearity, are not possible. Rarely are general methods of analysis, other than maximum likelihood or GMM, possible; methods are generally quite model-specific, exploiting special features of the data and problems addressed.

Microdata sets, derived from longitudinal surveys, have long been a staple of empirical labor economics (Devine and Kiefer, 1991); Heckman (1978b), presented at the 1977 Paris Conference, is an example of early attention in labor economics to econometric problems especially associated with the use of panel data.[60] This literature is too voluminous and diverse for me to attempt to survey it here. Chamberlain (1984) has a section on nonlinear models in which he treats random-effects probit models, fixed-effects logit models, and duration models, giving examples from the literature; Maddala (1987b) covers logit, probit, and tobit models using panel data, but excludes duration and hazard models; Arellano and Honoré (2001) survey the literature of the 1970s and 1980s, as well as more recent contributions to the analysis of

[59] For example, in psychology, "item response analysis" is a collective name for a number of models that describe the response of an individual subject as a probability function of subject and item variables (Rasch, 1961). Some of these, such as "ability" or "intelligence," may be latent and specific to the particular individual respondent. The dimensions relevant to the inquiry are individual and item, rather than individual and time. See Hamerle and Ronning (1995) for a good general survey of panel methods and models in the social sciences.

[60] See also Heckman and Willis (1975, 1977). Although these papers preceded the 1977 Paris Conference historically, I discuss them in Section 4.c(2–3).

nonlinear panel models.[61] I cover here examples, very selectively chosen, of logit, probit, tobit and, briefly, hazard and duration panel models from the period between the two Paris conferences. But first a short digression on the problem of incidental or nuisance parameters, which, because individual effects cannot easily be eliminated by transforming the problem in the non-linear case, figure prominently in the discussion.

(1) Incidental or Nuisance Parameters[62]. Consider an infinite sequence of in-dependent random variables with parametrically specified probability laws whose nature we wish to infer. The Neyman-Scott (1948) definition divides the parameters on which the distributions depend into two groups: (1) those that appear in every probability distribution; and (2) those that appear in only a finite number of the distributions. The parameters in the first group are those in which we are interested, and are called by N-S, in an unfortunate use of terminology, *structural*; the second type are called in the general statistics liter-ature *incidental*, and by Neyman and Scott, *inconsistent observations*, because as the sequence of RVs grows, information about these parameters stops accu-mulating. "Nuisance" parameters, more generally, are parameters we would like to eliminate from consideration in making inferences about the subset of parameters in which we are interested; "incidental" parameters are a partic-ularly troublesome subclass of nuisance parameters whose number increases with sample size. For example, in the case of a linear panel data regression in-volving only exogenous explanatory variables, fixed individual-specific effects considered as parameters are an example of incidental parameters because they are of no interest in themselves and their number grows as $N \to \infty$.[63]

    The critical problem is how to eliminate the nuisance or incidental para-meters so one can focus on the parameters of primary interest. One way of

---

[61] Note that the term *fixed effects* in Arellano and Honoré (2001) refers to individual-specific effects generally, *both* random and fixed in the terminology used here. They write (2001, p. 44, Footnote 19): "Even though one often imagines a random sample of individuals, and hence random draws of the individual specific effects, it is customary [at least in the circles in which Arellano and Honoré move] to call the effect 'fixed' when no assumptions are made on its relationship with other explanatory variables. A random effect is one which has been modeled in some manner."

[62] Lancaster (2000), written to mark the fiftieth anniversary of the publication of Neyman and Scott (1948), is an excellent survey and is the primary basis for this short section.

[63] The classic example, given in Neyman-Scott, looks very much like a panel data problem with fixed effects in which the number of individuals grows as sample size increases but not the number of time periods for which each individual is observed:

$$x_{it} \underset{\sim}{iid} \frac{1}{\sqrt{2\pi\sigma^2}} e^{\left\{ -\frac{1}{2\sigma^2} (x_{it} - \mu_i)^2 \right\}}, \quad i = 1, \ldots, N, \quad t = 1, \ldots, T_i, \quad N \to \infty.$$

If we're not interested in the μ_i per se but only in σ^2, maximum likelihood breaks down because ML estimates of σ^2 are inconsistent.

looking at a random-effects model is as a reformulation of the problem of an individual-specific-effects model in terms of a smaller number of parameters. This is what Basu (1977) calls *marginalization*, by which he means replacing the original "experiment" by an alternative.[64] Short of such a drastic reformulation of the basic model, however, one can regard the fixed-effects model as a DGP that generates the individual-specific effects and the observed variables of the model jointly. A fixed-effects formulation is then obtained by conditioning on the individual specific effects, then eliminating them as parameters. One way, in the context of ML estimation, which will be familiar to econometricians, is by "concentrating" the likelihood function (i.e., "maximizing out" the parameters of no interest per se, namely, these conditioning variables).[65] This is not a very satisfactory way in the case of incidental parameters because their number grows with sample size. Since the problem of incidental parameters does not arise in the case of random-effects models, following Lancaster (2000) I'll focus in this subsection on fixed-effects models, leaving more general discussion of various nonlinear models with random or fixed effects to the subsections that follow.[66] Of course, the fact that the incidental-parameters problem does not arise for random-effects models makes one wonder why so much attention in recent work has been devoted to getting around the problem in a fixed-effects context.[67] Lancaster (2000) provides an interesting answer to this question, which I describe in the next section.

In the following examples, μ_i is a fixed individual-specific effect: The *linear model, in which all explanatory variables are exogenous,* is simply the regression

---

[64] Of course, this is precisely what Balestra and Nerlove (1966) did when they replaced a model with state-specific fixed-effects by a random-effects model and estimated the parameters of the distribution of the unobserved effects.

[65] Basu (1977) lists ten ways of which "concentrating" the likelihood function is the ninth listed. The concentrated likelihood function is referred to as the "profile likelihood" in the general statistical literature.

[66] It does not arise for the fixed-effects model in a Bayesian framework either: Simply formulate a prior noninformative with respect to the nuisance parameters, calculate the posterior distribution, then integrate out the nuisance parameters. This is called *marginalization*. See Bernardo and Smith (1994, pp. 479–481). As Lancaster (2000, p. 403) remarks, however, "This is straightforward in principle, like all Bayesian calculations, but unfortunately does not, in general, solve the econometric issue of consistency." The two examples Lancaster gives are (1) in panel logit or probit in which the prior on the fixed individual-specific effects is uniform (proportional to a constant), the model of the marginal posterior with respect to β is not consistent; and (2) in a dynamic linear model the same prior yields a marginal posterior whose mode in γ and ρ is not consistent. Perhaps consistency is too much to ask for, but it's pretty minimal from a frequentist point of view.

[67] Arellano and Honoré (2001) focus "... on the extreme case where no assumptions are made on the relationship between the individual specific effect and the explanatory variables. Whether a more 'random' effects approach where some assumptions are made on how the distribution on this effect depends on the explanatory variables is more useful, depends on the context (and one's taste)."

model:

$$y_{it} = \mu_i + \beta x_{it} + \varepsilon_{it}, \qquad \varepsilon_{it} \underset{\sim}{iid} n\left(0, \sigma_\varepsilon^2\right).$$

ML, which is OLS in this case, is consistent for β but inconsistent for σ_ε^2. Cameron and Trivedi (1998) look at *count data models* of the form: y_{it} is *iid* Poisson with conditional mean (and variance) $\mu_i \exp\{\beta x_{it}\}$. The likelihood can be reparametrized so that the ML estimate of β, based on the transformed likelihood, is consistent for $N \to \infty$.[68] Chamberlain (1985) deals with a *duration model* in which the hazard of the occurrence of y_{it} is $\theta y^{\theta-1} \mu_i \exp\{\beta x_{it}\}$; that is, y_{it} has a Weibull distribution. ML estimates of both θ and β are inconsistent. Chamberlain suggests transforming the data to logarithmic first differences to get around this problem. We have looked at *dynamic linear models* extensively: ML estimates of all of the parameters conditional on the initial values in the sample are inconsistent.

Logit, probit, and related models for binary panel data have been considered by various authors since the early 1980s (Chamberlain, 1980; Heckman, 1981a, 1981b). The model is y_{it} binary with expectation conditional on $\{x_{it}\, i = 1, \ldots, N, t = 1, \ldots, T\}$:

$$E(y_{it} \mid \mu_i, \beta, \{x_{it}\, i = 1, \ldots, N, t = 1, \ldots, T\}$$
$$= F(\mu_i + \beta x_{it}), \quad i = 1, \ldots, N, \quad t = 1, \ldots, T,$$

for F a distribution function. ML is generally inconsistent for β.[69] But this is not true for probit, F normal, or in general.[70]

Dynamic models for binary panel data simply compound the difficulties encountered for linear panel data models with those encountered for binary panel data. The model is y_{it} binary with expectation conditional on $\{x_{it}\, i = 1, \ldots, N, t = 1, \ldots, T\}$:

$$E(y_{it} \mid \mu_i, \beta, \gamma, \{x_{it}\, i = 1, \ldots, N, t = 1, \ldots, T\})$$
$$= F(\mu_i + \beta x_{it} + \gamma y_{i,t-1}), \quad i = 1, \ldots, N, \quad t = 1, \ldots, T,$$

for F a distribution function. We would on this account expect fixed-effect methods to be inconsistent except possibly for logistic models and fixed initial conditions. Heckman's (1981) Monte Carlo results verify this.[71]

---

[68] See Greene (2000, pp. 887–889).

[69] But fixed effects, which is equivalent to ML conditional on the sufficient statistics for μ_i, $\bar{y}_{i.}$, is.

[70] Manski (1987) proposes a consistent semiparametric estimator of β for F in a broad class of distributions.

[71] In a forthcoming paper, Honoré and Kyriazidou (2000a) consider identification and estimation in panel discrete choice models when the explanatory variables include strictly exogenous variables, lagged values of endogenous variables, and individual-specific fixed effects. In Honoré and Kyriazidou (2000b), they apply similar techniques to finding consistent estimates of strictly nondynamic limited dependent variable models. This flurry of recent activity is more properly part of the future of panel data econometrics than its history.

As long as fixed effects are assumed, there is apparently no general solution for this problem except instrumental variables, and instruments are very difficult to find in a panel context.[72] At the very end of his survey of the incidental parameter problem in econometrics, Lancaster (2000, pp. 409–410) suggests a very interesting motivation for sticking with a fixed-effects formulation despite the terrible difficulties that it entails in contrast to the random-effects approach: He argues in effect that because the joint distribution of the random-effects is not specified when the likelihood is conditioned on the realized individual-specific effects, the approach is essentially semiparametric. ("...Neyman and Scott wrote the first semiparametric paper in econometric theory.") But motivation is not enough without a solution or solutions to what is a generally intractable problem.

(2) Logit and Probit Models

(a) NONDYNAMIC MODELS. Consider the following simple model: y_{it} is a binary variable with

$$prob[y_{it} = 1 \mid x, \beta, \mu] = F(x_{it}\beta + \mu_{it}), \tag{38}$$

where $F()$ is a cumulative distribution function such as logistic (logit) or unit normal (probit). x is assumed to consist of purely exogenous variables; no lagged values of the dependent variable are permitted.

An early application of a random-effects probit model, predating the 1977 Paris Conference, is Heckman and Willis (1975), who try to explain successive fertility decisions of couples using the full reproductive histories and associated economic histories. Their model reduces to

$$y_{it}^* = x_{it}\beta + \mu_i + \varepsilon_{it}, \quad i = 1, \ldots, N, \quad t = 1, \ldots, T$$

$$y_{it} = 1, \quad \text{if } y_{it}^* > 0, = 0, \quad \text{otherwise,}$$

$$\mu_i \sim iidN(0, \sigma_\mu^2) \text{ independent of } \varepsilon_{it} \sim iidN(0, \sigma_\varepsilon^2) \tag{39}$$

and both independent of x_{it}. They write (1975, p. 102):

---

[72] See the papers on nonlinear panel models in Mátyás and Sevestre (1996) and the recent unpublished paper by Heckman and Vytlacil (2000). When a sufficient statistic exists for the incidental parameters (which it frequently does not in many nonlinear panel models of interest in econometrics), an alternative method, *conditional maximum likelihood*, can be used to obtain consistent estimates. The existence of a minimal sufficient statistic for the incidental parameters can be viewed merely as facilitating partial maximization of the likelihood function in order to eliminate them. For example, in the linear nondynamic case, the individual group sums or means are sufficient for the individual-specific effects; conditioning on them is equivalent to working with deviations from these grouped means rather than the original observations; the estimates of the slopes are equivalent to the fixed-effects estimates and consistent. Conditional maximum likelihood is employed by Chamberlain (1980), discussed later, to obtain consistent estimates of the nonincidental parameters in the binary choice logistic model. See Cox and Hinkley (1974, pp. 292–294), Basu (1977), and Cox and Reid (1987). The method fails completely in the dynamic nonlinear case and in the dynamic linear case for fixed T (see Equation 30).

It is extremely important to account explicitly for sources of sample variation among individuals due to measured and unmeasured components. To avoid bias, it is especially important to take into account persistent variations in the monthly probability of conception among individuals caused by unmeasured differences in fecundity..., the frequency of coition, or efficiency of contraception, which, in turn are related to omitted economic variables and family characteristics which determine health, cost of contraception, and the demand for children.... Bias arises when persistent variation is ignored because of a selective mechanism which confounds changes in the behavior of an "average" couple in a sample caused by a change in an economic variable – the relationship we seek– with changes in the composition of the sample caused by differential probabilities of conception.

What Heckman and Willis are talking about is essentially the same point, but in a much subtler context, as that raised by Airy in 1861 or by Balestra and Nerlove in 1966.[73]

To formulate the likelihood function for the model (39), note that the model is identified only up to a scalar multiple of the variance. Let

$$\sigma^2 = \sigma_\mu^2 + \sigma_\varepsilon^2, \quad \rho = \frac{\sigma_\mu^2}{\sigma^2}, \quad v_{it} = \frac{\varepsilon_{it}}{\sigma_\varepsilon}, \quad m_i = \frac{\mu_{it}}{\sigma_\varepsilon}, \quad \beta^* = \frac{\beta}{\sigma}.$$

Then,

$$y_{it} = 1 \Rightarrow v_{it} = \frac{\varepsilon_{it}}{\sigma_\varepsilon} > \frac{-x_{it}\beta - \sigma_\mu m_i}{\sigma_\varepsilon}.$$

Define

$$\eta_{it} = \frac{-x_{it}\beta - \rho^{\frac{1}{2}} m_i}{\sqrt{1-\rho}}.$$

Thus,

$$y_{it} = 1 \Rightarrow v_{it} > \eta_{it}$$
$$y_{it} = 0 \Rightarrow v_{it} > \eta_{it}.$$

Conditional on the μ_i, the y_{it}^* are independent normal. The joint density of the y_{it} for i follows:

$$\prod_{t=1}^{T} [1 - \Phi(\eta_{it})]^{y_{it}} [\Phi(\eta_{it})]^{1-y_{it}}.$$

---

[73] In their rather lengthy paper, Heckman and Willis (1975, pp. 121–129) do worry about additional serial correlation in ε_{it} but not, as far as I can tell, about whether all the x_{it} might not be truly exogenous but correlated possibly with the μ_i. That concern was to appear later in Heckman and MaCurdy (1980) and, of course, it is explicit contemporaneously in Chamberlain and Griliches (1975). See Avery, Hansen, and Hotz (1983) for a treatment of the more general case with serially correlated ε_{it} by the method of moments. A generalization of the Heckman-Willis 1975 model to a simple two-equation simultaneous equations context is contained in Sickles and Taubman (1986).

Multiply by the density of the m_i and integrate to obtain the joint unconditional density of the y_{it}:

$$\prod_{i=1}^{N}\left(\int_{-\infty}^{\infty}\prod_{t=1}^{T}[1-\Phi(\eta_{it})]^{y_{it}}[\Phi(\eta_{it})]^{1-y_{it}}\left\{\frac{1}{\sqrt{2\pi}}e^{-m_i^2/2}\right\}dm_i\right), \qquad (40)$$

where $\Phi()$ is the standard normal cumulative distribution function.[74]

Heckman and Willis (1977) consider a similar problem of sequential quantal response but now in the context of labor-force participation of married women. Building on the theory of quantal choice and the well-known reservation wage/value of time theory of participation, they construct and estimate a logistic analogue of the model described previously.

An important landmark in the history of panel data econometrics in the period between the two Paris conferences is Chamberlain (1980), who applied the conditional maximum likelihood approach to binary and multinomial choice logistic models, an approch used earlier by Rasch (1961) to estimate a logistic model for intelligence test scores.[75] But this approach does not work for the probit model. Conditional maximum likelihood, which is equivalent to fixed individual-specific effects, yields consistent estimates of β, since the individual means are sufficient for the μ_i. Of course, the estimates are not efficient and the information matrix, which yields asymptotic standard errors, is hard to come by, since the μ_i have not actually been estimated (see Chamberlain, 1980, p. 230). This same approach is easily extended to the multivariate logistic, aka the *log-linear probability model*, which allows for interactions among the effects (Chamberlain, 1980, pp. 231–232). Chamberlain goes on to consider models in which a marginal distribution for the μ_i is specified, since the conditional ML approach does not always work; for example, when F is normal. He writes (1980, p. 233):

The main point I want to make here is that the random sampling specification is appropriate only as a marginal distribution for $[\mu]$. We must, however, specify a distribution for $[\mu]$ conditional on x. The conventional random-effects model assumes that $[\mu]$ is independent of x. But our interest in introducing the incidental parameters was motivated by missing variables that are correlated with x. If one mistakenly models $[\mu]$ as independent, then the omitted variable bias is not eliminated. So we want to specify a conditional distribution of $[\mu]$ given x, which allows for dependence.

One way to do so is to specify a simultaneous structural equations framework as is done in Chamberlain and Griliches (1975), discussed previously.[76]

---

[74] The only problem is the integral in (40). That wasn't so easy in 1975; but see Butler and Moffit (1980) for an early efficient algorithm.

[75] See Footnote 71.

[76] See also Chamberlain and Griliches (1977) and Chamberlain (1978).

An alternative, suggested by Mundlak (1978) and explored further by Chamberlain (1980), is to specify a regression relationship between the latent effects and the exogenous explanatory variables. In the simplest case of a linear nondynamic model, it is possible to get back the fixed-effects estimates as the ML estimates but, more generally (dynamic linear models or nonlinear models), this is not the case and alternative estimates are obtained (Chamberlain, 1980, p. 234; Maddala, 1987a, p. 305).

Although the same conditional ML technique that works for the logit model does not yield consistent estimates for the simple probit model, Manski (1987) showed how to obtain such estimates using the maximum score estimator (Manski, 1975, 1985). Indeed, the method proposed by Manski, *maximum score* (MS), achieves consistent estimates in a wide variety of nondynamic binary choice models for very general specifications of the marginal distribution F (Horowitz, 1998, pp. 65–100).[77] Unfortunately, the method as originally proposed by Manski does not converge very fast nor is it asymptotically normal (Kim and Pollard, 1990).

(b) DYNAMIC MODELS. Although the rationale for dynamic models of discrete choice was set forth rather early by Heckman (1978a, 1981a),[78] there was little follow-up until the 1990s, and then principally for limited dependent and sample selection models discussed later (Honoré, 1993; Kyriazidou, 1997a; Kyriazidou, 1997b; Honoré and Kryiazidou, 2000a). Heckman's paper (1978a), further elaborated in (1981a), laid the foundation for subsequent work. His own description of what he is up to is better than I can give (1978a, p. 228):

This paper considers simple answers to the following question. From an observed series of discrete events from individual histories, such as spells of unemployment experienced by workers or the labor-force participation of married women, is it possible to explain the frequently noted empirical regularity that individuals who experience an event in the past are more likely to experience the event in the future? There

---

[77] A brief and exceptionally clear discussion of the method of *maximum score* is given in Greene (2000, pp. 842–844): In the case of ordinary regression, we can view estimation as a method of maximizing the goodness of fit of the predicted to the observed values in the sample, in the sense of a quadratic form in the deviations. Such a criterion does not readily apply when the variable to be "predicted" is binary. Instead, Manski (1975, 1985, 1987) proposes to choose β in (38) so as to maximize

$$\sum_{i=1}^{N}\sum_{i=1}^{T}\{2y_{it} - 1 - (1 - 2\alpha)\}\, sign\,(x_{it}\beta),$$

where $0 < \alpha < 1$ is a preset quantile. For example, when $\alpha = 1/2$, the maximum score estimate of β maximizes the number of times the prediction $x_{it}\beta$ has the same sign as $2y_{it} - 1$. Assessment of significance or tests of hypotheses are problematic. Generally, a method called *bootstrapping* is employed (Horowitz, 1998, pp. 79–84).

[78] See my 1977 discussion of his contribution at the first Paris conference, reproduced in Appendix C.

are two distinct explanations for this regularity. One explanation is that individuals who experience the event are altered by their experience. A second explanation is that individuals may differ in their propensity to experience the event. If individual differences are stable over time, individuals who experience the event in the past are likely to experience the event in the future, even though the actual experience of the event has not modified individual behavior. The question considered in this paper is whether or not it is possible to determine which explanation is the more appropriate.

The answer is of profound significance for policies designed to affect the probabilities that different individuals will experience the events in question. For example, if spells of unemployment increase the probability of further spells of unemployment because the worker acquires less work experience, it is quite a different matter than if the worker is inherently less employable due to poor health or lack of education and, therefore, has a persistently higher probability to experience unemployment.

Consider a simple binary-choice model involving a lagged dependent variable among other explanatory variables:

$$y_{it}^* = x_{it}\beta + \gamma y_{it-1}^* + \mu_i + \varepsilon_{it}, \quad i = 1, \ldots, N, \quad t = 1, \ldots, T$$
$$y_{it} = 0, \quad \text{if } y_{it}^* < 0; \quad y_{it} = 1, \quad \text{if } y_{it}^* \geq 0. \tag{41}$$

To complete the model, we need to specify whether the μ_is are random or fixed and require some distributional assumptions on ε_{it} and on μ_i, if assumed random. The conditions for conditional maximum likelihood estimation for models such as (41) with fixed effects μ_i clearly fail even for serially independent logistically distributed errors ε_{it}, since the error in period t cannot be independent of the explanatory variables in $t-1$ if a lagged value of the dependent variable is one of them. Nor will the conditions for the consistency of the method of maximum score be satisfied.[79] Notwithstanding the difficulties of

---

[79] As Arellano and Honoré (2001, p. 63) remark, it is enough to drive one to the conclusion

> ... that it would be more fruitful to take a random-effect approach that makes more assumptions of the distribution of the individual specific effects. However, estimation of dynamic nonlinear models is very difficult even in that case. The main difficulty is the so-called initial conditions problem: if one starts observing the individuals when the process in question is already in progress, then the first observation will depend on the dependent variable in the period before the sample starts. ... One will have to deal with the relationship between the first lagged dependent variable and the individual-specific effect. The relationship will depend (in a complicated way) on the parameters of the model, but also on the distribution of the explanatory variables in periods prior to the start of the sample, which is typically unknown.

See Section 4.b(4) and Appendix E; Nerlove (1999c) gives a proposed solution to this problem in the linear case and implements it in the estimation of a growth convergence model using a cross-country panel data set. The problem is, of course, a great deal more difficult in a nonlinear context. Still, I would prefer to deal with it head on than to settle for

estimating a model such as (41) with either random or fixed effects, as Heckman (1978a) notes, the two sources of persistence have quite different implications for the sequences of events observed for each individual; consider (41) with $\beta = 0$. If there were no state dependence, to use Heckman's phrase, $\gamma = 0$, then the sequence $(0, 0, 1, 1)$ would be as likely as any other, for example, $(0, 1, 0, 1)$. If $\gamma > 0$, however, the first sequence is more likely than the second, and vice versa, if $\gamma < 0$. Heckman (1978a, pp. 239–257) thus proposed a runs test for distinguishing between true and spurious state dependence. Indeed, in 1978a and 1981a, he showed how to use the probability implications of the model to identify and estimate both β and γ in (41).[80]

(3) Limited Dependent Variables

(a) NONDYNAMIC MODELS. The basic structure of the censored regression or so-called tobit model is:

$$y_{it}^* = x_{it}\beta + \mu_i + \varepsilon_{it}, \quad i = 1, \ldots, N, \quad t = 1, \ldots, T$$
$$y_{it} = \text{max or min}(y_{it}^*, c) \tag{42}$$

c is often fixed a priori, often at 0, but note, for example, $c = -\infty$ yields an ordinary panel data regression model.[81] Let $c = 0$ and $\delta_{it} = 1$, if $y_{it}^* > 0$, 0, otherwise. The log likelihood is a straightforward generalization of (40):

$$\log L = const. + \sum_{i=1}^{N} \sum_{t=1}^{T} \left\{ (1 - \delta_{it}) \log \Phi \left(\frac{-\mu_i - x_{it}\beta}{\sigma} \right) \right.$$
$$\left. + \delta_{it} \left[-\frac{1}{2} \log \sigma^2 - \frac{1}{2} \left(\frac{y_{it} - \mu_i - x_{it}\beta}{\sigma} \right)^2 \right] \right\}. \tag{43}$$

Note that the assumption $c = 0$ replaces the earlier normalization by dividing by σ.

Amemiya (1985, Chapter 9) gives a "catalogue" of various types of limited dependent or sample selection or tobit models for the pure cross-section case and numerous examples of each type, as well as methods of estimation alternative to maximum likelihood. Appendix F to this chapter contains a brief summary. Although in principle it is possible to generalize any of the random-effects probit models[82] to random-effects tobit models, there are few examples to be found in the period between the Paris conferences. One notable exception is the paper by Hausman and Wise (1979), although this model is rather simple in that it allows only two periods and for sample attrition between the two periods. Moreover, appropriate estimation techniques and likelihood functions

---

some rather complicated procedure that could be counted on only to yield estimates with the weak property of consistency.

[80] See also Honoré and Kyriazidou (2000a).

[81] One might be tempted to allow c to vary by individual, but then the model is not identified.

[82] See Footnote 73.

differ case by case for attrition models (see Maddala, 1983, Chapter 9). Given the rather strong assumptions imposed on the distributions of the random effects, there is no difficulty in principle in employing likelihood methods, but the computational burdens may be severe. The likelihood functions (or moments, if a method-of-moments methods are employed) typically involve multivariate integrals, although not generally of a very high order. This is one of the reasons for the recent popularity of simulation-based methods of inference. See, for example, Hajivassilou and Ruud (1994) and Keane (1993, 1994).

Although Heckman and Willis (1975, 1977) formulated random-effects probit and logistic models, Heckman (1981a) and Heckman and MaCurdy (1980) work with fixed-effects models, perhaps influenced by Mundlak (1978).[83] Heckman and MaCurdy (1980) is an early example of a fixed-effects tobit model; they (1980, p. 56 and Footnote 17) are quite explicit in preferring fixed effects because of the possibility of correlation between the explanatory variables included and the individual effects.[84] More recently, the fields of nondynamic fixed-effects tobit models have been well plowed by Honoré (1992, 1993), Kyriazidou (1997), Honoré and Kryiazidou (2000b), and Honoré, Kryiazidou, and Udry (1997).[85]

---

[83] Heckman (1981b) is well aware of the incidental-parameters problem but argues on the basis of Monte Carlo evidence that the inconsistency of maximum likelihood is not of great import (1981b, p. 180): "The issue here, as always, is whether or not the asymptotic theory provides a good guide in practical work." Heckman and MaCurdy (1980, p. 59) write:

> Fixed effects in nonlinear models pose difficult statistical problems if the number of time periods observed for each household is small, as is true for our sample. One such difficulty is the 'incidental parameters' problem first discussed by Neyman and Scott (1948). Since the number of observations per household is fixed, it is not possible to consistently estimate fixed effects. In non-linear models – in contrast with linear models – it is *in general* not possible to devise estimators that are not functions of the fixed effects. It this case, the inconsistency in the estimated fixed effects is transmitted to the estimated structural parameters.

[84] They write: "Using panel data, one can eliminate the fixed effect, and hence purge the analysis of unobservable variables that are bound to be correlated with the included variables.... For this reason, it is inappropriate to treat... [the former] as a random effect that is uncorrelated with explanatory variables."

[85] In the case of linear models, Chamberlain (1984) proposes estimators that make assumptions intermediate to purely fixed effects and fully parametrically specified random effects. His suggestions have received an extended treatment in Crépon and Mairesse (1996) and in connection with nonlinear models in Lechner and Breitung (1996). The essential idea is to specify the random individual-specific effects as some unknown linear function of the explanatory variables subject to error independently of the remainder effects. In the LDV case, one can apply a semiparametric estimator to the data for each time period to estimate the model parameters and those of the auxiliary relationship up to a scale factor; these are then combined using a minimum-distance estimator to obtain the estimates for the joint sample. Still more "semi" semiparametric estimators have been proposed by Newey (1994) and others. Other estimators alternative to pure fixed effects have been proposed, *inter alia*, by Lee (1999).

(b) DYNAMIC MODELS. There has been very little work on dynamic limited-dependent variable models to date. Generally speaking, random effects are considered only as a "backdrop" to a fixed-effects approach, which then is viewed as semiparametric. Dynamic discrete choice models with such fixed effects are explored in Honoré and Kryiazidou (2000a). Kyriazidou (1999) extends her (Kryiazidou, 1997) model to encompass dynamics in both the relationship to be estimated and the sample selection process. I am not aware of any attempt to estimate a fully parametric nonlinear dynamic random-effects panel model. As Arellano and Honoré (2001, p. 71) remark, the ". . . approach is problematic in a dynamic model if one does not observe the start of the process." Then, as remarked in Section 4.b(4) and Appendix E, one has to model explicitly the process generating the data before observation of the panel begins. Nonlinearity of the process being studied greatly complicates this modeling.[86]

(4) Hazard and Duration Models. One of the most important areas associated with panel data econometrics is the literature, which developed in the eighties and more recently, dealing with the analysis of duration data. Yet discussion of this literature is largely eschewed or given short shrift in major surveys of panel data econometrics (Maddala, 1987a; Baltagi, 1985). I'll not deal with it except extremely briefly. The problem is that there is too much of it and, while the question of heterogeneity is clearly related to the problem of individual-specific latent effects, a point already clarified by Heckman (1978a), the relation to the corresponding issues arising in panel data econometrics is not always obvious.[87] The literature draws heavily on statistical reliability theory and the biostatistical literature, not always, according to Heckman and Singer (1984), with an adequate appreciation of the sometimes subtle differences that arise in the context of inference from nonexperimental data. Heckman and Singer (1984) discuss the distinction between single-spell and multiple-spell models. The latter bring out the "panel" character of the analytical issues even if the data themselves are retrospective cross sections.

While some of the earliest work on the "in-and-out" character of female labor-force participation can be viewed as precursor, the beginning of duration analysis in econometrics can be dated from the papers by Lancaster (1979) and Nickell (1979) on unemployment durations. The methods are of potentially very wide substantive applicability. Kiefer (1988, p. 648) gives the following catalogue:

. . . duration of marriages, spacing of births, time to adoption of new technologies, time between trades in financial markets, product durability, geographical or occupational mobility (time between moves), lifetimes of firms, time to invention from research

---

[86] Wooldridge (2000) suggests a very general way of estimating nonlinear dynamic random-effects panel models with feedback to endogenous explanatory variables but, as he himself states, in practice the methods he suggests may be difficult to implement.

[87] Chamberlain (1985) emphasizes the problem of individual heterogeneity in studying transition and duration data.

investment, payback periods for overseas loans, duration of wars, time in office for congressmen and other elected officials, time from initiation to resolution of legal cases, spacing of purchases of durable goods (or replacement capital), time in rank and length of stay in graduate school.

In some sense, event histories, duration of spells, and similar data gathered from surveys, whether by one-time survey with retrospection or by repeated sampling of the same individuals over time, are subject to the same problems of individual heterogeneity as panel data in general. In his broad survey of panel data problems and approaches, Chamberlain (1984) devotes only three pages to duration analysis. More comprehensive surveys are Heckman and Singer (1984) and Kiefer (1988), although panel issues are not emphasized.[88] Lancaster (1990) deals at length with heterogeneity problems. Tuma, Hannan, and Groeneveld (1979) give a summary of the extensive sociological literature in the area, generally referred to there as "event histories." More recently, Fougère and Kamionka (1996) have given a "state-of-the-art" summary that does emphasize the panel data aspects of the problem. Allowing for latent individual heterogeneity is very difficult in a cross section even if retrospective data are collected on spells and transitions.

d. The Second Paris Conference, 1997

The twentieth anniversary of the 1977 Paris Conference was celebrated in Paris in 1997 with most of the original participants in attendance plus many of those who had made significant contributions in the intervening years. Many of the papers were published in Sevestre (1999). In his introduction to the volume, Sevestre identifies elements of continuity and change. First, many members of the cast of characters in 1977 and 1997 were the same: those who were interested in the subject in 1977 were still interested in 1997, although this conclusion is a bit disingenuous since invitations were issued to all those who participated in the first conference. Second, Sevestre points to the strong economic motivation behind the questions being asked. He says that most of the papers presented at the 1997 conference, like those given in 1977, "... contain an application which goes well beyond simple illustration." While I would agree that although this is, by and large, a fair assessment of the papers at the 1997 conference, it has not been generally true of recent developments in panel data econometrics, which have become increasing motivated by the internal methodological logic of the subject. Finally, the principal changes noted by Sevestre have to do with the increasing availability of panel data sets: cross-country and dense financial compendia, in particular.

5. BEYOND PARIS

In his paper, "Panel Data Econometrics: A Successful Past and a Promising Future," presented at the 2000 Geneva Conference, Alain Trognon (2000)

---

[88] Greene (2000, pp. 937–950) bases his brief exposition largely on Kiefer's survey.

emphasized the development of panel data econometrics in terms of its internal methodological momentum rather than in response to the availability of panel data sets and questions that can be better answered by such data than by alternatives. I certainly agree with this assessment with respect to recent years but not with respect to the earlier years. Indeed, on the basis of my reading of the history of the subject, I would argue that the development of the subject has followed a typical pattern: in the beginning, there are relatively few papers. Some are "dry wells," others important sources for the stream of research that soon emerges. The flow soon broadens, and becomes a wide river. But at some point, rapids, rocks, and eddies are encountered. Research is increasingly preoccupied with methodological issues such as the problem of incidental parameters in nonlinear fixed-effects models. Less and less attention is devoted to formulating econometric models relevant to important economic issues and data. Perhaps this assessment is too harsh. There are, no doubt, major exceptions to such "an end to history"; for example, Heckman's recent work on the evaluation of social programs (2001).

In his work on agricultural experiments, Fisher introduced the idea of randomization, which eventually became the norm, in contrast to the systematic experimental design that had prevailed before. Fisher's battles with the establishment in which he argued that randomized experiments could provide more accurate and efficient estimates than the then-accepted systematic designs are described by Box (1978, pp. 140–166). It is my hope that our increased understanding of the consequences of and remedies for individual heterogeneity in panel data econometrics will inform and guide the collection of social and economic data, much as Fisher's statistical theory informed and guided the design of agricultural experiments in the twenties.

References

Airy, G. B. (1861), *On the Algebraical and Numerical Theory of Errors of Observations and the Combination of Observations*, Cambridge and London: Macmillan and Co.

Aldrich, J. C. (1999), "Fisher and Fixed X Regression," unpublished discussion paper, University of Southampton, November 24.

Amemiya, T. (1971), "The Estimation of the Variances in a Variance-Components Model," *International Economic Review, 12*: pp. 1–13.

Amemiya, T. (1985), *Advanced Econometrics*, Cambridge, MA: Harvard University Press.

Amemiya, T., and T. E. MaCurdy (1986), "Instrumental-Variable Estimation of an Error-Components Model," *Econometrica, 54*: pp. 1377–1398.

Anderson, R. E. (1979), *Studies on the Estimation of Variance Components*, Ph.D. dissertation, Cornell University, Ithaca, 1978. Summarized in "On the History of Variance Component Estimation," pp. 19–57, in *Variance Components and Animal Breeding*, L. D. Van Vleck and S. R. Searle (Eds.), Ithaca: Cornell University.

Anderson, R. L., and T. A. Bancroft (1952), *Statistical Theory in Research*, New York: McGraw-Hill.

Anderson, T. W., and C. Hsiao (1981), "Estimation of Dynamic Models with Error Components," *Journal of the American Statistical Association, 76*: 598–606.

Anderson, T. W., and C. Hsiao (1982), "Formulation and Estimation of Dynamic Models Using Panel Data," *Journal of Econometrics, 18*: 47–82.

Arellano, M., and B. Honoré (2001), "Panel Models: Some Recent Developments," forthcoming in J. J. Heckman and E. E. Leamer, *Handbook of Econometrics, Vol. 5*, Amsterdam: North-Holland.

Avery, R. B., L. P. Hansen, and V. J. Hotz (1983), "Multiperiod Probit Models and Orthogonality Condition Estimation," *International Economic Review, 24*: pp. 21–35.

Balestra, P. (1967), *The Demand for Natural Gas in the United States: A Dynamic Approach for the Residential and Commercial Market.* Amsterdam: North-Holland Publishing.

Balestra, P. (1980), "A Note on the Exact Transformation Associated with the First-Order Moving Average Process," *Journal of Econometrics, 14*: pp. 381–394.

Balestra, P., and M. Nerlove (1966), "Pooling Cross Section and Time Series Data in the Estimation of a Dynamic Model: The Demand for Natural Gas," *Econometrica, 34*: pp. 585–612.

Baltagi, B. H. (1995), *Econometric Analysis of Panel Data*, New York: Wiley.

Baltagi, B. H., and Q. Li (1991a), "A Transformation That Will Circumvent the Problem of Autocorrelation in an Error Component Model," *Journal of Econometrics, 48*: pp. 385–393.

Baltagi, B. H., and Q. Li (1991b), "A Joint Test for Serial Correlation and Random Individual Effects," *Statistics and Probability Letters, 11*: pp. 277–280.

Basu, D. (1977), "On the Elimination of Nuisance Parameters," *Journal of the American Statistical Association, 72*: pp. 355–366.

Beggs, J. J. (1980), "Pooling Time Series and Cross-Sectional Data in Dynamic Econometric Models," doctoratal dissertation, Department of Economics, Northwestern University.

Beggs, J. J., and M. Nerlove (1988), "Biases in Dynamic Models with Fixed Effects," *Economics Letters, 26*: pp. 29–31.

Bernardo, J. M., and A. F. M. Smith (1994), *Bayesian Theory*, New York: Wiley.

Bhargava, A., L. Fanzini, and W. Narendranathan (1982), "Serial Correlation and the Fixed-Effects Model," *Review of Economic Studies, 49*: pp. 533–549.

Bhargava, A., and J. D. Sargan (1983), "Estimating Dynamic Random-Effects Models from Panel Data Covering Short Time Periods," *Econometrica, 51*: pp. 1635–1659.

Blundell, R., and R. J. Smith (1991), "Conditions Initiales et Estimation Efficace dans les Modèles Dynamiques sur Données de Panel," *Annales d'Économie et de Statistique, 20–21*: pp. 109–124.

Box, J. F. (1978), *R. A. Fisher: The Life of a Scientist*, New York: Wiley.

Breusch, T. S. (1987), "Maximum Likelihood Estimation of Random-Effects Models," *Journal of Econometrics 36*: pp. 383–389.

Breusch, T. S., G. E. Mizon, and P. Schmidt (1989), "Efficient Estimation Using Panel Data," *Econometrica, 57*: pp. 695–700.

Bronfenbrenner, M. (1944), "Production Functions: Cobb-Douglas, Interfirm, Intrafirm," *Econometrica, 12*: pp. 35–44.

Butler, J. S., and R. Moffit (1982), "A Computationally Efficient Quadrature Procedure for the One-Factor Multinomial Probit Model," *Econometrica, 50*: pp. 761–764.

Cameron, A. C., and P. K. Trivedi (1998), *Regression Analysis of Count Data*, New York: Cambridge University Press.

Chamberlain, G. (1975), "Unobservables in Econometric Models," unpublished doctorate dissertation, Department of Economics, Harvard University.

Chamberlain, G. (1978), "Omitted Variable Bias in Panel Data: Estimating the Returns to Schooling," in Colloque International du CNRS, pp. 49–82.

Chamberlain, G. (1980), "Analysis of Covariance with Qualitative Data," *Review of Economic Studies, 47*: pp. 225–238.

Chamberlain, G. (1984), "Panel Data," in Z. Griliches and M. Intriligator, (Eds.) *Handbook of Econometrics, Vol. 2*, pp. 1247–1318. Amsterdam: North-Holland.

Chamberlain, G. (1985), "Heterogeneity, Omitted Variable Bias, and Duration Dependence," in Heckman and Singer, pp. 3–38.

Chamberlain, G., and Z. Griliches (1975), "Unobservables with a Variance-Components Structure: Ability, Schooling, and the Economic Success of Brothers," *International Economic Review, 16*: pp. 422–449.

Chamberlain, G., and Z. Griliches (1977), "More on Brothers," in P. Taubman, ed., *Kinometrics: The Determinants of Socioeconomic Success Within and Between Families*, pp. 97–124, Amsterdam: North-Holland Publishing.

Chauvenet, W. (1960), *A Manual of Theoretical and Practical Astronomy: Embracing the General Problems of Spherical Astronomy, the Special Applications to Nautical Astronomy, and the Theory and Use of Fixed and Portable Astronomical Instruments, with an Appendix on the Method of Least Squares*, 1st edition, Philadelphia: J. B. Lippincott and Co., 1863. The fifth edition, 1889, reprinted by Dover Publications, New York.

Colloque International du CNRS (1978), "L'Économétrie des Données Individuelles Temporelles," *Annales de l'INSEE*, pp. 30–31.

Cox, D. R. (1974), "Partial Likelihood," *Biometrika, 62*: pp. 269–276.

Cox, D. R., and D. V. Hinkley (1974), *Theoretical Statistics*, London: Chapman and Hall.

Cox, D. R., and N. Reid (1987), "Parameter Orthogonality and Approximate Conditional Inference," *Journal of the Royal Statistical Society, Ser. B, 49*: pp. 1–39.

Crépon, B., and J. Mairesse (1996), "The Chamberlain Approach," in Mátyás and Sevestre, pp. 323–391.

Daniels, H. E. (1939), "The Estimation of Components of Variance," *Supplement to the Journal of the Royal Statistical Society, 6*: pp. 186–197.

de Finetti, B. (1930), "Problemi Determinati e Indeterminati nel Calculo delle Probabilità," *Rend. R. Acc. Naz. Lincei*, Series 6, Vol. 12, fasc. 9.

de Finetti, B. (1990), *Teoria delle Probabilità*, Torino: Giulio Einaudi, 1970; translated as *Theory of Probability*, New York: Wiley.

Devine, T. J., and N. M. Kiefer (1991), *Empirical Labor Economics: The Search Approach*, New York: Oxford University Press.

Dhrymes, P. J. (1971), *Distributed Lags: Problems of Estimation and Formulation*, San Francisco: Holden-Day.

Edgeworth, F. Y. (1885), "On Methods of Ascertaining Variations in the Rate of Births, Deaths, and Marriages," *Journal of the Royal Statistical Society, 48*: pp. 628–649.

Eisenhart, C. (1947), "The Assumptions Underlying the Analysis of Variance," *Biometrics, 3*: pp. 1–21.

Eisner, R. (1978), *Factors in Business Investment*, New York: National Bureau of Economic Research.

Fisher, F. M., and C. Kaysen (1962), *The Demand for Electricity in the United States*, Amsterdam: North-Holland Publishing.

Fisher, R. A. (1918a), "The Correlation Between Relatives on the Supposition of Mendelian Inheritance," *Transactions of the Royal Society of Edinburgh, 52*: pp. 399–433.

Fisher, R. A. (1918b), "The Causes of Human Variability," *Eugenics Review, 10*: pp. 213–220.

Fisher, R. A. (1990), *Statistical Methods for Research Workers*, 1st ed., Edinburgh and London: Oliver and Boyd, 1925. Reprinted in *Statistical Methods, Experimental Design, and Scientific Inference*, Oxford: University Press.

Fougère, G., and T. Kamionka (1996), "Individual Labour Market Transitions," in Mátyás and Sevestre, pp. 771–809.

Fuller, W. A., and G. E. Battese (1974), "Estimation of Linear Models with Crossed-Error Structure," *Journal of Econometrics, 2*: pp. 67–78.

Galton, F. (1889), *Natural Inheritance*, London: Macmillan.

Gauss, C. F. (1963), *Theoria Motus Corporum Celestium*, Hamburg: Perthes und Besser, 1809. Translation by C. H. Davis in *Theory of Motion of Heavenly Bodies*, New York: Dover.

Godfrey, L. G. (1988), *Misspecification Tests in Econometrics: The Lagrange Multiplier Principle and Other Approaches*, Cambridge, UK: Cambridge University Press.

Goldberger, A. S. (1964), *Econometric Theory*, New York: Wiley.

Goldberger, A. S. (1971), "Econometrics and Psychometrics: A Survey of Communalities," *Psychometrika, 36*: pp. 83–107.

Goldberger, A. S. (1972), "Structural Equation Methods in the Social Sciences," *Econometrica, 40*: pp. 979–1002.

Goldberger, A. S. (1974), "Unobservable Variables in Econometrics," in P. Zarembka (Ed.), *Frontiers in Econometrics*, New York: Academic Press, pp. 193–213.

Goldberger, A., and O. D. Duncan, eds. (1973), *Structural Equation Models in the Social Sciences*, New York: Seminar Press.

Greene, W. (2000), *Econometric Analysis*, 4th ed., Upper Saddle River, NJ: Prentice-Hall.

Griliches, Z. (1974), "Errors in Variables and Other Unobservables," *Econometrica, 42*: pp. 971–998.

Griliches, Z., and W. Mason (1972), "Education, Income, and Ability," *Journal of Political Economy, 80(3) Part II*: pp. S74–S103.

Griliches, Z. (1977), "Estimating the Returns to Schooling: Some Econometric Problems," *Econometrica, 45*: pp. 1–22.

Grunfeld, Y. (1958), *The Determinants of Corporate Investment in the U.S.*, unpublished doctorate thesis, Department of Economics, University of Chicago.

Haavelmo, T. (1944), "The Probability Approach in Econometrics," supplement to *Econometrica, 12*.

Hahn, J. (1999), "How Informative Is the Initial Condition in a Dynamic Panel Model with Fixed Effects?" *Journal of Econometric, 93*: pp. 309–326.

Hajivassilou, V., and P. Ruud (1994), "Classical Estimation Methods for LDV Models Using Simulation," in R. F. Engle and D. L. McFadden, *Handbook of Econometrics, Vol. 4*, pp. 2383–2441. Amsterdam: Elsevier.

Hald, A. (1998), *A History of Mathematical Statistics from 1750 to 1930*, New York: Wiley.

Halperin, M. (1951), "Normal Regression Theory in the Presence of Intra-Class Correlation," *Annals of Mathematical Statistics, 22*: pp. 573–580.

Hamerle, A., and G. Ronning (1995), "Panel Analysis for Qualitative Variables," in G. Arminger, C. C. Clogg, and M. Sobel, *Handbook of Statistical Modeling for the Social and Behavioral Sciences*, pp. 401–451, New York: Plenum Press.

Hartley, H. O., and J. N. K. Rao (1967), "Maximum Likelihood Estimation for the Mixed Analysis of Variance Model," *Biometrika, 54*: pp. 93–108.

Harville, D. A. (1972), "Maximum Likelihood Approaches to Variance Component Estimation and to Related Problems," with a comment by J. N. K. Rao and a rejoinder by Harville, *Journal of the American Statistical Association, 72*: pp. 320–340.

Hause, J. C. (1977), "The Covariance Structure of Earnings and the On-the-Job Training Hypothesis," *Annals of Economic and Social Measurement, 6*: pp. 335–365.

Hausman, J. A. (1978), "Specification Tests in Econometrics," *Econometrica, 46*: pp. 1251–1271.

Hausman, J. A., and W. E. Taylor (1981), "Panel Data and Unobservable Individual Effects," *Econometrica, 49*: pp. 1377–1398.

Hausman, J. A., and D. Wise (1979), "Attrition Bias in Experimental and Panel Data: The Gary Income Maintenance Experiment," *Econometrica, 47*: pp. 455–474.

Heckman, J. (1976), "The Common Structure of Statistical Models of Truncation, Sample Selection, and Limited Dependent Variables and a Simple Estimator for Such Models," *Annals of Economic and Social Measurement, 5*: pp. 475–492.

Heckman, J. (1978a), "Simple Statistical Models for Discrete Panel Data Developed and Applied to Test the Hypothesis of True State Dependence Against the Hypothesis of Spurious State Dependence," in Colloque International du CNRS, pp. 227–269.

Heckman, J. (1978b), "Dummy Endogenous Variables in a Simultaneous Equations System," *Econometrica, 46*: pp. 931–959.

Heckman, J. (1981a), "Statistical Models for Discrete Panel Data," in C. F. Manski and D. McFadden, *Structural Analysis of Discrete Data with Econometric Applications*, pp. 114–178. Cambridge, MA: MIT Press.

Heckman, J. (1981b), "The Incidental Parameter Problem and the Problem of Initial Conditions in Estimating a Discrete Time – Discrete Data Stochastic Process," in C. F. Manski and D. McFadden, *Structural Analysis of Discrete Data with Econometric Applications*, pp. 179–195. Cambridge, MA: MIT Press.

Heckman, J. (2001), "Accounting for Heterogeneity, Diversity and General Equilibrium in Evaluating Social Programms," *Economic Journal*, 111: pp. F654–F699.

Heckman, J., and T. E. MaCurdy (1980), "A Life Cycle Model of Female Labour Supply," *Review of Economic Studies, 47*: pp. 47–74.

Heckman, J., and B. Singer, eds. (1982), *Econometric Analysis of Longitudinal Data*, special issue of the *Journal of Econometrics, 18*: pp. 1–190.

Heckman, J., and B. Singer (1984), "Econometric Duration Analysis," *Journal of Econometrics*, *24*: pp. 63–132.

Heckman, J., and B. Singer, eds. (1985), *Longitudinal Analysis of Labor Market Data*, Cambridge, UK: Cambridge University Press.

Heckman, J., and E. J. Vytlacil (1999), "Local Instrumental Variables," paper presented at the North American Summer Meeting of the Econometric Society.

Heckman, J., and R. Willis (1975), "Estimation of a Stochastic Model of Reproduction: An Econometric Approach," in N. Terleckyj, *Household Production and Consumption*, pp. 99–138, New York: National Bureau of Economic Research.

Heckman, J., and R. Willis (1977), "A Beta Logistic Model for the Analysis of Sequential Labor Force Participation by Married Women," *Journal of Political Economy*, *85*: pp. 27–58.

Hemmerle, W. J., and H. O. Hartley (1973), "Computing Maximum Likelihood Estimates for the Mixed AOV Model Using the W-Transformation," *Technometrics*, *15*: pp. 819–831.

Henderson, C. R. (1953), "Estimation of Variance and Covariance Components," *Biometrics*, *9*: pp. 226–252.

Henderson, C. R. (1971), "Comment on 'The Use of Error Components Models in Combining Cross Section with Time Series Data'," *Econometrica*, *39*: pp. 397–401.

Hildreth, C. (1949), "Preliminary Considerations Regarding Time Series and/or Cross Section Studies," *Cowles Commission Discussion Paper, No. 333*, July 18.

Hildreth, C. (1950), "Combining Cross Section Data and Time Series," *Cowles Commission Discussion Paper, No. 347*, May 15.

Hoch, I. (1955), "Estimation of Production Function Parameters and Testing for Efficiency," paper presented to the Econometric Society, Montreal Meeting, September 10, 1954. Reported *Econometrica*, *23*: pp. 325–326.

Hoch, I. (1958), "Simultaneous Equations Bias in the Context of the Cobb-Douglas Production Function," *Econometrica*, *26*: pp. 566–578.

Hoch, I. (1962), "Estimation of Production Function Parameters Combining Time-Series and Cross-Section Data," *Econometrica*, *30*: pp. 34–53.

Holly, A. (1982), "A Remark on Hausman's Specification Test," *Econometrica*, *50*: pp. 749–760.

Honoré, B. E. (1992), "Trimmed LAD and Least Squares Estimation of Truncated and Censored Regression Models with Fixed Effects," *Econometrica*, *60*: pp. 533–565.

Honoré, B. E. (1993), "Orthogonality Conditions for Tobit Models with Fixed Effects and Lagged Dependent Variables," *Journal of Econometrics*, *59*: pp. 35–61.

Honoré, B. E., and E. Kyriazidou (2000a), "Panel Data Discrete Choice Models with Lagged Dependent Variables," *Econometrica*, *68*: pp. 839–874.

Honoré, B. E. and E. Kyriazidou (2000b), "Estimation of Tobit-Type Models with Individual Specific Effects," *Econometric Reviews*, *19*: pp. 341–366.

Honoré, B. E., E. Kyriazidou, and C. Udry (1997), "Estimation of Type 3 Tobit Models Using Symmetric Trimming and Pairwise Comparisons," *Journal of Econometrics*, *76*: pp. 107–128.

Horowitz, J. L. (1998), *Semiparametric Methods in Econometrics*, New York: Springer-Verlag.

Hsiao, C. (1996), *Analysis of Panel Data*, Cambridge, UK: Cambridge University Press.

Jöreskog, K. G. (1973), "A General Method for Estimating a Linear Structural Equation System," in A. S. Goldberger and O. D. Duncan, pp. 85–112.

Jöreskog, K. G., and D. Sörbom (1976), *LISREL-III: Estimation of Linear Structural Equation Systems by Maximum Likelihood*, Chicago: International Educational Services.

Karlsson, S., and J. Skoglund (2000), "Maximum-Likelihood Based Inference in the Two-Way Random-Effects Model with Serially Correlated Time Effects," unpublished discussion paper, Department of Economic Statistics, Stockholm School of Economics, January 29.

Keane, M. P. (1993), "Simulation Estimation for Panel Data Models with Limited Dependent Variables," in G. S. Maddala, C. R. Rao, and H. D. Vinod, *Handbook of Statistics, Vol. 11*, pp. 545–571, Amsterdam: Elsevier.

Keane, M. P. (1994), "A Computationally Practical Simulation Estimator for Panel Data," *Econometrica, 62*: pp. 95–116.

Keane, M. P., and D. E. Runkle (1992), "On the Estimation of Panel Data Models When Instruments Are Not Strictly Exogenous," *Journal of Business and Economic Statistics, 10*: pp. 1–9.

Kendall, M. G. (1954), "Note on the Bias in the Estimation of Autocorrelations," *Biometrika, 41*: pp. 403–404.

Khuri, A. I., and H. Sahai (1985), "Variance Components Analysis: A Selective Literature Survey," *International Statistical Review, 53*: pp. 279–300.

Kiefer, N. (1988), "Economic Duration Data and Hazard Functions," *Journal of Economic Literature, 26*: pp. 646–679.

Kiefer, N., and G. R. Neumann (1981), "Individual Effects in a Nonlinear Model: Explicit Treatment of Heterogeneity in the Empirical Job-Search Model," *Econometrica, 49*: pp. 965–979.

Kiefer, J., and J. Wolfowitz (1956), "Consistency of the Maximum Likelihood Estimator in the Presence of Infinitely Many Incidental Parameters," *Annals of Mathematical Statistics, 27*: pp. 887–906.

Kim, J., and D. Pollard (1990), "Cube Root Asymptotics," *Annals of Statistics, 18*: pp. 191–219.

Koopmans, T. C., and W. C. Hood (1953), "The Estimation of Simultaneous Linear Economic Relationships," in W. C. Hood and T. C. Koopmans, *Studies in Econometric Method*, Chap. 6, pp. 112–199, New York: Wiley.

Kuh, E. (1959), "The Validity of Cross-Sectionally Estimated Behavior Equations in Time Series Applications," *Econometrica, 27*: pp. 197–214.

Kyriazidou, E. (1997), "Estimation of a Panel Data Sample Selection Model," *Econometrica, 65*: pp. 1335–1364.

Kyriazidou, E. (1999), "Estimation of Dynamic Panel Data Sample Selection Models," available at http://www.econ.ucla.edu/kyria/dsele/dsele.pdf.

Lancaster, T. (1990), *The Econometric Analysis of Transition Data*, Cambridge, UK: Cambridge University Press.

Lancaster, T. (2000), "The Incidental Parameter Problem Since 1948," *Journal of Econometrics, 95*: pp. 391–413.

Lechner, M., and J. Breitung (1996), "Some GMM Estimation Methods and Specification Tests for Nonlinear Models," in Mátyás and Sevestre, pp. 583–612.

Lee, L. F. (1981), "Efficient Estimation of Dynamic Error Components Models with Panel Data," in O. D. Anderson and M. R. Perryman, *Time-Series Analysis*, pp. 267–285, Amsterdam: North-Holland.

Lee, M-J. (1999), "A Root-N Consistent Semiparametric Estimator for Related-Effect Binary Response Panel Data, *Econometrica, 67*: pp. 427–434.

Legendre, A. M. (1805), *Nouvelles Méthodes pour la Détermination des Orbites des Comètes*, Paris: Courcier.

Lillard, L. A., and Y. Weiss (1979), "Components of Variance in Panel Data Earnings Data: American Scientists, 1960–1970," *Econometrica, 47*: pp. 437–454.

Lillard, L. A., and R. J. Willis (1978), "Dynamic Aspects of Earnings Mobility," *Econometrica, 46*: pp. 985–1012.

Lindley, D. V., and M. R. Novick (1981), "The Role of Exchangeability in Inference," *Annals of Statistics, 9*: pp. 45–58.

Maddala, G. S. (1971a), "The Use of Variance Components Models in Pooling Cross Section and Time Series Data," *Econometrica, 39*: pp. 341–358.

Maddala, G. S. (1971b), "The Likelihood Approach to Pooling Cross Section and Time Series Data," *Econometrica, 39*: pp. 939–953.

Maddala, G. S. (1994), "Some Problems Arising in Pooling Cross-Section and Time Series Data," discussion paper, University of Rochester, 1975, first published in Vol. 1, pp. 223–245, G. S. Maddala, *Econometric Methods and Applications*, Aldershot: Edward Elgar Publishers.

Maddala, G. S. (1987a), "Recent Developments in the Econometrics of Panel Data Analysis," *Transportation Research, Ser. A, 21A*: pp. 303–326.

Maddala, G. S. (1987b), "Limited Dependent Variable Models Using Panel Data," *Journal of Human Resources, 12*: pp. 307–338.

Maddala, G. S. (1993), Introduction to Vol. 1, *The Econometrics of Panel Data*, Vols. 1–2, Aldershot: Edward Elgar Publishers.

Maddala, G. S., and T. D. Mount (1973), "A Comparative Study of Alternative Estimators for the Variance Components Model Used in Econometric Applications," *Journal of the American Statistical Association, 68*: pp. 324–328.

Manski, C. (1975), "The Maximum Score Estimation of the Stochastic Utility Model of Choice," *Journal of Econometrics, 3*: pp. 205–228.

Manski, C. (1977), "Semiparametric Analysis of Discrete Response: Asymptotic Properties of the Maximum Score Estimator," *Journal of Econometrics, 27*: pp. 313–333.

Manski, C. (1987), "Semiparametric Analysis of Random-Effects Linear Models from Binary Panel Data," *Econometrica, 55*: pp. 357–362.

Marschak, J., and W. H. Andrews (1944), "Random Simultaneous Equations and the Theory of Production," *Econometrica, 12*: pp. 143–205.

Mátyás, L., and P. Sevestre (1996), *The Econometrics of Panel Data: A Handbook of the Theory with Applications*, 2nd revised ed., Dordrecht: Kluwer Academic Publishers.

Mazodier, P. A. (1971), "The Econometrics of Error Components Models," unpublished doctorate dissertation, Department of Economics, Harvard University, Cambridge, MA.

Mazodier, P. A. (1972), "L'Estimation des Modèles à Erreurs Composées," *L'Annales de l'INSEE, 7*: pp. 43–72.

Moon, H. R., and P. C. B. Phillips (1999), "Maximum Likelihood Estimation in Panels with Incidental Trends," *Oxford Bulletin of Economics and Statistics*, Special Issue, pp. 711–747.

Moran, P. A. P., and C. A. B. Smith (1966), *Commentary on R. A. Fisher's Paper on "The Correlation Between Relatives on the Supposition of Mendelian Inheritance,"*

London: Published for the Galton Laboratory, University College London by the Cambridge University Press.

Mundlak, Y. (1961), "Empirical Production Functions Free of Management Bias," *Journal of Farm Economics, 43*: pp. 44–56.

Mundlak, Y. (1963), "Estimation of Production and Behavioral Functions from a Combination of Cross-Section and Time-Series Data," in C. Christ, *et al., Measurement in Economics: Studies in Mathematical Economics and Econometrics in Memory of Yehuda Grunfeld*, pp. 138–166, Stanford: Stanford University Press.

Mundlak, Y. (1964), *An Economic Analysis of Established Family Farms in Israel, 1953–1958*, The Falk Project for Economic Research in Israel, Jerusalem.

Mundlak, Y. (1978a), "On the Pooling of Time Series and Cross Section Data," *Econometrica, 46*: pp. 69–85.

Mundlak, Y. (1978b), "Models with Variable Coefficients: Integration and Extension," in Colloque International du CNRS, *op. cit.*, pp. 483–509.

Mundlak, Y., and I. Hoch (1965), "Consequences of Alternative Specifications in Estimation of Cobb-Douglas Production Functions," *Econometrica, 33*: pp. 824–828.

Nerlove, M. (1958), *The Dynamics of Supply: Estimation of Farmers' Response to Price*, Baltimore: Johns Hopkins Press.

Nerlove, M. (1965), *Estimation and Identification of Cobb-Douglas Production Functions*, Chicago: Rand McNally.

Nerlove, M. (1967), "Experimental Evidence on the Estimation of Dynamic Economic Relations from a Time-Series of Cross Sections," *Economic Studies Quarterly, 18*: pp. 42–74.

Nerlove, M. (1971a), "Further Evidence on the Estimation of Dynamic Economic Relations from a Time Series of Cross Sections," *Econometrica, 39*: pp. 359–82.

Nerlove, M. (1971b), "A Note on Error Components Models," *Econometrica, 39*: pp. 383–396.

Nerlove, M. (1999a), *Likelihood Inference in Econometrics*, partially completed manuscript.

Nerlove, M. (1999b), "Properties of Alternative Estimators of Dynamic Panel Models: An Empirical Analysis of Cross-Country Data for the Study of Economic Growth," in C. Hsiao, K. Lahiri, L-F. Lee, and M. H. Pesaran, *Analysis of Panels and Limited Dependent Variable Models*, pp. 136–170. New York: Cambridge University Press.

Nerlove, M. (1999c), "Likelihood Inference for Dynamic Panel Models," *Annales d'Économie et de Statistique, 55–56*: pp. 369–410.

Nerlove, M., and P. Balestra (1996), "Formulation and Estimation of Econometric Models for Panel Data," introductory essay in Mátyás and Sevestre, pp. 3–22.

Nerlove, M., and S. J. Press (1978), Review of *Discrete Multivariate Analysis: Theory and Practice*, by Y. M. M. Bishop, S. E. Fienberg, and P. W. Holland, Cambridge, MA: MIT Press, 1976, in *The Bulletin of the American Mathematical Society, 84*: pp. 470–480.

Nerlove, M., and S. J. Press (1986), "Multivariate Log-Linear Probability Models in Econometrics," in *Advances in Statistical Analysis and Statistical Computing: Theory and Applications, 1*: pp. 117–171, R.S. Mariano (Ed.), Greenwich, CT: JAI Press.

Newey, W. K. (1994), "The Asymptotic Variance of Semiparametric Estimators," *Econometrica, 62*: pp. 1349–1382.

Neyman, J., and E. L. Scott (1948), "Consistent Estimates Based on Partially Consistent Observations," *Econometrica, 16*: pp. 1–32.

Nickell, S. (1981), "Biases in Dynamic Models with Fixed Effects." *Econometrica, 49*: pp. 1417–1426.

Pesaran, M. H. (1973), "Exact Maximum Likelihood Estimation of a Regression Equation with a First-Order Moving-Average Error," *Review of Economic Studies, 40*: pp. 529–535.

Rao, C. R. (1946), "On the Linear Combination of Observations and the General Theory of Least Squares," *Sankhyā, 7*: pp. 237–256.

Rao, C. R. (1952), *Advanced Statistical Methods in Biometric Research*, New York: Wiley.

Rao, C. R. (1970), "Estimation of Heteroscedastic Variances in Linear Models," *Journal of the American Statistical Association, 65*: pp. 161–172.

Rao, C. R. (1971a), "Estimation of Variance and Covariance Components – MINQUE Theory," *Journal of Multivariate Analysis, 1*: pp. 257–275.

Rao, C. R. (1971b), "Minimum Variance Quadratic Unbiased Estimation of Variance Components," *Journal of Multivariate Analysis, 1*: pp. 445–456.

Rao, C. R. (1972), "Estimation of Heteroscedastic Variances in Linear Models," *Journal of the American Statistical Association, 67*: pp. 112–115.

Rao, C. R. (1979), "MINQUE Theory and its Relation to ML and MML Estimation of Variance Components," *Sankhyā B, 41*: pp. 138–153.

Rao, P. S. R. S. (1997), *Variance Components Estimation: Mixed Models, Methodologies and Applications*, London: Chapman & Hall.

Rasch, G. (1961), "On General Laws and the Meaning of Measurement in Psychology," in *Proceedings of the Fourth Berkeley Symposium on Mathematical Statistics and Probability, Vol. 4*, pp. 321–333, Berkeley: University of California Press.

Revankar, N. S. (1979), "Error Component Models with Serially Correlated Time Effects," *Journal of the Indian Statistical Association, 17*: pp. 137–160.

Ridder, G., and T. Wansbeek (1990), "Dynamic Models for Panel Data," in R. van der Ploeg (Ed.), *Advanced Lectures in Quantitative Economics*, pp. 557–582, New York: Academic Press.

Sahai, H. (1979), "A Bibliography on Variance Components," *International Statistical Review, 47*: pp. 177–222.

Sahai, H., A. I. Khuri, and C. H. Kapadia (1985), "A Second Bibliography on Variance Components," *Communications in Statistical Theory and Methods, 14*: pp. 63–115.

Scheffé, H. (1956), "Alternative Models for the Analysis of Variance," *Annals of Mathematical Statistics, 27*: pp. 251–271.

Scheffé, H. (1959), *The Analysis of Variance*, New York: Wiley.

Schott, J. R. (1997), *Matrix Analysis for Statistics*, New York: Wiley.

Searle, S. R. (1979), "Notes on Variance Components Estimation. A Detailed Account of Maximum Likelihood and Kindred Methodology," *Technical Report BU-673-M*, Biometrics Unit, Cornell University, Ithaca, NY.

Searle, S. R., and H. V. Henderson (1979), "Dispersion Matrices for Variance Components Models," *Journal of the American Statistical Association, 74*: pp. 465–470.

Searle, S. R., G. Casella, and C. E. McCullough (1992), *Variance Components*, New York: Wiley.

Sevestre, P. (1983), "Modèles Dynamiques á Erreurs Composées," Thése pour le Doctorat de Troisième Cycle, Université Paris I.

Sevestre, P. ed. (1999), "Économétrie des Données de Panel," Numéro spécial d'*Annales d'Économie et de Statistique*, pp. 55–56.

Sevestre, P., and A. Trognon (1983), "Propriétiés de Grands Échantillons d'une Classe d'Estimateurs des Modèles Autorégressifs à Erreurs Composées," *Annales de l'INSEE, 50*: pp. 25–49.

Sevestre, P., and A. Trognon (1985), "A Note on Autoregressive Error Components Models," *Journal of Econometrics, 28*: pp. 231–245.

Sevestre, P., and A. Trognon (1996), "Dynamic Linear Models," in Mátyás and Sevestre, *op. cit.*, pp. 120–144.

Shaman, P. (1969), "On the Inverse of the Covariance Matrix of the First-Order Moving Average," *Biometrika, 56*: pp. 595–600.

Sickles, R. C., and P. Taubman (1986), "A Multivariate Error Components Analysis of the Health and Retirement Status of the Elderly," *Econometrica, 54*: pp. 1339–1356.

Snedecor, G. W. (1934), *Calculation and Interpretation of Analysis of Variance and Covariance*, Ames, IA: Collegiate Press.

Snedecor, G. W. (1937–1980), *Statistical Methods*, 7 editions, Ames, IA: Iowa State College Press.

Sobel, D. (1995), *Longitude*, New York: Penguin Books.

Stigler, S. (1999), *Statistics on the Table: The History of Statistical Concepts and Methods*, Cambridge, MA: Harvard University Press.

Stigum, B. P. (1974), "Asymptotic Properties of Dynamic Stochastic Parameter Estimates – III," *Journal of Multivatiate Analysis, 4*: pp. 351–381.

Stigum, B. P. (1976), "Least Squares and Stochastic Difference Equations," *Journal of Econometrics, 4*: pp. 349–370.

Thiele, T. N. (1931), *Theory of Observations*, London: Layton, 1903. Reprinted in *Annals of Mathematical Statistics, 2*: pp. 165–307.

Tobin, J. (1958), "Estimation of Relationships for Limited Dependent Variables," *Econometrica, 26*: pp. 24–26.

Trognon, A. (1978), "Miscellaneous Asymptotic Properties of Ordinary Least Squares and Maximum Likelihood Methods in Dynamic Error Components Models," *Annales de l'INSEE, 30–31*: pp. 631–657.

Trognon, A. (2000), "Panel Data Econometrics: A Successful Past and a Promising Future," paper presented at the Ninth International Conference on Panel Data, June 22–23. Geneva, Switzerland.

Wallace, T. D., and A. Hussain (1969), "The Use of Error Components Models in Combining Cross Section with Time Series Data," *Econometrica, 37*: pp. 55–72.

Wilks, S. S. (1962), *Mathematical Statistics*, Princeton: Princeton University Press, 1943. Second, greatly augmented edition, New York: Wiley.

Wooldridge, J. M. (2000), "A Framework for Estimating Dynamic, Unobserved Effects Panel Data Models with Possible Feedback to Future Explanatory Variables," *Economics Letters, 68*: pp. 245–250.

Wright, S. (1921), "Correlation and Causation," *Journal of Agricultural Research, 20*: pp. 557–585.

Zellner, A., J. Kmenta, and J. Dreze (1966), "Specification and Estimation of Cobb-Douglas Production Function Models," *Econometrica, 34*: pp. 784–795.

Appendices to "The History of Panel Data Econometrics, 1861–1997"

Decomposition of the Sum of Squares of a Variable Observed in a Two-Dimensional Panel[1]

Let x_{it} be a typical observation associated with a panel consisting of N individuals, on each of which we have T observations. Denote

$$\text{the mean across time for individual } i: \bar{x}_i = \frac{1}{T}\sum_1^T x_{it},$$

$$\text{the mean across individuals for time period } t: \bar{x}_t = \frac{1}{N}\sum_1^N x_{it},$$

the overall mean across individuals and over time periods t: $\bar{x}$

$$= \frac{1}{NT}\sum_1^T\sum_1^N x_{it}. \tag{1}$$

The following notation is useful: a single parameter or observation, even if on a random variable, is denoted by a lower case latin or greek letter, with or without subscripts for individuals (groups) and/or time dimension. Matrices are generally denoted by upper-case latin letters. It will generally be true that vectors and scalars can be given in the same notation without ambiguity and great saving in time, although many authors are at pains to distinguish. The identity matrix of order K is denoted by I_K, a vector of K ones by ℓ_K, and a $K \times K$ matrix of ones by $J_K = \ell_K \ell'_K$. I make extensive use of the kronecker product of two matrices.

Using the notation introduced in the preceding paragraph and the vector $x = (x_{11}, \ldots, x_{1T}, \ldots, x_{N1}, \ldots, x_{NT})'$ of "stacked" observations, we can describe the variability of the observations x in terms of the following decomposition of the sum of squares:

---

[1] This appendix is adapted from Chapter 19 of Nerlove (1999a).

overall SS around the general mean:

$$\sum_{1}^{N}\sum_{1}^{T}(x_{it}-\bar{x})^2 = x'\left[I_{NT}-\frac{J_{NT}}{NT}\right]x;$$

within-group SS, around the group means:

$$\sum_{1}^{N}\sum_{1}^{T}(x_{it}-\bar{x})^2 = x'\left[I_{NT}-\left(I_N\otimes\frac{J_T}{T}\right)\right]x;$$

between-group SS, variation of group means around the overall mean:

$$\sum_{1}^{N}\sum_{1}^{T}(\bar{x}_i-\bar{x})^2 = x'\left[\left(I_N-\otimes\frac{J_T}{T}\right)-\frac{J_{NT}}{NT}\right]x;$$

within-period SS, around period means:

$$\sum_{1}^{N}\sum_{1}^{T}(x_{it}-\bar{x})^2 = x'\left[I_{NT}-\left(\frac{J_N}{N}\otimes I_T\right)\right]x;$$

between-period SS, variation of period means around the overall mean:

$$\sum_{1}^{N}\sum_{1}^{T}(\bar{x}_t-\bar{x})^2 = x'\left[\left(\frac{J_N}{N}\otimes I_T\right)-\frac{J_{NT}}{NT}\right]x;$$

residual SS:

$$\sum_{1\,.\,1}^{N\ T}(x_{it}-\bar{x}_i-\bar{x}_t+\bar{x})^2 = x'\left[I_{NT}-\left(I_N\otimes\frac{J_T}{T}\right)-\left(\frac{J_N}{N}\otimes I_T\right)+\frac{J_{NT}}{NT}\right]x.$$

$$(2)$$

The matrices of the quadratic forms decomposing the total SS of the variable x are, more compactly,

$$V = \left[I_{NT}-\frac{J_{NT}}{NT}\right], \quad rank = NT-1;$$

$$B_N = \left[I_{NT}-\left(I_N\otimes\frac{J_T}{T}\right)\right] = \left(I_N-\frac{J_N}{N}\right)\otimes\frac{J_T}{T}, \quad rank = (T-1)N;$$

$$B_T = \left[\left(I_N\otimes\frac{J_T}{T}\right)-\frac{J_{NT}}{NT}\right] = \frac{J_N}{N}\otimes\left(I_T-\frac{J_T}{T}\right), \quad rank = N-1;$$

$$W_N = \left[I_{NT}-\left(\frac{J_N}{N}\otimes I_T\right)\right] = I_N\otimes\left(I_T-\frac{J_T}{T}\right), \quad rank = T(N-1);$$

$$W_T = \left[\left(\frac{J_N}{N}\otimes I_T\right)-\frac{J_{NT}}{NT}\right] = \left(I_N-\frac{J_N}{N}\right)\otimes I_T, \quad rank = T-1;$$

$$W^* = \left[I_{NT} - \left(I_N \otimes \frac{J_T}{T} \right) - \left(\frac{J_N}{N} \otimes I_T \right) + \frac{J_{NT}}{NT} \right]$$

$$= \left(I_N - \frac{J_N}{N} \right) \otimes \left(I_T - \frac{J_T}{T} \right), \quad rank = (N-1)(T-1). \tag{3}$$

The properties of the matrices, all of which are symmetric and idempotent, defined in (3), that are useful in obtaining the spectral decomposition of the variance-covariance matrix of the disturbances in a general three-component random-effects model, are

$$V = W_N + W_T = B_N + B_T = W^* + W_T + B_T;$$

$$W_N B_N = W_T B_T = W^* B_N = W^* B_T = B_N B_T = 0;$$

$$V \frac{J_{NT}}{NT} = W^* \frac{J_{NT}}{NT} = W_N \frac{J_{NT}}{NT} = W_T \frac{J_{NT}}{NT} = B_N \frac{J_{NT}}{NT} = B_T \frac{J_{NT}}{NT} = 0. \tag{4}$$

From the decomposition (2), we see that the information contained in the sum of squares or cross products among panel variables can be decomposed into six parts as detailed there. These pieces of information are more or less valuable according to the amount of "noise" in the system related to the different components of the variation. What an error-components model does is to weight these bits inversely according to their error variances. What maximum likelihood does is to estimate the weights and the relationship among observed variables simultaneously. What fixed-effects models do is to throw away a part of the observable variation bearing on the relationship to be estimated as if the error associated with that component were very large. All this in the name of avoiding correlation between the error components and the explanatory variables, which is the very source of the information being discarded.

Alternative Formulations of the Concentrated Likelihood Function for the Two-Component Random-Effects Model

Consider the model

$$y_{it} = \alpha + \beta x_{it} + \mu_i + \varepsilon_{it}, \quad i = 1, \dots, N, \quad t = 1, \dots, T, \tag{1}$$

where $\sigma^2 = \sigma_\mu^2 + \sigma_\varepsilon^2$, and $\rho = \sigma_\mu^2 / \sigma^2$ and the variance covariance matrix of the disturbances in the stacked model is

$$Euu' = \sigma^2 \Omega = \sigma^2 \begin{pmatrix} A & \cdots & 0 \\ \vdots & \ddots & \vdots \\ 0 & \cdots & A \end{pmatrix}, \quad \text{where } A \text{ is a } T \times T \text{ matrix}$$

$$A = \begin{pmatrix} 1 & \cdots & \rho \\ \vdots & \ddots & \vdots \\ \rho & \cdots & 1 \end{pmatrix}.$$

Suppressing the constant term α by taking deviations from the overall means and assuming u follows a multivariate normal distribution with mean zero and variance-covariance matrix $\sigma^2 \Omega$, the log likelihood is

$$\log L\left(\beta, \sigma_\mu^2, \sigma_\varepsilon^2 \mid y_{11}, \dots, y_{NT}; x_{11}, \dots, x_{NT}\right)$$
$$= -\frac{NT}{2} \log 2\pi - \frac{NT}{2} \log \sigma^2 - \frac{1}{2} \log |\Omega^{-1}| - \frac{1}{2\sigma^2} \sum_{i=1}^{N} \sum_{t=1}^{T} (y_{it} - \beta x_{it})^2. \tag{2}$$

Transforming the observations to

$$y_{it} = \xi^{-1/2} \bar{y}_{i.} + \eta^{-1/2}(y_{it} - \bar{y}_{i.}),$$
$$x_{it} = \xi^{-1/2} \bar{x}_{i.} + \eta^{-1/2}(x_{it} - \bar{x}_{i.}), \quad i = 1, \dots, N, \quad t = 1, \dots, T,$$

where $\xi = 1 - \rho + T\rho$, $\eta = 1 - \rho$, and $\bar{x}_{i.}$ and $\bar{y}_{i.}$ are the group means yields the likelihood:

$$\log L(\beta, \rho, \sigma^2 \mid y_{11}, \ldots, y_{NT}; x_{11}, \ldots x_{NT}; y_{10}, \ldots, y_{N0})$$

$$= -\frac{NT}{2}\log 2\pi - \frac{NT}{2}\log\sigma^2 - \frac{N}{2}\log\xi - \frac{N(T-1)}{2}\log\eta$$

$$- \frac{1}{2\sigma^2}\sum_{i=1}^{N}\sum_{t=1}^{T}(y_{it}^* - \beta X_{it}^*)^2. \tag{3}$$

While Balestra and Nerlove (1966) worked in terms of the transformed observations, I now believe replacing the final term in (3) by its equivalent in terms of the moments or sums of squares of the untransformed observations would be preferable from the standpoint of numerical calculation, both faster and more accurate.

In Maddala's (1971a) notation, the within-group sums of squares of y and x and of cross-products, respectively, are W_{yy}, W_{xx}, and W_{xy}, and of the group means, or "between" SS and sums of cross-products, respectively, B_{yy}, B_{xx}, and B_{xy}. Using this notation, the final term of (3) can be rewritten as

$$- \frac{1}{2\sigma^2}\left\{\left(\frac{W_{yy}}{\eta} + \frac{B_{yy}}{\xi}\right) - 2\left(\frac{W_{yx}}{\eta} + \frac{B_{yx}}{\xi}\right)\beta + \left(\frac{W_{xx}}{\eta} + \frac{B_{xx}}{\xi}\right)\beta^2\right\}.$$

Holding ρ fixed and maximizing $\log L$ with respect to β and σ^2, we obtain

$$\hat{\beta}(\rho) = \left[\frac{W_{xx}}{\eta} + \frac{B_{xx}}{\xi}\right]^{-1}\left(\frac{W_{xy}}{\eta} + \frac{B_{xy}}{\xi}\right)$$

$$\hat{\sigma}^2(\rho) = \frac{1}{NT}\left(\frac{W_{yy}}{\eta} + \frac{B_{yy}}{\xi}\right) - \left(\frac{W_{xy}}{\eta} + \frac{B_{xy}}{\xi}\right)'$$

$$\times \left[\frac{W_{xx}}{\eta} + \frac{B_{xx}}{\xi}\right]^{-1}\left(\frac{W_{xy}}{\eta} + \frac{B_{xy}}{\xi}\right),$$

which are functions of ρ because ξ and η are. Substituting in (3) gives us the *concentrated* log likelihood function of ρ and the data alone:

$$\log L^*(\rho \mid x, y) = -\frac{NT}{2}\log 2\pi - \frac{N}{2}\log\xi - \frac{N(T-1)}{2}\log\eta$$

$$- \frac{NT}{2}\log\left\{\frac{1}{NT}\left(\frac{W_{yy}}{\eta} + \frac{B_{yy}}{\xi}\right) - \left(\frac{W_{xy}}{\eta} + \frac{B_{xy}}{\xi}\right)'\right.$$

$$\left.\times \left[\frac{W_{xx}}{\eta} + \frac{B_{xx}}{\xi}\right]^{-1}\left(\frac{W_{xy}}{\eta} + \frac{B_{xy}}{\xi}\right)\right\}. \tag{4}$$

This being a function only of the parameter ρ, which is bounded between 0 and 1, given the data, it is very easy to maximize graphically.

Maddala (1971a), however, argues not in terms of ρ but in terms of

$$\theta = \frac{\eta}{\xi} = \frac{1-\rho}{1-\rho+T\rho}.^1$$

After some algebra and using the relation $\sigma_\varepsilon^2 = \eta\sigma^2$, we can derive the log likelihood counterpart to (3):

$$\log L\left(\beta, \theta, \sigma_\varepsilon^2 \mid y_{11}, \ldots, y_{NT}; x_{11}, \ldots x_{NT}; y_{10}, \ldots, y_{N0}\right)$$

$$= -\frac{NT}{2}\log 2\pi - \frac{NT}{2}\log \sigma_\varepsilon^2 - \frac{N}{2}\log\theta$$

$$- \frac{1}{2\sigma_\varepsilon^2}\{(W_{yy} + \theta B_{yy}) - 2(W_{yx} + \theta B_{yx})\beta + (W_{xx} + \theta B_{xx})\beta^2\}, \quad (5)$$

hence,

$$\hat{\beta}(\theta) = [W_{xx} + \theta B_{xx}]^{-1}(W_{xy} + \theta B_{xy})$$

and

$$\hat{\sigma}_\varepsilon^2(\theta) = \frac{1}{NT}(W_{yy} + \theta B_{yy}) - (W_{xy} + \theta B_{xy})'[W_{xx} + \theta B_{xx}]^{-1}(W_{xy} + \theta B_{xy}),$$

so that the concentrated log likelihood function is

$$\log L^*(\theta \mid y_{11}, \ldots, y_{NT}; x_{11}, \ldots x_{NT}; y_{10}, \ldots, y_{N0})$$

$$= -\frac{NT}{2}(\log 2\pi + 1) - \frac{N}{2}\log\theta$$

$$- \frac{NT}{2}\log\left\{\frac{1}{NT}(W_{yy} + \theta B_{yy}) - (W_{xy} + \theta B_{xy})'[W_{xx} + \theta B_{xx}]^{-1}\right.$$

$$\left. \times (W_{xy} + \theta B_{xy})\right\}. \quad (6)$$

For $T = 20$, the relationship between ρ and θ is graphed in Figure 1.

It is clear that, for large values of ρ, θ varies relatively little, whereas the opposite is true for small values of ρ. So when ρ is very small, it should be easier to estimate using the θ-formulation, and vice versa.

Here is a numerical example showing that the two formulations function about equally well numerically:

$$\begin{bmatrix} B_{yy} & B_{yx} \\ B_{xy} & B_{xx} \end{bmatrix} = \begin{bmatrix} 355780. & [2.2116*10^6 \quad 230819] \\ \begin{bmatrix} 2.2116*10^6 \\ 230819. \end{bmatrix} & \begin{bmatrix} 1.6038*10^7 & 1.62779*10^6 \\ 1.62779*10^6 & 363501. \end{bmatrix} \end{bmatrix}$$

---

[1] Alternatively, $\rho = \frac{-(1-\theta)}{1-\theta+T\theta}$

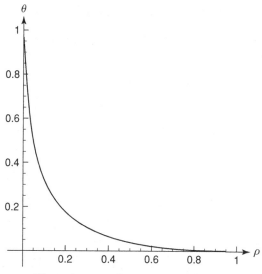

Figure 1. θ as a Function of ρ, $T = 20$.

$$\begin{bmatrix} W_{yy} & W_{yx} \\ W_{xy} & W_{xx} \end{bmatrix} = \begin{bmatrix} 2.24435*10^6 & \begin{bmatrix} 4.38196*10^6 & 3.99373*10^6 \end{bmatrix} \\ \begin{bmatrix} 4.38196*10^6 \\ 3.99373*10^6 \end{bmatrix} & \begin{bmatrix} 2.30778*10^7 & 5.93598*10^6 \\ 5.93598*10^6 & 1.0772*10^7 \end{bmatrix} \end{bmatrix}.$$

The results of plotting the concentrated likelihood function and the values β, σ^2, and θ or ρ obtained at the maximum are presented in Figures 2 and 3: It is apparent that the differences are very minor.

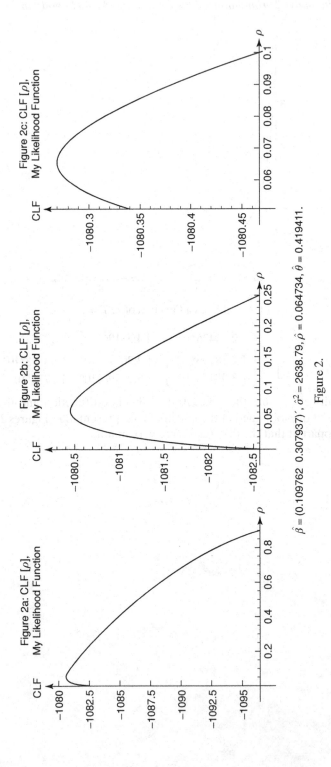

$\hat{\beta} = (0.109762 \quad 0.307937)', \hat{\sigma}^2 = 2638.79, \hat{\rho} = 0.064734, \hat{\theta} = 0.419411.$

Figure 2.

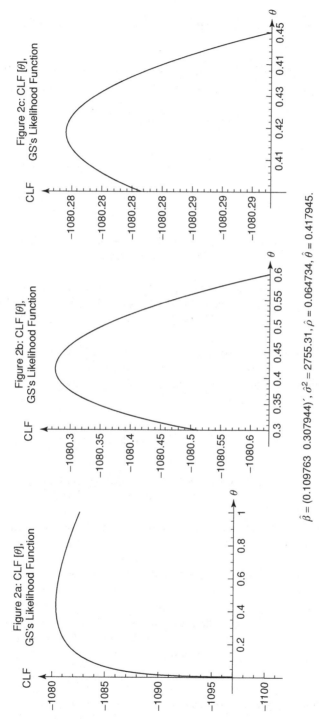

$\hat{\beta} = (0.109763 \ 0.307944)'$, $\hat{\sigma}^2 = 2755.31$, $\hat{\rho} = 0.064734$, $\hat{\theta} = 0.417945$.

Figure 3.

Introduction to *The Econometrics of Panel Data*, Colloque International du CNRS, INSEE, Paris 22–24 August 1977

"Econometric Analysis of Longitudinal Data: Approaches, Problems, and Prospects," by Marc Nerlove

This paper presents a selective summary of the twenty-seven papers and discussions presented at the Colloque International sur L'Économétrie des Données Individuelles Temporelles, held in Paris, at INSEE, August 22–24, 1977, under the auspices of the Centre National de la Recherche Scientifique. The main themes of the conference papers are outlined and attention is drawn to a number of especially interesting points or promising approaches, as well as to a number of problems inherent in using the extraordinarily rich bodies of data afforded by longitudinal sources.

1. INTRODUCTION

Twenty-seven papers dealing with various aspects of the econometric analysis of longitudinal data were presented during the Colloquium; twenty-five of them are published here.[1] Many of the papers deal with methodological problems, including the appropriate formulation of models, in the exploitation of the rich sources of data now available, consisting essentially of time series for individual economic agents or areas. These include discussions of latent, or unobserved variables, sample selectivity, and categorical variables, as well as general models and computational problems. Other papers deal with the statistical properties of various estimation methods within the context of particular models and extensions of existing estimation techniques. Applications are presented of longitudinal data to the study of investment, technical progress, length of life of capital equipment, dividend behavior of firms, spatial income determination, consumer demand, life-time income profiles, returns

---

[1] Unless otherwise specified, references are to papers presented at the Colloquium. General references have been included in the general list of references for this essay.

to schooling, retirement decisions, female labor-force participation decisions, and banks' portfolio behavior. The great variety of applied topics covered testifies to the value of longitudinal data resources and the power of existing statistical procedures to draw inferences from such sources in many different circumstances.

2. SUMMARY

a. Methodological Papers

One major theme of the methodological papers presented is in the development of highly general models into which previous models and discussions of appropriate estimation procedures can be fitted as special cases.

Jöreskog described a general model involving structural equations among several jointly dependent variables assumed to be observable over several time periods. These variables are, in principle, directly observable and continuously measurable in character (i.e., not categorical). The explanatory variables are also assumed to be observable, may vary or not vary over time, and may have effects that vary or do not vary over time. The structural equations are assumed subject to unobserved shocks that consist of a time-invariant effect and a serially correlated disturbance. The model is, thus, somewhat less general than Jöreskog has discussed on earlier occasions (Jöreskog, 1973), in which explanatory variables may be subject to error, so that the possibility of *latent* explanatory variables with possibly several indicators is permitted. This more general approach and an associated maximum-likelihood procedure (Jöreskog and Sörbom, 1976) is used, in part, by Chamberlain in his study of the relation between schooling and earnings in relation to the unobserved, latent variables "ability" and the "anticipated future wage advantge" of additional schooling.

Mundlak develops a similar, although in some respects more general, model in which, however, only a single dependent variable is assumed. Some parameters are assumed to be constant across individuals and over time periods; others are permitted to vary across individuals only. The disturbances are assumed to be uncorrelated both across individuals and serially. Mundlak distinguishes the following cases: (1) only variables with constant coefficients occur (ordinary regression), or only variables with varying parameters occur; (2) independent variables are continuously variable or categorical; (3) variable coefficients are fixed or random; and (4) the independent variables are related to the coefficients. His framework permits Mundlak to summarize conveniently a variety of results previously obtained by himself and others.

Wansbeek and Kapteyn treat a similar general model involving parameters constant over both individuals and over time, time-varying parameters, and time-invariant, individual varying parameters. There is only one dependent variable and the disturbances in the equation are assumed to be both serially and cross-sectionally uncorrelated. The primary emphasis of the authors is on problems of prediction when varying parameters are assumed to be "fixed effects" or "random effects."

Harvey discusses what are essentially time-series problems within the context of longitudinal data, and he shows how Kalman filtering techniques may be extended to the multivariate case and adapted to provide additional scope for investigating the nature of time variation in the parameters of a suitable model in this context.

A second general methodological theme is represented in Maddala's paper on selectivity problems in the analysis of longitudinal data. In many surveys, the data themselves are generated by individuals making certain choices or having certain characteristics so that those included in the survey may be self-selected. The most common example is female labor-force participation in which wage rates are measured only for women who actually participate. Other examples include measurement of returns to college education (in which account must be taken of why those who choose not to go to college make that choice), migration, and the demand for owner-occupied versus rental housing. Maddala develops a unified framework in which to discuss selectivity problems and biases and the various identification and estimation problems in models of self-selection, sample truncation, or attrition. The general structure of the model that Maddala introduces is "that there are two systems of equations A and B describing the behavior of individuals and there is a choice function C that determines which group the individual belongs to." In general, "the error in C is correlated with the errors in A and/or B." And, in many cases, "C involves the endogenous variables in A and B." Maddala's approach thus represents an extension, generalization, and development of that of Heckman (1976).

The paper by Griliches, Hall, and Hausman represents perhaps the most important and well-worked-out example of a selectivity model applied to the problem of estimating the economic returns to schooling using data from the National Longitudinal Survey of Young Men. The principal selectivity problems involved in their study are changing sample size over time due to attrition and the self-selection to "work" of the out-of-school subsample, the only part of the data for which an earnings function could be computed. In particular, the decision to remain in school for a longer period before going to work is not independent of an unobserved, latent variable termed "ability" nor are the earnings of such individuals once they go to work nor of their counterparts who enter the world of work earlier independent of "ability," Of particular interest in the paper by Griliches, *et al.*, are the measures presented of the extent to which self-selection "to work" may bias the estimates of the effects of schooling on earnings. While a number of other papers involve the issues raised by Maddala, none do so as explicitly, although the paper by Chamberlain, as noted, treats a similar theme using the same body of data and a model involving two latent variables.

While the paper by Chevaillier and Paelinck dealing with "spatial econometrics" involves some potentially important new methodological problems (two-dimensional spatial correlation is fundamentally different from one-dimensional serial correlation), it does not treat these issues from a general point of view and may more properly be considered as an application.

Perhaps the most significant methodological paper of the conference is the paper by Heckman on the distinction between true state dependence versus spurious state dependence due to unobserved differences among individuals. The question addressed is essentially how to distinguish between two possible explanations for the empirical regularity that individuals who experience an event in the past are more likely to experience that event in the future: (1) One possible explanation is that implicit in the variance-components type of model for continuous data, namely, that for various, and possibly unobserved reasons, individuals differ in their propensity to experience the event. (2) A second and more interesting explanation is that the probabilities of experiencing the event at a given point in time are altered by past experience, or lack of experience, of the event. Thus, for example, the probability that a woman is presently in the labor force is strongly related to her past labor-force experience, either because she has an exceptionally high (or low) propensity to participate, in general, for reasons we cannot fully account for in terms of measured differences, or because, having participated (or not) in the past affects the terms on which she can currently participate, through, for example, accumulation (or depreciation) of human capital in the form of work experience. The phrasing of the question clearly presupposes that the event experienced is a categorical random variable, although, in principle, the framework of analysis could be extended to encompass continuously measured variables by supposing that the probability law governing their generation depended either on certain unobserved, latent random variables reflecting individual differences, or on past experience (essentially, a distributed lag), or both. By concentrating on the discrete or categorical case, however, Heckman makes explicit the central importance of the probability law governing the generation of the observations.[2] Heckman develops his model in terms of a continuous latent random variable for which the observed event occurs when the latent variable crosses some threshold for the individual in question. Such a formulation is consistent with his other recent work in which he shows that the introduction of latent variables allows the combination of both continuous and categorical jointly dependent variables

---

[2] This point was stressed more in earlier econometric discussions (Haavelmo, 1944) than it has been in recent ones. Indeed, the discussion of Balestra and Nerlove (1966), which lies behind much of the other work presented at the conference, is essentially an "equation formulation" of the general problem Heckman is discussing. In the Balestra-Nerlove formulation, the role of "state dependence" is effected by the inclusion of a simple distributed lag, while individual differences affecting the probability governing the value of the dependent variable (propensity to experience the event) are described by an unobserved component of residual variance.

in a common structural equation model (Heckman, 1978b). Heckman's analysis is applied to a study of the dynamics of female labor supply using data from the Michigan Panel on Income Dynamics, in which he concludes that there is evidence of both true state dependence and of temporal persistence of unmeasured factors that determine the probability of labor-force participation.

b. Papers on Properties of Estimators and Computational Problems

A number of papers deal with primarily computational problems or with properties of estimators.

Bronwyn Hall describes a very general computer program for the analysis of longitudinal data. Hall's program is capable of estimating linear or nonlinear models with fixed or with random effects, including probit models involving categorical variables and models with variable coefficients. However, the program is restricted to the case in which, while intercepts, slopes, and variances are allowed to vary across individuals, they may not do so over time. This assumption allows a convenient computational simplification in data storage. Several estimation procedures are available within the program.

Glejser discusses briefly the problem of truncation remainders in the estimation of distributed-lag models from panel data in which the time series on each individual is very short and in which the disturbances in the relation to be estimated are, in general, autocorrelated. The problem of truncation remainder arises when the distributed-lag model is specified in a form in which the dependent variable is a specified function of lagged values of the independent variables, in principle an infinite number, but the series must be truncated due to the finite temporal dimension of the sample.[3] A number of Monte Carlo experiments are performed in order to assess a particular estimation procedure proposed. Unfortunately, no alternative estimates are considered, nor are the experiments guided by any analysis of the sort for example undertaken by Trognon; consequently, the results are inconclusive.

Mazodier and Trognon show to what extent the results obtained by Nerlove (1971b) on generalized least-squares estimation in three-component error-components models may or may not be extended to situations in which the variances of the individual and period error components are not constant, but may vary across strata consisting of a number of individuals or periods, a special case being strata that contain only one individual or period. When each stratum contains only one individual or time period, it is not, in general, possible to estimate the heteroskedastic variances and, even when each stratum contains sufficient information to compute these variances, it is not possible to transform the data so as to compute simply a generalized least-squares estimate. The situation is altered when individual or period-specific constant

---

[3] See Dhrymes (1971, p. 98).

effects are included in the model, although this *may* render the variance components unidentifiable.

Trognon's paper deriving asymptotic properties of ordinary least-squares and maximum-likelihood estimators in dynamic error-components models is an analytic *tour de force*. In two papers, Nerlove (1971a, 1967) explored experimentally the properties of various types of estimators, including ordinary least squares and maximum likelihood, in a simple distributed-lag two-component-error model, both including and excluding an exogenous explanatory variable. One of the purposes of these experiments was to ascertain whether the peculiar properties of ordinary least squares, and especially of maximum likelihood, found in Balestra and Nerlove (1966) could be reproduced. Trognon uses powerful results recently obtained by Stigum (1974, 1975) to deduce the asymptotic properties of these estimators under various circumstances. The principal finding in Nerlove (1967) was that, when the proportion of variance contributed by the individual, time-invariant component was large, the OLS estimate of the coefficient of the lagged dependent variable in the case with no exogenous variable present was sharply biased upward, thus confirming the finding of the implausible behavior the OLS estimate found by Balestra and Nerlove (1966). But the prevalence of boundary solutions for the maximum-likelihood estimators was confirmed only when an exogenous variable was present and only in the case of certain parameter combinations by Nerlove (1971a). Trognon succeeds in reproducing all of these results analytically, including a demonstration of the properties of the maximum-likelihood estimators for various combinations of parameter values in the case of an exogenous variable present and generated in nearly the same fashion as in Nerlove (1971a).[4]

Trognon's results demonstrate the power of asymptotic methods in the study of alternative estimators in the context of longitudinal data analysis, in contradiction to the opinion expressed in Nerlove (1971a, p. 364) that "…existing large sample asymptotic results are not helpful in problems of this sort." However, it should be noted that Trognon's conclusions are derived from analytic approximations, whose validity depends on the number of time periods being large, but in which the bias as computed goes to zero as T increases indefinitely, so that the "asymptotic" conclusions in the usual sense are indeed not helpful. The importance of pushing analytical approximations as far as possible before undertaking Monte Carlo experiments, or as an aid to understanding Monte Carlo results, is underscored by Trognon's work. It is to be hoped that the techniques that he uses may be applied to the elucidation of other puzzles in the study of estimation from longitudinal data, such as why the prevalence of boundary solutions in the maximum-likelihood case disappears when the likelihood function is based on an approximation to the *unconditional* probability

---

[4] Analytic results could not be derived for the case actually considered in Nerlove (1971a) because the exogenous variable was generated by a nonstationary process.

of the sample observations rather than on the probability conditional on the initial values of the dependent variable.

c. Applications

As indicated previously, a great variety of applications are included among the conference papers: altogether seventeen of the twenty-seven papers dealt primarily with applied topics, and most of the papers classified as methodological contain at least one empirical illustration.

Lipsey gives a detailed description of the problems encountered in creating a microdata set for a sample of U.S. firms by linking commercial and Census data sources on firms and establishments. The problems of merger, dissolution, name-change, and reconciliation of enterprise and establishment series through employment data are explored. Perhaps the most important lesson to be learned from Lipsey's fascinating account is how important are the problems of sample selectivity discussed by Maddala and by Griliches, *et al.*

Seven papers deal with the behavior of firms, including banks, as estimated from longitudinal data sets. Eisner continues his investigation of the determinants of business investment using data on approximately seven hundred firms over a fourteen-year period from the McGraw Hill Capital Expenditure Surveys.[5] Missing data on particular variables and incomplete series because of mergers on nonresponse significantly reduce the number of observations available on individual firms in any one year. Indeed, dynamic behavior cannot readily be estimated using the microdata because the individual time series are broken and short; nonetheless, by constructing time series for firms with more than one year of observations and pooling deviations of these observations about the firms means for years in which observations are available, Eisner is able to draw conclusions about the effects of past sales, profits, and depreciation, as well as reported sales expectations. It would be a useful addition to his study to examine the effects of sample selectivity on his results using methods such as are suggested by Maddala.

Oudiz, Mairesse, Atkinson and Mairesse, and Henin use time series for individual French firms to investigate investment behavior, technical progress, length of life of capital equipment, and dividend behavior. With panel data for 195 French industrial firms for the years 1963–75 and for 124 firms for 1966–75, Oudiz tests Eisner's specification against an alternative specification in which investment is made to depend on current retained earnings, lagged retained earnings, and the change in long-term debt other than bonds plus bonds outstanding. The great advantage of the French data, as compared with those Eisner has used, is that there are no gaps or missing observations for the firms

---

[5] Eisner (1978).

included in the sample, although this, of course, does not imply the absence of any selectivity bias. Oudiz pools the data for each sample in three broad industry groups and investigates deviations from year means, firm means, and overall means. On the whole, Eisner's conclusions from the larger but lower quality U.S. sample are supported, although comparisons with the alternative formulation suggest greater imperfections in the French capital market.

Mairesse uses the same data as Oudiz for the period 1966–1975 to estimate production functions involving technological change, both disembodied and embodied (that is, which depends on the amount of new capital formation through gross investment). Mairesse's stochastic specification is of the components-of-variance type in which firm-specific time-invariant random effects are considered. These are rather important in this connection since the purpose of the investigation is to disentangle the two types of technological progress. A number of alternative specifications and estimation procedures are examined; in general, the results with respect to disembodied technical progress are insensitive to the manner in which firm differences are accounted for or removed, but the same is not true for embodied technical progress. Some of these differences may, perhaps, be understood in terms of the results obtained by Nerlove (1971a) by interpreting past investments as a form of distributed lag. A companion study with Atkinson deals with the implications of one of the two samples for the estimation of the length of life of capital equipment in French manufacturing industry.

The paper by Henin uses data on only forty firms over a seven-year period, 1967–1973, to test various alternative specifications based on the Lintner model of firm dividend behavior. While the author makes use of relatively elaborate stochastic specifications, he consistently reports the value of Durbin-Watson statistics (testing for serial correlation), and on the results of the method of Cochrane and Orcutt to remove serial correlation, without adequate explanation. Additional discussion is surely required in view of the fact that the value of the D-W statistic and the results of the Cochrane-Orcutt procedure depend crucially on the order of the observations: while the observations for *each* firm are naturally ordered with respect to time, the firms themselves have *no natural order*.

Papers by Chevaillier and Paelinck on spatial-income determination, Chamberlain on ability and schooling, and Griliches *et al.* on the returns to schooling and ability have previously been commented on in connection with the discussion of methodological papers in Section 1. A different approach to the question of returns to schooling is taken by Smith and Welch. Their paper examines the earnings behavior of new labor-market entrants in the 1967–1974 period, using data from the *Current Population Surveys*, cross-classified by industry and area. Although only eight years of time-series observations are available, the authors attempt to "simulate" cyclical effects cross-sectionally on the assumption that local labor-market conditions vary sufficiently to do so. Although the cross-sectional estimates are highly erratic, the authors draw rather strong conclusions about the cyclic nature of wage changes and employment, and cast considerable doubt on the widely accepted theory that there has been a massive decline in the returns to college education, regarding this as possibly a largely cyclic phenomenon.

The paper by Jonsson and Klevmarken on the relationship between cross-sectional and cohort earnings profiles and with what can be inferred about the former from the latter is of related interest in connection with all of the papers that deal with inferences about earnings from relatively short time series "multiplied" cross-sectionally. The data that they use in the empirical part of the study, however, refer to Swedish engineers only over a relatively short fifteen-year period, so that, in general, it proved difficult and of dubious value to estimate cohort specific effects.

As indicated, a number of the methodological papers, such as Heckman's, deal with labor-force participation behavior. Both papers by Lillard, on permanent and transitory responses in labor supply, and by Shapiro and Mott on working young mothers, deal with similar related problems within the context of longitudinal data analysis. In the development of a model that introduces the distinction between permanent and transitory wage differences and dynamic supply responses to such differences, Lillard makes the greatest use of the riches afforded by panel data and adds a new methodological dimension to the conference.

Finally, Salvas-Bronsard, in her paper estimating systems of demand equations for individual French households, 1965–1972, stratified by income class and socioeconomic status, provides a potentially but, unfortunately, unrealized application of the methodological results of Mazodier and Trognon. Hester, in an interesting paper only somewhat tangentially related to the major themes of the conference, uses data on individual banks over time to show how individual and aggregate behavior may rather substantially differ.

3. CONCLUSIONS

While it is difficult to draw any general conclusions from such a large and diversified series of papers, I should like to use this occasion to make a few remarks on problems and on what seem to me to be promising approaches and prospects.

First, there is clearly a need when dealing with a relatively new, unfamiliar, and rich course of data to go back to "basics." As emphasized by Griliches in many oral comments, as well as his paper, it is important to understand and to model the sources of stochastic variation, as well as the relations among observed variables. Moreover, as brought out most clearly in Heckman's paper, but also well in Maddala's comprehensive discussion of selectivity problems, it is useful if not essential to describe the problem of inference as concerned with the underlying probability laws governing the generation of the observed data. Both attention to the behavioral character of the sources of stochastic variation and the explicit modeling of the underlying structure of the probability law require a rather specific context for proper implementation. Yet, as the papers by Jöreskog, Maddala, and Mundlak show, there is nonetheless considerable scope for generalized modeling efforts that attempt to reduce most specific problems to special cases within a general analytic framework.

Perhaps the most significant general issue to arise at the conference, in my view, is that of sample selection, especially as viewed within a general framework in which latent, unobserved variables trigger responses that may be categorical in character. Models of this sort apply to labor supply as analyzed by Heckman, earnings-schooling relations as analyzed by Chamberlain and Griliches *et al.*, as well as to the more explicit cases of missing data and truncated samples. Nearly all of the applications presented at the conference involve this issue, although few authors have taken account of it explicitly. In many instances, it will be difficult to model the relevant behavior or to explore the implications of this phenomenon, but it represents, perhaps, the most widespread problem discussed and the greatest prospect for further advance, both methodologically and empirically.

Finally, the power of analytic techniques, such as those employed by Trognon, to illuminate and extend results heretofore obtained by Monte Carlo experimentation is, indeed, impressive.

We are clearly on the frontier of a great and largely unexplored area of econometric research. The papers presented at this conference cast much light into some of the nooks and crannies of this vast space, but much remains in shadow or only tangentially and partially illuminated. What we see now so dimly and from the corners of our eyes may yet prove to be the most fascinating and exciting new knowledge to be gained by further research.

Derivation of the Likelihood Function for the Three-Component Random-Effects Nondynamic Panel Model with Serially Correlated Period Effects[1]

Consider the model given by equations (15)–(16) of the text:

$$y_{it} = \alpha + \beta x_{it} + u_{it}, \quad i = 1, \ldots, N, \quad t = 1, \ldots, T, \tag{1}$$

with disturbances

$$u_{it} = \mu_i + \lambda_t + \varepsilon_{it}$$

(i) $\mu_i \sim iid(0, \sigma_\mu^2)$

$\mu = [\mu_i]$ is a $N \times 1$ vector

(ii) $\varepsilon_{it} \sim iid(0, \sigma_\varepsilon^2)$

$\varepsilon_i = [\varepsilon_{it}]$ is a $T \times 1$ vector, and

$\varepsilon = [\varepsilon_i]$ is a $TN \times 1$ vector

(iii) $\lambda = [\lambda_t]$ is a $T \times 1$ vector

such that $E\lambda = 0$ and $E\lambda\lambda' = \sigma_\psi^2 A$, positive definite

(iv) $\mu_i, \lambda_t, \varepsilon_{it}$ are mutually independent.

For example, in the case of first-order autocorrelated time effects considered in the text,

$$\lambda_t = \varphi \lambda_{t-1} + \psi_t, \quad \text{where } |\varphi| \leq 1, \quad \psi_t \sim iid(0, \sigma_\varphi^2) \text{ so}$$

$$A = \begin{bmatrix} 1 & \varphi & \cdots & \varphi^{T-1} \\ \varphi & 1 & \cdots & \varphi^{T-2} \\ \vdots & \vdots & & \vdots \\ \varphi^{T-1} & \varphi^{T-2} & \cdots & 1 \end{bmatrix}$$

---

[1] This appendix reproduces in notation consistent with the text the results of Karlsson and Skogland (2000, Section 2). The results of Karlsson and Skogland parallel those of Balestra's unpublished notes.

To derive the log likelihood function, we will later assume that they are independently normally distributed.

Let ℓ_K, for any positive integer K be the $K \times 1$ vector of ones; $J_K = \ell_K \ell'_K$; $I_K =$ the $K \times K$ identity matrix; $M_K = I_K - J_K/K$. Note, $J_K J_K = K J_K$, $M_K M_K = M_K$ and $M_K J_K = 0$. Stacking y_{it}, x_{it}, and u_{it} first with respect to i, then with respect to t, the model can be written in compact form as

$$y = Z\delta + u$$
$$u = (I_N \otimes \ell_T)\mu + (\ell_N \otimes I_T)\lambda + \varepsilon, \tag{2}$$

where $Z = [\ell_{NT} \ x]$ and $\delta = [\alpha \ \beta]'$. Thus, the variance-covariance matrix of u is

$$\begin{aligned}
\Omega = E(uu') &= (I_N \otimes \ell_T)E(\mu\mu')(I_N \otimes \ell_T)' + (\ell_N \otimes I_T)E(\lambda\lambda') \\
&\quad \times (\ell_N \otimes I_T)' + E(\varepsilon\varepsilon') \\
&= \sigma_\mu^2(I_N \otimes J_T) + \sigma_\psi^2(J_N \otimes A) + \sigma_\varepsilon^2(I_N \otimes I_T). \tag{3}
\end{aligned}$$

Let

$$\begin{aligned}
R &= \sigma_\mu^2(I_N \otimes J_T) + \sigma_\varepsilon^2(I_N \otimes I_T) = I_N \otimes \left(\sigma_\mu^2 J_T + \sigma_\varepsilon^2 \otimes I_T\right) \\
&= I_N \otimes \left(\sigma_1^2\frac{J_T}{T} + \sigma_\varepsilon^2 M_T\right),
\end{aligned}$$

where $\sigma_1^2 = T\sigma_\mu^2 + \sigma_\varepsilon^2$. Then,

$$\Omega = R + \sigma_\varepsilon^2(\ell_N \otimes I_T)A(\ell'_N \otimes I_T).$$

It is easier to determine Ω^{-1} and $\det\Omega$ than to obtain the characteristic roots of Ω, although this would be the preferable route since it would permit a transformation of the observations along the lines suggested for the three-component model without serially correlated period effects.[2] Let

$$R^* = \frac{1}{\sigma_\varepsilon^2}M_T + \frac{1}{\sigma_1^2}\frac{J_T}{T}$$

R^* is only $T \times T$, which in many panel situations will be modest. Using some "well-known" results in matrix algebra (Schott, 1997, Chapter 7, Section 3), Karlsson and Skoglund show

$$R^{-1} = I_N \otimes R^*, \tag{4}$$

and, hence,

$$\Omega^{-1} = I_N \otimes R^* - \sigma_\psi^2(\ell_N \otimes R^*)\left[I_T + N\sigma_\varepsilon^2 AR^*\right]^{-1}A(\ell'_N \otimes R^*), \tag{5}$$

---

[2] Balestra goes part of the way: the characteristic roots of R are straightforward. The second term in Ω is what causes the difficulty. But the roots associated with this term can certainly be determined numerically in a particular case; for example, in terms of the parameter φ in the case of first-order autocorrelation.

and

$$\det \Omega = |R^*|^{-N} \left| \sigma_\psi^2 A \right| \left| \frac{1}{\sigma_\psi^2} A^{-1} + NR^* \right|$$

$$= \left(\sigma_\varepsilon^2 \right)^{N(T-1)} \left(\sigma_1^2 \right)^N \left| I_T + N\sigma_\psi^2 AR^* \right|. \tag{6}$$

Hence, the log likelihood function is

$$L\big(\delta, \sigma_\mu^2, \sigma_\psi^2, \sigma_\varepsilon^2, \varphi | Z\big) = \frac{-NT}{2} \ln(2\pi) - \frac{N(T-1)}{2} \ln\left(\sigma_\varepsilon^2\right) - \frac{N}{2} \ln\left(T\sigma_\mu^2 + \sigma_\varepsilon^2\right)$$

$$- \frac{1}{2} \ln \left| I_T + N\sigma_\psi^2 AR^* \right| - \frac{1}{2}(y - Z\delta)' \big[(I_N \otimes R^*) - (\ell_N \otimes R^*) $$

$$\times \big[I_T + N\sigma_\psi^2 AR^* \big]^{-1} \sigma_\psi^2 A(\ell_N' \otimes R^*) \big] (y - Z\delta). \tag{7}$$

It is clearly possible to concentrate out the δ by finding the GLS estimates using the matrix

$$\big[(I_N \otimes R^*) - (\ell_N \otimes R^*) \big[I_T + N\sigma_\psi^2 AR^* \big]^{-1} \sigma_\psi^2 A(\ell_N' \otimes R^*) \big].$$

But this still leaves the concentrated likelihood function a function of four parameters $\sigma_\mu^2, \sigma_\psi^2, \sigma_\varepsilon^2, \varphi$. Karlsson and Skoglund do an extensive Monte Carlo; so the maximization itself cannot be too difficult, but a graphical analysis may be much more problematic. My suggestion would be to reparametrize in terms of $\frac{\sigma_\psi^2}{1-\varphi^2}$ and examine the relationship between this variance of the period effects and the variance σ_μ^2 of the individual-specific effects and the maximizing values of the other parameters.

Likelihood for Stationary Panel Data-Generating Processes with Exogenous Variables and Individual-Specific Random Effects[1]

In this appendix, I present a method of maximum-likelihood estimation based on the density of the observations *unconditional on the initial or starting values of the dependent variable, in which the same process as that under investigation is assumed to generate the data prior to the point at which we begin to observe them.*[2] This approach fully takes into account what information the initial conditions contain about how the process has operated in the past and is thus of special relevance to short time-dimension ("shallow") panels.

For simplicity, I restrict attention to the simple model containing one exogenous variable x_{it} and one lagged value of the dependent variable y_{it-1} as explanatory. Extension to the case in which more than one exogenous explanatory variable is included presents no serious difficulty. The model is given in equation (26) of the text.

1. SPECIFICATION OF THE JOINT DISTRIBUTION OF THE OBSERVATIONS, BOTH CONDITIONAL AND UNCONDITIONAL ON THE INITIAL OBSERVATIONS[3]

If $|\gamma| \geq 1$ or the processes generating the x_{it} are not stationary, it will not make sense to assume that the process generating the y_{it} is the same prior to the period of observation as for $t = 1, \ldots, T$. I will assume that, possibly after some differencing, both the y_{it} and the x_{it} are stationary. In this case, the initial

---

[1] Based on Nerlove (1999a, Chapter 19, Section 6). Patrick Sevestre and Alain Trognon have been immensely helpful in the formulation presented here. The key ideas are found in various forms in Bhargava and Sargan (1983, pp. 1641–1644), Ridder and Wansbeek (1990, pp. 571–577), and related to those of Blundell and Smith (1991) concerning efficient estimation of panel models.

[2] The history of this problem is discussed fully in Section 4b(4) of the text.

[3] See also Ridder and Wansbeek (1990, esp. pp. 575–577).

observations are determined by

$$y_{i0} = \sum_{j=0}^{\infty} \gamma^j \beta x_{i,-j} + \frac{1}{1-\gamma}\mu_i + v_{i0}, \quad \text{where } v_{it} = \gamma v_{it-1} + \varepsilon_{it}.^{4,5} \quad (1)$$

The joint distribution of $y_{iT}, \ldots, y_{i1}, y_{i0}$ depends on the distribution of μ_i, ε_{it}, and x_{it}. If y_{i0} is literally taken as fixed, which is to deny the plausible assumption that it is generated by the same process as generates the y_{it} that are observed, the conditional likelihood function for the model is given by equation (9) in Section 4(e).

To proceed in a manner consistent with the hypothesis that the presample values are generated by the same process as the within-sample observations, we need to derive the joint distribution of $y_{iT}, \ldots, y_{i1}, y_{i0}$, from (1) and (4.1). Since, ε_{it} and μ_i are assumed to be independently normally distributed with mean zero and variances σ_ε^2 and σ_μ^2, respectively, matters depend on what is assumed about how the x_{it} are generated in the presample period, even though we may propose to condition on the observed values within the sample period. Consider a single individual i of the N observed. Various alternative specifications considered in the literature are reported and analyzed in Sevestre and Trognon (1996, pp. 136–138).[6] Considerable simplification, however, can be obtained if, following Nerlove (1971a), we are willing to assume that x_{it} follows a well-specified common stationary time-series model for all individuals i. The first term in (1) is

$$\varphi_{i0} = \beta \sum_{j=0}^{\infty} \gamma^j x_{i,-j}. \quad (2)$$

---

[4] For a particular time period T and the infinite past

$$y_{iT} = \gamma^\infty y_{i-\infty} + \sum_{j=0}^{\infty} \gamma^j \beta x_{i-j} + \frac{1-\gamma^\infty}{1-\gamma}\mu_i + v_{iT},$$

where

$$v_{iT} = \sum_{j=0}^{\infty} \gamma^j \varepsilon_{iT-j}.$$

Since $1 \geq |\gamma|$ and $v_{iT} = \sum_{j=0}^{\infty} \gamma^j \varepsilon_{iT-j}$ is the MA form of a first-order autoregression with white noise input, equation (2) follows.

[5] If all variables are expressed as deviations from their overall means, there is no need to include an intercept; if not, μ_i should be replaced by $\alpha + \mu_i$.

[6] One interesting possibility discussed by Sevestre (1983) and Sevestre and Trognon (1985; 1996, pp. 136–138) is to choose y_{i0} a linear function of some *observed* individual-specific time-invariant exogenous variables and a disturbance that is decomposed as the sum of the individual-specific disturbances μ_i and a remainder. The first-order equations for maximizing the likelihood then take on a simple recursive form when $\beta = 0$, and permit other simplification when $\beta \neq 0$. But if we knew some individual-specific time-invariant observed variables influenced behavior, why not incorporate them directly in (2), the equation to be estimated?

Hence, for any stationary processes x_{it}, which may be serially correlated,

$$\frac{\varphi_{it}}{\beta} = \gamma \frac{\varphi_{it-1}}{\beta} + x_{it}, \tag{3}$$

with variances that depend on the serial autocovariances of the exogenous variable in the presample period, say $\Gamma_i(j) = \text{cov}(x_{it}, x_{it-j})$,

$$\sigma_{\varphi_i}^2 = \frac{\beta^2 \sigma_{x_i}^2 + 2\gamma \sum_{j=0}^{\infty} \gamma^j \Gamma_i(j+1)}{1 - \gamma^2}. \tag{4}$$

If we suppose that each x_{it} follows a first-order autoregressive process common for all i,

$$x_{it} = \delta x_{it-1} + \omega_{it}, \quad \omega_{it} \; iid \sim \left(0, \sigma_\omega^2\right), \tag{5}$$

then the random variable

$$\phi_{it} = \sum_{j=0}^{\infty} \gamma^j \beta x_{it-j} \tag{6}$$

has a well-defined variance, which is the same for all i and a function of β, γ, and σ_x^2,

$$\sigma_0^2 = \frac{\beta^2 \sigma_x^2 (1 + \gamma \delta)}{(1 - \gamma^2)(1 - \gamma \delta)}.^7 \tag{7}$$

The joint distribution of

$$\begin{bmatrix} \mu_i + \varepsilon_{iT} \\ \vdots \\ \mu_i + \varepsilon_{i1} \\ y_{i0} \end{bmatrix} \quad \text{is } N(0, \Sigma), \tag{8}$$

where

$$\Sigma = \begin{bmatrix} \sigma_\varepsilon^2 I_T + \sigma_\mu^2 e_T e_T' & d^* e_T \\ d^* e_T' & \sigma_0^2 \end{bmatrix}, \quad e_T = \begin{bmatrix} 1 \\ \vdots \\ 1 \end{bmatrix},$$

---

[7] I am indebted to Alain Trognon for pointing this out to me. When the x_{it} are serially correlated more generally, the result is much more complicated. See Bhargava and Sargan (1983). Following, I assume that the xs are generated in the presample period by first-order autoregressions common to all individuals and estimate both the common variance and common serial correlation from the pooled within-sample variation of the xs. With only four or five time points, little else seems feasible. The first-order serial correlations are indeed rather small in many empirical situations so that this correction makes hardly any difference to the results as compared with those assuming the xs are random.

with

$$\sigma_0^2 = \frac{\beta^2 \sigma_x^2 (1 + \gamma \delta)}{(1 - \gamma^2)(1 - \gamma \delta)} + \frac{\sigma_\mu^2}{(1 - \gamma)^2} + \frac{\sigma_\varepsilon^2}{1 - \gamma^2} \quad \text{and} \quad d^* = \frac{\sigma_\mu^2}{1 - \gamma}.$$

The joint density of $y_{iT}, \ldots, y_{i1}, y_{i0}$, given the within-sample observations on $x_{iT}, \ldots, x_{i1}$, JPDF, may be factored into the product of the joint conditional on y_{i0}, CPDF, and the marginal of y_{i0}, MPDF, JPDF = CPDF × MPDF.

$$\text{MPDF} = \frac{1}{\sqrt{2\pi \sigma_0^2}} \exp\left\{ -\frac{1}{2\sigma_0^2} y_{i0}^2 \right\}, \tag{9}$$

and

$$\text{CPDF} = \frac{1}{(2\pi)^{\frac{T}{2}}} |S|^{-\frac{1}{2}} \exp\left\{ -\frac{1}{2} v' S^{-1} v \right\}, \tag{10}$$

where

$$v = \begin{bmatrix} y_{iT} - \beta x_{iT} - \gamma y_{iT-1} - \dfrac{c}{\sigma_0^2} y_{i0} \\ \vdots \\ y_{i1} - \beta x_{i1} - \gamma y_{i0} - \dfrac{c}{\sigma_0^2} y_{i0} \end{bmatrix}, \tag{11}$$

with $c = \frac{\sigma_\mu^2}{1 - \gamma}$, and where

$$S = \sigma_\varepsilon^2 I_T + \zeta^2 e_T e_T', \tag{12}$$

with

$$\zeta^2 = \sigma_\mu^2 - \frac{c^2}{\sigma_0^2}.$$

Note that while c cannot be negative as long as $|\gamma| < 1$, ζ^2 could be if the variance σ_0^2 were small enough, but this is unlikely for plausible values of the parameters β, γ, σ^2, and ρ.

2. THE JOINT LIKELIHOOD CONDITIONAL ON THE INITIAL OBSERVATIONS AND THE EXOGENOUS VARIABLES

The conditional likelihood, CLF, for the parameters β, γ, σ^2, and ρ is the log of the product of the CPDF's in (10) over individuals. Note that the problem has been reparameterized in terms of c, σ_0^2, ζ^2, and S, but these are all functions of the original four parameters and the observations within-sample of the dependent and explanatory variables; once the parameters β, γ, σ^2, and ρ are given, so are c, σ_0^2, ζ^2, and S, and the value of the CLF for the sample data. But the CLF is not so easy to calculate, since S, albeit block diagonal, is rather large and must be inverted. The usual trick in such cases is to diagonalize

S using an orthogonal transformation; provided we introduce two additional reparameterizations, we can cast the problem into the form used to formulate the GLS estimators. Let

$$q^2 = \sigma_\varepsilon^2 + \zeta^2 \quad \text{and} \quad \rho^* = \frac{\zeta^2}{q^2}, \quad \text{so that } 1 - \rho^* = \frac{\sigma_\varepsilon^2}{q^2}. \tag{13}$$

S is then diagonalized with the characteristic roots

$$\begin{aligned}
\xi^* &= 1 - \rho^* + \rho^* T, \\
\eta^* &= 1 - \rho^*,
\end{aligned} \tag{14}$$

along the diagonal by the transform

$$v_i^* = (\xi^*)^{\frac{1}{2}} \left(\frac{1}{T}\right) e_T e_T' v_i + (\eta^*)^{\frac{1}{2}} \left(I_T - \frac{1}{T} e_T e_T'\right) v_i. \tag{15}$$

The joint conditional likelihood, CLF, can now be written:

$$\begin{aligned}
\log L(&\beta, \gamma, \rho, \sigma^2 \mid y_{11}, \dots, y_{NT}; x_{11}, \dots, x_{NT}; y_{10}, \dots, y_{N0}) \\
&= -\frac{NT}{2} \log 2\pi - \frac{NT}{2} \log q^2 - \frac{N}{2} \log \xi^* - \frac{N(T-1)}{2} \log \eta^*. \\
&\quad - \frac{1}{2q^2} \sum_{i=1}^{N} \sum_{t=1}^{T} (v_{it}^*)^2.
\end{aligned} \tag{16}$$

(16) is the same form as (9) in the text above, but ξ, η, and q^2 as well as v^* are complex transforms of β, γ, σ^2, and ρ and the observations.

3. THE JOINT LIKELIHOOD UNCONDITIONAL ON THE INITIAL OBSERVATIONS

To obtain the joint unconditional likelihood, we may simply take the log of the product of the joint marginal PDFs of the initial observations and add it to the CLF in (16); thus,

$$\begin{aligned}
\log L(&\beta, \gamma, \rho, \sigma^2 \mid y_{11}, \dots, y_{NT}; x_{11}, \dots, x_{NT}; y_{10}, \dots, y_{N0}) \\
&= -\frac{NT}{2} \log 2\pi - \frac{NT}{2} \log q^2 - \frac{N}{2} \log \xi^* - \frac{N(T-1)}{2} \log \eta^* \\
&\quad - \frac{1}{2q^2} \sum_{i=1}^{N} \sum_{t=1}^{T} (v_{it}^*)^2 - \frac{N}{2} \log(\sigma_0^2) - \left[\frac{1}{2\sigma_0^2}\right] \sum_{i=1}^{N} y_{i0}^2.
\end{aligned} \tag{17}$$

Concentrating the likelihood function to permit a one- or two-dimensional grid search is not possible. Nor is it possible to graph the likelihood surface with respect to variations in all of the parameters. Although "slicing" the likelihood function along any hyperplane in the parameter space can reveal the trade-offs between any pair of parameters. If gradient or search procedures yield an interior maximum, the ML estimates obtained are consistent as long as the random variables $\phi_{it} = \sum_{j=0}^{\infty} \gamma^j \beta x_{i,t-j}$ have well-defined variances and covariances, which they will if the x_{it} are generated by a stationary process. It doesn't really matter what this process is as long as it is stationary. Besides, since the x_{it} are assumed to be exogenous, we really have no basis on which to model their determination and are likely to mis-specify this part of the model. In this sense, we ought to prefer this kind of "almost full-information" maximum likelihood. Still we have to assume something about the variance of the x process in order to proceed. I suggest estimating σ_x^2 from the sample data.

To generalize these results to the case in which there are several explanatory variables in addition to the lagged value of the dependent variable, assume that X_{it} follows a stationary VAR process and replace βx_{it}^* by $X_{it}^* \beta$ and $\beta^2 \sigma_x^2$ by $\beta' \Sigma_{XX} \beta$ in the previous formula.

The expression

$$\varphi^2 = \frac{\beta^2 \sigma_x^2 (1 + \gamma \delta)}{(1 - \gamma^2)(1 - \gamma \delta)} + \frac{\sigma_\mu^2}{(1 - \gamma)^2} + \frac{\sigma_\varepsilon^2}{1 - \gamma^2} \tag{18}$$

is the unconditional variance of the initial observations y_{i0}. The absolute value of the difference between the log of the unconditional likelihood function and the log of the conditional likelihood function is

$$f(\varphi^2) = \frac{N}{2} \left[\log 2\pi + \log \varphi^2 + \frac{\text{var } y_0}{\varphi^2} \right]. \tag{19}$$

$f(\varphi^2)$ is an increasing function of N and var y_0, but given N and var y_0, reaches a minimum for $\varphi^2 = \text{var } y_0$ (i.e., when the sample value is close to the true value of the unconditional variance of the initial observations). So the larger the number of cross-section observations and the larger the sample variance of the initial observations, the greater the information contained in them about the prior operation of the process that generated the data. But the closer are φ^2 and var y_0, the less informative are the initial observations on the dependent variable.

Amemiya's Classification of Limited Dependent Variable or Tobit Models

Amemiya (1985, Chapter 9) classifies limited dependent variable models into five types according to the form of the likelihood function to which they give rise. Such models are appropriate when the distribution of the observations (on the dependent variable in the univariate case) are truncated or censored. In the case of truncated regression models, observations outside a specified range on both the dependent and explanatory variables are lost, whereas in the case of censored regression, only the observations on the dependent variable are lost in the sense that they are set equal to the upper or lower bound defining their range of observed variation. The first econometric example of such a model was presented in Tobin (1958) and called by Goldberger (1964) tobit model by analogy with the term *probit*.

Type I:

Consider the censored regression model:

$$y_i^* = x_i \beta + u_i, \quad i = 1, \ldots, N$$
$$y_i = y_i^*, \quad \text{if } y_i^* > \eta_i,$$
$$= \eta_i, \quad \text{if } y_i^* \leq \eta_i, \tag{1}$$

$u_i \sim iid\, n(0, \sigma^2)$. Generally, it is assumed $\eta_1 = \eta_2 = \cdots = \eta_N$ are known and, without loss of generality if the model contains a constant term, $= 0$; if the η_i's are unknown parameters, the model is subject to the incidental parameters problem discussed in Section 4.c(1) of the text. In the censored subcase, it is assumed that y_i^* is essentially unobserved if $y_i^* \leq \eta_i$, but that the associated values of the explanatory variables, x_i are observed. Let $\eta_1 = \eta_2 = \cdots = \eta_N = 0$ and $\delta_i = 1$ if $y_i > 0, = 0$ if $y_i \leq 0$[1]; the likelihood function associated with

---

[1] I maintain this assumption and this notation throughout the remainder of this appendix.

(1) is:

$$L_{1c}(\beta, \sigma^2 \mid y_i, x_i, i = 1, \ldots, N) = \prod_{i=1}^{N} \left[1 - \Phi\left(\frac{x_i\beta}{\sigma}\right) \right]^{1-\delta_i} \left[\frac{\varphi(y_i - x_i\beta)}{\sigma} \right]^{\delta_i}$$

$$= \prod_{i=1}^{N} \left[1 - \Phi\left(\frac{x_i\beta}{\sigma}\right) \right]^{1-\delta_i} \left[\Phi\left(\frac{x_i\beta}{\sigma}\right) \right]^{\delta_i} \times \prod_{i=1}^{N} \left[\frac{\varphi(y_i - x_i\beta)}{\sigma} \middle/ \Phi\left(\frac{x_i\beta}{\sigma}\right) \right]^{\delta_i},$$

$$(2)$$

where $\varphi(\,)$ is the standardized normal density and $\Phi(\,)$ is the standardized cumulative normal. Note that the first of the two products in the second line of (2) is the likelihood function for the ordinary probit model for y_i, while the second product is the likelihood function (3) for the truncated tobit model of Type 1 in (3) following.

In the truncated regression model, the explanatory variables are unobserved for $y_i \leq 0$; the likelihood function becomes

$$L_{1c}(\beta, \sigma^2 \mid y_i, x_i, i = 1, \ldots, N) = \prod_{i=1}^{N} \left[\frac{\varphi(y_i - x_i\beta)}{\sigma} \middle/ \Phi\left(\frac{x_i\beta}{\sigma}\right) \right]^{\delta_i}. \quad (3)$$

Type II:

These models involve two unobserved variables, one of which, y_{1i}^*, does the censoring or sample selection:

$$y_{1i}^* = x_{1i}\beta_1 + u_{1i}$$
$$y_{2i}^* = x_{2i}\beta_2 + u_{2i}$$
$$y_{2i} = y_{2i}^*, \quad \text{if } y_{1i}^* > 0$$
$$\qquad = 0, \quad \text{if } y_{1i}^* \leq 0, \quad i = 1, \ldots, N, \quad (4)$$

where $(u_{1i}, u_{2i}) \sim iid\ N(0, \Omega)$, $\Omega = \begin{bmatrix} \sigma_{11} & \sigma_{12} \\ \sigma_{12} & \sigma_{22} \end{bmatrix} > 0$. Let $\delta_{1i} = 1$ if $y_{1i}^* > 0, = 0$ if $y_{1i}^* \leq 0$. The likelihood function is

$$L_{2c}(\beta_1, \beta_2, \Omega \mid y_{1i}, y_{2i}, x_{1i}, x_{2i}, i = 1, \ldots, N) = \prod_{i=1}^{N} \left[1 - \Phi\left(\frac{x_{1i}\beta_1}{\sigma_{11}^{\frac{1}{2}}}\right) \right]^{1-\delta_{1i}}$$

$$\times \left[\Phi\left(\frac{x_{1i}\beta_1}{\sigma_{11}^{\frac{1}{2}}} + \frac{\sigma_{12}}{\sigma_{11}^{\frac{1}{2}}\sigma_{22}^{\frac{1}{2}}}(y_{2i} - x_{2i}\beta_2)\right) \left(1 - \frac{\sigma_{12}}{\sigma_{11}^{\frac{1}{2}}\sigma_{22}^{\frac{1}{2}}}\right)^{-\frac{1}{2}} \frac{\varphi\left(\frac{y_{2i} - x_{2i}\beta_2}{\sigma_{22}^{\frac{1}{2}}}\right)}{\sigma_{22}^{\frac{1}{2}}} \right]^{\delta_{1i}}.$$

$$(5)$$

The first term is the probability that $y_{1i}^* \leq 0$, the second term is the marginal probability that $y_{1i}^* > 0$ times the density of y_{2i} conditional on y_{1i}^*. The likelihood function depends on σ_{11} only through $\frac{\beta_1}{\sigma_{11}^{\frac{1}{2}}}$ and $\frac{\sigma_{12}}{\sigma_{11}^{\frac{1}{2}}}$.

Type III:

These are doubly censored two-equation models with y_{1i}^* again performing the sample selection:

$$
\begin{aligned}
y_{1i}^* &= x_{1i}\beta_1 + u_{1i} \\
y_{2i}^* &= x_{2i}\beta_2 + u_{2i} \\
y_{1i} &= y_{1i}^* \quad \text{if } y_{1i}^* > 0 \\
&= 0 \quad \text{if } y_{1i}^* \leq 0 \\
y_{2i} &= y_{2i}^* \quad \text{if } y_{1i}^* > 0 \\
&= 0 \quad \text{if } y_{1i}^* \leq 0, \quad i = 1, \ldots, N,
\end{aligned}
\tag{6}
$$

where $(u_{1i}, u_{2i}, u_{3i}) \sim iid \, N(0, \Omega)$, $\Omega = \begin{bmatrix} \sigma_{11} & \sigma_{12} \\ \sigma_{12} & \sigma_{22} \end{bmatrix} > 0$. The difference between models of Type II and models of Type III is that y_{1i} is observed if $y_{1i}^* > 0$. Let $\delta_{1i} = 1$ if $y_{1i}^* > 0$, $= 0$ if $y_{1i}^* \leq 0$. The likelihood function is

$$
L_{3c}(\beta_1, \beta_2, \Omega \mid y_{1i}, y_{2i}, x_{1i}, x_{2i}, i = 1, \ldots, N)
$$

$$
= \prod_{i=1}^{N} \left[1 - \Phi\left(\frac{x_{1i}\beta_1}{\sigma_{11}^{\frac{1}{2}}} \right) \right]^{1-\delta_{1i}} \left[\varphi_2\left(\begin{bmatrix} y_{1i} - x_{1i}\beta_1 \\ y_{2i} - x_{2i}\beta_2 \end{bmatrix}, \Omega \right) \right]^{\delta_{1i}},
\tag{7}
$$

where $\varphi_2(\,)$ is the bivariate normal density with variance covariance matrix Ω.

Type IV:

These are triply censored three-equation models with y_{1i}^* again performing the sample selection. They differ from Type III only in that they involve a third variable y_{3i}^*, which is observed only when $y_{1i}^* > 0$.

$$
\begin{aligned}
y_{1i}^* &= x_{1i}\beta_1 + u_{1i} \\
y_{2i}^* &= x_{2i}\beta_2 + u_{2i} \\
y_{3i}^* &= x_{3i}\beta_3 + u_{3i} \\
y_{1i} &= y_{1i}^* \quad \text{if } y_{1i}^* > 0 \\
&= 0 \quad \text{if } y_{1i}^* \leq 0, \\
y_{2i} &= y_{2i}^* \quad \text{if } y_{1i}^* > 0 \\
&= 0 \quad \text{if } y_{1i}^* \leq 0 \\
y_{3i} &= y_{3i}^* \quad \text{if } y_{1i}^* > 0 \\
&= 0 \quad \text{if } y_{1i}^* \leq 0, \quad i = 1, \ldots, N
\end{aligned}
\tag{8}
$$

where $(u_{1i}, u_{2i}, u_{3i}) \sim iid\ N(0, \Omega)$, $\Omega = \begin{bmatrix} \sigma_{11} & \sigma_{12} & \sigma_{13} \\ \sigma_{21} & \sigma_{22} & \sigma_{23} \\ \sigma_{31} & \sigma_{32} & \sigma_{33} \end{bmatrix} > 0$. The likelihood function is a straightforward extension of (7).

Type V:

Models of Type V differ from those of Type IV only in that the sign of y_{1i}^* is observed and not its value when positive.

Amemiya (1985, Chapter 9) gives numerous examples of all of these models and discusses alternatives to maximum likelihood estimation.

TWO

Pooling Cross-Section and Time-Series Data in the Estimation of a Dynamic Model: The Demand for Natural Gas (with Pietro Balestra)[1]

Preface

"The wonder, Watson, is that the dog did not bark in the night."
Arthur Conan Doyle, *Hound of the Baskervilles*

Sometimes what we don't observe is as important as what we do.

This paper begins with the formulation of a very explicit theoretical model. While such a beginning is commonplace now, it was not in 1960. Moreover, the theoretical formulation played a key role in our assessment of the econometric results and in revision of the methods used. The theoretical model is manipulated in order to obtain an econometric formulation that can be fit to the data at hand. Although the model fits well by conventional standards when estimated by ordinary least squares, in terms of the theoretical interpretation, the coefficient of the lagged dependent variable – in this case, the consumption of natural gas – cannot be considered plausible. But, rather than reject the theory, Balestra and I were led to think more carefully about the stochastic formulation of the model in relation to the data. And from a revised stochastic formulation, we were led to alternative methods of estimation, results of which, in turn, were examined in accordance with the theoretical interpretation dictated by the model and repeatedly revised. Theory, stochastic formulation, and econometric methodology continually interact.

Although we do not cite Hildreth (1950) or, indeed, any of the many references in the earlier statistical literature discussed in the previous chapter, our stochastic reformulation is clearly in the Cowles tradition of Haavelmo and Marschak. We begin by considering the disturbance term as a representation of left-out variables and then asking what sorts of things those left-out variables might consist of. This leads very naturally to the notion that some of these left-out variables are individual-specific and relatively time-invariant. Although we mention the possibility of period-specific effects, which are also present in

---

[1] Reprinted with permission from *Econometrica*, Vol. 34, No. 3 (July 1966), 585–612.

Hildreth's (1950) formulation, we decided to focus on individual-specific effects and all the rest. Our first attempt to incorporate such individual-specific effects was to treat them as fixed effects; that is, estimate an equation with dummy variables for each individual (in this case, states). Recall that after rejecting the estimation of a random-effects model by maximum likelihood, Hildreth (1950) fell back on a fixed-effects formulation. Fortunately, we were ignorant of or didn't remember Hildreth's difficulties with ML in the case of random effects, so we next tried a random-effects model. The argument we give for doing so is couched in terms of saving degrees of freedom and is naive. We proceeded to develop the likelihood function for the random-effects model. However, we ignored the fact that in this sort of model the lagged value of the dependent variable cannot be considered independent and simply treated it as if it were just another explanatory variable, conditioning the likelihood function on its value. This mistake was to have far-reaching consequences, as detailed in the previous chapter; nonetheless, it did allow us to get on with resolution of the intractability of the first-order conditions that had so put off Hildreth (1950). He did not, after all, have any lagged values of the dependent variable to worry about.

To circumvent the apparent intractability of the likelihood function, we introduced two methods, neither of them new, but neither widely known in the econometric literature at that time. The first was to *concentrate* the likelihood function with respect to ρ, the ratio of the variance of the individual-specific effects to the overall disturbance variance, often called the *intraclass correlation*. The second was to transform the observations in such a way that the original block-diagonal variance-covariance matrix was reduced to diagonal form in the characteristic roots of the original matrix. This greatly simplified the likelihood function and reduced the problem of determining the inverse and determinant of the variance-covariance matrix to trivial proportions.

In the method of maximum likelihood, for example, it frequently turns out that, *given* the values of one or two of the parameters, it is very easy to maximize with respect to the remaining ones. Sometimes we say that we are "maximizing out" the deselected parameters. The best discussion of the technique of concentrating the likelihood function that I know of is found in Koopmans and Hood (1953, pp. 156–158), in which they derive the *limited information maximum likelihood estimates* for the parameters of a single equation of a system of simultaneous structural equations. I think the same idea is also implicit in Anderson and Rubin's (1949) original derivation of the limited information maximum-likelihood method, although that paper is so turgid it's difficult to tell.

The basic idea of two-step maximization, employed to reduce the dimension of a maximum problem, is straightforward: suppose we want to max $f(\theta_1, \theta_2)$ re: θ_1 and θ_2. Under very general conditions, we can "hold θ_2 fixed" and

$$\max_{\theta_1} f(\theta_1, \theta_2) = f(\theta_1(\theta_2)) = f^*(\theta_2)$$

where $\theta_1(\theta_2)$ is the value of θ_1 which maximizes $f(\theta_1, \theta_2 = \theta_2)$. Then varying θ_2, find

$$\max_{\theta_2} f^*(\theta_2) = f^*(\theta_1(\theta_2)) = f^{**}$$

is the maximum maximorum.

The function $f^*(\theta_2)$ is said to be "concentrated with respect to θ_1." That is, θ_1 has been "maximized out," so that the concentrated function is a function of θ_2 only.

Concentration of likelihood by partial maximization is discussed in the statistical literature of parametric inference under the heading of *likelihood profiles* (see Lindsey, 1996, pp. 111–114.) But I believe that this technique of parameter reduction was first employed in the econometric literature. David Hendry, who has made a careful study of the development of ideas in econometrics, agrees with me on this point. I had used the method in my work on agricultural supply functions (1958), which was probably why it occurred to me when Balestra and I were working out the details of this paper.

The second device we introduced for simplifying the likelihood function was to transform the observations so that the disturbance variance-covariance was rendered diagonal. This transformation, as our colleague at the time, Bill Madow, pointed out, was employed much earlier by Halperin (1951). Its real importance lay not in the simplification of the likelihood function that it afforded, but rather in the clarification of the relationship between fixed and random effects in terms of the information content of panel observations as described in Appendix A of the previous chapter.

So, in the end, we were able to fix the value of ρ and maximize the resulting likelihood quite easily with respect to the regression coefficients and overall residual variance, then plug those results back into the likelihood so that we could examine the concentrated likelihood directly. Unfortunately, one of those pesky boundary solutions, the existence of which Trognon (1978) was later to prove, occurred. This disconcerting finding put us off maximum likelihood and we were led finally to an instrumental variables approach that gave us estimates plausible from the standpoint of our theory.

To summarize the main results with respect to the estimation reported in this chapter:

(1) upward bias in the coefficient of the lagged dependent variable in the pooled OLS regression;
(2) downward bias in this coefficient in the fixed-effects regression;
(3) the occurrence of an unacceptable number of boundary solutions at a zero value of the intraclass correlation for maximum-likelihood estimates based on the likelihood function, which treated the initial values of the dependent variable as fixed;

(4) improved estimates based on feasible GLS using an estimate of the intraclass correlation derived from a first-stage instrumental variables regression.

These findings were the basis for the Monte Carlo experiments reported in the two papers that follow.

References

Anderson, T. W., and H. Rubin (1949), "Estimation of the Parameters of a Single Equation in a Complete System of Stochastic Equations," *Annals of Mathematical Statistics, 20*: pp. 46–63.

Halperin, M. (1951), "Normal Regression Theory in the Presence of Intraclass Correlation," *Annals of Mathematical Statistics, 22*: pp. 573–580.

Hildreth, C. (1950), "Combining Cross-Section Data and Time Series," *Cowles Commission Discussion Paper, No. 347*, May 15.

Koopmans, T. C., and W. C. Hood (1953), "The Estimation of Simultaneous Linear Economic Relationships," in W. C. Hood and T. C. Koopmans (Eds.), *Studies in Econometric Method*, pp. 112–199, New York: Wiley.

Lindsey, J. K. (1996), *Parametric Statistical Inference*, Oxford: Clarendon Press.

Nerlove, M. (1958), *The Dynamics of Supply: Estimation of Farmers' Response to Price*, Baltimore: The Johns Hopkins Press.

Trognon, A. (1978), "Miscellaneous Asymptotic Properties of Ordinary Least Squares and Maximum Likelihood Methods in Dynamic Error Components Models," *Annales de l'INSEE 30-31*: pp. 631–657.

Pooling Cross-Section and Time-Series Data in the Estimation of a Dynamic Model: The Demand for Natural Gas

Pietro Balestra and Marc Nerlove[1]

In this paper, we consider two basic aspects of demand analysis, with application to the demand for natural gas in the residential and commercial market. The more fundamental one consists in the formulation of a demand function for commodities – such as natural gas – whose consumption is technologically related to the stock of appliances. We believe that in such markets, the behavior of the consumer can be described best in terms of a dynamic mechanism.

Related to this is the more specific problem of estimating the parameters of the demand function, when the demand model is cast in dynamic terms and when observations are drawn from a time series of cross sections.

Accordingly, this paper is centered around these two major themes, although, as the title suggests, the emphasis is placed on the second one. In Section 1, we present the theoretical formulation of the dynamic model for gas. In Section 2, the results of the estimation of the gas model by ordinary least-squares methods are presented. These results, together with more fundamental theoretical considerations, suggest a different approach. The essence of this approach, which is not restricted to the gas model, is discussed in Section 3, whereas two alternative procedures for estimating the coefficients of the dynamic model in light of this new approach are proposed in Section 4. It is subsequently shown that the application of these procedures to the gas data produces results that are reasonable on the basis of *a priori* theoretical considerations.

[1] The research underlying this paper was performed in part under Grant NSF GS-142 from the National Science Foundation to Stanford University. We are indebted to Sherman H. Clark of Stanford Research Institute for his help in formulating the underlying framework in this study; to Zvi Griliches and L. G. Telser for pointing out a major error in a first draft; and to T. Amemiya, D. Blackwell, E. J. Hannan, H. Konijn, E. Kuh, C. R. Rao, and A. Zellner for helpful comments. Of course, responsibility for remaining errors is our own.

1. THE DYNAMIC MODEL OF GAS DEMAND

While it is true that natural gas is not a durable commodity (i.e., a commodity that is enjoyed repeatedly over a length of time or that may be stored for future use), yet it is also true that the consumption of gas, at least at the household level, is closely related to the stock of gas appliances in existence and that to a large extent it is governed by such stocks. It follows that the approach to the problem should be a dynamic one[2] and that the demand function should incorporate a stock effect and some assumptions about the adjustment of these stocks over time.

The approach underlying the dynamic model developed in this paper is consideration of the demand in the *new* market for gas (i.e., the incremental demand for gas), inclusive of demand due to the replacement of gas appliances and the demand due to net increases in the stock of such appliances. The rationale of this approach is that, given the particular characteristics of the gas market, it is unrealistic to assume that the consumer's choice is determined in the manner suggested by traditional (static) demand theory. In the gas market, for instance, a short-run change in the relative price of gas does not induce many consumers to revise choices once made, because of the high transfer costs involved in the shift to a different type of fuel. More specifically, once a major appliance is installed in a home, there is little or no substitution between the different types of fuels. And because the demand for space heating is probably highly inelastic, we would expect a very low short-run price elasticity of demand from current gas consumers.

In the planning stage, on the other hand, the relative price of the different fuels surely has some effect on the decision-making process and, at least at this stage, we should observe a pattern of behavior consistent with traditional demand theory. Therefore, the demand function considered here must be understood in an *ex ante* sense.[3] It describes the behavior of a consumer not committed by past contracts to any particular form of technique (or type of service).

We assume that the new demand for gas, G^*, is a function of the relative price of gas,[4] p, and the total new requirements for all types of fuel, F^*. In

---

[2] Apart from theoretical considerations, actual experimentation with a static model yielded insignificant or even positive price elasticities in most cases.

[3] The same notion has been applied in the study of investment decisions, a field in many respects similar to the one presently under investigation. See P. J. Dhrymes and M. Kurz, "Technology and Scale in Electricity Generation," *Econometrica*, Vol. 32, No. 3, July 1964, pp. 287–315.

[4] Two different definitions of the price variable were tried: (1) the price of gas deflated by the consumer price index, and (2) the price of gas deflated by the price of the substitutes. Since the results are quite similar (although a different interpretation must necessarily apply), only those corresponding to the first definition are reported here.

symbols,

$$G^* = f(p, F^*).[5] \tag{1}$$

Note that equation (1) implies that the price variable has an effect primarily on the rate of change of gas consumption rather than on its absolute levels.

The problem is to define the concepts of new demand and new market and incorporate them into a model expressed in terms of observable variables.

Let F_t be the demand for all types of fuel in period t. The increment in total fuel consumption between any two periods is given by

$$\Delta F_t = F_t - F_{t-1}. \tag{2}$$

The quantity ΔF_t represents the change in total fuel demand between period t and period $(t-1)$, but it does not express the total *new* demand for fuels. The reason is that not all of the demand prevailing in period $(t-1)$ is also committed in period t, as some of the installations that existed in period $(t-1)$ are retired during the course of the year, because of obsolesence or simple wear and tear.

To clarify this matter, consider explicitly the stock of appliances. Let W_{t-1} be the average stock of appliances in period $(t-1)$ and λ_{t-1} the rate of utilization of these appliances in the same period. Then, by definition,

$$F_{t-1} = \lambda_{t-1} W_{t-1}. \tag{3}$$

Of the stock of appliances W_{t-1} (assuming a constant, proportional rate of depreciation r in the aggregate), only $(1-r)W_{t-1}$ will be present in period t and, given the rate of utilization λ_t, will be associated with a fuel consumption of

$$\lambda_t(1-r)W_{t-1}. \tag{4}$$

The quantity in (4) expresses the portion of fuel consumption that in period t is associated with the stock of appliances already in existence at the beginning of the period (and not yet retired).

In period t, the average stock of appliances will be W_t. This stock of appliances is associated with a total fuel consumption of

$$F_t = \lambda_t W_t. \tag{5}$$

---

[5] One of the referees has questioned the connection between the demand for fuel and the demand for a particular sort of fuel, namely gas, which is expressed by (1). The rationale for considering the demand for a component of an aggregate category will become clearer as we progress. It is, essentially, that the demand for gas is a *derived demand*, derived from the demand for space heating. Total fuel demand is a surrogate for the total demand for space heating; equation (1) thus, in more conventional terms, simply expresses the demand for a "factor of production" as a function of its price relative to other factors and "output."

The new demand for fuel, F_t^*, may then be defined as the difference between the total demand for fuel and the "committed" demand for fuel:

$$F_t^* = \lambda_t W_t - (1 - r)\lambda_t W_{t-1}. \tag{6}$$

The rate of utilization, λ, is not likely to vary violently from one period to the next. On the contrary, it may be safely assumed for gas that the rate of utilization is relatively constant, because a high (and therefore constant) efficiency of combustion is easily attained for gas fuels.[6] It may be true for other types of fuel that the rate of utilization is affected by technological progress. It is unlikely, however, for the relatively short time period encompassed in this study that this effect causes appreciable variation in the rate of utilization. We, therefore, assume

$$\lambda_t = \lambda, \quad \text{all } t. \tag{7}$$

Equation (6) may now be expressed in terms of fuel variables alone, since

$$\lambda_t W_{t-1} = \lambda_{t-1} W_{t-1} = F_{t-1}. \tag{8}$$

Thus, the total new demand for fuel becomes

$$F_t^* = F_t - (1 - r)F_{t-1}. \tag{9}$$

It is clear that the total new demand for fuel as defined here is larger than the incremental change in fuel consumption, $F_t - F_{t-1}$. Equation (9) may be rearranged as follows:

$$F_t^* = (F_t - F_{t-1}) + r F_{t-1}. \tag{10}$$

The total new demand for fuel then appears as the sum of the incremental change in consumption (the terms in parentheses) and "replacement" demand (expressed by $r F_{t-1}$). The quantity $r F_{t-1}$ represents that portion of the total demand for fuel "freed" by the retirement (and replacement) of old appliances.

By an analogous argument, the new demand for gas, G^*, may be defined as

$$G_t^* = G_t - (1 - r_g)G_{t-1}. \tag{11}$$

The depreciation rate for gas appliances, r_g, is not necessarily the same as the depreciation rate appropriate to fuel-consuming appliances generally. Two factors account for this discrepancy. First, the lifetime of a given installation (appliance) using a particular type of fuel may be different from the lifetime of another installation using a different type of fuel. Second, the rate of depreciation for an aggregate stock is clearly related to the average age of the stock. The average age of the stock of appliances is certainly lower in a new market (e.g., gas) than in an older one (e.g., coal).

---

[6] We, of course, abstract from variations in weather conditions. It should be emphasized in this connection that all fuel variables have been normalized for weather changes in the statistical analyses reported here.

Assuming linearity,[7] equation (1) may be rewritten

$$G_t^* = \beta_0 + \beta_1 p_t + \beta_2 F_t^*, \tag{12}$$

or, equivalently,

$$\begin{aligned} G_t &= \beta_0 + \beta_1 p_t + \beta_2 [F_t - (1 - r) F_{t-1}] + (1 - r_g) G_{t-1} \\ &= \beta_0 + \beta_1 p_t + \beta_2 \Delta F_t + \beta_2 r F_{t-1} + (1 - r_g) G_{t-1}. \end{aligned} \tag{13}$$

Equation (13) portrays the basic dynamic mechanism of the model. The parameters r and r_g need not be known *a priori*, since estimates of them are provided by (13) itself.

Total fuel consumption, however, is not given *a priori*, as fuel consumption itself is a function of several other variables. On the basis of theoretical considerations and actual experimentation (both in this study and in others), it was found that total fuel consumption may be well approximated by an equation of the form

$$F_t = \gamma_0 + \gamma_1 N_t + \gamma_2 Y_t, \tag{14}$$

where N_t and Y_t stand, respectively, for total population and per capita income. Price effects are found to be negligible. Substituting (14) in (13), we obtain

$$G_t = \alpha_0 + \alpha_1 p_t + \alpha_2 \Delta N_t + \alpha_3 N_{t-1} + \alpha_4 \Delta Y_t + \alpha_5 Y_{t-1} + \alpha_6 G_{t-1}. \tag{15}$$

Equation (15) is in a form suitable for estimation. The implicit parameter r, however, is now overidentified, since estimates of it are provided by both ratios α_3/α_2 and α_5/α_4. A constrained maximization is thus necessary. This may be accomplished by defining

$$\begin{cases} N_t^* = N_t - (1 - r) N_{t-1}, \\ Y_t^* = Y_t - (1 - r) N_{t-1}. \end{cases} \tag{16}$$

Equation (15) becomes

$$G_t = \alpha_0 + \alpha_1 p_t + \alpha_2 N_t^* + \alpha_4 Y_t^* + \alpha_6 G_{t-1}. \tag{17}$$

Equation (17) is now estimated for values of r in the admissible interval and the value so chosen as to maximize the likelihood function (which, in this case, is the same as maximizing the R^2).

2. ESTIMATION BY ORDINARY LEAST-SQUARES METHODS

Before turning to a discussion of estimation proper, we discuss two subsidiary questions: (1) the type of data to which the model developed is applied; and

---

[7] The assumption of linearity is necessary to ensure appropriate identification of the parameters. Certain nonlinearities, however, might be introduced later in the estimating equation. A few that were tried did not change the results appreciably.

(2) the question of the identification of the demand equation, which involves a discussion of the conditions under which gas is supplied.

The investigation reported here is based on data by state and covers the period 1950–1962.[8] We thus think of the demand relationship as applicable to a "representative" consumer at the state level. All fuel variables are expressed in quantities (10^{12} Btu) and are normalized for weather changes within each state and between states. The price variables are given in cents per million Btu and are deflated by the consumer price index. The population variable is expressed in thousands and, finally, the per capita income variable is given in constant 1961 dollars.

Thirteen observations are available on each state (only thirty-six states, however, have enjoyed gas consumption over the entire time span). To obtain an adequate number of degrees of freedom, estimation by individual states must be abandoned. Instead, all observations are grouped together and estimation (though not necessarily by ordinary least squares) is performed on the combined sample of cross section and time series.[9]

The problem of identifying the demand relation when considering a market involving both demand and supply relationships is a serious one in studies of the type reported here. Nonetheless, it may plausibly be argued that regulation of the gas market by federal and state commissions, coupled with the heavily capitalized nature of the gas industry, suggests that a recursive system of Wold's type may not be an unrealistic representation of the working of the gas market, at least in the residential and commerical sector.[10] Furthermore, because sales of natural gas are made to the industrial sector on an interruptible basis (and thus represent a buffer for possible expansion in the residential-commercial sector) and because of the existence of excess capacity (which is typically generated in the expansion process of a heavily capitalized industry), it is plausible to consider the supply of gas to the residential-commercial sector as nearly perfectly elastic. However, to ensure a perfect elasticity of supply (which is a property holding only for sufficiently short periods in this market), it is necessary to divide the time period under investigation into two technologically different periods corresponding to two stages of development: an innovating stage and a mature stage. During the latter period (1957–1962), all states included in the sample are reasonably homogeneous as far as gas availability is concerned, and the assumption of perfectly elastic supply is approximated. Only the results for this latter period are reported here.

[8] These data were compiled by Stanford Research Institute on the basis of published statistics and other information available to the Institute.

[9] A similar set of data (a combination of cross-section and time-series data by states) was also used in a recent study of the demand for electricity by F. M. Fisher and C. Kaysen, *The Demand for Electricity in the United States, A Study in Econometrics*, Contributions to Economic Analysis, Amsterdam: North-Holland Publishing Co., 1962.

[10] H. Wold and L. Juréen, *Demand Analysis: A Study in Econometrics*, New York: John Wiley and Sons, Inc., 1953.

Bearing these considerations in mind, let us examine various estimates of the gas equation. Parameter estimates corresponding to equation (15) are shown in line 1 of Table 1, while those corresponding to equation (17) are shown in line 2 (for the maximizing value of r).

In both cases, the estimated coefficient of the lagged endogenous variable is above one, a result that is incompatible with theoretical expectations because it implies a negative depreciation rate for gas appliances. It may be argued that this result is due to partial incorporation of a time trend in the coefficient of G_{t-1}. However, the explicit introduction of a time effect into the equation (by either a time trend or dummy variables for years) did not change the results appreciably. Similarly, other attempts to incorporate special factors, such as the difference in weather conditions, did not yield statistically significant effects. On the other hand, the estimation rate of depreciation for all fuel-consuming appliances (11 per cent) is not unreasonable.

Under certain restrictive conditions, one could argue that the coefficient of G_{t-1} may be very close to unity. Such might be the case, for example, because of inertia factors, the relatively young age of the stock of gas appliances, and gas apparently is not losing its own replacement market. Then, the variable G_{t-1} may be shifted to the left-hand side of the equation. The estimated coefficients for both equations (15) and (17) corresponding to this model are shown in lines 3 and 4 of Table 1.[11]

It should be remembered that the demand function used here refers to the new demand for gas. Therefore, the average price elasticity, $\bar{\varepsilon}$, is

$$\bar{\varepsilon} = \frac{\partial G^*}{\partial p} \frac{\bar{p}}{\bar{G}^*}, \tag{18}$$

where $G^* = G_t - (1 - r_g)G_{t-1}$ is the relevant consumption variable and not G_t. The estimated average elasticity of new gas demand for the various forms listed in Table 1 ranges from 0.58 to 0.69. But the average price elasticity appears to be increasing over time. A higher price elasticity, for instance, is obtained for the period 1957–1962 than for the period 1950–1956. Furthermore, when only the data for the years 1961–1962 are considered, the average price elasticity is above unity.

One possible explanation for the results thus far obtained is that, when cross-section and time-series data are combined in the estimation of a regression equation, certain "other effects" may be present in the data.[12] A natural way to account for these "other effects" is to introduce explicitly into the equation individual shift variables. The rationale of this procedure is that the

---

[11] The R^2 given here are not those for the regressions actually performed but reflect the "explanation" of G_t rather than $G_t - G_{t-1}$. The R_1^2 appropriate for the latter variable as dependent were 0.400 and 0.398, respectively.

[12] E. Kuh and J. R. Meyer, "How Extraneous Are Extraneous Estimates," *The Review of Economics and Statistics*, Vol. 39, November, 1957, especially p. 381.

Table 1. *Various Estimates of the Parameters of the Gas Model from the Pooled Sample, 1957–62**

Based on	α_0	α_1	α_2	α_3	α_4	α_5	α_6	Maximizing value or r	R^2
Equation (15) No constraints	-3.650 (3.316)	-.0451 (.0270)	.0174 (.0093)	.00111 (.00041)	.0183 (.0080)	.00326 (.00197)	1.010 (.014)	—	0.994
Equation (17) No constraints	-2.300 (2.295)	-.03887 (.02518)	.01149 (.00302)	—	.01945 (.00751)	—	1.012 (.0135)	11%	0.994
Equation (15) α_6 constrained at 1	-3.654 (3.312)	-.0566 (.0221)	.0187 (.0091)	.00135 (.00025)	.0189 (.0079)	.00371 (.00188)	1.0	—	0.994
Equation (17) α_6 constrained at 1	-2.066 (2.260)	-.0111 (.0212)	.0128 (.0012)	—	.0206 (.0072)	—	1.0	12%	0.994
Equation (15) Including Dummy Variables for States	—	-.2026 (.0532)	-.0135 (.0215)	.0327 (.0046)	.0131 (.0084)	.0044 (.0101)	.6799 (.0633)	—	0.996

* Figures in parentheses are standard errors of the corresponding coefficients above.

data contain an additive effect specific to the individual (state). To account for such effects, dummy variables corresponding to the thirty-six different states may be introduced explicitly into the model. It is moot, however, whether the dummy-variable method is appropriate in the case of a dynamic model. The presence of lagged endogenous variables may make it difficult, if not impossible, to separate the individual (state) effects from the effect induced by the lagged variable.

The results of including thirty-six dummy variables in equation (15) are shown in line 5 of Table 1.[13] As expected, the estimated coefficient of the lagged endogenous variable is drastically reduced, but to such a low level that it implies a depreciation rate of gas appliances of more than 30 per cent – highly implausible.[14] The coefficient of the price variable, on the other hand, is increased.

Despite its limitations, the dummy-variable experiment suggests that the coefficient of the lagged consumption variable (in the general pooled model) may indeed reflect in part a *regional* effect rather than a true lag effect. The problem with dummy variables is that they appear to reflect too much and thus to reduce the coefficient of the lagged gas variable to too low a level.[15] The idea of a regional (individual) effect, however, may be introduced in an alternative fashion.

3. THE RESIDUAL MODEL

The problem of estimating dynamic relationships from a time series of cross sections is more general than the material in the preceding sections would suggest. For this reason, it seems best to discuss the problem in a somewhat

---

[13] Note that the overall constant term has been omitted, obviating the necessity for constraining the thirty-six state coefficients to sum to zero.

[14] E. Kuh has pointed out that regarding the coefficient of G_{t-1} as a superposition of an ordinary distributed lag and the depreciation effect (rather than as a pure depreciation effect as we have done) renders the very low value of the estimated coefficient plausible. Inasmuch as we have expressed the model in terms of the "new" demand for gas, however, it is difficult to see why any additional distribution of lag should arise. Indeed, what we have actually done is to build a model that has a distributed lag effect as a *consequence*.

[15] Another way of looking at this problem is to say that the use of dummy variables wastes degrees of freedom since we are not really interested in the values of their coefficients, but only in the coefficients of lagged gas consumption, price, income, etc. What we imply is that boiling this effect down to one parameter as we do in the next section is somehow more efficient. Clearly, however, this is a small sample question, since in large samples when the number of observations increases faster than the number of regions, it cannot really matter how many parameters are estimated (as long as there are only a finite number). Unfortunately, there is no small sample theory for stochastic difference equations of the sort estimated here, and it is thus not possible to prove the assertion of greater efficiency. Monte Carlo experiments may, however, yield evidence on the matter and will be attempted by one of the authors at a future date.

more general setting. In this section, therefore, we develop in general terms a model that includes as special cases both ordinary time-series and ordinary cross-section analysis, along lines suggested originally by E. Kuh.[16] In Section 4, we present two alternative estimation procedures, together with applications to the gas model. A modification of the second procedure is also suggested but not applied to the gas model.

Suppose we have observations on N individuals, $n = 1, 2, \ldots, N$, taken over T periods of time, $t = 1, 2, \ldots, T$. Although in this study we are concerned with states, the individuals may be firms, consumers, regions, or any other statistical entity. We denote the variable to be explained by y_{nt}. This variable we assume is explained by K truly exogenous variables $z_{nt}^{(1)}, \ldots, z_{nt}^{(k)}$, including one that is identically one, so that no constant term need be included, and θ lagged values of the dependent variable. It is, incidentally, the presence of such lagged values that produces the essential difficulty of the problem, and which distinguishes it from the type of problem discussed in recent econometric literature.

To express the relation to be estimated in matrix form, we may write:

$$
y = \begin{bmatrix} y_1 \\ \vdots \\ y_N \end{bmatrix} = \begin{bmatrix} y_{11} \\ \vdots \\ y_{1T} \\ \vdots \\ y_{N1} \\ \vdots \\ y_{NT} \end{bmatrix},
$$

an $NT \times 1$ vector.

$$
Z = \begin{bmatrix} z_{11}^{(1)} & \cdots & z_{11}^{(K)} \\ \vdots & & \vdots \\ z_{NT}^{(1)} & \cdots & z_{NT}^{(K)} \end{bmatrix},
$$

an $NT \times K$ matrix of purely exogenous variables.

$$
Y_\theta = \begin{bmatrix} y_{1-1} & \cdots & y_{1-\theta} \\ \vdots & & \vdots \\ y_{1T-1} & \cdots & y_{1T-\theta} \\ \vdots & & \vdots \\ y_{NT-1} & \cdots & y_{NT-\theta} \end{bmatrix},
$$

[16] E. Kuh, "The Validity of Cross-Sectionally Estimated Behavior Equations in Time-Series Application," *Econometrica*, Vol. 27, April 1959, pp. 197–214.

an $NT \times \theta$ matrix of lagged values of the dependent variable.

$$u = \begin{bmatrix} u_1 \\ \vdots \\ u_N \end{bmatrix} = \begin{bmatrix} u_{11} \\ \vdots \\ u_{NT} \end{bmatrix},$$

an $NT \times 1$ vector of residuals. We also let α be a $K \times 1$ vector of constant coefficients of the exogenous variables, and β a $\theta \times 1$ vector of coefficients for the lagged endogenous variables. Throughout much of the discussion, we shall further simplify by writing $X = [Z : Y_\theta]$, an $NT \times K + \theta$ matrix, and

$$\gamma = \begin{bmatrix} \alpha \\ \beta \end{bmatrix},$$

a $K + \theta \times 1$ vector.

The relationship to be estimated from the combination of time-series and cross-section data then takes the form:

$$y = Z\alpha + Y_\theta\beta + u = X\gamma + u. \tag{19}$$

Of course, the statistical properties of various estimates, and indeed the real meaning of the model, are determined by what we assume about the properties of the residual vector u. We assume that each residual u_{nt} may be decomposed into two statistically independent parts: an individual effect and a remainder. Thus,

$$u_{nt} = \mu_n + v_{nt}. \tag{20}$$

We could also allow for a separate time effect, say λ_t, but this would greatly complicate the analysis without adding any essential generality. As indicated, the random variables μ_n and v_{nt} are assumed to have zero means, and to be independent,[17] from which it follows that

$$E\mu_n v_{nt} = 0, \quad \text{all } n, t. \tag{21}$$

We further assume that there is no serial correlation among the v_{nt}, and that

---

[17] The assumption of zero means, especially for v_{nt}, is a rather important one. If $Ev_{nt} = m_n \neq 0$, it is necessary to introduce certain shift variables for $N - 1$ of the individuals into the matrix Z. There should be $n - 1$ of these variables, if an overall constant term is allowed, one for all values of t in the nth block, and zero otherwise, except for the Nth block. If such variables are introduced, we may define new residuals with components v_{nt}, which do have zero mean. Assuming no shift variables of this sort, however, is not the same thing as the assumption of zero variance, σ_μ^2, (i.e., $\varrho = 0$). In this case, $\Omega = \sigma^2 I$, and ordinary least-squares estimates of α and β would be appropriate despite the presence of lagged values of the dependent variable (under certain standard conditions, of course). One might be tempted to assume zero variance, σ_μ^2, if shift variables had been included in the Z matrix. In Section 3 of this study, however, it was found that such an assumption led to economically implausible results. Hence, it seems better to adopt the more general mode.

these are independent from one individual to another; thus,

$$Ev_{nt}v_{n't'} = \begin{cases} \sigma_v^2, & n = n' \text{ and } t = t', \\ 0, & \text{otherwise.} \end{cases} \tag{22}$$

Similarly,

$$E\mu_n\mu_{n'} = \begin{cases} \sigma_\mu^2, & n = n' \\ 0, & \text{otherwise.} \end{cases} \tag{23}$$

Perhaps the most dubious assumption is that μ_n are independent of themselves for different individuals. For example, if the individuals are geographical regions with arbitrarily drawn boundaries, as they are here, we would not expect this assumption to be well satisfied. Nonetheless, we shall adopt it in what follows.

Equation (21) implies that the variance-covariance matrix of the residuals u may be written

$$Euu' = \Omega = \sigma^2 \begin{bmatrix} A & 0 & \dots & 0 \\ 0 & A & \dots & 0 \\ \vdots & \vdots & & \vdots \\ 0 & 0 & \dots & A \end{bmatrix}, \tag{24}$$

where

$$Eu_n u_n' = \sigma^2 A = \sigma^2 \begin{bmatrix} 1 & \rho & \rho & \dots & \rho \\ \rho & 1 & \rho & \dots & \rho \\ \vdots & \vdots & & & \vdots \\ \rho & \rho & \rho & \dots & 1 \end{bmatrix} \tag{25}$$

is a $T \times T$ matrix, and where

$$\begin{cases} \sigma^2 = \sigma_\mu^2 + \sigma_v^2, \\ \rho = \sigma_\mu^2/\sigma^2. \end{cases} \tag{26}$$

Note that in a pure cross section, there is only one time period for each individual, say the first, and we have only the upper left-hand corner one of each A; hence, in this case, $\Omega = \sigma^2 I$, where I is an $N \times N$ identity matrix. Furthermore, if there is only one individual, we cannot, in principle, ever distinguish between "individual" and "remainder" effects; hence, no generality is lost by assuming $\mu_n \equiv 0$ and thus $\sigma_\mu^2 \equiv 0$. In this case, then, too, $\Omega = \sigma^2 I$, where I is a $T \times T$ identity matrix, and ordinary least squares would, under fairly general circumstances, be an appropriate method of estimation.

Were no lagged values of the dependent variable y included among the explanatory variables in (19) (i.e., if β were identically zero), ordinary least-squares estimates of the coefficients, α, would be unbiased and consistent under the usual assumptions. They would not, however, be minimum variance or, in general, asymptotically efficient. Furthermore, the standard estimates of the variance-covariance matrix of the estimated coefficients, $\widehat{V(\alpha)}$, say, would be biased and inconsistent. If the true variance-covariance matrix of the residuals u, Ω, were known up to a multiplicative constant – in this case σ^2 – the minimum-variance, linear, unbiased estimators of α are given by

$$\hat{\alpha} = [Z'\Omega^{-1}Z]^{-1}Z'\Omega^{-1}y. \tag{27}$$

An unbiased estimate of $V(\hat{\alpha}) = E(\hat{\alpha} - \alpha)(\hat{\alpha} - \alpha)'$ is

$$\widehat{V(\hat{\alpha})} = \frac{\hat{u}'\,\Omega^{*-1}\hat{u}}{NT - K} \cdot [Z'\,\Omega^{*-1}Z]^{-1}, \tag{28}$$

where $\sigma^2\Omega^* = \Omega$ and $\hat{u} = y - Z\hat{\alpha}$.[18]

Provided we assume that the u's are distributed according to a multivariate normal distribution with zero means and variance-covariance matrix $\sigma^2\Omega^*$, $\hat{\alpha}$ given by (27) is the maximum-likelihood estimate of α, and

$$\hat{\sigma}^2 = \frac{\hat{u}'\Omega^{*-1}\hat{u}}{NT} \tag{29}$$

is the maximum-likelihood estimate of σ^2. Under quite unrestrictive conditions, these estimates are (i) functions of sufficient statistics, (ii) consistent, (iii) asymptotically normal, and (iv) efficient.[19]

Unfortunately, however, Ω is not known up to a multiplicative constant, and the question is whether it may be possible to derive estimators having some or all of the desirable properties of the least squares, or the maximum-likelihood estimates by estimating Ω up to a multiplicative factor.[20] In our case, this simply involves estimating the single parameter ρ, namely, the fraction of the overall residual variance accounted for by individual differences, as Ω depends only on this parameter and on σ^2, which can be estimated for known ρ by (29). The case in which *no lagged endogenous variables appear* in the regression has been discussed by Zellner[21] and Telser.[22] Zellner's idea is simply to estimate by two stages: first, using the ordinary least-squares estimates of

[18] A. C. Aitken, "On Least Squares and Linear Combinations of Observations," *Proceedings of the Royal Society of Edinburgh*, Vol. 55, 1934–1935, pp. 42–48. See also A. Goldberger, *Econometric Theory*, New York: John Wiley, 1964, pp. 231–235.

[19] M. G. Kendall and A. Stuart, *The Advanced Theory of Statistics*, Vol. 2, London: Charles Griffen, 1961, pp. 36–46.

[20] For possible approaches when Ω is not known, see H. Theil, *Economic Forecasting and Policy*, Amsterdam: North-Holland Publishing Company, 1961, pp. 221–225.

[21] A. Zellner, "An Efficient Method of Estimating Seemingly Unrelated Regressions and Tests for Aggregation Bias," *Journal of the American Statistical Association*, Vol. 57, 1962, pp. 348–368.

[22] L. G. Telser, "Iterative Simultaneous Estimation of Sets of Linear Regressions," *Journal of the American Statistical Association*, Vol. 59, September 1964, pp. 845–862.

α, and under suitable restrictions on the form of Ω, he obtains estimates of the variances and covariances of the residuals.[23] Since the ordinary least-squares estimates of α are consistent under general conditions, the estimates of the variances and covariances of the us are also. Thus, second, the matrix Ω may be replaced in (27) by a consistent estimate and new estimates of α derived. Zellner discusses the asymptotic properties of such two-stage estimators and shows that the gain in efficiency depends on the values of the off-diagonal elements in Ω (in our case, the extent to which ρ differs from zero), and on the correlation of the independent variables for the different individuals (blocks). If the independent variables for each individual are perfectly correlated, Zellner's results show that if no shift variables are included, the asymptotic efficiency of the ordinary least-squares estimators is the same as that of the proposed two-stage estimators. Such perfect correlation will rarely be the case, however.

Telser develops alternative computational procedures for estimates of the general type proposed by Zellner, and shows that these are Best Asymptotically Normal (BAN) estimators in much the same way that we show a related type of estimator is asymptotically maximum likelihood in the following subsection.[24]

The difficulty with the Zellner two-stage procedure and the Telser iterative procedure in connection with the present problem is the necessity of beginning with consistent estimates of the regression coefficients. Only in this way can consistent estimates of the residual variances and covariances be obtained, and such are essential if desirable asymptotic properties of the final estimates are to be achieved. When lagged endogenous variables are included among the explanatory variables of y in (19), it is no longer true that the ordinary least-squares estimates of $\gamma = [\begin{smallmatrix} \alpha \\ \beta \end{smallmatrix}]$ are consistent unless there is no serial correlation of any kind. In this case, of course, there is no possibility either of increasing the efficiency of the estimates by any sort of iteration.

There are two possible approaches to this problem, both of which are explored in Section 4. First, we may try to find estimators of the coefficients γ in (19) that are consistent despite the presence of lagged endogenous variables. We can then obtain a consistent estimate of ρ and, using Ω so determined, find

$$\gamma = [X'\Omega^{-1}X]^{-1}X'\Omega^{-1}y, \tag{30}$$

which we show will have desirable properties. Alternatively, since the structure

---

[23] Zellner's model is different from the one developed in this study in two important respects. First, Zellner postulates different sets of regression coefficients for each (cross section) equation and zero restrictions on the coefficients occurring in other equations. Second, Zellner does not assume constancy of the parameter ϱ for different years.

[24] Zellner himself shows that these estimates are asymptotically normal and have the same asymptotic distribution as the minimum-variance unbiased estimates. A discussion of BAN estimators and their properties is given in connection with the discussion of our estimates in the following subsection.

of our problem is much simpler than the more general one considered by Zellner and Telser by virtue of the fact that Ω^* depends only on a single parameter ρ, we may try to obtain simultaneous maximum-likelihood estimates for γ, σ^2, and ρ. These will have all the desirable asymptotic properties we seek, and an easily determined asymptotic variance-covariance matrix as well.

4. ESTIMATION PROCEDURES

Maximum-Likelihood Estimates

We suppose, as is usual in such discussions, that the values of y_{nt} for $t \leq 0$ and all n are fixed. The $z_{nt}^{(k)}$ are assumed to be nonstochastic. If the u_{nt} are distributed according to a multivariate normal distribution with zero means and variance-covariance matrix Ω, their probability density may be written

$$p(u) = (2\pi)^{-NT/2} |\Omega^{-1}|^{\frac{1}{2}} e^{-\frac{1}{2} u' \Omega^{-1} u}. \tag{31}$$

Consequently, using u as a shorthand notation for $y - X\gamma$, the logarithmic likelihood function for the parameters, γ, ρ, and σ^2 may be written

$$L(\gamma, \rho, \sigma^2) = -\frac{NT}{2} \log 2\pi - \frac{1}{2} \log |\Omega| - \frac{1}{2} u' \Omega^{-1} u. \tag{32}$$

The maximum of L with respect to γ is clearly obtained when the quadratic form

$$u' \Omega^{-1} u = [y - X\gamma]' \Omega^{-1} [y - X\gamma]$$

is at a minimum. This occurs for

$$\hat{\gamma} = (X' \Omega^{-1} X)^{-1} X' \Omega^{-1} y.^{25} \tag{33}$$

$\hat{\gamma}$ is the maximum-likelihood estimate of γ for Ω known up to a scalar multiple. For unknown Ω, (33) is *one* of a series of equations that must be solved simultaneously to find the maximum-likelihood estimate of γ, ρ, and σ^2.

The appropriate equation for σ^2 may be found by writing $\Omega = \sigma^2 \Omega^*$, differentiating L with respect to σ^2, and setting the result to zero. This yields

$$\sigma^2 = \frac{[y - X\gamma]' \Omega^{*-1} [y - X\gamma]}{NT}. \tag{34}$$

It may be verified that the second derivative of L with respect to σ^2 is negative at this point as required for a maximum, given γ and ρ.

---

[25] This is a standard result that follows from the fact that $X' \Omega^{-1} X$ is positive definite.

It is a trifle more difficult to find the final equation of those determining the maximum-likelihood estimates.[26] The derivation of the final expressions for ρ and σ^2 given by maximizing the likelihood function is contained in the appendix to this paper, where we find that the maximum-likelihood estimates for ρ and σ^2 are given by

$$\rho = \frac{\sum_{n=1}^{N}\left\{\left[\sum_{t=1}^{T} u_{nt}\right]^2 - \sum_{t=1}^{T} u_{nt}^2\right\}}{(T-1)\sum_{n=1}^{N}\sum_{t=1}^{T} u_{nt}^2},$$

$$\sigma^2 = \frac{\sum_{n=1}^{N}\sum_{t=1}^{T} u_{nt}^2}{NT}. \tag{35}$$

The reader should bear in mind that the *u*s appearing in (35) are merely shorthand expressions for the appropriate combination of γs, ys, and xs.[27]

Equations (33) and (35) determine the maximum-likelihood estimates of γ, ρ, and σ^2. Unfortunately, they are highly nonlinear in the γs and ρ. While there are numerical methods for solving such systems of nonlinear equations, the computational burden is very great. Fortunately, the interpretation of the parameter ρ as the ratio of a component of variance to an overall variance, which forces ρ to lie in the interval $[0, 1]$, suggests a much simpler procedure. For any ρ lying in this interval, we may determine those values of γ and σ^2 that maximize the likelihood function. As indicated, these values will be given by equations (33) and (34). Inserting the values so obtained in the likelihood function, we obtain a *partially maximized* likelihood, say $\hat{L}$, which we may write purely as a function of ρ:

$$\hat{L}(\rho) = -\frac{NT}{2}\{1 + \log 2\pi\} - \frac{NT}{2}\log \hat{\sigma}^2(\rho) - \frac{N}{2}\log\{(1-\rho)^{T-1}[(1-\rho)+T\rho]\},$$

$$\tag{36}$$

where $\hat{\sigma}^2(\rho)$ is given by (34) when γ is chosen, as in (33), for a particular value of ρ. It has been written with a hat and as a function of ρ to remind us that it

---

[26] Considering a model in which the variance-covariance matrix of the residuals is identical to our Ω, M. Halperin states: "The maximum likelihood equations...are of such a formidable character that an explicit solution does not appear possible" (p. 574). However, Halperin then shows that, for the case of no lagged endogenous variables, the least-squares estimators and certain tests of significance are still valid. In his proofs, Halperin makes use of the same orthogonal transformation as the one adopted in the next subsection. It should be pointed out, however, that Halperin does not allow for lagged endogenous variables and, also, that he introduces individual shift variables. In such a case, it may be shown, indeed, that the least-squares estimators of the coefficients and the maximum-likelihood estimators are computationally the same. M. Halperin, "Normal Regression Theory in the Presence of Intraclass Correlation," *The Annals of Mathematical Statistics*, Vol. 22, No. 4, December, 1951, pp. 573–580. William Madow was kind enough to call Halperin's paper to our attention.

[27] The expression for σ^2 in (35) differs from that in (34) because the maximum-likelihood estimate of ϱ, *given* γ, has been inserted.

is both an optimized value and dependent on ρ. Since ρ varies over the closed interval, $\hat{L}(\rho)$ must reach a maximum within the interval or on the boundary, provided it is continuous throughout the interval. Except, possibly, on a set measure of zero, $\hat{L}(\rho)$ is indeed continuous on the half-open interval $(0, 1)$; at $\rho = 1$, however, Ω is singular and $\hat{L}(\rho)$ is therefore undefined.

It follows from these remarks that if $\hat{L}(\rho)$ reaches a maximum *within* the interval $[0, 1]$, we can find the value of ρ for which this occurs by computing $\hat{L}(\rho)$ numerically for a sufficient number of points ρ within the interval. Unfortunately, however, there is no guarantee, for any particular observed y and X, that the maximum of $\hat{L}(\rho)$ so defined actually lies within $[0, 1]$. It is clear, too, from (35) that there is no guarantee either that ρ as given there in terms of the u_{nt} will lie in the interval $[0, 1]$, although σ^2 must be positive, as it should be.

We have thus come to the following conclusion: If, for given observations on y and X, the likelihood function $\hat{L}(\gamma, \rho, \sigma^2)$, defined in (32), has a maximum with respect to γ, ρ, and σ^2 such that the maximizing value of ρ lies between zero and one, the procedure of maximizing $\hat{L}(\rho)$, defined in (36), will yield that maximum.[28] If, however, the maximum of $\hat{L}(\gamma, \rho, \sigma^2)$ does not occur for a value of between zero and one, the maximum-likelihood procedure outlined in this section is inapplicable, and alternative methods of estimation must be employed.

The application of the suggested procedure to the gas data reveals, indeed, that the ML method may lead in practice to inadmissible results. In Table 2, the column labelled L^* gives the values of $\hat{L}(\rho)$ – omitting the constant term – for 20 values of ρ. The figures show that the likelihood function does not reach a maximum in the interval of the *a priori* admissible values of ρ. Hence, the ML method should be abandoned and an alternative procedure adopted.

It is interesting to note, however, the pattern displayed by the coefficient of the lagged consumption variable. This coefficient gradually declines as ρ increases; for a sufficiently high value of ρ, it becomes smaller than unity.

Alternative Estimates

The desirable properties of maximum-likelihood estimates, apart from the intrinsic appeal of the method and the fact that they are functions of sufficient

---

[28] The asymptotic variance-covariance matrix of the maximum-likelihood estimators, $\hat{\gamma}$, $\bar{\varrho}$, and $\hat{\sigma}^2$ satisfying (33) and (35) simultaneously, is given by the inverse of the matrix of second derivatives of L, defined in (32), evaluated at $\gamma = \hat{\gamma}$, $\sigma^2 = \hat{\sigma}^2$, $\varrho = \hat{\varrho}$:

$$\begin{bmatrix} \dfrac{\partial^2 L}{\partial \varrho^2} & \dfrac{\partial^2 L}{\partial \varrho \partial \sigma^2} & \dfrac{\partial^2 L}{\partial \varrho \partial \gamma'} \\[2ex] \dfrac{\partial^2 L}{\partial \varrho \partial \sigma^2} & \dfrac{\partial^2 L}{(\partial \sigma^2)^2} & \dfrac{\partial^2 L}{\partial \sigma^2 \partial \gamma'} \\[2ex] \dfrac{\partial^2 L}{\partial \varrho \partial \gamma} & \dfrac{\partial^2 L}{\partial \sigma^2 \partial \gamma} & \dfrac{\partial^2 L}{\partial \gamma \partial \gamma'} \end{bmatrix}^{-1} .$$

See Kendall and Stuart, *op. cit.*, p. 55.

Table 2. *Estimated Value of the Likelihood Function for 20 Values of ϱ, 1957–1962*

Assumed Value of ϱ	L^{*a}	Const.	P_t	N_{t-1}	ΔN_t	Y_{t-1}	ΔY_t	G_{t-1}
				Regression Coefficients				
.00	−58.663	−3.650	−.0451	.00111	.0174	.00325	.0183	1.010
.05	−58.786	−3.582	−.0480	.00119	.0168	.00331	.0181	1.008
.10	−58.918	−3.517	−.0509	.00127	.0160	.00337	.0180	1.006
.15	−59.052	−3.455	−.0536	.00136	.0152	.00341	.0179	1.004
.20	−59.185	−3.396	−.0564	.00145	.0144	.00345	.0178	1.002
.25	−59.319	−3.339	−.0591	.00155	.0134	.00348	.0177	.999
.30	−59.453	−3.286	−.0617	.00165	.0124	.00351	.0176	.997
.35	−59.587	−3.240	−.0644	.00177	.0114	.00354	.0176	.994
.40	−59.724	−3.200	−.0670	.00190	.0102	.00355	.0175	.991
.45	−59.863	−3.172	−.0697	.00204	.00897	.00357	.0174	.988
.50	−60.007	−3.161	−.0724	.00220	.00765	.00357	.0174	.984
.55	−60.157	−3.174	−.0751	.00238	.00624	.00357	.0173	.980
.60	−60.316	−3.227	−.0779	.00258	.00473	.00357	.0172	.975
.65	−60.487	−3.338	−.0807	.00282	.00311	.00356	.0172	.970
.70	−60.674	−3.545	−.0837	.00311	.00135	.00355	.0171	.964
.75	−60.884	−3.913	−.0860	.00347	−.00055	.00354	.0170	.957
.80	−61.128	−4.568	−.0902	.00393	−.00262	.00355	.0170	.949
.85	−61.427	−5.794	−.0942	.00460	−.00492	.00358	.0169	.937
.90	−61.824	−8.361	−.0996	.00571	−.00478	.00367	.0168	.921
.95	−62.446	−15.464	−.1101	.00827	−.01039	.00389	.0166	.891

[a] Constant $(-NT/2) \log 2\pi$ suppressed.

statistics, are all asymptotic: consistency, asymptotic normality, and asymptotic efficiency. But as we have just seen by example, "Blind adherence to the principle of maximum likelihood...may lead to more difficult computations and still yield less accurate estimates than other methods of estimation."[29] It was precisely such difficulties that led Neyman to consider what other estimates possessed the same desirable asymptotic properties as maximum-likelihood estimates: consistency, asymptotic normality, and efficiency, but more optimal computational or small sample properties.[30] He called estimates with these large sample properties Best Asymptotically Normal (BAN) estimates.

Although there are a number of methods currently available for deriving BAN estimates, in this context the simplest procedure is to find a set

[29] T. S. Ferguson, "A Method of Generating Best Asymptotically Normal Estimates with Application to the Estimation of Bacterial Densities," *Annals of Mathematical Statistics*, Vol. 29, 1958, p. 1047.

[30] J. Neyman, "Contribution to the Theory of the χ^2 Test," *Proceedings of the Berkeley Symposium on Mathematical Statistics and Probability*, Berkeley: University of California Press, 1949, pp. 239–273.

of estimates asymptotically equivalent to the maximum-likelihood estimates (AML).[31] It will then follow that such estimates have all the desirable asymptotic properties of maximum-likelihood estimates except perhaps efficiency. We continue to assume, as before, that the residuals u_{nt} are distributed according to (31).

Suppose that $m = NT \to \infty$, and that if $N \to \infty$ then it does so in such a way that $N/T \to 0$. Let us further suppose we are given a consistent estimate S_m of the residual variance-covariance matrix Ω. Thus, as $T \to \infty$, $S_m \to \Omega$ in probability, and $S_m^{-1} \to \Omega^{-1}$. However, Ω^{-1} depends on T and can be shown to be block diagonal with blocks of the form

$$
C' \mathrm{diag}\left\{\frac{1}{\xi}, \frac{1}{\eta}, \ldots, \frac{1}{\eta}\right\} C = [e/\sqrt{T}C_1'] \begin{bmatrix} 1/\xi & 0 & \cdots & 0 \\ 0 & 1/\eta & \cdots & 0 \\ \vdots & \vdots & & \\ 0 & 0 & \cdots & 1/\eta \end{bmatrix} \begin{bmatrix} e'/\sqrt{T} \\ C_1 \end{bmatrix}
$$

$$
= \frac{ee'}{\xi T} + \frac{C_1' C_1}{\eta} = \frac{ee'}{\xi T} + \frac{1}{\eta}\left\{I - \frac{ee'}{T}\right\}
$$

$$
\to \frac{1}{\eta}I = \frac{1}{\sigma^2(1-\rho)}I,
$$

as $m \to \infty$, by equation (A.6) of the appendix. The matrices $C_1 C_1$ and the variables ξ and η are also defined there.

It follows that replacing Ω by a consistent estimate of itself in (30) leads asymptotically to the ordinary least-squares estimates based on the pooled sample and that these are the same in the limit as the maximum-likelihood estimates.[32] The estimates so obtained may very well have more desirable small sample properties than the direct maximum-likelihood estimates although we have not, other than empirically, succeeded in demonstrating these. Furthermore, $[x' S_m^{-1} X]^{-1}$ will be a consistent estimate of the asymptotic variance-covariance matrix of these estimates. It follows then that our only problem is to obtain a consistent estimate of the residual variance-covariance matrix Ω. Once this is obtained, we can proceed to a "second round" estimate,

$$
\gamma = \left[X' S_m^{-1} X\right]^{-1} X' S_m^{-1} y. \tag{37}
$$

If there were no lagged values of y present in the X matrix (i.e., if $\beta = 0$), moments of the calculated residuals, $\hat{u} = y - Z(Z'Z)^{-1}Z'y$, from the ordinary

---

[31] We are indebted to T. Amemiya who pointed out an error in our original proof, which was based on a theorem of C. L. Chiang, "On Regular Best Asymptotically Normal Estimates," *Annals of Mathematical Statistics*, Vol. 27, 1956, pp. 336–351.

[32] The assumption of normality, of course, makes the proof that our estimates are AML quite trivial. It is possible, however, to derive AML estimates in cases where normality is not assumed but then rather tedious regularity conditions must be checked. In essence, one must show asymptotic normality; we here assume normality from the start.

least-squares regression would be consistent estimates of the corresponding elements of the matrix Ω. Hence, as Telser has shown, under appropriate restrictions on the form of Ω sufficient to enable one to compute estimates of its elements from moments of the calculated residuals, the second-stage estimates are BAN.[33] Unfortunately, however, there will generally be lagged values of y present among the independent variables of the regression equation (19); under these circumstances, the ordinary least squares estimates of the coefficients are inconsistent estimates of the elements of Ω from moments of the calculated residuals from the ordinary least-squares regression.

Suppose, on the other hand, that consistent estimates of γ were available. The calculated residuals from (19) could then be used to compute, for example by (35), consistent estimates of ρ and σ^2. These in turn would form the matrix S_m to be used in a second round producing estimates of γ. To ensure, however, that the estimated ρ would lie between zero and one, we might wish to depart somewhat from the estimates given in (35). The following, for example, would also lead to consistent estimates of ρ:

$$\rho = \frac{\sum_{n=1}^{N} \sum_{t=1}^{T} \sum_{t'=1}^{T} \hat{u}_{nt}\hat{u}_{nt'} - \frac{1}{N}\left(\sum_{n=1}^{N}\sum_{t=1}^{T}\hat{u}_{nt}\right)^2}{NT^2\hat{\sigma}^2}, \tag{38}$$

where $\hat{\sigma}^2$ is given by the second equation in (35) and $\hat{u}_{nt}$ is a residual calculated from (19) by inserting consistent estimates for γ.[34]

There are a variety of ways in which one may obtain consistent estimates of γ. We shall discuss only two here, one of which is inspired by Theil's two-stage least squares; the second method has been suggested by E. J. Hannan. Only the first of the two, however, can be applied to the gas model.

Equation (20) suggests that the residual u_{nt} may be divided into two parts: one, μ_n, represents the individual effect common, for a given individual n, to all time periods for which we observe him. The other, v_{nt}, represents the remainder. The reason that ordinary least-squares estimates are inconsistent when lagged variables are included is that these variables are correlated with the current values of the residuals u_{nt} since they are determined to the same degree as the current value of the dependent variables by μ_n. Precisely the same sort of difficulty arises in the estimation of one of a system of structural

[33] Telser, *op. cit.*

[34] Note that the corresponding estimate from (35) is really quite similar to (38), for it can be written:

$$\frac{\sum_{n=1}^{N}\sum_{t=1}^{T}\sum_{t'=1}^{T}\hat{u}_{nt}\hat{u}_{nt'} - \sum_{n=1}^{N}\sum_{t=1}^{T}\hat{u}_{nt}^2}{T(T-1)N\hat{\sigma}^2}.$$

Thus, it is mostly a question of the appropriate adjustment to

$$\sum_{n=1}^{N}\left(\sum_{t=1}^{T}\hat{u}_{nt}\right)^2 = \sum_{n=1}^{N}\sum_{t=1}^{T}\sum_{t'=1}^{T}\hat{u}_{nt}\hat{u}_{nt'}.$$

equations involving more than one endogenous variable of the system. In this case, if one of the endogenous variables is chosen as dependent, and the rest are treated *as if* independent in a least-squares regression, the results are inconsistent because of the correlation between the endogenous variables treated as independent and the residual of the equation. One solution to this difficulty is to use as *instrumental variables* a sufficient number of other exogenous or (in the absence of serially correlated residuals) lagged endogenous variables appearing elsewhere in the system in the formation of the "normal" equations so that the current endogenous variables in the equation need not be used for this purpose. The difficulty, of course, is that there are usually more than enough predetermined variables for this purpose, and a choice must be made among them. One of Theil's contributions in the development of two-stage least squares was to show how such a choice could be avoided by selecting as instrumental variables those linear combinations of all predetermined variables most highly correlated with the current endogenous variables whose values they replaced in forming normal equations.[35]

We do not, of course, deal here with one of a system of simultaneous equations containing several endogenous variables. It is thus not readily apparent how additional exogenous variables should be obtained. The key to the solution is found in the idea that the lagged values of the dependent variables are determined in a sense by other equations, although these are just lagged versions of the equation we are trying to estimate. Thus, under certain restrictions, the tth of equations (19) for the nth individual,

$$y_{nt} = \sum_{k=1}^{K} \alpha_k z_{nt}^{(k)} + \sum_{\tau=1}^{\theta} \beta_\tau y_{nt-\tau} + u_{nt} \tag{39}$$

has the solution

$$y_{nt} = \sum_{k=1}^{K} \sum_{\tau=0}^{\infty} \lambda_\tau^{(k)} z_{nt-\tau}^{(k)} + w_{nt}. \tag{40}$$

Equations (40) for $n = 1, \ldots, N$, and $t = 1, \ldots, T$, may be thought of as the reduced form for equation (39), $n = 1, \ldots, N, t = 1, \ldots, T$. If some of the lagged zs are linear combinations of each other (e.g., when some were shift variables), the solutions would only involve independent variables. Because the zs are nonstochastic, they are independent of the current and past values of the residuals u_{nt}. The residuals w_{nt} are merely linear combinations of the current and lagged values of u_{nt}; hence, in principle it would be proper to estimate the coefficients $\lambda_\tau^{(k)}$ by ordinary least squares. Of course, an infinite

[35] L. R. Klein, "On the Interpretation of Theil's Method of Estimating Economic Relationships," *Metroeconomica*, Vol. 7, 1955, pp. 147–153. For a more systematic and transparent derivation of Klein's result, among others, see A. Madansky, "On the Efficiency of Three-Stage Least-Squares Estimation," *Econometrica*, Vol. 32, Jan.–April, 1964, pp. 51–56.

past history of zs is not available so that truncation of the infinite series of them in (40) must occur at some point in practice. Since we are generally very short of time periods in a time series of cross sections, it is suggested that only the current zs be used to estimate the coefficients $\lambda_0^{(k)}$ and the remaining terms in (40) be neglected.

When estimates $\hat{\lambda}_0^{(k)}$ and perhaps others, $\hat{\lambda}_\tau^{(k)}$, $\tau > 0$, have been obtained, we have certain linear combinations of exogenous variables:

$$y_{nt}^* = \sum_{k=1}^{K} \hat{\lambda}_0^{(k)} z_{nt}^{(k)} + \cdots; \tag{41}$$

the lagged values of which may be used as instrumental variables in generating normal equations for the estimation of α and β in (19). In effect, we replace the tth equation for the nth individual (39) by

$$
\begin{aligned}
y_{nt} &= \sum_{k=1}^{K} \alpha_k z_{nt}^{(k)} + \sum_{\tau=1}^{\theta} \beta_\tau Y_{nt-\tau}^* + u_{nt} \\
&= \sum_{k=1}^{K} \alpha_k z_{nt}^{(k)} + \sum_{\tau=1}^{\theta} \sum_{k=1}^{K} \beta_\tau \hat{\lambda}_0^k z_{nt-\tau}^{(k)} + \cdots + u_{nt},
\end{aligned}
\tag{42}
$$

in which it is appropriate to estimate the coefficients α_k and β_τ by ordinary least squares, provided the moment matrix of the zs is nonsingular and satisfies certain other regularity conditions. In this case, the estimates of α_k and β_τ so obtained will be consistent and enable us to construct consistent estimates S_m of Ω to be used in the second stage of this estimation of γ given in (37).[36]

The application of the first stage of this suggested estimating procedure to the gas data yields an estimate of ρ of 0.7667. It is interesting to note that the value of ρ so obtained is considerably larger than the corresponding value obtained by Kuh in his analysis of investment functions.[37] This high value of ρ is not, as one may be tempted to think, due to the exclusive influence of weather differences among states, since an explicit variable accounting for these differences was introduced in (39).

When this value of ρ is used in the second stage, plausible estimates of the coefficients of both the price variable and lagged gas consumption are obtained (Table 3). For several reasons, the rate of depreciation in the gas

---

[36] It may be shown directly that the second-round estimates are consistent; that is, that

$$\operatorname{plim} X'\Omega^{-1}u = \operatorname{plim} \sum_{n} X_n' A^{-1} u_n = 0.$$

where $X_n = [Z_n : Y_{\theta n}]$ is the nth block of the matrix $X = [Z : Y_\theta]$. While comforting, however, the demonstration is unnecessary because consistency is a property of AML estimates.

[37] "...The individual firm effects are important, being in the present instance one-quarter to one-third as large as the time varying errors." E. Kuh, "The Validity of Cross Sectionally Estimated Behavior Equations in Time Series Applications," *op. cit.*, p. 201.

Table 3. *AML Estimates of Gas Equation, 1957–1962*
(Standard errors in parentheses)
Coefficient of

Const.	P_t	N_{t-1}	ΔN_t	Y_{t-1}	ΔY_t	G_{t-1}
−4.091	−.0879	.00360	−.00122	.00354	.0170	.9546
(11.544)	(.0468)	(.00129)	(.0190)	(.00622)	(.0080)	(.0372)

market should not be expected to be very high. From the estimate of the coefficient of G_{t-1} in Table 3, we may derive an estimated depreciation rate of approximately 4.5 percent.

The high standard errors associated with one income variable and one population variable would suggest that the estimating procedure is quite sensitive to collinearity. To circumvent such difficulties, one might use the estimated depreciation rate for all fuel using appliances of 11 percent (obtained in Section 3) to construct the variables N_t^* and Y_t^* and then proceed to the estimation of a constrained version of the gas equation. The results of such computation are shown in Table 4. All coefficients have small standard errors. As compared to the unconstrained model, this new method yields a smaller coefficient for the price variable and a higher coefficient for the lagged consumption variable.

Application of the residual model to the gas data produces estimates that are in agreement with the theoretical expectations. It may be emphasized that the estimated coefficient of lagged gas consumption (as given by the residual model) is smaller than unity. This result lends support to the basic hypothesis embodied in the dynamic model of gas demand.

Unfortunately, the method just outlined breaks down if there are no truly exogenous variables in the problem, apart from constant terms, trends, or shift variables, for the lagged values of these are linear combinations of their current values and the moment matrix of independent variables in (42) will be singular. It is, therefore, useful to develop an alternative approach that does not require the presence of true exogenous variables, although we do not need it in the particular case of the gas model. (Furthermore, given the limited number of observations available over time, this new approach is inapplicable to the gas model.)

Table 4. *AML Estimates: Constrained Case,*
1957–1962 (Standard errors in parentheses)
Coefficient of

Const.	P_t	N_t^*	Y_t^*	G_{t-1}
−1.148	−.0695	.02163	.01801	.9786
(5.250)	(.0441)	(.00789)	(.00794)	(.0321)

Originally, it was thought that the first-difference transformation, suggested earlier by A. Walters,[38] could be used to obtain consistent estimates needed for the first round of the AML procedure. Regrettably, however, this proved not to be the case.[39] Nonetheless, provided a sufficient number of observations over time on each individual is available, consistent estimates may be found. The six years of gas data, our second period, are unfortunately insufficient considering the number of parameters to be estimated; nevertheless, the method may be useful in other contexts and is as follows:

Rewrite (39) as

$$y_{nt} = (\alpha_1 + \mu_n) + \sum_{k=z}^{K} \alpha_k z_{nt}^{(k)} + \sum_{\tau=1}^{\theta} \beta_\tau y_{nt-\tau} + v_{nt}. \tag{43}$$

Since the v_{nt} are serially independent, provided sufficient observations over time are available, the ordinary least-squares estimates in (43) for each individual may be found and are certainly consistent. Let these be denoted by $\hat{\alpha}_k^n$ and $\hat{\beta}_\tau^{(n)}$, the superscript indicating the estimates refer to the nth individual. The following series of estimates of parameters in (39) may be shown to be consistent:

$$
\begin{cases}
\hat{\alpha}_k = \dfrac{1}{N} \sum_{n=1}^{N} \hat{\alpha}_k^{(m)}, \quad k = 2, \ldots, K, \\[2ex]
\hat{\beta}_\tau = \dfrac{1}{N} \sum_{n=1}^{N} \hat{\beta}_\tau^{(n)}, \quad \tau = 1, \ldots, \theta, \\[2ex]
\hat{\alpha}_1 = \dfrac{1}{N} \sum_{n=1}^{N} \left\{ \bar{y}_n - \sum_{k=2}^{K} \hat{\alpha}_k \bar{z}_n^{(k)} - \sum_{\tau=1}^{\theta} \hat{\beta}_\tau \bar{y}_{n,-\tau} \right\}, \\[2ex]
\text{where } \bar{y}_{n,-\tau} = \dfrac{1}{T} \sum_{\tau=1}^{T} y_{n,t-\tau}, \quad \tau = 0, \ldots, \theta, \quad \text{and} \quad \bar{z}_n^k = \dfrac{1}{T} \sum_{t=1}^{T} z_{nt}^{(k)}, \\[2ex]
\hat{\sigma}_\mu^2 = \dfrac{1}{N} \sum_{n=1}^{N} \left[\left(\bar{y}_n - \sum_{k=2}^{K} \hat{\alpha}_k \bar{z}_n^{(k)} - \sum_{\tau=1}^{\theta} \hat{\beta}_\tau \bar{y}_{n,-\tau} \right) - \hat{\alpha}_1 \right]^2, \\[2ex]
\sigma^2 = \dfrac{1}{NT} \sum_{n=1}^{N} \sum_{t=1}^{T} \left[y_{nt} - \hat{\alpha}_1 - \sum_{k=2}^{K} \hat{\alpha}_k z_{nt}^{(k)} - \sum_{\tau=1}^{\theta} \beta_\tau y_{n,t-\tau} \right]^2, \\[2ex]
\hat{\rho} = \hat{\sigma}_\mu^2 / \hat{\sigma}^2.^{40}
\end{cases}
\tag{44}
$$

[38] A. A. Walters, "Some Notes on the Cobb-Douglas Production Function," *Metroeconomica*, Vol. 13, 1961, pp. 122–138.

[39] As was pointed out by Z. Griliches and L. G. Telser.

[40] If we let

$$u_{nt} = y_{nt} - \alpha_1 - \sum_{k=z}^{} \alpha_k Z_{nt}^{(k)} - \sum_{\tau=1}^{\theta} \beta y_{n,t-\tau}.$$

The final estimate of $\hat{\rho}$ may be used in a second round of estimates in the manner suggested to obtain AML estimates.

5. CONCLUSIONS

In this paper, we have developed a dynamic model of the demand for natural gas in the residential and commercial sector. Point estimates of the parameters of the model based on a pooled sample of thirty-six states over six years suggest an implausible, negative rate of depreciation on gas appliances. Introduction of state shift variables results in an estimated rate of 30 percent per year – also implausible. After several attempts to incorporate other variables (not reported here), we concluded that time-invariant but perhaps unobservable state effects were responsible for biasing the coefficient of lagged gas consumption in the demand equation.

A model suggested by E. Kuh was explored in some detail and several different methods for estimating its parameters in the presence of lagged endogenous variables were proposed. Of these, the maximum-likelihood method was shown to lead, in the case of gas demand, to an unacceptable boundary solution. An alternative method, however, was proposed that led to theoretically plausible results. The final results obtained suggested that time-invariant regional effects account for about three quarters of the total residual variance in the gas-demand equation. The estimated rate of depreciation on gas appliances (mainly furnaces) is in the order of 5 percent per year. The estimated net long-run price and income elasticities of new gas demand are 0.63 and 0.62, respectively, in the unconstrained case, and 0.63 and 0.44, when the depreciation rate is assumed to be 11 percent for all fuel-consuming appliances. In this case, the depreciation on gas appliances is estimated at slightly more than 2 percent per year.

then ϱ may be written suggestively as

$$\varrho = \frac{\sum_{n=1}^{N} \left(\sum_{t=1}^{T} u_{nt} \right)^2}{T \sum_{n=1}^{N} \sum_{t=1}^{T} u_{nt}^2}.$$

The perceptive reader will note that this is the same as ϱ in (38) apart from rounding errors.

Derivation of the Maximum-Likelihood
Estimates of ρ and σ^2

Rather than differentiate directly with respect to ρ, which will involve us in the explicit evaluation of Ω^{-1} and $|\Omega|$, it is useful to reparameterize the problem by making a particular kind of orthogonal transformation of the variables. Since the Jacobian of an orthogonal transformation is unity, the probability density of the transformed variables is given simply by (31) with appropriate substitutions, and thus the likelihood function of the new parameters will be given by making the corresponding substitutions in (32).

Let C be a $T \times T$ orthogonal matrix, every element of the first row of which is $1/\sqrt{T}$. If e is a $T \times 1$ vector consisting entirely of ones,

$$e = \begin{bmatrix} 1 \\ 1 \\ \vdots \\ 1 \end{bmatrix},$$

we may write C as

$$C = \begin{bmatrix} e'/\sqrt{T} \\ C_1 \end{bmatrix}, \tag{A.1}$$

where C_1 is a $T - 1 \times T$ matrix. There is an infinite number of such matrices; for example, one is

$$\begin{bmatrix} \dfrac{1}{\sqrt{T}} & \dfrac{1}{\sqrt{T}} & \dfrac{1}{\sqrt{T}} & \cdots & \dfrac{1}{\sqrt{T}} \\[2ex] \dfrac{1}{\sqrt{1\times 2}} & \dfrac{-1}{\sqrt{1\times 2}} & 0 & \cdots & 0 \\[2ex] \dfrac{1}{\sqrt{2\times 3}} & \dfrac{1}{\sqrt{2\times 3}} & \dfrac{-2}{\sqrt{2\times 3}} & \cdots & 0 \\[2ex] \vdots & \vdots & \vdots & & \\[2ex] \dfrac{1}{\sqrt{(T-1)T}} & \dfrac{1}{\sqrt{(T-1)T}} & \dfrac{1}{\sqrt{(T-1)T}} & \cdots & \dfrac{-(T-1)}{\sqrt{(T-1)T}} \end{bmatrix}.$$

It is unnecessary, however, to specify which one of all those we choose, as only the fact that all the elements in the first row are $1/\sqrt{T}$ and the orthogonality of the matrix as a whole are ever used. Because C is orthogonal, we have

$$CC' = \begin{bmatrix} e'/\sqrt{T} \\ C_1 \end{bmatrix} [e/\sqrt{T} \; C_1'] = \begin{bmatrix} 1 & \dfrac{e'C_1'}{\sqrt{T}} \\ \dfrac{C_1 e}{\sqrt{T}} & C_1 C_1' \end{bmatrix} = \begin{bmatrix} 1 & 0 \\ 0 & I \end{bmatrix},$$

so that

$$\begin{cases} C_1 e = 0, \\ C_1 C_1' = I, \end{cases} \tag{A.2}$$

where I is a $T-1 \times T-1$ identity matrix. In a similar way, we can show that $C_1' C_1 = I - ee'/T$, where I is $T \times T$.

Let C^* be an $NT \times NT$ orthogonal matrix defined as

$$C^* = \begin{bmatrix} C & 0 & \dots & 0 \\ 0 & C & \dots & 0 \\ \vdots & \vdots & & \\ 0 & 0 & \dots & C \end{bmatrix}.$$

The transformation we wish to make is from u to v (implying corresponding transformations in y and X), where

$$v = C^* u. \tag{A.3}$$

Because C^* is orthogonal, we also have, of course, $C^{*\prime} v = u$.

By equation (25),

$$\sigma^2 A = \sigma^2 \{(1 - \rho)I + \rho \, ee'\}. \tag{A.4}$$

Hence, by (A.2), we deduce

$$\sigma^2 C A C' = \sigma^2 \{(1 - \rho)CC' + \rho C \, ee' C'\}$$

$$= \sigma^2 \left\{ (1 - \rho)I + \rho \begin{bmatrix} T/\sqrt{T} \\ C_1 e \end{bmatrix} [T/\sqrt{T} \, e' \, C_1'] \right\}$$

$$= \sigma^2 \left\{ (1 - \rho)I + \rho \begin{bmatrix} T & 0 & \dots & 0 \\ 0 & 0 & \dots & 0 \\ \vdots & \vdots & & \\ 0 & 0 & \dots & 0 \end{bmatrix} \right\}. \tag{A.5}$$

Thus, we let

$$\begin{cases} \xi = \sigma^2 [(1 - \rho) + T\rho], \\ \eta = \sigma^2 (1 - \rho). \end{cases} \tag{A.6}$$

Note that there is a one-to-one correspondence between the parameters, ξ and η, and the original parameters, σ^2 and ρ:

$$\begin{cases} \rho = \dfrac{\xi - \eta}{\xi + \eta(T-1)}, \\ \sigma^2 = \dfrac{\xi + \eta(T-1)}{T}. \end{cases} \tag{A.7}$$

Since maximum-likelihood estimates have the property that the estimate of a one-to-one function of a parameter is the function of the maximum-likelihood estimate, it follows that such estimates of the parameters ρ and σ^2 may be obtained by estimating ξ and η instead. Actually, since σ^2 is estimated so readily by (34) once γ and ρ are known, we will need only to obtain ρ from (41), and ξ and η.

The next step in our analysis must be to rewrite the likelihood function in terms of the parameters ξ and η. First, evaluate $|\Omega|$ as

$$|\Omega| = |C^*||\Omega||C^{*\prime}| = |C^*\Omega C^{*\prime}| = \det \begin{bmatrix} \sigma^2 CAC' & 0 & \dots & 0 \\ 0 & \sigma^2 CAC' & \dots & 0 \\ \vdots & \vdots & & \\ 0 & 0 & \dots & \sigma^2 CAC' \end{bmatrix}$$

$$= \det \begin{bmatrix} \xi & 0 & \dots & 0 \\ 0 & \eta & \dots & 0 \\ & & & \\ 0 & 0 & \dots & \eta \end{bmatrix} = \xi^N \eta^{N(T-1)}. \tag{A.8}$$

Next, evaluate $u'\Omega^{-1}u$:

$$u'\Omega^{-1}u = v'C^*\Omega^{-1}C^{*\prime}v = v'[C^*\Omega C^{*\prime}]^{-1}v. \tag{A.9}$$

Finally, $C^*\Omega C^{*\prime} = \mathrm{diag}\{\xi, \eta, \ldots, \eta, \ldots, \xi, \eta, \ldots, \eta\}$, so that

$$[C^*\Omega C^{*\prime}]^{-1} = \mathrm{diag}\left\{\frac{1}{\xi}, \frac{1}{\eta}, \ldots, \frac{1}{\eta}, \ldots, \frac{1}{\xi}, \frac{1}{\eta}, \ldots, \frac{1}{\eta}\right\}. \tag{A.10}$$

Thus, reparameterized, the likelihood function is

$$L(\gamma, \xi, \eta) = -\frac{NT}{2}\log 2\pi - \frac{N}{2}\log \xi - \frac{N(T-1)}{2}\log \eta - \frac{1}{2}\left\{\frac{M_1(\gamma)}{\xi} + \frac{M_2(\gamma)}{\eta}\right\}, \tag{A.11}$$

where

$$M_1(\gamma) = \sum_{n=1}^{N} v_{n1}^2,$$
$$M_2(\gamma) = \sum_{n=1}^{N}\sum_{t=2}^{T} v_{nt}^2. \tag{A.12}$$

If we now differentiate with respect to ξ and η and set the resulting expressions to zero, we obtain

$$\xi = \frac{M_1(\gamma)}{N},$$
$$\eta = \frac{M_2(\gamma)}{N(T-1)}. \tag{A.13}$$

One may readily verify that at this point the second-order conditions for a maximum of L will generally be satisfied if γ is given. If ξ and η from (A.13) are inserted in (A.7), the maximum-likelihood equations for ρ and σ^2 are obtained.

$$\begin{cases} \rho = \dfrac{(T-1)M_1(\gamma) - M_2(\gamma)}{(T-1)[M_1(\gamma) + M_2(\gamma)]}, \\[2ex] \sigma^2 = \dfrac{M_1(\gamma) + M_2(\gamma)}{NT}. \end{cases} \tag{A.14}$$

To complete the derivation of the equations for the determination of the maximum-likelihood estimate, it is necessary to express $M_1(\gamma)$ and $M_2(\gamma)$ of (A.14) in terms of the vector $u = y - X\gamma$ appearing in (33) and (34). From

(A.3) and partitioning v conformably with the earlier partition of u, we have

$$
v_n = \begin{bmatrix} v_{n1} \\ \vdots \\ v_{nT} \end{bmatrix} = Cu_n = \begin{bmatrix} e'/\sqrt{T} \\ C_1 \end{bmatrix} u_n = \begin{bmatrix} \dfrac{1}{\sqrt{T}} \displaystyle\sum_{t=1}^{T} u_{nt} \\ C_1 u_n \end{bmatrix}, \tag{A.15}
$$

so that

$$
M_1(\gamma) = \sum_{n=1}^{N} v_{n1}^2 = \frac{1}{T} \sum_{n=1}^{N} \sum_{t=1}^{T} \sum_{t'=1}^{T} u_{nt} u_{nt'},
$$

$$
M_2(\gamma) = \sum_{n=1}^{N} \sum_{t=2}^{T} v_{nt}^2 = \sum_{n=1}^{N} u_n' C_1' C_1 u_n = \sum_{n=1}^{N} \left\{ \sum_{t=1}^{T} u_{nt}^2 - \frac{\left[\sum_{t=1}^{T} u_{nt} \right]^2}{T} \right\},
$$

$$\tag{A.16}$$

since $C_1' C_1 = I - ee'T$. Equation (35) of the text follows from (A.14) by inserting these results.

THREE

Experimental Evidence on the Estimation of Dynamic Economic Relations from a Time Series of Cross Sections[1]

Preface

> Anyone who considers arithmetical methods of producing random digits, is, of course, in a state of sin.
>
> *John von Neumann*, 1951

Stochastic simulation has been around longer than history. Prior to the nineteenth century, it was used, as in Buffon's needle experiment, to verify a theoretical result, but not until the nineteenth century is stochastic simulation used in a serious attempt to learn about a process by analogy (Stigler, pp. 141–156). Perhaps the most famous example is William S. Gosset's 1908 attempt to discover the properties of the t-distribution. Yule (1926) used stochastic simulation to study the sampling properties of time-series regressions. The term "Monte Carlo" appears to have been introduced by Metropolis and Ulam (1949). Early examples of Monte Carlo in econometrics include Orcutt and Cochrane (1949), Wagner (1958), and Summers (1965). Since the advent of high-speed computers, such studies have become ubiquitous in econometrics (see David Hendry's 1984 survey). The next two chapters reprinted here continue what was to become a commonplace mode of econometric inquiry in the 1970s and 1980s.

Many years ago, when computers were in their infancy, a science-fiction tale appeared that described a computer-simulation model of a human society, complete in every detail and in which individual simulated people existed and went about their daily affairs. The social scientists who created this little world used it experimentally to determine the outcome of various social and economic policies and institutions, but were frustrated in their work by the simulated people who objected to experimentation without representation. The revolt of the simulated people was cut short when the scientists

[1] Reprinted with permission from *The Economic Studies Quarterly, 18*: pp. 42–74, 1967.

rebooted. When statisticians engage in Monte Carlo experimentation, their object is to re-create inside the computer the imagined world of repeated "experiments" of classical, Neyman-Pearson statistical theory: In a Monte Carlo or sampling study, the researcher specifies a theoretical statistical model that reflects the underlying sampling process, *generates* samples of data (each of size, say, T) consistent with this process, develops estimates of the unknown parameters consistent with one or more rules, and analyzes the estimates to determine sampling characteristics. In a stochastic world, economic relationships are disturbed randomly (i.e., what we observe is the outcome of a stochastic data generation process [DGP]); twenty years of data on consumption and income is the outcome of such a DGP; to assess the properties of different estimates of the marginal propensity to consume, we must imagine that the DGP is run again and again, each time generating a sequence of T = 20 observations on consumption and income. If for example, we want to describe the OLS estimates of the marginal propensity to consume from one such run of the DGP that generated the twenty years of data we observe, we must *derive* the distribution of that estimate, or at least some of its moments or other properties, from assumptions on the DGP, *including* its stochastic part. We may not be able to do this analytically, as we can in the case of OLS under standard assumptions about the DGP, but we may be able to approximate certain moments or other properties of the distribution by expansions in powers, possibly fractional, of 1/T; that is to say, *asymptotically*. The problem with asymptotic results is, of course, that they are only approximate; in the case of approximations in powers of 1/T, or *large T asymptotics*, these approximations become better and better as T gets large. But how much better is better and how large does T have to be in order to ensure a certain level of approximation? Sometimes this question can be answered analytically, but more often not. When all the analytical options have been exhausted, all that is left is to turn to a computer simulation of the imaginary Neymann-Pearson world in which experiments are endlessly repeated. Of course, results obtained this way are themselves only approximations and suffer many limitations.

One of the most serious limitations is failure to formulate an experiment that truly captures the essence of the problem. More often than not, this is due to an imperfect *analytical* understanding of the structure of the problem. But, of course, this is why we turn to Monte Carlo in the first place. In the first study, I report a Monte Carlo investigation of the estimation of a simple first-order autoregression from repeated simulated panels. There are no exogenous explanatory variables included. The autoregression to be estimated is assumed to be stationary. The samples used in estimation are produced by starting off the process for whatever parameter values have been chosen at a random observation having the mean and variance of the unconditional distribution, but then run for twice as long as the panel is assumed to be observed. As

Maddala (1975) was later to point out in connection with the derivation of the maximum-likelihood estimates, this does not help resolve the problem of basing the likelihood function on the distribution of the observations conditional on the initial values.

Of the four "problems" raised by the Balestra-Nerlove paper:

(1) upward bias in the coefficient of the lagged dependent variable in the pooled OLS regression
(2) downward bias in this coefficient in the fixed-effects regression
(3) the occurrence of an unacceptable number of boundary solutions at a zero value of the intraclass correlation for maximum-likelihood estimates based on the likelihood function that treated the initial values of the dependent variable as fixed
(4) improved estimates based on feasible GLS using an estimate of the intraclass correlation derived from a first-stage instrumental variables regression

only the first two are reproduced in this study. Boundary solutions for the maximum-likelihood estimates were not obtained. Instrumental variables estimates were unavailable because there were no exogenous explanatory variables present. Although the bias of the fixed-effects estimate was replicated, the Monte Carlo experiment did not reveal the reason for this behavior. Understanding of the nature of that problem had to wait for the publication of Nickell (1981).

References

Gosset, W. S. (1908), "The Probable Error of the Mean," *Biometrika, 6*: pp. 1–24.

Hendry, D. F. (1984), "Monte Carlo Experimentation in Econometrics," in Z. Griliches and M. D. Intriligator, *Handbook of Econometrics, Vol. II*, Chapter 16, pp. 937–976. Amsterdam: Elsevier.

Maddala, G. S. (1994), "Some Problems Arising in Pooling Cross-Section and Time-Series Data," discussion paper, University of Rochester, 1975, first published in Vol. 1, pp. 223–245, G. S. Maddala, *Econometric Methods and Applications*, Aldershot: Edward Elgar Publishers.

Metropolis, N., and S. Ulam (1949), "The Monte Carlo Method," *Journal of the American Statistical Association, 44*: pp. 335–341.

Neumann, J. von (1951), "Various Techniques Used in Connection with Random Digits," *Bureau of Standards Applied Mathematics Series 12*, pp. 36–38.

Nickell, S. (1981), "Biases in Dynamic Models with Fixed Effects." *Econometrica, 49*: pp. 1417–1426.

Orcutt, G. H., and D. Cochrane (1949), "A Sampling Study of the Merits of Autoregressive and Reduced Form Transformations in Regression Analysis," *Journal of the American Statistical Association, 44*: pp. 356–372.

Stigler, S. M. (1999), *Statistics on the Table*, Chapter 7, "Stochastic Simulation in the Nineteenth Century," pp. 141–156. Cambridge, MA: Harvard University Press.

Summers, R. (1965), "A Capital Intensive Approach to the Small Sample Properties of Various Simultaneous Equation Estimators," *Econometrica, 33*: pp. 1–41.

Wagner, H. M. (1958), "A Monte Carlo Study of Estimates of Simultaneous Linear Structural Equations," *Econometrica, 26*: pp. 117–133.

Yule, G. U. (1926), "Why Do We Sometimes Get Nonsense Correlations Between Time Series? – A Study in Sampling and the Nature of Time Series," *Journal of the Royal Statistical Society, 89*: pp. 1–64.

Experimental Evidence on the Estimation of Dynamic Economic Relations from a Time Series of Cross Sections*

By Marc Nerlove

1. BACKGROUND

Data on a number of individual units (e.g., firms, households, geographical areas) over several periods of time are becoming increasingly available. Very often we would like to use such data to estimate a behavior relationship containing an autoregressive component due, possibly, to a distributed lag or other dynamic factor affecting economic behavior. In an earlier study, Balestra and I (1966) studied the demand for natural gas using data on thirty-six states of the United States, over a six-year period. We encountered a number of rather serious methodological problems in attempting to estimate a distributed lag model, which appear to be of more general interest in view of the growing availability of data for individual units over serveral time periods. This paper reports the first of a series of experimental studies designed to explore the general methodological issues involved in studies of this type.

The analysis of Balestra and Nerlove (1966) suggested that consumer demand for natural gas was basically a derived demand from the demand for space heating. Of the two factors of production used to produce space heating, fuel and heating plant, only the former was systematically observable. However, the durability of the second, unobserved factor, led to a model in which there was a distributed lag in the substitution of gas for other fuels. The distribution of lag in the demand for gas was closely related to the depreciation rate for the durable factor in space heating. This interpretation proved crucial in the assessment of various methods of estimation employed.

* Research undertaken at the Cowles Foundation for Research in Economics at Yale University with the support of National Science Foundation Grant GS–818. The author is indebted to Mrs. E. Bockelman for programming assistance and to W. Brainard, F. M. Fisher, E. J. Hannan, T. Koopmans, L. J. Savage, J. Tobin, K. F. Wallis, and A. Zellner for helpful comments. None should be held responsible for remaining errors or other shortcomings; these are the author's alone.

Although the actual model used in the gas study was considerably more complicated than what follows, the latter serves well to illustrate all the essential features. Let observations be available on N individuals (e.g., consuming units, firms, geographical areas, industries) over a period of T time periods. For the i-th individual and the t-th year, we suppose the following relation to hold between the endogenous variable y, the exogenous variable x, and the latent variable u:

$$y_{it} = \alpha y_{it-1} + \beta x_{it} + u_{it}, \quad i = 1, \ldots, N; \ t = 1, \ldots, T. \tag{1}$$

Note that we suppose the autoregressive structure and relation of the endogenous variable y to the exogenous variable x to be the same for every individual at every point in time; we do not, however, argue that the disturbances are independent for all i and t. Indeed, such independence is especially implausible in the present context for, as usual, u_{it} represents, among other things, variables that are left out of the analysis including, in particular, those factors that reflect individual differences that persist through time.[1]

In our investigation of natural-gas demand, we supposed that the disturbances u_{it} were composed of two stochastically independent components with mean zero: an individual, time-invariant effect, μ_i, and a remainder, v_{it}. We further supposed that the μ's were independent for different individuals and that the v_{it} were as well and also serially independent. Thus, it follows that

$$
\begin{cases}
u_{it} = \mu_i + v_{it} \\
E\mu_i = Ev_{it} = 0, \quad \text{all } i \text{ and } t, \\
E\mu_i v_{it} = 0, \quad \text{all } i, i', \text{ and } t, \\
E\mu_i \mu_{i'} = \begin{cases} \sigma_\mu^2, & i = i' \\ 0, & i \neq i', \end{cases} \\
Ev_{it} v_{i't'} = \begin{cases} \sigma_v^2, & i = i', t = t' \\ 0, & \text{otherwise.} \end{cases}
\end{cases}
\tag{2}
$$

Except for the fact that the disturbances u_{it} cannot be observed directly, but only inferred as residuals in the relation between y_{it} and y_{it-1} and x_{it}, the model used in the gas study is a classical one in components of variance analysis and a special case of the so-called random-effects model in the analysis of variance (Fisher, 1946, pp. 222–226). Kuh (1959) used a similar one in his work on the relation between time-series and cross-section estimates, except he did not assume independence of the individual effects, μ_i and time-varying effects, v_{it}, for fixed i. The complexity in our problem, in contrast to both the classical situation and the problem investigated by Kuh, arises because the u_{it}

---

[1] In actual empirical investigations one must, of course, try to take into account explicitly all factors reflecting individual differences that can be measured. In the study of gas demand, for example, weather differences, population, income, and relative prices were used as independent variables. Nonetheless, it is generally impossible to measure and to take into account *all* relevant factors causing time-persistent individual differences; hence, the need for models such as the one described.

can only be inferred by estimation of a relation containing an autoregressive component.[2]

If the observations are arrayed first by individual and then by period, the assumptions of the model can be written in convenient matrix form. Thus, let

$$y' = (y_{11}, \ldots, y_{1T}, \ldots, y_{NT}), \quad y'_{-1} = (y_{10}, \ldots, y_{1T-1}, \ldots, y_{NT-1}),$$
$$x' = (x_{11}, \ldots, x_{1T}, \ldots, x_{NT}), \quad \text{and}$$
$$u' = (u_{11}, \ldots, u_{1T}, \ldots, u_{NT});$$

then (1) and (2) may be written as

$$y = \alpha y_{-1} + \beta x + u$$
$$Eu = 0$$
$$Euu' = \sigma^2 \begin{bmatrix} A & 0 & \cdots & 0 \\ 0 & A & \cdots & 0 \\ \vdots & & & \\ 0 & 0 & \cdots & A \end{bmatrix} = \Omega, \tag{3}$$

where Euu' is a block-diagonal matrix consisting of N blocks of identical matrices A, which are $T \times T$ of the form

$$A = \{(1 - \rho)I_T + \rho e e'\}, \tag{4}$$

---

[2] Note that the way of introducing individual time-invariant effects is as a shift in the *relation* between y_{it} and y_{it-1} and x_{it}. An alternative, suggested to me by J. Tobin, would be to regard the latent variable μ_i as affecting the *level* of y_{it} but not the relation between current and past values of the endogenous variable or the current value and the exogenous variable. Thus, instead of (1) we might have

$$(y_{it} - \mu_i) = \alpha(y_{it-1} - \mu_i) + v_{it}. \tag{1'}$$

The effect of this change is to alter our interpretation of the variance of the disturbance in (1), for now the overall variance of this disturbance becomes

$$\sigma^{*2} = (1 - \alpha)^2 \sigma_\mu^2 + \sigma_v^2,$$

which now depends on α. What we later interpret as the "intraclass correlation" becomes

$$\rho^* = \frac{(1 - \alpha)^2 \sigma_\mu^2}{\sigma^{*2}} \leq \frac{\sigma_\mu^2}{\sigma_\mu^2 + \sigma_v^2}$$

if $0 \leq \alpha \leq 1$.

Tobin's suggestion cannot affect the validity of the findings presented here because, of course, the model (1)–(2) was assumed to be true in the generation of the experimental observations. However, the relevance of these results to the empirical findings of the gas study may be affected, although not necessarily so. Those findings concerning the methods of least squares and least squares with individual constant terms are unaffected; whereas, the maximum-likelihood and two-round methods described later involve a correct interpretation of the disturbance variance and would result in different estimates if (1') rather than (1) were known to be true. The relation between these two types of estimates will be explored in a subsequent paper on the effects of various types of specification errors.

where I_T is an identity matrix of order T, e is a $T \times 1$ vector consisting entirely of ones, and where

$$\rho = \sigma_\mu^2/\sigma^2, \qquad \sigma^2 = \sigma_\mu^2 + \sigma_\nu^2. \tag{5}$$

ρ is the so-called "intraclass correlation." If, in addition, we suppose that the random variables u_i and ν_{it} are normally distributed, it follows that the disturbance vector u will have a multivariate normal distribution with mean vector zero and variance-covariance matrix Ω, as specified in (3)–(5).

In this paper, we consider only cases in which (3)–(5) are assumed to represent a correct specification. Needless to say, (3)–(5) may not correctly characterize the real world as analyzed in our study of the demand for gas, and such misspecification may account for many of the puzzling results we obtained. It is of interest, however, to see whether some or all of the features of our earlier investigation can be reproduced without introducing the possibility of specification error.

It is clear at once that, unless the intraclass correlation ρ is zero, ordinary least squares will yield estimates that are seriously deficient. In particular, the estimate of α should be biased upward for any size sample since ρ, being a ratio of a component of total variance to the total, must necessarily lie between zero and one. Analogously to the more standard situation of first-order serial correlation, we might also expect that the estimate of σ^2 derived from the ordinary least-squares regression should prove too low. In the gas study, the ordinary least-squares estimate of α turned out to be greater than one, thus implying a negative rate of depreciation for the durable factor in space heating. The following Monte Carlo results reported confirm that our earlier rejection of ordinary least squares on the ground of the economic implausibility of negative depreciation was well founded. They also confirm a serious downward bias in the estimate of σ^2 and of the standard error of the estimated α.

In the previous model, the $NT \times 1$ vector of disturbances $u = (u_{11}, \ldots, u_{NT})'$ is assumed to be a sample of one from a multivariate normal population with mean zero and variance-covariance matrix Ω. Now there are several ways to generate such a vector that are completely indistinguishable for fixed N and T, but which may have different implications when N and/or T are allowed to vary. In the Monte Carlo investigations reported, the method of generating u amounted to drawing an $NT \times 1$ vector from the appropriate multivariate normal population; call this way "Mechanism I." An alternative method of generating the vector u, but one precisely equivalent to Mechanism I for fixed N and T, is as follows: Consider two univariate normal populations with means zero and variances σ_μ^2 and $\sigma_\nu^2 = (\frac{1-\rho}{\rho})\sigma_\mu^2$, respectively. Draw a sample of N values μ_i, $i = 1, \ldots, N$ from the first population and a sample of NT values ν_{it}, $i = 1, \ldots, N$, $t = 1, \ldots, T$ from the second. Form the values u_{it} by the sum $u_{it} = \mu_i + \nu_{it}$. Call this way of generating the vector $u = (u_{11}, \ldots, u_{NT})'$ "Mechanism II." For fixed N and T, the properties of the vector u generated either by Mechanism I or by Mechanism II are identical. However, suppose that holding N fixed we were to increase T; we might be tempted in using Mechanism II to leave the original set of $\mu_i's$ and merely to draw additional $v_{it}'s$. In so doing, we create a distinguishable difference between the vectors u generated by the two mechanisms. However, if in increasing T, we drew new $\mu_i's$ as well, the distinction between the two mechanisms would again disappear.

If Mechanisms I and II produce indistinguishable vectors u for fixed N and T, why should we artificially draw a distinction between the two? Indeed, we should not, but an improper interpretation of Mechanism II leads us to an estimation procedure that is seemingly natural but which, in the case of a relation containing an autoregressive component, produces very low-quality estimates of the autoregressive parameter. If we think of the $\mu_i's$ as fixed, is it not natural to treat them as parameters? Then, it would seem that an appropriate estimation procedure would be to introduce separate constant terms for each individual and apply ordinary least squares to the resulting relationship. Thus, let e_i be an $N_T \times 1$ vector consisting entirely of zeros except for the ith block, which consists of ones: $e_i' = (0, \ldots, 0, \ldots, 1, \ldots, 1, \ldots, 0, \ldots, 0)$; then we may rewrite the model as

$$
\begin{cases}
y = \alpha y_{-1} + \beta x + \sum_{i=1}^{N} \mu_i e_i + v \\
\sum_{i=1}^{N} \mu_i = 0 \\
Ev = 0 \\
Evv' = \sigma_v^2 I_{NT},
\end{cases}
\tag{6}
$$

where $v' = (v_{11}, \ldots, v_{1T}, \ldots, v_{NT})$, e_i is a column vector of T ones, and the constraint that the μ's sum to zero has been imposed to preserve the original assumption that the constant term in (1) is zero.[3] As long as N is not very large in relation to T, estimation of α and β by ordinary least squares from a relation containing individual constant terms should be feasible.

Unfortunately, the least-squares estimates of α obtained from a regression including individual constant terms in the gas study turned out to be implausibly low, suggesting an average length of life of only about three years for the durable factor in space heating. We remarked at the time that "The presence of lagged endogenous variables may make it difficult, if not impossible, to separate the individual effects from the effect induced by the lagged variable." Yet, as several critics pointed out, our defense of the rejection of this method was a weak one, especially in view of the apparent naturalness of the use of individual constants. Perhaps the most significant finding in the Monte Carlo experiments reported later is the extent to which estimates of α based on least-squares regressions including individual constant terms are biased

---

[3] Actually, all estimation procedures discussed allow for a nonzero constant, although all experimental data were generated using a relation having a zero constant term.

downward for a wide range of values of both α and the intraclass correlation. Although it is not clear precisely why such underestimation of the autoregressive parameter occurs, the following argument can be made: We are not, in fact, interested in the individual μ_i's but rather only in ρ or σ_μ^2, (i.e., the extent to which variation in the μ_i's causes y_{it} to vary). By treating the μ_i's as constants and estimating them, we must inevitably overestimate σ_μ^2 on account of errors of estimation of each individual μ_i. For T, very large relative to N, this effect should be very slight, but typically N will be substantially larger than T in applications of economic relevance.[4] If such overestimation of σ_μ^2 does not result in a compensating understimation of σ_v^2, there is simply too little variation in y_{it} left over to be explained by variation in y_{it-1} and x_{it}. Thus, α and β should tend to be underestimated in absolute value. Judging from the Monte Carlo results reported, this is precisely what occurs, but it is still a puzzle as to why compensating underestimation of σ_v^2 does not occur. In any event, both our earlier results and those reported here clearly suggest that the information about the stochastic structure of the μ_i's afforded by the model is too important to neglect in estimation.[5]

To use the information on the stochastic structure of the μ_{it}'s most effectively, a maximum-likelihood approach would seem desirable despite its computational complexity. On the assumption that the random variables μ_i and v_{it} are normally and independently distributed, the logarithmic likelihood function, conditional on the initial values $y_{i0}, i = 1, \ldots, N$, is

$$L(\alpha, \beta, \rho, \sigma^2 \mid y, y_{-1}, x) = -\frac{NT}{2} \log 2\pi - \frac{NT}{2} \log |\Omega| - \frac{1}{2} Q(\alpha, \beta, \rho, \sigma^2),$$

(7)

where

$$Q(\alpha, \beta, \rho, \sigma^2) = (y - \alpha y_{-1} - \beta x)' \Omega^{-1} (y - \alpha y_{-1} - \beta x).$$

If ρ were a known value, the maximum-likelihood estimates of α and β would

[4] It is shown that the estimate of α based on a least-squares regression with individual constant terms tends to the same value as the maximum-likelihood estimate of α for known ρ as $T \to \infty$ and $N/T \to 0$ (e.g., fixed N and $T \to \infty$). This is a natural result, inasmuch as the estimate of σ_μ^2 must improve as T increases relative to N.

[5] It might be thought that transformation of the time series for each individual by taking first differences of the original observations would eliminate the problem of the individual time-invariant effects. This approach is used, for example, by Houthakker and Haldi (1960). Unfortunately, such a transformation, while eliminating the individual time-invariant effects, introduces serial correlation into the new disturbance term, which now becomes $v_{it} - v_{it-1}$. If v_{it} is assumed serially uncorrelated to start with, then, of course, the variance-covariance matrix of the new disturbances is known and Aitken's generalized least squares may be applied. Unfortunately, except for the "end-effect" due to the loss of one observation for each individual, the resulting estimates are the same as those obtained when least squares with individual constant terms is employed.

be obtained by minimizing the quadratic form Q (i.e., they would be just the Aitken generalized least-squares estimates). The maximum-likelihood estimate of σ^2 would be obtained as

$$\hat{\sigma}^2 = \frac{(y - \hat{\alpha}y_{-1} - \hat{\beta}x)'\Omega^{*-1}(y - \hat{\alpha}y_{-1} - \hat{\beta}x)}{NT}, \tag{8}$$

where $\Omega^* = \Omega/\sigma^2$. Despite the presence of a lagged endogenous variable, these estimates are asympotically efficient in the sense that the asymptotic distribution is normal and has variance-covariance matrix equal to the Cramèr-Rao lower bound. However, if Ω^* is not known, but merely replaced by a consistent estimate, the resulting estimates of α and β are not generally fully efficient (see Amemiya and Fuller, 1965). The meaning of the asymptotic distribution is not completely clear in this case; for N fixed and $T \to \infty$, it can be shown that the least-squares regressions with individual constant terms and the Aitken generalized least-squares estimates tend to a common value. However, it is questionable whether we would wish to consider the case in which T alone increased. Rather, T and N might increase with the ratio $N/T \to 0$. It has not been shown, at this time, whether estimates of α and β obtained by replacing Ω^* by a consistent estimate are or are not fully efficient.

Even if ρ and, therefore, Ω^* is unknown, the joint maximum-likelihood estimate of $(\alpha, \beta, \rho, \sigma^2)$ is asymptotically efficient in this case, provided such exists (Kendall and Stuart, 1961, pp. 54–56). Since the intraclass correlation is the ratio of a component of total variance to the total, it should lie between zero and one. (While the lower bound might conceivably obtain, the upper cannot if the distribution of u is to remain nonsingular.) Thus, on the assumption that the likelihood function is sufficiently well behaved, the wellknown method of step-wise maximization may be employed (Hood and Koopmans, 1953, pp. 156–158). In the present context, this method amounts to computing the generalized least-squares estimates of α and β and the corresponding estimate of σ^2 for various fixed values of ρ, and then replacing the parameters in L by these estimates and the fixed values of ρ. The maximum value of the likelihood function may then be determined numerically. Those values of α, β, σ^2, and ρ that lead to the maximum are, of course, the joint maximum-likelihood estimates.

While full maximum likelihood no doubt possesses considerable appeal, there are at least three possible complications: First, for a particular given set of observations that maximum of L may fail to occur for values of ρ within the half-open interval $[0, 1)$. Were the interval closed, we could be sure a maximum with respect to ρ would occur either within or on the boundary of $[0, 1]$ provided L were a continuous function of ρ throughout that interval. Unfortunately, L is not a continuous function of ρ at $\rho = 1$, nor is the interval fully closed. Furthermore, a maximum may occur at the boundary point $\rho = 0$ or fail to exist altogether with positive probability even though the true value of ρ lies well within the interval. The former possibility is disturbing both in light of the fact that we know the ordinary least-squares estimates are seriously deficient and because it will be impossible to obtain any sort of asymptotic standard errors should the maximum actually occur at the lower boundary point since derivatives of the likelihood function fail to exist there. Second, it is not at all clear that the maximum-likelihood estimates will possess desirable small-sample properties. In particular, if the true value of ρ is close to one, we might expect that at least some of the maximum likelihood estimates may become exceedingly erratic simply because the expression $1 - \rho$ is involved in $|\Omega^*|$ and Ω^{*-1} (explained later). Third, it is plausible in view of these possibilities that the maximum-likelihood method may be extremely sensitive to errors of specification. Such sensitivity has, in fact, been demonstrated in numerous other contexts (e.g., Tiao and Tan, 1965).

While the Monte Carlo results reported do not shed any light on the robustness of the maximum-likelihood approach in this context, they do suggest that our distrust is not entirely without foundation on other grounds. Furthermore, the earlier results of the gas study led to rejection of the maximum-likelihood approach on grounds of the economic implausibility of the estimates. When the numerical procedure outlined previously was employed on the gas data, we found that – at least for the particular set of observations at hand – the maximum value of the likelihood function for values of ρ in $[0, 1)$ occurred at the boundary point $\rho = 0$. The result thus implied that the ordinary least-squares estimates, correct only for $\rho = 0$, were, in fact, the full maximum-likelihood estimates.[6] These we had already rejected since they implied a negative rate of depreciation for the durable factor in space heating. That these unfortunate results might be due to specification error, rather than any inherent defect of the method, was suggested by some rather whimsical calculations in which we estimated ρ and α neglecting all exogenous variables originally appearing in the problem. In this case, the likelihood function reversed its direction of increase and did not achieve any maximum at all for ρ in $[0, 1)$. The Monte Carlo results suggest that both the first and the second possible source of difficulty mentioned in the preceding paragraph may be of practical importance when both ρ and α are large.

Despite the fact that a two-step estimation procedure in which Ω^* is estimated consistently and then inserted in (7) which is then maximized with respect to α and β, does not generally result in estimates which are fully efficient nor ones for which it is easy to obtain good approximations to the relevant

[6] In an apparently similar but actually different context, Konijn (1963) demonstrated that this sort of boundary solution with $\rho = 0$ must occur. However, an important element in his proof is that the individual means (over time) of each independent variable must be equal for any pair of individuals. (Konijn has them all zero, but this represents no loss of generality beyond the assumption of equality.) Not only is this rather unlikely in most meaningful economic contexts, but it is also simply impossible when the regression equation contains an autoregressive component. In this case, initial differences in the values of the disturbance term must produce differences in the means of y_{it-1} over time among individuals.

standard errors, the difficulties with maximum likelihood suggest at least a fair trial. In the gas study we used an instrumental variable approach to obtain a consistent estimate of Ω^* which was then used in a generalized least-squares calculation to obtain second-round estimates of α and β. The results turned out to accord fully with our economic intuition. Given the tortuous route by which we arrived at our procedure, however, it seems worthwhile to explore its properties in other contexts and in considerably more detail before recommending its general use. It is to this end that the present series of experiments is directed. In those reported here, exogenous variables are not included in the relationship to be estimated; however, a very close relative of the instrumental variable, two-round approach employed in the gas study is investigated. The results are sufficiently encouraging to warrant a more detailed series of Monte Carlo experiments on the instrumental variable two-round procedure, and these will be reported in a subsequent paper.

2. DESIGN OF THE EXPERIMENTS

The series of experiments reported here involved the implementation of three types of decisions: (1) the choice of model; (2) the manner in which observations would be generated and quantity in which they would be generated; and (3) the methods of estimation that would be analyzed and the manner of the analysis. All of these aspects of the design and analysis of the initial set of experiments reported are discussed in this subsection.

a. Generation of the Observations

As indicated the model chosen for the first series of experiments involved no exogenous variables. Furthermore, no attempt was made in this series to investigate the effects of specification error. The model was

$$y = \alpha y_{-1} + u, \tag{9}$$

where the $NT \times 1$ vector u was distributed according to a multivariate normal distribution with mean vector 0 and variance-covariance matrix Ω defined in (3)–(5). It was necessary to generate a series of NT observations on the endogenous variable (i.e., a $NT \times 1$ vector y) for various assumed numerical values of α, ρ, and σ^2, it was necessary to repeat this step many times so that the distributions of various estimators of α, ρ, and σ^2 might be numerically determined. Since N is several times as large as T in most economically relevant contexts, we chose $N = 25$ and $T = 10$.

The basic starting point for all Monte Carlo calculations is the random number generator. Only a true random process may, of course, produce real random numbers. To approximate such a process digitally in machines with a thirtysix-bit word recursion relations of the form

$$R_{n+1} = C R_n (\mod 2^{35})$$ (10)

are used to produce a sequence of numbers $R_0, R_1, R_2, \ldots$ which simulate the behavior of a true random sequence (i.e., so-called "pseudorandom numbers"). (For a discussion of various methods for generating pseudorandom numbers and the problems arising, see Hammersley and Handscomb, 1964, pp. 25–42). Not only do such sequences repeat after a certain point, but they also tend to exhibit certain forms of nonrandom behavior. Hence, when generating long sequences of such numbers, it is desirable to use several generators (i.e., relations of the form [10]) with differently chosen C and R_0. In the calculations reported here, five such generators were used in such a way that no generator was ever started at a previous starting point, and in such a way that the particular generator used to produce a number in the ultimate sequence was itself determined through the use of one of the generators. It is believed that the sequence of numbers thus obtained is subject to very few of the difficulties and problems to which most sequences of pseudorandom numbers are beset. The numbers resulting were transformed into pseudorandom variables uniformly distributed on the interval $[0, 1]$. Pairs of such numbers were in turn transformed to independent normal variates with mean zero and variance one by means of the transformation

$$\begin{cases} w_1 = (-2\log v_1)^{\frac{1}{2}} \cos(2\pi v_2) \\ w_2 = (-2\log v_1)^{\frac{1}{2}} \sin(2\pi v_2), \end{cases}$$ (11)

where (v_1, v_2) is a pair of uniformly and independently distributed random variables (Hammersley and Handscomb, 1964).

Because the present series of experiments was designed to examine the properties of various estimators of α, ρ, and σ^2 assuming correct specification of the underlying model, the squence of w's, independent normal, zero mean, unit variance, had next to be transformed into $NT \times 1$ vectors u distributed according to a multivariate normal with mean vector zero and variance-covariance matrix Ω as given in (3)–(5). Naturally, this transformation was dependent on the particular values of ρ and σ^2 chosen. In general, the best way in which to obtain a vector u coming from a population $N(\theta, \Omega)$ on the basis of a series of random variables $w_i \sim n(0, 1)$ is to make use of the unique decomposition of any real, positive semidefinite matrix into the product of a lower triangular matrix and its transpose:

$$\Omega = \sigma^2 T T'.$$ (12)

Then $u = Tw + \theta \sim N(\theta, \Omega)$, where each element of w is $n(0, 1)$. The elements of T may be found by a simple system of recursions. Such a general solution to the problem, however, does not permit us to take advantage of the very simple structure of Ω, in particular of the fact that it depends on only two parameters.

Thus, in these experiments we made use of the square root of Ω defined as that matrix with characteristic roots equal to the square roots of the characteristic roots of Ω (all real and positive because of the positive definiteness of Ω).

To obtain $\Omega^{\frac{1}{2}}$, one makes use of the orthogonal transformation

$$C = \begin{bmatrix} e'/\sqrt{T} \\ C_1 \end{bmatrix}, \tag{13}$$

where e is a $T \times 1$ vector consisting entirely of ones and C_1 is a $T - 1 \times T$ matrix such that

$$\begin{cases} C_1 e = 0 \\ C_1 C_1' = I_{\tau-1} \\ C_1' C_1 = I_{\tau - ee'} / T. \end{cases} \tag{14}$$

As shown in Balestra and Nerlove (1966)

$$\sigma^2 C A C' = \begin{bmatrix} \xi & 0 & \cdots & 0 \\ 0 & \eta & & \\ \vdots & \vdots & & \\ 0 & 0 & \cdots & \eta \end{bmatrix}, \tag{15}$$

where

$$\begin{cases} \xi = \sigma^2[(1-\rho) + T\rho] \\ \eta = \sigma^2(1-\rho). \end{cases} \tag{16}$$

Thus, we have

$$\Omega^{\frac{1}{2}} = \begin{bmatrix} B & 0 & \cdots & 0 \\ 0 & B & \cdots & 0 \\ \vdots & \vdots & & \vdots \\ 0 & 0 & \cdots & B \end{bmatrix}, \tag{17}$$

where each of the N blocks B is a $T \times T$ matrix of the form

$$B = C' \text{diag}\{\sqrt{\xi}, \sqrt{\eta}, \dots, \sqrt{\eta}\}C \tag{18}$$

$$= \sqrt{\eta} I_T + \frac{\sqrt{\xi} - \sqrt{\eta}}{T} ee'.$$

Thus, an element of the $NT \times 1$ vector u is obtained as

$$u_{it} = \frac{\sqrt{\xi} - \sqrt{\eta}}{T} \sum_{h=1}^{T} w_h + \sqrt{\eta} w_\tau, \quad t = 1, \dots, T, \tag{19}$$

where $w_1, \dots, w_\tau$ is a sequence of independent normal variables with zero mean and unit variance. Note that N such sets of Tw's are required to generate the full $NT \times 1$ vector u.

Having obtained a set of NT variables u_{it} with the required property, the observations y_{it} may now be generated from (9) given N initial values y_{i0}, $i = 1, \ldots, N$. The initial values were determined for each choice of α, ρ, and σ^2 by taking

$$y_{i0} = \frac{u_{i0}}{\sqrt{1 - \alpha^2}}, \quad i = 1, \ldots, N. \tag{20}$$

T was chosen twice as large as the number of observations used in each experiment; only the last half of each set of observations on y_{it} was used to remove any possible transient. Actually, such precautions might be considered excessive in view of (20), which, for $|\alpha| < 1$, implies y_{i0} has the same variance as any y_{it} no matter how far out in the sequence.

b. Parameter Values

In the experiments reported here, $T = 10$, $N = 25$ and α was chosen to have the values 0.0, 0.1, 0.5, and 0.9. For each value of α so chosen, ρ was given successive values of 0.00, 0.05, 0.10 (0.10), 0.90, 0.95, and 0.99. Throughout, we took $\sigma^2 = 1$. For each set of parameter values, fifty sets of observations were generated and for each of these sets, five different estimates of α and σ^2 and two of ρ were computed. As it turned out, there is some evidence that fifty runs was not sufficient to produce a stable distribution for certain true values of the parameters. This is discussed in more detail in the next subsection.

c. Methods of Estimation

As indicated in the previous subsection, were ρ a known value, the generalized least-squares of α and the corresponding estimate of σ^2 would possess a large number of desirable properties. Unbiasedness of α for finite samples is not one, however. Both to assess the extent of the small sample bias in the estimate of α under ideal conditions and to have a useful standard of comparison for other methods of estimation, the generalized least-squares estimates were computed.

Table 1 summarizes the moments used in the calculation of the various estimates. Tables 2 through 5 summarize the formulae used to compute the estimates of α, ρ, and σ^2 and the standard error of the estimated α by generalized least squares, ordinary least squares, least squares with individual constant terms, and a two-round procedure in which ρ is replaced by a consistent estimate based on the variance of the individual constant terms in a least-squares regression equation containing such terms. Maximum-likelihood estimates of α, ρ, and σ^2 were obtained numerically as shown in Table 2.

Since the intraclass correlation lies in the interval $[0, 1)$ and since given a value of ρ, the maximum-likelihood estimates of α and σ^2 are those given in

Table 1. *Moments Used in*
Calculating the Estimates

$$\bar{y}_{i\cdot} = \frac{1}{T}\sum_{\tau} y_{it}$$

$$\bar{y}_{i-1} = \frac{1}{T}\sum_{\tau} y_{it-1}$$

$$\bar{y}_{\cdot\cdot} = \frac{1}{NT}\sum_{i,t} y_{it}$$

$$\bar{y}_{\cdot-1} = \frac{1}{NT}\sum_{i,t} y_{it-1}$$

$$M_{00} = \frac{1}{NT}\sum_{i,t} (y_{it} - \bar{y}_{\cdot\cdot})^2$$

$$M_{01} = \frac{1}{NT}\sum_{i,t} (y_{it} - \bar{y}_{\cdot\cdot})(y_{it-1} - \bar{y}_{\cdot-1})$$

$$M_{11} = \frac{1}{NT}\sum_{i,t} (y_{it-1} - \bar{y}_{\cdot-1})^2$$

Table 2. *Generalized Least-Squares Estimates*

Estimate of α:

$$\hat{\alpha} = \frac{M_{01} - \frac{\delta}{N}\sum_i (\bar{y}_{i\cdot} - \bar{y}_{\cdot\cdot})(\bar{y}_{i-1} - \bar{y}_{\cdot-1})}{M_{11} - \frac{\delta}{N}\sum_i (\bar{y}_{i1} - \bar{y}_{\cdot-1})^2},$$

where

$$\delta = \frac{T\sigma}{1 - \rho + T\sigma}.$$

Estimate of σ^2:

$$\hat{\sigma}^2 = \frac{1}{1-\rho}\left\{ [M_{00} - \hat{\alpha} M_{01}] \right.$$
$$\left. - \frac{T\sigma}{1 - \rho + T\sigma}\left[\frac{\sum_i (\bar{y}_{i\cdot} - \bar{y}_{\cdot\cdot})^2}{N} - \hat{\alpha}\frac{\sum_i (\bar{y}_{i\cdot} - \bar{y}_{\cdot\cdot})(\bar{y}_{i-1} - \bar{y}_{\cdot-1})}{N} \right]\right\}.$$

Estimate of the standard error of $\hat{\alpha}$:

$$S.E._{\hat{\alpha}} = \left[\frac{(1-\rho)\hat{\sigma}^2}{M_{11} - \frac{\delta}{N}\sum_i (\bar{y}_{i-1} - \bar{y}_{\cdot-1})_2} \right]^{\frac{1}{2}}.$$

Table 3. *Ordinary Least-Squares Estimates*

Estimate of α:

$$a = \frac{M_{01}}{M_{11}}.$$

Estimate of σ^2:

$$s^2 = M_{00} - a\,M_{01}^*.$$

Estimate of the standard error of a:

$$S.E._c = \left[\frac{s^2}{M_{11}}\right]^{\frac{1}{2}}.$$

---

* Note that there is no correction for loss of degrees of freedom in order that this estimate be comparable with all the other estimates of σ^2.

Table 2, namely the generalized least-squares estimates $\hat{\alpha}$ and $\hat{\sigma}^2$, the obvious procedure is to pick a value of ρ, say ρ_0. Then we compute $\hat{\alpha}(\rho_0)$ and $\hat{\sigma}(\rho_0)$ as the generalized least-squares estimates using the formulae in Table 2 for $\rho = \rho_0$. The likelihood function we wish to maximize with respect to α, σ^2, and

Table 4. *Estimates Based on Least-Squares Regressions Containing Individual Constant Terms*

Estimate of α:

$$a_c = \frac{\sum_{i,t}(y_{it} - \bar{y}_{i\cdot})(y_{it-1} - \bar{y}_{i-1})}{\sum_{i,t}(y_{it-1} - \bar{y}_{i-1})^2}.$$

Estimate of ρ:

$$r = \frac{\sum_i (b_i - \bar{b})^2}{\sum_i (b_i - \bar{b})^2 + N s_v^2},$$

where

$$b_i = \bar{y}_{i\cdot} - a_c \bar{y}_{i-1},$$

and s_v^2 is an estimate of σ_v^2.
Estimate of σ^2:

$$s_c^2 = \frac{1}{1-r}\left\{\frac{\sum_{i,t}(y_{it} - \bar{y}_{i\cdot})^2}{NT} - a_c \frac{\sum_{i,t}(y_{it} - \bar{y}_{i\cdot})(y_{it-1} - \bar{y}_{i-1})}{NT}\right\}.$$

Estimate of the standard error of a_c:

$$S.E._{a_c} = \left[\frac{(1-r)s_c^2}{\sum_{i,t}(y_{it-1} - \bar{y}_{i-1})^2/NT}\right]^{\frac{1}{2}}.$$

Table 5. *Two-Round Estimates Using an Estimate of ρ Derived from Least-Squares Regressions Containing Individual Constant Terms*

Estimate of α:

$$\hat{\alpha} = \frac{M_{01} - \frac{d}{N}\sum_i(\bar{y}_i. - \bar{y}..)(\bar{y}_{i-1} - \bar{y}._{-1})}{M_{11} - \frac{d}{N}\sum_i(\bar{y}_{i-1} - \bar{y}._{-1})^2},$$

where

$$d = \frac{Tr}{1 - r + Tr}.$$

r being defined in Table 4.
Estimate of σ^2:

$$\hat{\sigma}^2 = \frac{1}{1-r}\left\{[M_{00} - \hat{\alpha}M_{01}] - d\left[\frac{\sum_i(\bar{y}_i. - \bar{y}..)^2}{N} - \hat{\alpha}\frac{\sum_i -(\bar{y}_i.\bar{y}..)(\bar{y}_{i-1} - \bar{y}._{-1})}{N}\right]\right\}$$

No estimate of the standard error of $\hat{\alpha}$ is obtained.

ρ is:

$$L(\alpha, \rho, \sigma^2 \mid y, y_{-1}) = -\frac{NT}{2}\log 2\pi - \frac{N}{2}\log\xi - \frac{N(T-1)}{2}\log\eta$$
$$-\frac{1}{2}Q(\alpha, \rho, \sigma^2 \mid y, y_{-1}), \tag{21}$$

where

$$\xi = \sigma^2[(1 - \rho) + T\rho],$$
$$\eta = \sigma^2(1 - \rho),$$

and

$$\frac{1}{NT}Q(\alpha, \rho, \sigma^2 \mid y, y_{-1}) = \frac{1}{\eta}[M_{00} - 2\alpha M_{01} + \alpha^2 M_{11}] + \left(\frac{1}{\xi} - \frac{1}{\eta}\right)$$
$$\times\left[\sum_i\frac{(\bar{y}_i. - \bar{y}..)^2}{N} - 2\alpha\sum_i\frac{(\bar{y}_i. - \bar{y}..)(\bar{y}_{i-1} - \bar{y}._{-1})}{N}\right.$$
$$\left. + \alpha^2\sum_i\frac{(\bar{y}_{i-1} - \bar{y}._{-1})^2}{N}\right].$$

Inserting $\hat{\alpha}(\rho_0)$ and $\hat{\sigma}^2(\rho_0)$, we obtain the concentrated likelihood function:

$$\hat{L}(\rho_0) = -\frac{NT}{2}\log 2\pi - \frac{N}{2}\log\hat{\sigma}^2(\rho_0)[(1 - \rho_0) + T\rho_0]$$
$$-\frac{N(T-1)}{2}\log\hat{\sigma}^2(\rho_0)[1 - \rho_0] - \frac{NT}{2}. \tag{22}$$

The moments M_{00}, M_{01}, and M_{11} are defined in Table 1. Provided ρ_0 is in $[0, 1)$, $\hat{L}(\rho_0)$ has a well-defined value. This value may be computed for any ρ_0 in $[0, 1)$ and that value of ρ_0 found for which $\hat{L}(\rho_0)$ is the largest. Provided the function $\hat{L}(\rho_0)$ actually reaches a maximum within the interval (it may not since the interval is open at one end and $\hat{L}$ is not continuous there), the maximizing value of ρ, say $\hat{\rho}$, can be approximated as closely as one wishes. Clearly, $\hat{\alpha}(\hat{\rho})$, $\hat{\sigma}^2(\hat{\rho})$, and $\hat{\rho}$ are the maximum-likelihood estimates. In the following computations, a twenty-one-point grid was laid down in the interval $[0, 1]$ consisting of the points 0.00, $(.05)$, 0.95, and 0.99. For ρ_0 equal each of these values $\hat{L}(\rho_0)$ was computed. A finer grid would clearly have given more accurate results, but would probably not have altered the conclusions reached. Needless to say, however, more experience is needed in this sort of computation before we can say very definitively whether the increased sensitivity of a finer grid (or of a gradient procedure) is a net gain or a net loss on balance.

Provided the maximizing value of ρ is not on the boundary of the set $[0, 1)$, the asymptotic variance-covariance matrix of the estimates is given by the standard result (Kendall and Stuart, 1961, p. 55). In this case, for var $(\hat{\alpha})$ the formula reduces to

$$\text{var}(\hat{\alpha}) = \frac{\frac{\partial^2 L}{\partial \eta^2} \cdot \frac{\partial^2 L}{\partial \xi^2}}{\left(\frac{\partial^2 L}{\partial \eta \partial \alpha}\right)^2 \cdot \frac{\partial^2 L}{\partial \xi^2} + \left(\frac{\partial^2 L}{\partial \xi \partial \alpha}\right)^2 \cdot \frac{\partial^2 L}{\partial \eta^2} - \frac{\partial^2 L}{\partial \alpha^2} \cdot \frac{\partial^2 L}{\partial \eta^2} \cdot \frac{\partial^2 L}{\partial \xi^2}}, \tag{23}$$

where the partial derivatives of L in (21) are evaluated at $\alpha = \hat{\alpha}(\hat{\rho})$, $\xi = \hat{\sigma}(\hat{\rho})[(1 - \hat{\rho}) + T\hat{\rho}]$, and $\eta = \hat{\sigma}(\hat{\rho})[1 - \hat{\rho}]$. This result can be written down solely in terms of the quantities $M_{00} \cdots y_{.-1} \cdots y_i. \cdots$ etc. defined previously, but to do so would serve no purpose here. Other elements of the asymptotic variance-covariance matrix can also be derived, but these were not computed in the experiments reported here. The asymptotic standard error of $\hat{\alpha}$ is obtained by taking the square root of $\text{var}(\hat{\alpha})$.

While Tables 1 through 5 are largely self-explanatory, a number of points deserve special comments:

First, note that the generalized least-squares estimates of α, as reported in Table 1, are obtained by correcting the numerator and denominator of the least-squares estimate by factors that depend on ρ and the deviations of the "within-group" means from the overall means. When $\rho = 0$, $\hat{\alpha}$ reduces to the ordinary least-squares estimate, as it does also when $\bar{y}_{i-1} = \bar{y}_{.-1}$ for $i = 1, \ldots, N$.[7] We see also that $\delta \to 1$ as $T \to \infty$; for fixed N, it thus follows from the definitions of M_{01} and M_{11} that $\hat{\alpha} \to a_c$ as $T \to \infty$. Thus, for fixed N, the generalized least-squares estimates and the estimates based on ordinary

---

[7] The condition $\bar{y}_{i-1} = \bar{y}_{.-1}$ corresponds to the condition required to prove Konijn's result referred to in Footnote 6. Clearly, this condition is not relevant in most economic applications nor even possible of realization in the present Monte Carlo calculations.

least-squares but applied to equations containing individual constant terms, tend to a common value. Furthermore, since r is a consistent estimate of ρ, for $N, T \to \infty$ such that $N/T \to 0$, the two-round estimate of $\hat{\alpha}$ will tend in probability to this common value as will the maximum-likelihood estimate if one exists, the limit being taken for $N, T \to \infty$ in such a way that $N/T \to 0$.

Second, it is also true for fixed N, that $\hat{\sigma}^2 \to s_c^2$ as $T \to \infty$, and the probability limit of the maximum likelihood estimate, if it exists, for $N, T \to \infty$ such that $N/T \to 0$, is this common value.

Finally, since the two-round estimates are not maximum-likelihood, the usual convenient results regarding asymptotic standard errors are not available. Furthermore, since the second-round estimates are not generally fully efficient asymptotically when a lagged dependent variable is present, we cannot use the result of Table 2 either. Although theoretically possible, it would be quite difficult to obtain even asymptotic results in this case and standard errors for α estimated by the two-round method have not been computed.

3. THE RESULTS

For each set of parameter values chosen, fifty sets of observations (y, y_{-1}) were generated as described in the previous subsection. For each of these sets of observations, five different estimates of α and σ^2 were computed according to the formulae presented in the previous subsection. In all cases, $T = 10$, $N = 25$. For all of the methods but the last, asymptotic standard errors were computed. Finally, two of the methods, least squares with individual constant terms and maximum likelihood, permitted estimation of the intraclass correlation, ρ. Thus, for each set of parameter values, we had sixteen estimates computed for each of fifty samples. Since every set of computations was repeated for fifty-two parameter values:

$$\begin{cases} \alpha = 0.0, 0.1, 0.5, 0.9 \\ \rho = 0.0, 0.05, 0.1(0.1), 0.9, 0.95, 0.99, \\ \sigma^2 = 1, \end{cases} \tag{24}$$

there were altogether $52 \times 16 \times 50 = 41{,}600$ numbers to summarize.

For each of the $52 \times 16 = 832$ distributions, the maximum, minimum, median, and first and third quantiles were computed. Except, however, in a few instances these summary measures did not prove very useful, principally because except in the few instances referred to the distributions were more or less symmetrical. For each of the 832 distributions, the mean value was computed. Except for the $4 \times 52 = 208$ distributions of estimated standard errors, the mean-square error (squared bias plus variance) was also computed. For the distributions of estimated standard errors, on the other hand, only the variance of the distribution was computed. The entire distribution for each set of parameter values was printed out so that different methods of estimation might be compared for the same set of observations. However, this has not led to any useful insights as yet.

Tables A.1–E. 2 in the appendix to this paper contain a number of summary measures. The first letter refers to the method of estimation, the second to the parameter being estimated. Thus,

A———generalized least squares
B———ordinary least squares
C———least squares with individual constant terms
D———maximum likelihood, 21-point grid
E———two-round using ρ estimated from least-squares regression including individual constant terms.

The first table of each two-table set reports the mean and mean-square error for the estimate of α obtained by the method in question for each of the fiftytwo combinations of α and ρ (recall $\sigma^2 = 1$ throughout). In the first four sets of tables (i.e., all except those for the two-round method), the mean of the estimated standard error of the α estimate is reported in parentheses to one side of the mean of the distribution of α estimates for that combination of parameter values. The variances of the distributions of the standard errors were exceedingly small and it did not seem worthwhile to report these results in any detail. In the two tables referring to least-squares with individual constant terms and maximum likelihood, the mean and mean-square error of the estimated intraclass correlation is also reported in a column just to the right of the corresponding results for the estimate of α. Standard errors were not computed for the estimates of ρ and, therefore, are not reported.

The second table of each two-table set reports the estimates of σ^2 for each parameter combination for the method in question. These estimates are important primarily because of the frequent reliance on measures of goodness of fit in the assessment of results. Because the variance of y_{it} depends on the parameters α and ρ, the correlation between y_{it} and y_{it-1} does also. It seems desirable to have a measure of goodness of fit that does not depend on the parameters. This might be accomplished in either of two ways: given α and ρ, a value of σ^2 might be chosen so as to make the true correlation of y_{it} and y_{it-1} equal to a fixed constant; or we may simply hold σ^2 fixed in all experiments and examine various estimates of it rather than estimates of the correlation. The latter alternative has been chosen in the series of experiments reported here. Both the mean and the mean-square error are reported for each method of estimation and combination of parameter values. Note that the estimate presented in Table C.2 for least squares with individual constant terms is not the usual estimate of residual variance, but that plus the variance of the individual constant terms.

In what follows, we examine the results obtained by each method in turn and then compare methods for various parameter combinations.

a. Generalized Least Squares

As indicated earlier, although the generalized least-squares estimates are not relevant from a practical point of view, they do offer a useful standard of comparison. In particular, the small sample bias known to exist even under ideal circumstances in the estimation of autoregressive models may be evaluated for the model considered here. Tables A.1 and A.2 present estimates of $\hat{\alpha}$ and $\hat{\sigma}^2$ for this method.

For all combinations of parameter values, the mean-square error is extremely small in the estimation of α, never amounting to more than 0.006. The smallest mean-square errors of estimate are obtained for the larger values of α. The pattern of bias is not completely systematic, which leads one to suspect that fifty repetitions of each experiment may have been too small a number. In general, $\hat{\alpha}$ appears to understate α for small values of ρ and to overstate it for large, the point at which the change occurs is sooner the higher the true value of α. In all cases, however, the bias is very slight. This should perhaps have been expected for $\rho = 0$, for then, in effect, the sample is a large one ($= 25 \times 10 = 250$). On the other hand, as ρ increases, there is a sense in which the effective sample size falls. This should but does not appear to be reflected in increasing small sample bias. Only in the case of $\alpha = 0.90$ and intermediate values of ρ do the bias and the rather small standard errors give a misleading picture.

The mean-square errors of the estimates of σ^2 are noticeably larger than those for $\hat{\alpha}$. On the whole, there is a distinct tendency to underestimate σ^2, albeit very slightly.

b. Ordinary Least Squares

Except in the case $\rho = 0$ when they are equal to the generalized least-squares estimates, the estimates obtained by ordinary least squares are known to be seriously deficient. Just how awful the ordinary least-squares estimates are, however, is difficult to appreciate *a priori*. For low a, the estimate progressively deteriorates with increasing ρ; indeed, for $\alpha = 0.0$ and 0.1, α appears to be a better estimate of ρ than of α. For larger values of α, the situation is somewhat improved; although a consistently overestimates α by substantial amounts, the extent of overestimation is reduced the larger α. As one might expect, the estimated standard error of a gives no hint as to its serious shortcomings. The estimates of residual variance derived from these regressions substantially underestimate σ^2. The larger ρ, the more serious the underestimation, and the larger α, the more serious the underestimation when $\rho \geq 0.20$. It may be that the apparent anomaly for $\rho < 0.20$ is due simply to the fact that fifty repetitions are not sufficient to establish the regularity in this range.

c. Least Squares with Individual Constant Terms

Perhaps the most important and striking finding of the present series of experiments is the extent of the deficiencies in the estimates obtained by least squares with individual constant terms. In the original gas study, we thought the implausibility of the estimates obtained in this way might be due to deficiencies connected with the loss of an excessive number of degrees of freedom. It is clear, however, from the results presented here that the difficulties with these estimates stem from more fundamental causes and have more far-ranging implications.

It will be seen from Table C. 1 that the estimate of α is systematically biased downward, while the estimate of ρ obtained from the estimates of the constants and of the residual variance is systematically biased upward. The severity of the bias in both cases is less for large values of both α and ρ. However, for fixed ρ, the larger α, the greater the bias in ρ. Indeed, for small ρ, the effect is quite substantial. On the other hand, for fixed α the bias in a_c hardly seems to vary with ρ at all, while for fixed ρ, the bias and mean-square error of a_c exhibits a complex pattern generally rising with α for the lower values of ρ, but falling with α for the larger values of ρ after an initial rise. Although the estimated standard errors of a_c are, for the most part, substantially larger than for ordinary least squares, they too give little indication of the deficiencies in the estimate.

The estimates of σ^2 reported in Table C.2 are substantial overestimates. Furthermore, the estimates exhibit extremely erratic behavior with respect to variations in α and ρ, and particularly with respect to variations in ρ for $\alpha = 0.90$. Overestimation of ρ by r is clearly responsible for the overestimation of σ^2 by s_c^2. Some of the reasons for this overestimation are the subject of previous comments. It is the interplay between errors in the estimation of ρ and those in the estimation of σ_v^2 that result in the erratic behavior of s_c^2. Just what determines this, however, must be the subject of further investigation.

d. Maximum Likelihood

Tables D.1 and D.2 report the maximum likelihood estimates of α, ρ, and σ^2 based on a 21-point grid for ρ in the interval $(0, 1)$, as described in the previous subsection. As in the case of least squares with individual constant terms, there is a definite tendency to underestimate α and to overestimate ρ, at least for small and moderate values of ρ. For larger values of ρ, there appears to be a slight tendency to overestimate α when it is low and to underestimate it when it is high. On the other hand, the estimates of ρ appear to improve. Appearances are deceptive, however, and a closer examination of the distributions of ρ suggest that the apparent improvement is simply the result of having a grid in which the largest value of ρ was 0.99. In every instance when the true value was 0.99 and even for lower values, the distributions were highly skewed, especially for larger values of α. In the gas study, it will be recalled, we found that the maximum likelihood estimate had a most disturbing tendency to hit up against a boundary point, in that case $\rho = 0$. Here, of course, the set of admissible values does not include the boundary point $\rho = 1.0$, but the same tendency exists. Such behavior does not rule out the method by any means, but it does suggest that the results may be quite difficult to interpret properly for certain combinations of the parameters.

Turning to Table C.2, we see that, especially for large values of ρ and α, the maximum likelihood estimates of σ^2 are quite wild. This is perhaps to be expected in view of the form of the likelihood function, and suggests yet another reason for distrust of the method. The rise and then fall of $\hat{\sigma}^2$ for $\alpha = 0.50$ and $\alpha = 0.90$ for successively higher values of ρ is due in all probability to the fact that ρ is constrained to be 0.99 or less. Were ρ allowed beyond the interval, a more monotonic pattern might have resulted.

e. Two Round

Tables E.1 and E.2 report similar results for the two-round method of estimation. The estimate of α is biased downward, but the bias decreases as the value of ρ increases. The mean-square error of the estimate decreases with increasing ρ for $\alpha = 0.9$; its behavior is nonmonotonic and somewhat erratic for smaller values of α. Mean-square error tends to increase for fixed ρ and increasing α when ρ is 0.6 or less, but shows a nonmonotonic pattern for ρ larger than 0.6. Estimates of σ^2 follow much the same pattern as the corresponding maximum-likelihood estimates, but the bias for large α is substantially less. When α is large, the variance of y_{it} becomes very large; hence, an upward bias in the estimate of residual variance may reflect only the effect of the slight downward bias in α applied to a much more variable y_{it}.

f. Comparison of Various Methods

Generalized least squares represents an unattainable ideal, but provides a useful standard against which to assess the remaining four methods.

With respect to the estimation of α: ordinary least squares fails abysmally in comparison with the other three feasible methods. Both maximum likelihood using a 21-point grid and the two-round procedure offer considerable improvement, both in terms of bias and mean-square error over least squares with individual constant terms for all values of α and ρ. Indeed, for small values of α and all values of ρ, the mean-square errors of both are roughly the same as for generalized least squares. On the other hand, for large values of α and low to moderate values of ρ, both maximum likelihood and the two-round procedure are distinctly inferior to generalized least squares. Except for very high values of ρ, however, the two-round procedure has a slight edge over the maximum likelihood in terms of both bias and mean-square error for $\alpha = 0.90$, while the reverse is true for $\alpha = 0.50$. The reason for this difference becomes apparent on examination of the estimates of ρ obtained from least-squares regressions with individual constant terms and those obtained by the maximum likelihood method: the bias in the former, upon which the two-round estimates are based, is greater for $\alpha = 0.50$ than the bias in the latter, whereas the reverse is true when $\alpha = 0.90$.

The results do not thus appear to offer a clear choice between the two-round procedure and maximum likelihood, at least as far as the estimation of α is concerned. To the extent that relatively large values of α and moderate values of ρ are deemed plausible on *a priori* grounds, one might tend to give the two-round procedure a slight edge. Clearly, however, further exploration of the relation between α and the two estiamtes would be desirable using both a denser α-net and a larger number of repetitions per experiment.

Although the really implausible behavior of maximum likelihood found in the gas study did not occur here, the estimates of ρ do tend to bunch near a boundary point far too soon when α is large. This does not occur for least squares with constant terms upon which the two-round procedure is based and may, therefore, provide some reason to prefer the latter to maximum likelihood.

When we consider estimates of σ^2, the picture is far from encouraging. The unattainable estimates of residual variance from the generalized least-squares regressions are quite good, although biased slightly downward probably due to the absence of any adjustment for loss of degrees of freedom. (Use of the maximum likelihood estimate for known ρ leads to a biased estimate, but one which has a minimum expected squared error). The least-squares estimates of σ^2 are very bad, being far too low especially for large values of ρ. Perhaps the greates disappointment of the series of experiments reported here, however, is that the estimate of σ^2 obtained by other methods is generally even worse, especially for large values of α. Of the three remaining methods, maximum likelihood turns in the worst performance and the two-round procedure the best, but none can be said to be even remotely satisfactory.[8]

4. CONCLUSIONS

In the present series of Monte Carlo investigations, we set out to obtain some insight into the earlier findings in Balestra and Nerlove (1966). The basic model of that study was simplified by eliminating all exogenous variables. We also assumed a correctly specified model in connection with all estimation procedures studied. The results reported here do confirm the inadequacy of both ordinary least squares and least squares with constant terms in the estimation

---

[8] More than one friendly critic suggested that these results might be due to numerical error; however, since the computation uses essentially the same piece of program used by the generalized least-squares estimate of σ^2, this clearly cannot be the case.

of the autoregressive parameter. Maximum likelihood and a two-round procedure similar to the two-round procedure used in Balestra and Nerlove (1966) yield much better estimates of α but surprisingly poor estiamtes of σ^2. The inquiry fails to confirm the inadequacy of maximum likelihood as compared with a two-round procedure, although there is some evidence that it is distinctly worse than the two-round procedure for values of the parameters that might often be encountered in practice.

In future investigations in this series, it is clearly necessary to study models containing exogenous variables and to see whether such are sufficient without the introduction of specification error to reproduce the earlier difficulties experienced with the method of maximum likelihood and thus to allow a clear choice. However, there is no reason to be optimistic in this connection, for the difference between individual constant terms and exogenous variables is merely one of degree of smoothness. Hence, it is likely that the choice between maximum likelihood and some variant of the two-round procedure will rest largely on some robustness criterion.

Yale University

References

Amemiya, T., and W. Fuller (1965), "A Comparative Study of Alternative Estimators in a Distributed Lag Model," Technical Report 12 (NSF-GS-142, June), Institute for Mathematical Studies in Social Science, Stanford University, Stanford.

Balestra, P., and M. Nerlove (1966), "Pooling Cross-Section and Time-Series Data in the Estimation of a Dynamic Model: The Demand for Natural Gas," Technical Report No. 8, Institute for Mathematical Studies in Social Science, Stanford University, Stanford, December 21, 1964; published in revised form in *Econometrica, 34*: July, pp. 585–612.

Fisher, R. A. (1946), *Statistical Methods for Research Workers*, Edinburgh: Oliver and Boyd.

Hammersley, J. M., and D. C. Handscomb (1964), *Monte Carlo Methods*, London: Methuen.

Hill, B. M. (n.a.), "Constrained Sampling in the Random-Effects Model," unpublished.

Hood, W. C., and T. C. Koopmans, eds. (1953), *Studies in Econometric Method*, New York: John Wiley.

Houthakker, H. S., and J. Haldi (1960), "Household Investment in Automobiles: An Intertemporal Cross-Section Analysis," in Friend, I., and R. Jones (Eds.), *Proceedings of a Conference on Consumption and Savings*, Vol. I, Philadelphia: University of Pennsylvania Press, pp. 175–224.

Irwin, J. O. (1946), "On the Interpretation of Within- and Between-Class Analysis of Variance When the Intraclass Correlation is Negative," *Journal of the Royal Statistical Society,* 109: pp. 157–158.

Kendall, M. G., and A. Stuart (1961), *The Advanced Theory of Statistics*, Vol. II, London: Charles Griffin.

Konijn, H. S. (1963), "Note on the Nonexistence of a Maximum-Likelihood Estimate," *Australian Journal Statistics 5*: November, pp. 43–46.

Kuh, E. (1959), "The Validity of Cross Sectionally Estimated Behavior Equations in Time-Series Applications," *Econometrica, 27*: April, pp. 197–214.

Tiao, G. C., and W. Y. Tan (1965), "Bayesian Analysis of Random-Effects Models in the Analysis of Variance II. Effect of Autocorrelated Errors," Technical Report 54, Department of Statistics, University of Wisconsin, August.

Parameter Values

$T = 10$
$N = 25$
$\alpha = 0.0, 0.1, 0.5, 0.9$
$\rho = 0.0, 0.05, 0.1 \ (0.1), 0.9, 0.95, 0.99$
$\sigma^2 = 1$

Table A.1. *Means and M.S.E. of the Generalized Least-Squares Estimates of* α^*

$\rho =$	Item	$\alpha = 0.00$	$\alpha = 0.10$	$\alpha = 0.50$	$\alpha = 0.90$
0.00	Mean	−.004 (.063)	0.083 (.063)	0.495 (.055)	0.892 (.029)
	M.S.E.	0.005	0.004	0.002	0.001
0.05	Mean	−.005 (.063)	0.102 (.063)	0.508 (.055)	0.917 (.026)
	M.S.E.	0.004	0.002	0.003	0.001
0.10	Mean	−.013 (.063)	0.095 (.063)	0.490 (.055)	0.926 (.025)
	M.S.E.	0.003	0.004	0.003	0.001
0.20	Mean	0.007 (.063)	0.094 (.063)	0.510 (.054)	0.947 (.023)
	M.S.E.	0.005	0.004	0.004	0.003
0.30	Mean	0.019 (.063)	0.111 (.063)	0.505 (.054)	0.936 (.024)
	M.S.E.	0.004	0.004	0.003	0.002
0.40	Mean	0.008 (.063)	0.103 (.063)	0.520 (.054)	0.945 (.023)
	M.S.E.	0.005	0.003	0.004	0.002
0.50	Mean	−.004 (.063)	0.089 (.063)	0.509 (.054)	0.943 (.023)
	M.S.E.	0.004	0.003	0.003	0.002
0.60	Mean	0.010 (.063)	0.103 (.063)	0.518 (.054)	0.945 (.023)
	M.S.E.	0.004	0.004	0.003	0.003
0.70	Mean	0.004 (.063)	0.112 (.063)	0.524 (.054)	0.950 (.021)
	M.S.E.	0.006	0.006	0.005	0.003
0.80	Mean	0.017 (.063)	0.107 (.063)	0.513 (.055)	0.944 (.021)
	M.S.E.	0.005	0.004	0.004	0.002
0.90	Mean	−.002 (.063)	0.109 (.063)	0.524 (.054)	0.937 (.019)
	M.S.E.	0.004	0.004	0.004	0.002
0.95	Mean	−.008 (.063)	0.119 (.063)	0.516 (.054)	0.925 (.010)
	M.S.E.	0.005	0.005	0.003	0.001
0.99	Mean	0.013 (.063)	0.118 (.063)	0.515 (.054)	0.908 (.010)
	M.S.E.	0.004	0.005	0.003	0.000

* Figures in parentheses following $\hat{\alpha}$s are mean estimated S.E.

Table A.2. *Means and M.S.E. of the Estimates of σ^2 from Generalized Least-Squares Regressions*

$\rho =$	Item	$\alpha = 0.00$	$\alpha = 0.10$	$\alpha = 0.50$	$\alpha = 0.90$
0.00	Mean	0.995	0.984	0.999	1.007
	M.S.E.	0.008	0.007	0.007	0.010
0.05	Mean	0.987	0.995	0.987	0.995
	M.S.E.	0.009	0.008	0.005	0.010
0.10	Mean	0.976	1.004	0.979	1.022
	M.S.E.	0.009	0.008	0.008	0.008
0.20	Mean	0.987	1.010	1.009	0.981
	M.S.E.	0.010	0.007	0.006	0.010
0.30	Mean	1.000	0.982	0.976	0.970
	M.S.E.	0.008	0.008	0.008	0.012
0.40	Mean	1.004	1.004	0.981	0.949
	M.S.E.	0.006	0.007	0.008	0.009
0.50	Mean	1.000	1.007	0.995	0.956
	M.S.E.	0.010	0.007	0.006	0.010
0.60	Mean	0.981	1.002	1.006	0.958
	M.S.E.	0.010	0.008	0.006	0.011
0.70	Mean	0.981	0.999	0.989	0.951
	M.S.E.	0.010	0.006	0.006	0.011
0.80	Mean	0.992	0.990	0.999	0.960
	M.S.E.	0.009	0.006	0.008	0.009
0.90	Mean	1.007	0.992	0.993	0.957
	M.S.E.	0.007	0.007	0.010	0.012
0.95	Mean	0.990	1.022	0.995	0.971
	M.S.E.	0.006	0.009	0.008	0.012
0.99	Mean	0.985	0.986	0.992	0.982
	M.S.E.	0.010	0.008	0.009	0.007

Table B.1. *Means and M.S.E. of the Ordinary Least-Squares Estimates of α**

$\rho =$	Item	$\alpha = 0.00$	$\alpha = 0.10$	$\alpha = 0.50$	$\alpha = 0.90$
0.00	Mean	−.004 (.063)	0.083 (.063)	0.495 (.055)	0.892 (.029)
	M.S.E.	0.005	0.004	0.002	0.001
0.05	Mean	0.040 (.063)	0.149 (.063)	0.563 (.053)	0.941 (.023)
	M.S.E.	0.006	0.006	0.008	0.002
0.10	Mean	0.078 (.063)	0.192 (.062)	0.597 (.051)	0.965 (.019)
	M.S.E.	0.010	0.013	0.013	0.005
0.20	Mean	0.192 (.062)	0.291 (.061)	0.699 (.045)	0.995 (.014)
	M.S.E.	0.044	0.042	0.042	0.009
0.30	Mean	0.298 (.060)	0.393 (.058)	0.762 (.041)	0.999 (.012)
	M.S.E.	0.005	0.092	0.071	0.010
0.40	Mean	0.397 (.058)	0.479 (.056)	0.825 (.036)	1.010 (.010)
	M.S.E.	0.108	0.149	0.108	0.012
0.50	Mean	0.472 (.056)	0.559 (.052)	0.860 (.032)	1.012 (.009)
	M.S.E.	0.231	0.217	0.131	0.013
0.60	Mean	0.586 (.051)	0.647 (.048)	0.899 (.028)	1.017 (.007)
	M.S.E.	0.350	0.305	0.160	0.014
0.70	Mean	0.670 (.047)	0.753 (.042)	0.932 (.023)	1.019 (.005)
	M.S.E.	0.455	0.430	0.187	0.014
0.80	Mean	0.786 (.039)	0.825 (.035)	0.956 (.018)	1.021 (.004)
	M.S.E.	0.621	0.528	0.208	0.015
0.90	Mean	0.884 (.029)	0.916 (.025)	0.981 (.013)	1.022 (.003)
	M.S.E.	0.783	0.666	0.231	0.015
0.95	Mean	0.941 (.021)	0.961 (.018)	0.990 (.009)	1.023 (.002)
	M.S.E.	0.886	0.741	0.240	0.015
0.99	Mean	0.989 (.009)	0.992 (.008)	0.999 (.004)	1.023 (.001)
	M.S.E.	0.977	0.796	0.249	0.015

* Figures in parentheses following $\hat{\alpha}$s mean estimated S.E.

Table B.2. *Means and M.S.E. of the Estimates of σ^2 from Ordinary Least-Squares Regressions*

$\rho =$	Item	$\alpha = 0.00$	$\alpha = 0.10$	$\alpha = 0.50$	$\alpha = 0.90$
0.00	Mean	0.995	0.984	0.999	1.007
	M.S.E.	0.008	0.007	0.007	0.010
0.05	Mean	0.992	0.997	0.985	0.991
	M.S.E.	0.009	0.008	0.005	0.010
0.10	Mean	0.972	0.996	0.962	0.977
	M.S.E.	0.009	0.008	0.009	0.006
0.20	Mean	0.950	0.968	0.929	0.863
	M.S.E.	0.015	0.007	0.010	0.025
0.30	Mean	0.908	0.877	0.822	0.758
	M.S.E.	0.018	0.023	0.037	0.064
0.40	Mean	0.849	0.821	0.725	0.635
	M.S.E.	0.028	0.039	0.081	0.135
0.50	Mean	0.752	0.737	0.632	0.541
	M.S.E.	0.068	0.074	0.138	0.212
0.60	Mean	0.630	0.611	0.517	0.433
	M.S.E.	0.142	0.155	0.235	0.324
0.70	Mean	0.499	0.482	0.387	0.323
	M.S.E.	0.254	0.270	0.376	0.459
0.80	Mean	0.357	0.332	0.264	0.220
	M.S.E.	0.415	0.447	0.542	0.609
0.90	Mean	0.194	0.175	0.132	0.112
	M.S.E.	0.650	0.680	0.753	0.788
0.95	Mean	0.099	0.091	0.067	0.059
	M.S.E.	0.812	0.827	0.870	0.885
0.99	Mean	0.020	0.018	0.013	0.016
	M.S.E.	0.960	0.965	0.973	0.968

Table C.1. *Mean and M.S.E. of the Least-Squares Estimates of* α *and Associated Estimates of* ρ *from Regressions Containing Individual Constant Terms**

$\rho =$	Item	$\alpha = 0.00$		$\alpha = 0.10$	
		a_c	r	a_c	r
0.00	Mean	−.099 (.066)	0.113	−.027 (.067)	0.122
	M.S.E.	0.013	0.013	0.021	0.016
0.05	Mean	−.106 (.066)	0.167	−.006 (.067)	0.167
	M.S.E.	0.015	0.016	0.013	0.016
0.10	Mean	−.115 (.066)	0.216	−.019 (.067)	0.219
	M.S.E.	0.017	0.015	0.018	0.017
0.20	Mean	−.097 (.066)	0.310	−.023 (.067)	0.324
	M.S.E.	0.014	0.017	0.018	0.020
0.30	Mean	−.086 (.066)	0.400	−.002 (.067)	0.403
	M.S.E.	0.011	0.015	0.015	0.016
0.40	Mean	−.104 (.066)	0.511	−.012 (.067)	0.493
	M.S.E.	0.015	0.018	0.016	0.016
0.50	Mean	−.109 (.066)	0.580	−.027 (.066)	0.588
	M.S.E.	0.016	0.012	0.020	0.015
0.60	Mean	−.010 (.066)	0.674	−.008 (.067)	0.656
	M.S.E.	0.014	0.012	0.016	0.009
0.70	Mean	−.097 (.067)	0.739	−.005 (.067)	0.759
	M.S.E.	0.015	0.005	0.016	0.005
0.80	Mean	−.089 (.066)	0.833	−.003 (.067)	0.828
	M.S.E.	0.012	0.003	0.015	0.002
0.90	Mean	−.106 (.066)	0.916	−.013 (.066)	0.919
	M.S.E.	0.015	0.001	0.017	0.001
0.95	Mean	−.111 (.066)	0.956	−.001 (.067)	0.959
	M.S.E.	0.017	0.000	0.015	0.000
0.99	Mean	−.091 (.066)	0.992	0.001 (.067)	0.992
	M.S.E.	0.012	0.000	0.014	0.000

* Figures in parentheses following $\hat{\alpha}$s are mean estimated S.E.

Essays in Panel Data Econometrics

Table C.1. *Continued*

$\rho =$	Item	$\alpha = 0.50$		$\alpha = 0.90$	
		a_c	r	a_c	r
0.00	Mean	0.339 (.063)	0.151	0.664 (.050)	0.347
	M.S.E.	0.029	0.025	0.059	0.130
0.05	Mean	0.344 (.063)	0.212	0.645 (.051)	0.525
	M.S.E.	0.028	0.030	0.069	0.236
0.10	Mean	0.319 (.063)	0.279	0.648 (.050)	0.623
	M.S.E.	0.037	0.037	0.066	0.280
0.20	Mean	0.336 (.063)	0.388	0.665 (.049)	0.750
	M.S.E.	0.032	0.040	0.059	0.307
0.30	Mean	0.329 (.063)	0.491	0.663 (.048)	0.799
	M.S.E.	0.033	0.043	0.060	0.255
0.40	Mean	0.333 (.063)	0.595	0.682 (.047)	0.848
	M.S.E.	0.031	0.044	0.052	0.204
0.50	Mean	0.326 (.062)	0.670	0.689 (.046)	0.876
	M.S.E.	0.034	0.036	0.049	0.144
0.60	Mean	0.338 (.063)	0.735	0.709 (.044)	0.908
	M.S.E.	0.031	0.024	0.040	0.096
0.70	Mean	0.339 (.063)	0.817	0.741 (.041)	0.933
	M.S.E.	0.029	0.016	0.027	0.055
0.80	Mean	0.328 (.064)	0.877	0.772 (.037)	0.942
	M.S.E.	0.034	0.008	0.019	0.021
0.90	Mean	0.346 (.063)	0.937	0.814 (.030)	0.962
	M.S.E.	0.027	0.002	0.009	0.004
0.95	Mean	0.337 (.063)	0.969	0.846 (.023)	0.974
	M.S.E.	0.030	0.001	0.003	0.001
0.99	Mean	0.322 (.063)	0.994	0.887 (.011)	0.992
	M.S.E.	0.037	0.000	0.000	0.001

Table C.2. *Means and M.S.E. of the Estimates of σ^2 from Regressions Containing Individual Constant Terms*

$\rho =$	Item	$\alpha = 0.00$	$\alpha = 0.10$	$\alpha = 0.50$	$\alpha = 0.90$
0.00	Mean	1.121	1.081	1.091	1.135
	M.S.E.	0.026	0.015	0.017	0.034
0.05	Mean	1.104	1.204	1.159	2.036
	M.S.E.	0.023	0.057	0.033	1.127
0.10	Mean	1.074	1.163	1.051	2.083
	M.S.E.	0.016	0.039	0.012	1.207
0.20	Mean	1.206	1.076	1.222	2.961
	M.S.E.	0.054	0.016	0.058	3.932
0.30	Mean	1.349	1.283	1.889	6.286
	M.S.E.	0.136	0.092	0.824	28.339
0.40	Mean	1.418	1.226	1.517	3.059
	M.S.E.	0.190	0.063	0.286	4.311
0.50	Mean	1.173	1.080	1.655	3.516
	M.S.E.	0.045	0.016	0.444	6.423
0.60	Mean	1.273	1.661	1.906	5.102
	M.S.E.	0.093	0.461	0.845	17.090
0.70	Mean	1.777	1.215	2.398	3.610
	M.S.E.	0.640	0.055	1.995	6.936
0.80	Mean	1.426	0.733	1.732	8.389
	M.S.E.	0.202	0.075	0.564	55.126
0.90	Mean	1.031	1.260	0.784	1.951
	M.S.E.	0.010	0.077	0.053	0.946
0.95	Mean	1.506	1.958	0.662	1.931
	M.S.E.	0.274	0.959	0.118	0.915
0.99	Mean	1.239	1.486	5.094	2.088
	M.S.E.	0.075	0.257	17.098	1.218

Table D.1. *Means and M.S.E. of the Maximum-Likelihood Estimates of α and ρ Based on a 21-Point Grid for ρ**

$\rho =$	Item	$\alpha = 0.00$		$\alpha = 0.10$	
		$\hat{\alpha}$	$\hat{\rho}$	$\hat{\alpha}$	$\hat{\rho}$
0.00	Mean	−.035 (.060)	0.051	0.047 (.060)	0.053
	M.S.E.	0.005	0.003	0.007	0.003
0.05	Mean	−.021 (.061)	0.076	0.082 (.061)	0.083
	M.S.E.	0.004	0.002	0.002	0.004
0.10	Mean	−.021 (.061)	0.114	0.079 (.061)	0.129
	M.S.E.	0.004	0.002	0.004	0.004
0.20	Mean	−.001 (.062)	0.214	0.075 (.062)	0.243
	M.S.E.	0.004	0.005	0.004	0.007
0.30	Mean	0.011 (.062)	0.316	0.096 (.062)	0.335
	M.S.E.	0.004	0.006	0.004	0.007
0.40	Mean	−.006 (.063)	0.430	0.088 (.063)	0.434
	M.S.E.	0.004	0.009	0.004	0.010
0.50	Mean	−.009 (.063)	0.504	0.070 (.062)	0.539
	M.S.E.	0.004	0.007	0.005	0.010
0.60	Mean	−.001 (.062)	0.615	0.090 (.063)	0.619
	M.S.E.	0.004	0.008	0.004	0.008
0.70	Mean	0.001 (.063)	0.694	0.095 (.063)	0.731
	M.S.E.	0.006	0.005	0.005	0.004
0.80	Mean	0.012 (.063)	0.799	0.100 (.063)	0.806
	M.S.E.	0.004	0.002	0.004	0.002
0.90	Mean	−.008 (.063)	0.899	0.092 (.063)	0.905
	M.S.E.	0.005	0.001	0.004	0.001
0.95	Mean	−.005 (.063)	0.945	0.121 (.063)	0.948
	M.S.E.	0.005	0.000	0.005	0.000
0.99	Mean	0.013 (.062)	0.990**	0.118 (.062)	0.990**
	M.S.E.	0.004	0.000	0.005	0.000

* Figures in parentheses following $\hat{\alpha}$s are mean estimated asymptotic S.E.
** Median = 0.99.

Table D.1. *Continued*

$\rho =$	Item	$\alpha = 0.50$		$\alpha = 0.90$	
		$\hat{\alpha}$	$\hat{\rho}$	$\hat{\alpha}$	$\hat{\rho}$
0.00	Mean	0.416 (.060)	0.120	0.714 (.045)	0.529
	M.S.E.	0.010	0.018	0.037	0.291
0.05	Mean	0.424 (.057)	0.208	0.698 (.046)	0.714
	M.S.E.	0.009	0.030	0.044	0.445
0.10	Mean	0.403 (.058)	0.286	0.701 (.046)	0.794
	M.S.E.	0.013	0.042	0.042	0.484
0.20	Mean	0.420 (.058)	0.428	0.716 (.045)	0.880
	M.S.E.	0.011	0.057	0.037	0.464
0.30	Mean	0.413 (.058)	0.537	0.713 (.044)	0.906
	M.S.E.	0.010	0.063	0.038	0.369
0.40	Mean	0.418 (.058)	0.651	0.732 (.043)	0.935
	M.S.E.	0.010	0.068	0.031	0.287
0.50	Mean	0.412 (.058)	0.718	0.741 (.042)	0.947
	M.S.E.	0.011	0.053	0.028	0.200
0.60	Mean	0.425 (.058)	0.784	0.762 (.040)	0.956
	M.S.E.	0.010	0.037	0.027	0.127
0.70	Mean	0.423 (.058)	0.857	0.773 (.037)	0.978**
	M.S.E.	0.009	0.027	0.018	0.078
0.80	Mean	0.419 (.059)	9.902	0.797 (.034)	0.987**
	M.S.E.	0.010	0.012	0.013	0.035
0.90	Mean	0.450 (.058)	0.945	0.838 (.027)	0.990**
	M.S.E.	0.005	0.002	0.005	0.008
0.95	Mean	0.417 (.058)	0.976**	0.869 (.021)	0.990**
	M.S.E.	0.012	0.001	0.001	0.002
0.99	Mean	0.515 (.054)	0.990**	0.908 (.010)	0.990**
	M.S.E.	0.002	0.000	0.00	0.000

** Median = 0.99.

Table D.2. *Means and M.S.E. of the Maximum-Likelihood Estimates of σ^2 Based on a 21-Point Grid for ρ*

$\rho =$	Item	$\alpha = 0.00$	$\alpha = 0.10$	$\alpha = 0.50$	$\alpha = 0.90$
0.00	Mean	1.003	0.996	1.099	2.026
	M.S.E.	0.008	0.007	0.020	1.229
0.05	Mean	0.996	1.019	1.162	3.143
	M.S.E.	0.009	0.008	0.037	4.994
0.10	Mean	0.983	1.032	1.215	4.299
	M.S.E.	0.009	0.011	0.067	11.787
0.20	Mean	1.005	1.062	1.395	6.676
	M.S.E.	0.017	0.014	0.186	37.083
0.30	Mean	1.027	1.041	1.474	7.788
	M.S.E.	0.021	0.021	0.279	54.978
0.40	Mean	1.062	1.083	1.695	8.996
	M.S.E.	0.025	0.036	0.582	69.711
0.50	Mean	1.026	1.117	1.823	9.412
	M.S.E.	0.032	0.057	0.887	91.961
0.60	Mean	1.052	1.095	1.932	11.954
	M.S.E.	0.053	0.061	1.095	212.205
0.70	Mean	1.007	1.143	2.197	19.668
	M.S.E.	0.057	0.063	1.873	424.088
0.80	Mean	1.041	1.068	2.212	16.112
	M.S.E.	0.075	0.061	2.014	242.114
0.90	Mean	1.086	1.199	1.877	8.797
	M.S.E.	0.141	0.260	0.885	61.610
0.95	Mean	0.998	1.014	3.303	4.528
	M.S.E.	0.261	0.018	7.988	12.696
0.99	Mean	0.985	0.985	0.992	0.982
	M.S.E.	0.010	0.008	0.009	0.007

Table E.1. *Means and M.S.E. of the Second-Round Estimates of α Using r Estimated from Least-Squares Regressions with Individual Constant Terms*

$\rho =$	Item	$\alpha = 0.00$	$\alpha = 0.10$	$\alpha = 0.50$	$\alpha = 0.90$
0.00	Mean	−.055	0.021	0.405	0.749
	M.S.E.	0.007	0.011	0.012	0.025
0.05	Mean	−.053	0.051	0.423	0.743
	M.S.E.	0.007	0.005	0.009	0.029
0.10	Mean	−.056	0.046	0.404	0.749
	M.S.E.	0.007	0.007	0.013	0.025
0.20	Mean	−.030	0.050	0.431	0.766
	M.S.E.	0.006	0.006	0.010	0.021
0.30	Mean	−.014	0.076	0.427	0.763
	M.S.E.	0.005	0.005	0.009	0.020
0.40	Mean	−.029	0.070	0.436	0.782
	M.S.E.	0.005	0.005	0.008	0.018
0.50	Mean	−.032	0.055	0.430	0.789
	M.S.E.	0.005	0.006	0.009	0.016
0.60	Mean	−.021	0.077	0.446	0.805
	M.S.E.	0.005	0.005	0.008	0.012
0.70	Mean	−.017	0.083	0.447	0.831
	M.S.E.	0.006	0.006	0.006	0.006
0.80	Mean	−.007	0.087	0.439	0.854
	M.S.E.	0.005	0.005	0.009	0.004
0.90	Mean	−.024	0.076	0.458	0.880
	M.S.E.	0.005	0.005	0.005	0.001
0.95	Mean	−.029	0.093	0.448	0.895
	M.S.E.	0.006	0.006	0.007	0.001
0.99	Mean	−.009	0.092	0.433	0.904
	M.S.E.	0.004	0.005	0.010	0.000

Table E.2. *Means and M.S.E. of Second-Round Estimates of σ^2 Using r Estimated from Least-Squares Regressions with Individual Constant Terms*

$\rho =$	Item	$\alpha = 0.00$	$\alpha = 0.10$	$\alpha = 0.50$	$\alpha = 0.90$
0.00	Mean	1.050	1.043	1.085	1.371
	M.S.E.	0.012	0.010	0.016	0.185
0.05	Mean	1.070	1.079	1.119	1.818
	M.S.E.	0.016	0.015	0.024	0.825
0.10	Mean	1.071	1.080	1.155	2.234
	M.S.E.	0.016	0.025	0.041	1.725
0.20	Mean	1.113	1.152	1.260	3.047
	M.S.E.	0.039	0.035	0.092	5.055
0.30	Mean	1.144	1.130	1.296	3.397
	M.S.E.	0.050	0.043	0.130	6.933
0.40	Mean	1.209	1.181	1.416	3.849
	M.S.E.	0.074	0.072	0.249	10.138
0.50	Mean	1.188	1.227	1.514	4.191
	M.S.E.	0.085	0.111	0.420	13.610
0.60	Mean	1.224	1.194	1.551	4.383
	M.S.E.	0.126	0.114	0.487	13.923
0.70	Mean	1.159	1.247	1.636	4.261
	M.S.E.	0.096	0.107	0.555	12.108
0.80	Mean	1.232	1.184	1.702	3.609
	M.S.E.	0.164	0.108	0.734	8.960
0.90	Mean	1.260	1.360	1.691	2.706
	M.S.E.	0.206	0.362	0.794	3.602
0.95	Mean	1.235	1.316	1.737	1.953
	M.S.E.	0.223	0.210	0.798	1.203
0.99	Mean	1.246	1.279	1.945	1.292
	M.S.E.	0.197	0.186	1.567	0.246

Further Evidence on the Estimation of Dynamic Economic Relations from a Time Series of Cross Sections[1]

Preface

"Here is the guess of their true strength and forces
By diligent discovery; ..."
King Lear, V. i. 52

Because I did not succeed in replicating all of the salient characteristics of the different methods of estimation Balestra and I had employed, in particular the boundary maxima of the likelihood function, I felt compelled to continue the study of the various panel estimators under more realistic assumptions. The principal source of unreality in the paper reprinted in the last chapter is clearly the absence of any other source of variation other than the disturbances and the lagged values of the dependent variables themselves. But it was far from obvious how one ought to include a source of exogenously determined additional variation. After all, when all is said and done, the chief characteristic of exogenous variation is that we don't know or cannot specify how it is generated. But as Trognon (1978) was later to show in his analytic derivation of the existence of boundary maxima of the likelihood function, the characteristics of the process generating the exogenous variation are crucial. Indeed, in the paper reprinted as Chapter 8 of this volume, I make fairly strong assumptions about the mechanism generating the exogenous variation. In the paper reprinted here, the exogenous variables were generated by choosing a random variable ω_{it}, uniformly distributed on the interval $[-\frac{1}{2}, \frac{1}{2}]$ and forming

$$x_{it} = 0.1t + 0.5x_{it-1} + \omega_{it},$$

where the value x_{i0} was chosen as $5 + 10\omega_{i0}$. Now it was possible to explore the efficacy of an instrumental variables approach. And, of course, the most important finding is the existence of boundary solutions to maximization of the likelihood, conditional on the initial observations.

[1] Reprinted with permission from *Econometrica*, *39*: 359–382, 1971.

At the time this paper was written, many properties of econometric estimators were known only asymptotically, for large samples. In particular, anything good that could be said about instrumental variable estimators was asymptotic. (A good survey, c. 1980, is Bowden and Turkington, 1984.) But to what extent were the large-sample asymptotics a guide to what one might observe in practice?

In many cases, it is not possible to determine the exact distribution of certain sampling statistics or estimators, but it may be possible to approximate that distribution. The properties of most estimators, that is to say their distributions, usually depend on the size of the sample or the number of observations on which they are based. Even when such distributions cannot be obtained exactly, we may be able to find an approximation that gets better, that is more accurate, as the sample size increases. Let T be the sample size. Then we seek the properties of distributions to which the exact, unknown distributions converge as $T \to \infty$. Distributions exact for finite T are called *small-sample* distributions. Distributions that are limiting as $T \to \infty$ are sometimes called *large-sample* or *asymptotic* distributions. Often we can determine only or are only interested in certain properties such as the mean or variances of the asymptotic distributions. These properties are also said to be large sample or asymptotic.

The general idea behind the use of asymptotic theory in econometrics is to obtain *approximations* to the distribution of an estimator of interest. In the case of *large-sample asymptotics*, the approximation gets better as the sample size, T, is increased. But there is another little-used approach to obtaining approximations to the moments of finite sample distributions of estimators of interest. We might instead consider approximations that get better as a scalar multiple, σ, of the variance of the disturbance in the model gets smaller. For example, in the regression model

$$y_t = \alpha y_{t-1} + \beta x_t + u_t, \qquad t = 1, \ldots, T,$$

where $Eu_t u_t' = \sigma^2$, for $t = t'$, $= 0$, otherwise, the properties of the OLS estimates of α and β are deduced as $T \to \infty$, so that $x_1, \ldots, x_T$ cannot be treated as fixed in repeated samples but must be assumed also to follow some stochastic process. We could, however, instead consider the properties of the OLS estimates for fixed sample size as $\sigma \to 0$, thus permitting a different treatment of the variable x_t. Such asymptotics are called small-sigma asymptotics. Key references are the work of J. B. Kadane (1966, 1970, 1971) on properties of certain simultaneous-equations estimators; Jon K. Peck (1972), who worked out the small-sigma asymptotics for the panel data model considered in the paper reprinted here; and Bent Jørgensen (1987), who worked out the theory of small-sigma asymptotics for an extended class of generalized linear models.

A program of research for deriving analytical results corresponding to the essentially finite-sample Monte Carlo results presented in the paper reprinted here is laid out in Footnote 8 (p. 198). This was later carried out in Peck's

1972 Yale University Ph.D. dissertation. Peck essentially verified the small-sample results of the Monte Carlo investigation reported here, except the presence of boundary solutions of the likelihood maximization, but including the rather interesting findings with respect to the instrumental variable estimates reported on pp. 213–214. These are presented in detail in Appendix Tables A.5, A.11, B.5, B.11, C.5, C.11, and D.1–D.9, available on the internet at http://www.arec.umd.edu/mnerlove/Tables1971.ZIP(23.1mb). The instrumental variable estimates illustrate clearly the implications of asymptotic efficiency and consistency for the behavior of estimates in small samples. These properties do in fact serve as a guide as to what to expect even when the samples are small. Inconsistency is reflected in bias; inefficiency implies erratic small-sample behavior.

References

Bowden, R. J., and D. A. Turkington (1984), *Instrumental Variables*, New York: Cambridge University Press.

Jørgensen, Bent (1987), "Small Dispersion Asymptotics," *Revista Brasileira de Probabilidade e Estatistica, 1*: pp. 59–90.

Kadane, J. B. (1966), "Comparison of Estimators in Simultaneous Equations Econometric Models When the Residuals are Small," unpublished Ph.D. dissertation, Stanford, CA, Stanford University.

Kadane, J. B. (1970), "Testing Overidentifying Restrictions When the Disturbances are Small," *Journal of the American Statistical Association, 65*: pp. 182–184.

Kadane, J. B. (1971), "Comparison of k-Class Estimators When the Disturbances are Small," *Econometrica, 39*: pp. 723–737.

Peck, J. K. (1972), "A Comparison of Alternative Estimators for a Dynamic Relationship Estimated from a Time Series of Cross Sections When the Disturbances are Small," *Cowles Foundation Discussion Paper*, p. 325.

Trognon, A. (1978), "Miscellaneous Asymptotic Properties of Ordinary Least Squares and Maximum Likelihood Methods in Dynamic Error Components Models," *Annales de l'INSEE, 30–31*: pp. 631–657.

Further Evidence on the Estimation of Dynamic Economic Relations from a Time Series of Cross Sections[1]

Marc Nerlove

"... the Dodo suddenly called out, 'the race is over!' and they all crowded
round it, panting, and asking, 'But who has won?'"

Alice's Adventures in Wonderland

Availability of data on a large number of individuals, but on each individual
only over a very short period of time, has become increasingly common in a
number of different fields in economics. Very often we would like to use such
data to study behavioral relationships that are dynamic in character (i.e., that
contain a distributed lag or other form of autogressive relationship). Since
only a few observations are available over time, but a great many observations
are available for different individuals at a point in time, it is exceptionally
important to make the most efficient use of the data across individuals to
estimate that part of the behavioral relationship containing variables that differ
substantially from one individual to another, in order that the lesser amount
of information over time can be used to best advantage in the estimation of
the dynamic part of the relationship studied. As it turns out, the problem is

[1] The research on which this paper is based was carried out in part at the Cowles Foundation
for Research in Economics at Yale University with the support of the National Science
Foundation and the Ford Foundation, and, in part, during the author's tenure as Frank W.
Taussig Research Professor of Economics at Harvard University, during 1967–1968, and with
the financial support of the Department of Economics, Harvard University.

   I am indebted to Mrs. E. Bockelman for programming assistance and to William Raduchel
for his considerable help in the design and programming of the gradient procedure used to
obtain the maximum likelihood estimates. I have also benefited greatly from the critical
comments of G. S. Maddala contained in his unpublished papers, "Pooling Cross-Section
and Time Series Data – Comments on the Balestra-Nerlove Approach" and "On the Use
of Random-Effects Models in Pooling Cross-Section and Time-Series Data." Some of the
interpretation of the asymptotic properties of the estimates considered is based on Maddala's
work. I am also indebted to J. D. Sargan for pointing out an earlier error in my interpretation
of some of his results, and to C. W. Bischoff for helpful comments and suggestions. None but
the author should be held responsible for remaining errors.

far from simple: obvious devices such as the pooling of all observations and estimation by ordinary least squares, or the introduction of dummy variables for individuals, produce estimates having serious small-sample bias. In earlier papers, the author and others have formulated a simple variance-components model for the disturbance term in a relationship to be estimated from cross-section data over time. This paper presents a series of Monte Carlo studies designed to explore the small-sample properties of various types of estimates within this context. Not only is the bias of the obvious methods of estimation previously mentioned confirmed, but also certain serious deficiencies of the maximum likelihood approach that had been suspected earlier are confirmed. A two-round estimation procedure is proposed that appears to work well for a wide variety of parameter values.

1. INTRODUCTION

Data on a number of individual units (e.g., firms, households, geographical areas) over several periods of time are becoming increasingly available. Very often we would like to use such data to estimate a behavioral relationship containing an autoregressive component due, possibly, to a distributed lag or other dynamic factor affecting economic behavior. In an earlier study, Balestra (1966) and the present author studied the demand for natural gas using data on thirty-six states of the United States, over a six-year period. We encountered a number of rather serious methodological problems in attempting to estimate a distributed-lag model that appear to be of more general interest in view of the growing availability of data for individual units over several time periods. This paper reports the second of a series of experimental studies designed to explore the general methodological issues involved in studies of this type.

The first series of experiments, reported in Nerlove (1967), dealt with estimation of the following simple model:

$$y_{it} = \alpha y_{it-1} + u_{it} \qquad (i = 1, \ldots, N; t = 1, \ldots, T), \qquad (1.1)$$

where the u_{it} are unobserved random variables such that

$$u_{it} = \mu_i + v_{it},$$

$$E\mu_i = Ev_{it} = 0, \qquad \text{all } i \text{ and } t,$$

$$E\mu_i v_{i't} = 0, \qquad \text{all } i, i', \text{ and } t,$$

$$E\mu_i \mu_{i'} = \begin{cases} \sigma_\mu^2, & i = i', \\ 0, & i \neq i', \end{cases}$$

$$Ev_{it} v_{i't'} = \begin{cases} \sigma_v^2, & i = i', t = t', \\ 0, & \text{otherwise.} \end{cases} \qquad (1.2)$$

In the typical economic application, the number of individuals, N, is much larger than the number of time periods, T; and in the first set of experiments and in those reported here, N has been chosen two and one-half times as large as $T : N = 25, T = 10$.

The random variables u_{it}, which disturb the autoregressive relationship (1.1), are supposed to represent the net effects of variables whose explicit inclusion was not possible in the analysis. When one considers a pure cross section and fits, for example, a simple linear relationship to the data, it is standard practice to assume that the large number of factors that affect the individuals in the sample and the value of the dependent variable observed for each of them, but that have not been explicitly included as independent variables, may be appropriately summarized by a random disturbance.[2] The assumed stochastic mechanism generating the disturbances becomes, then, a basis for econometric analysis. To be sure, it is important to consider carefully just what the disturbances may or may not represent, but their *stochastic* nature is a necessary assumption for econometric analysis.[3]

When time-series data are considered, a similar argument is made for the inclusion of stochastic disturbances in the relation or relations to be estimated. So much is well known and widely understood, but when numerous individual units are observed over time, the problem of specifying the stochastic nature of the disturbances becomes conceptually more difficult. It is clear in the abstract that some of the omitted variables will represent factors peculiar to both the individual units and the time periods for which observations are obtained, while other variables reflect individual differences that tend to affect the observations for a given individual in more or less the same fashion over more than one, and perhaps all, periods of time. Still other variables may reflect factors peculiar to specific time periods but affecting individual units more or less equally. A three-component model naturally suggests itself:

$$u_{it} = \mu_i + \lambda_t + v_{it},$$

where μ_i represents the more or less time invariant, individual effects, λ_t represents the period specific and more or less individual invariant effects, and v_{it} represents the remaining effects that are assumed to vary over both individuals

[2] This elementary and old point (see Haavelmo, 1944, pp. 50–51) is stressed here because the nature of the disturbances in the analysis of cross sections over time has proved to be a source of considerable confusion when lagged values of the endogenous variables enter the relationships to be estimated.

[3] It is also standard to assume that the relationship to be estimated is homogenous from observation to observation, even though disturbed. That is, the parameters excepting the constant term do not vary from individual to individual in, for example, a cross section. It is possible, of course, to adopt a more general specification in which the coefficients in the relationship to be estimated are also random variables and we estimate only certain of their moments (see Hildreth and Hauck, 1968, and Nerlove, 1971, for example), but such models have not proved highly productive. The simplification that the disturbing elements affect only the level and not the form of the functional relationship is the basis of nearly all econometric work.

and time periods. The fundamental question that must be answered prior to econometric analysis is whether or not to treat μ_i and λ_t as parameters or as random variables. If we treat them as parameters, we may or may not wish to estimate their values explicitly; if we treat them as random variables, we may, of course, only estimate certain moments of their joint distribution. This question is not a trivial one, for it makes a surprising amount of difference in the estimates of the other parameters in dynamic relations and to their small-sample properties, depending on which approach is adopted.[4]

The model, (1.1) and (1.2), investigated in the first series of experiments assumed period, individual invariant effects, λ_t, to be absent, and assumed that μ_i and v_{it} were uncorrelated random variables with zero means. The assumed absence of period effects is largely a question of judgment in any particular application; however, what happens to the estimates when such effects are erroneously assumed to be absent will be the subject of further investigation. (See Nerlove, 1971, for a preliminary analysis.) That μ_i and v_{it} are assumed uncorrelated is essentially definitional and involves no loss of generality. (The covariance between μ_i and v_{it} is not identified.) The assumed absence of serial correlation among the v_{it} is more fundamental. When the random variables u_{it} are arranged in vector form, first by individuals, then according to period,

$$u = (u_{11}, \ldots, u_{1T}, u_{21}, \ldots, u_{2T}, \ldots, u_{N1}, \ldots, u_{NT})',$$

it can be seen that the variance-covariance matrix of these variables takes the following form:

$$Euu' = \sigma^2 \begin{bmatrix} A & 0 & \ldots & 0 \\ 0 & A & \ldots & 0 \\ \vdots & \vdots & & \vdots \\ 0 & 0 & \ldots & A \end{bmatrix} \tag{1.3}$$

where $\sigma^2 = \sigma_\mu^2 + \sigma_v^2$,

$$A = \begin{bmatrix} 1 & \rho & \ldots & \rho \\ \rho & 1 & \ldots & \rho \\ \vdots & \vdots & & \vdots \\ \rho & \rho & \ldots & 1 \end{bmatrix},$$

and $\rho = \sigma_\mu^2/\sigma^2$. The parameter ρ is the so-called "intraclass correlation coefficient" of the classical random-effects model in the analysis of variance

---

[4] Henderson's paper (1953) contains a suggestive discussion of the differences between the "fixed-effects" model and the "random-effects" model (see especially pp. 234–235). Searle (1968) gives a somewhat more transparent exposition of Henderson's results in matrix notation, together with certain extensions. I am indebted to a referee for these references.

(Fisher, 1946, pp. 222–226). (The model in this form was used by Kuh [1959] in his work on the relation between time-series and cross-section estimates, except that he did not assume that the individual effects, μ_i, and the time-varying effects, v_{it}, were uncorrelated.) It can be seen that the assumptions made concerning the u_{it} amount to the assumption of a very specific form of serial correlation; indeed, one might argue that the model is simply an approximation to a more realistic one that allows rather pronounced serial dependence among the disturbances for the same individual, but only a negligible amount of dependence among disturbances for different individuals. To achieve a good approximation, it may be necessary to allow, for example, some negative serial correlation among the disturbances v_{it} for the same individual to counterbalance the exceptionally rigid formulation involving the random effect μ_i, assumed to persist for all time periods over which a given individual is observed. The effects of misspecification in this direction will also be the subject of further investigation.

The question of whether the individual effects may be treated as constant parameters for the purpose of statistical analysis is related, not only to the nature of the approximation discussed previously, but also to the underlying mechanism assumed and the purpose of the analysis. Thus, for example, consider a number of individuals; for each of these we suppose some stochastic mechanism chooses certain individual effects, μ_i, and another mechanism chooses a number of further disturbances, v_{it}, for each. These two effects are then summed to give us NT disturbances, T for each of N individuals. If we think of extending the sample by θ periods for the same individual units by choosing θ more v_{it}'s, but retaining the same μ_i with which we began, it is apparent that something useful can be said about the new observations by explicitly estimating the values $\mu_i, i = 1, \ldots, N$ (i.e., treating these *as parameters* in the problem). This is analogous to the problem of predicting from a regression equation in which the disturbances are known to be serially correlated. For such prediction, it is helpful not only to have good estimates of the coefficients (i.e., estimates that consider the serial correlation of the disturbances), but also estimates of past values of the disturbances themselves.[5] Estimation, however, is not quite the same as prediction and it is far from clear that treating the μ_is as parameters will lead to good estimates of the true parameters of the system. Indeed, it was found in the series of experiments reported in Nerlove (1967) that downward-biased estimates of α were obtained when each μ_i was estimated explicitly. If the standard econometric approach is taken to the disturbances u_{it}, no part, not even the μ_i, should be regarded as nonstochastic or

---

[5] Of course, the problem can always be cast in the form of a prediction conditional on past values of the dependent variable and the independent variables alone, but the calculated residuals provide equivalent information if the regression coefficients have been correctly calculated.

fixed in repeated samples. Treating part as if it were fixed but unobserved is one possible approach to estimation, but it is only one and it is far from clear *a priori* that it is better than some other approach.[6]

Several investigations have examined the question of estimation in models similar to (1.1) and (1.2). Wallace and Hussain (1969) and Hussain (1966) consider estimation of nondynamic relationships from cross sections over time; in the latter, various approaches applicable to simultaneous equations are considered; the former compared analytically a method equivalent to treating μ_i (and λ_t) as parameters, and one based explicitly on the notion that these are random variables. In the second case, estimates of the moments of μ_i and ν_{it} (and λ_t) are obtained from the calculated residuals of ordinary least squares, and the estimated variance proportions are then used to transform the data before running a second regression. Wallace and Hussain show that, provided the moment matrix of the independent variables (all assumed nonstochastic) tends to a positive definite matrix as both N and T tend to infinity, both methods lead to asymptotically equivalent estimates with asymptotically equal variance-covariance matrices. Under suitable additional assumptions, both methods yield asymptotically normal estimates. Wallace and Hussain do not consider situations in which a lagged value of the dependent variable is one of the explanatory variables. Unfortunately, examples of this sort are exceptionally common in the analysis of economic data, and a great deal of complexity is introduced into the problem when a dynamic structure is postulated.

Amemiya (1967) considered the problem of estimating a model such as (1.1) and (1.2) (i.e., one including a lagged value of the dependent variable). His model also includes truly exogenous explanatory variables as well. Amemiya obtains the asymptotic distribution *for fixed N* and $T \to \infty$ for the following three estimates of the regression coefficients: (i) maximum likelihood; (ii) least squares, assuming the μ_i are fixed constants; and (iii) generalized least squares based on a consistently estimated value of ρ (what I have called the two-round estimates) or even one that is arbitrarily guessed. Not unexpectedly, Amemiya shows that it is impossible to obtain separate consistent estimates of ρ and σ^2 when N is fixed. That this is so should be intuitively obvious since the distributional properties of the random variables can hardly be determined with greater precision as the sample size is increased, as long as the sample size is not permitted to increase in a direction that could yield more information about the number of individuals. When both N and T are allowed to tend to infinity, Amemiya shows that all three estimates are consistent and

---

[6] We shall see, in fact, that estimation of the parameters of the model, other than those characterizing the disturbances, by means of regressions equivalent to those including fixed coefficients to represent the μ_is, "wastes" certain information contained in the relations among individual means.

asymptotically efficient provided that the moment matrix of the independent variables converges to a positive definite matrix, *regardless of the way in which N and T increase.*[7]

Asymptotic results are useful largely to the extent that they can serve as a guide to what we may find in the samples of small or moderate size with which we typically deal in econometrics.[8] It is apparent that the results of Wallace and Hussain and Amemiya may not serve us well in this respect since, asymptotically, they do not distinguish between various estimation procedures. Indeed, Amemiya's results suggest that full maximum likelihood, two-round procedures using an estimated value of ρ or arbitrary nonzero value of ρ, and methods based on treating the μ_i as constant parameters to be estimated, are all asymptotically equivalent. Since it was found in Nerlove (1967) that ordinary least squares, either ignoring the μ_is or treating them as constants to be estimated, gave exceedingly poor estimates of α for relevant sample sizes, it is apparent that existing large-sample asymptotic results are not helpful in problems of this sort. Consequently, I believe that Monte Carlo experiments of the type described here and in Nerlove (1967) may serve a useful purpose in increasing our understanding of the problems of estimation of dynamic economic relations from a time series of cross sections.

In the experiments reported in Nerlove (1967), no exogenous variable was included. This not only made it impossible to ascertain the properties of

---

[7] Although Amemiya apparently states that the value of ρ may be chosen in a completely arbitrary fashion and his result nonetheless follows, this is not quite true. The intraclass correlation may indeed be chosen arbitrarily as long *as it is not taken to be zero.* For $\rho = 0$, the ordinary least squares, the maximum likelihood, and the generalized least-squares estimates are all equivalent; whereas for $\rho \neq 0$, ordinary least squares without individual constant terms is never a suitable estimate, while maximum likelihood, generalized least squares, and a method equivalent to least squares with individual constant terms all lead to the same results asymptotically, as Amemiya says. For a long time, I was puzzled by the fact that N and T may tend to infinity arbitrarily, and this result still apparently holds. Essentially, one appears to be estimating a number of parameters tending to infinity at the same or a faster rate than the number of observations. The clue to resolution of the puzzle is to observe that the asymptotic results refer not to ρ and σ^2, but only to α (or any other coefficients of truly independent variables). Indeed, ρ and σ^2 are not identified asymptotically if N and T tend to infinity in an arbitrary fashion.

[8] *Large-sample* asymptotic results are, in fact, only one form of asymptotic theory. Essentially, what we try to do is to approximate the finite sample moments of our estimators, or some function thereof, by the first few terms in an expansion in powers of the reciprocal of sample size. It is possible to make similar calculations using expansions in powers of a scalar factor in the variance-covariance matrix of disturbances. This amounts to an asymptotic result for the variance of the disturbances tending to zero rather than sample size to infinity. Often, these results provide a better approximation to the finite sample distributions obtained in Monte Carlo experiments than do the large sample asymptotics. An explanation of the method and application to certain problems in the estimation of simultaneous equations is contained in Kadane (1966). At a later date, an attempt will be made to derive asymptotic results of this sort for the present model and compare them with the experimental sampling distributions reported here.

instrumental variable estimates and related two-round procedures, but also may very well have significantly affected the properties of those estimates whose distributions were investigated.[9] Indeed, as we shall see, the relative performance of full maximum likelihood and two-round procedures is affected by the inclusion of an exogenous variable.

Five methods of estimation were compared in the initial set of experiments: (1) generalized least-squares estimates employing the true value of ρ (used to generate the observations); (2) ordinary least-squares estimates, which are the same as (1) for $\rho = 0$; (3) least-squares estimates of α and an overall constant term obtained from regressions containing individual constant terms (i.e., analyses treating the μ_i as parameters to be estimated); (4) two-round estimates based on a value of ρ estimated by means of the individual constants from (3) by computing a variance of these constants and forming the ratio of this estimate to the sum of this estimate and the estimated residual variance of the regression (i.e., the same as (1) but using $\rho = \hat{\sigma}_\mu^2/(\hat{\sigma}_\mu^2 + \hat{\sigma}_v^2)$); and (5) maximum-likelihood estimates based on a search procedure for ρ in the interval $[0, 1)$.

In Nerlove (1967), it was noted that *for fixed N*, the estimates obtained by (1) and those obtained by (3) tend to a common value. For $N, T \to \infty$ such that $N/T \to 0$, estimates (1), (4), and (5) tend to a common value in probability. Thus, asymptotic theory casts relatively little light on the comparative small-sample properties of the estimates. In the experiments reported in Nerlove (1967), the following conclusions regarding these small-sample properties emerged:

1. Despite the small number of observations over time, the small-sample bias known to exist in the estimation of autoregressive schemes is surprisingly small for generalized least squares using the true value of ρ. While this method is not one that may be used in practice, the result does indicate the importance of information concerning the value of ρ and the great relevance of that information in estimation.
2. Ordinary least-squares estimates of α are seriously biased upward when ρ is different from zero. The corresponding estimates of σ^2 based on the calculated residuals from an ordinary least-squares regression are strongly biased toward zero.
3. Least squares with individual constant terms yield estimates of α biased toward zero. Furthermore, the implied estimate of ρ, based on the "variance" of the constant terms and the estimated residual variance, is biased upward despite the fact that the implied estimate of $\sigma^2 = \sigma_\mu^2 + \sigma_v^2$ is also biased upward.

---

[9] For example, Malinvaud (1966, pp. 463–464) shows that the asymptotic bias of the ordinary least-squares estimate of the coefficient of a lagged dependent variable in a regression containing exogenous variables is smaller than when no exogenous variables are present.

4. The distribution of the two-round estimates of α and the distribution
   of the maximum-likelihood estimates are very similar. There is some
   bias downward for large true α and some upward for small true α. The
   estimates of σ^2 are highly erratic for the maximum-likelihood method
   and somewhat less so for the two-round method. The very implausible
   behavior of the maximum-likelihood method found in the study of the
   demand for natural gas (Balestra and Nerlove, 1966) was not, however,
   reproduced in the experiments.

The experiments reported here differ from the earlier series in three respects. First, an exogenous variable is introduced in the relationship to be estimated. Second, the presence of an exogenous variable allows us to explore the
behavior of instrumental variable estimates and of two-round estimates based
on an instrumental variable first stage. Third, a gradient procedure for obtaining the maximum-likelihood estimates is used. The findings confirm the bias
of the ordinary least-squares estimates and those based on least squares with
individual constant terms. Furthermore, contrary to the conjecture expressed
in Nerlove (1967) that the curious behavior of the maximum-likelihood estimates found in Balestra and Nerlove (1966) could probably not be reproduced
without the introduction of specification error, we find here that such behavior
occurs with non-negligible frequency when exogenous variables with the sorts
of time paths assumed here are introduced.

2. DESIGN OF THE EXPERIMENTS

a. Generation of the Observations

Except for inclusion of an exogenous variable, the model used to generate the
observations was that previously employed. Arranging the observations first
by individual, then according to period, and defining

$$y = (y_{11}, \ldots, y_{1T}, \ldots, y_{N1}, \ldots, y_{NT})',$$

$$y_{-1} = (y_{10}, \ldots, y_{1T-1}, \ldots, y_{N0}, \ldots, y_{NT-1})',$$

$$x = (x_{11}, \ldots, x_{1T}, \ldots, x_{N1}, \ldots, x_{NT})',$$

$$u = (u_{11}, \ldots, u_{1T}, \ldots, u_{N1}, \ldots, u_{NT})',$$

the model becomes

$$y = \alpha y_{-1} + \beta x + u, \tag{2.1}$$

with

$$Euu' = \sigma^2 \begin{bmatrix} A & 0 & \cdots & 0 \\ 0 & A & \cdots & 0 \\ \vdots & \vdots & & \vdots \\ 0 & 0 & \cdots & A \end{bmatrix} = \sigma^2 \Omega, \tag{2.2}$$

where

$$A = \begin{bmatrix} 1 & \rho & \cdots & \rho \\ \rho & 1 & \cdots & \rho \\ \vdots & \vdots & & \vdots \\ \rho & \rho & \cdots & 1 \end{bmatrix}.$$

The first step in the generation of the observations for various sets of parameter values α, β, ρ, and σ^2 was the generation of a set of exogenous variables, *held fixed through the entire set of experiments.* While a set of real exogenous variables, say state employment figures over the last ten or twenty years, could have been used, there are several advantages in using an artificially generated series. The exact characteristics of the exogenous variables may be controlled if they are artificially generated. This means that the series may have many of the properties of real exogenous variables, serial correlation, trend, and the like, without some of the undesirable properties found in particular series. To be sure, we have to live with these undesirable properties in real estimation problems; but, in real estimation problems, we generally have more than one exogenous variable. The extreme smoothness and trend-like character of, say, state employment figures is not characteristic of some linear combination of, for example, these employment figures, prices, and weather variables. Since the nature of the exogenous variables present may quite profoundly affect the character of the estimates obtained by various methods, it is important not only to know this nature exactly, but also to be able to vary it systematically. Such variation is not attempted here, but will form the basis of subsequent experiments.

The exogenous variables were generated by choosing a random variable ω_{it}, uniformly distributed on the interval $[-\frac{1}{2}, \frac{1}{2}]$ and forming

$$x_{it} = 0.1t + 0.5x_{it-1} + \omega_{it}, \tag{2.3}$$

where the value x_{i0} was chosen as $5 + 10\omega_{i0}$. This was done for $i = 1, \ldots, 25$ and $t = 1, \ldots, 20$. In the experiments reported here $N = 25$, but $T = 10$. The additional ten exogenous variables were used in a manner described later.[10]

The next step in each repetition was the generation of random variables u_{it} with variance-covariance matrix given in (2.2). Since the maximum-likelihood

---

[10] The values of the exogenous variables used in all experiments for all parameter values are contained in an appendix to this paper (see Footnote 17).

estimates, the properties of which are explored later, are based on the assumption of normality, and since specification error was not being investigated in this series of experiments, the u_{it}s were assumed to follow a multivariate normal distribution. Given values for σ^2 and ρ, there are two ways in which random variables u_{it} may be computed starting with independent random variables uniformily distributed on the interval $[0, 1]$. From the uniformly distributed random variables, it is easy to obtain independent normal variables with zero mean and unit variance.[11] At this point, there are two possibilities. Suppose we wish to generate five hundred values $u_{it}, i = 1, \ldots, 25; t = 1, \ldots, 20$. We may first choose twenty-five μ_is such that

$$\mu_i \sim N(0, \rho\sigma^2),$$

then obtain five hundred v_{it}s such that

$$v_{it} \sim N(0, (1 - \rho)\sigma^2),$$

and finally form

$$u_{it} = \mu_i + v_{it} \qquad (i = 1, \ldots, 25; t = 1, \ldots, 20).$$

An alternative method to the foregoing is to transform the sequence of independent normal, zero mean, unit variance random variables (call these w_j), directly into a vector u having the desired variance-covariance matrix, $\sigma^2\Omega$ in (2.2).

---

[11] Only a true random process may, of course, produce real random numbers. To approximate such a process digitally in machines with a thirty-six-bit word, recursion relations of the form

$$R_{n+1} = CR_n(\bmod 2^{35})$$

are used to produce a sequence of numbers $R_0, R_1, R_2, \ldots$ which simulate the behavior of a true random sequence (i.e., so-called "pseudorandom numbers"). (For a discussion of various methods for generating pseudorandom numbers and the problems arising, see Hammersley and Handscomb, 1964, pp. 25–42.) Not only do such sequences repeat after a certain point, but they also tend to exhibit certain forms of nonrandom behavior. Hence, when generating long sequences of such numbers, it is desirable to use several generators (i.e., relations of the form given above with differently chosen C and R_0). In the calculations reported here, five such generators were used in such a way that no generator was ever started at a previous starting point and in such a way that the particular generator used to produce a number in the ultimate sequence was itself determined through the use of one of the generators. It is believed that the sequence of numbers thus obtained is subject to very few of the difficulties and problems that beset most sequences of pseudorandom numbers. The numbers resulting were transformed into pseudorandom variables uniformly distributed on the interval $[0, 1]$. Pairs of such numbers were in turn transformed to independent normal variates with mean zero and variance one by means of the transformation,

$$w_1 = (-2 \log v_1)^{\frac{1}{2}} \cos(2\pi v_2),$$
$$w_2 = (-2 \log v_1)^{\frac{1}{2}} \sin(2\pi v_2),$$

where (v_1, v_2) is a pair of uniformly and independently distributed random variables (Hammersley and Handscomb, 1964, p. 39).

In general, the best way in which to obtain a vector u coming from a population $N(\theta, \Omega)$ on the basis of a series of random variables $w_i \sim n(0, 1)$ is to make use of the unique decomposition of any real, positive semidefinite matrix into the product of a lower triangular matrix H and its transpose:

$$\sigma^2 \Omega = \sigma^2 H H'.$$

Then $u = Hw + \theta \sim N(\theta, \sigma^2 \Omega)$ where each element of w is $n(0, 1)$. The elements of H may be found by a simple system of recursions. Such a general solution to the problem, however, does not permit one to take advantage of the very simple structure of Ω, in particular of the fact that it depends on only two parameters. Thus, it is preferable in this case to make use of the square root of Ω defined as the matrix with characteristic roots equal to the square roots of the characteristic roots of Ω (all real and positive because of the positive definiteness of Ω).

To obtain $\Omega^{\frac{1}{2}}$, one makes use of the orthogonal transformation

$$C = \begin{bmatrix} e'/\sqrt{T} \\ C_1 \end{bmatrix}, \tag{2.4}$$

where e is a $T \times 1$ vector consisting entirely of ones, and C_1 is a $(T-1) \times T$ matrix such that

$$C_1 e = 0,$$
$$C_1 C_1' = I_{T-1}, \tag{2.5}$$
$$C_1' C_1 = I_T - ee'/T.$$

As shown in Balestra and Nerlove (1966):

$$\sigma^2 C A C' = \begin{bmatrix} \xi & 0 & \cdots & 0 \\ 0 & \eta & & \\ \vdots & \vdots & & \\ 0 & 0 & \cdots & \eta \end{bmatrix}, \tag{2.6}$$

where

$$\xi = \sigma^2[(1 - \rho) + T\rho],$$
$$\eta = \sigma^2(1 - \rho). \tag{2.7}$$

Thus, we have

$$\sigma \Omega^{\frac{1}{2}} = \begin{bmatrix} B & 0 & \cdots & 0 \\ 0 & B & \cdots & 0 \\ \vdots & \vdots & & \vdots \\ 0 & 0 & \cdots & B \end{bmatrix}, \tag{2.8}$$

where each of the N blocks B is a $T \times T$ matrix of the form

$$B = C' \text{diag}\{\sqrt{\xi}, \sqrt{\eta}, \ldots, \sqrt{\eta}\} C \qquad (2.9)$$

$$= \sqrt{\eta} I_T + \frac{(\sqrt{\xi} - \sqrt{\eta})}{T} ee'.$$

Thus, an element of the $NT \times 1$ vector u is obtained as

$$u_{it} = \frac{\sqrt{\xi} - \sqrt{\eta}}{T} \sum_{k=1}^{T} w_k + \sqrt{\eta} w_t \qquad (t = 1, \ldots, T), \qquad (2.10)$$

where $w_1, \ldots, w_T$ is a sequence of independent normal variables with zero mean and unit variance.[12] Note that N such sets of Tws are required to generate the full $NT \times 1$ vector u.

It is important to note that *the u_{it}s generated in either of the two ways have exactly the same distribution.* Given a particular starting point for the random-number generator used to obtain the initial uniformly distributed pseudorandom numbers with which both methods begin, the actual u_{it}s generated will differ in value (since the original pseudorandom numbers enter in each somewhat differently); however, the distributions will both be $N(0, \Omega)$. Hence, there is no way one could distinguish between two sets of such numbers – one generated one way, the other in the other fashion. The only ground for choice is thus computational convenience. Obtaining the u_{it}s by the first method requires the computation of $N + NT$ values of two different random normal variables and NT additions, whereas the computation of the u_{it}s by the second method requires only NT values of a random zero-mean, unit-variance, normal variable, and $N + NT$ additions. Thus, the second method trades N additions for the generation of N additional random values. Given the complexity of the pseudorandom-number of routines, it is obviously a considerable computational saving to use the second method.

Given the values of the exogenous variables, fixed for the entire series of experiments, and given the disturbances, computed for each repetition of

---

[12] An analogous result for

$$\Omega^{-1/2} = \begin{bmatrix} H & 0 & \cdots & 0 \\ 0 & H & \cdots & 0 \\ \vdots & \vdots & & \vdots \\ 0 & 0 & \cdots & H \end{bmatrix},$$

where

$$H = \frac{1}{\sqrt{\eta}} \left(I_T - \frac{ee'}{T} \right) + \frac{1}{\sqrt{\xi}} \frac{ee'}{T},$$

may be used to define a transformation of the original variables such that ordinary least-squares estimates are equal to the generalized least-squares estimates. Since $(1/\sqrt{\xi}) \to 0$ as $T \to \infty$, the transformed variables of generalized least squares become more and more like simple deviations from individual means. This result is useful in the interpretation of the properties of various estimates discussed later.

a single experiment involving certain parameter values, the next step is to compute the values of the series y and y_{-1} for each individual and for the number of time periods, T, involved in the experiments. If the relationship to be estimated were a pure autoregression, as in the first series of experiments reported in Nerlove (1967), it would be easy to choose the starting value y_{i0} in such a way that its variance would be exactly the same as the variance of any other y_{it} for the same individual. The presence of an exogenous variable, however, complicates matters. The initial value y_{i1} was taken to be

$$y_{i1} = \beta x_{i1} + \frac{u_{i1}}{\sqrt{1 - \alpha^2}}, \tag{2.11}$$

which would yield an appropriate value for $\beta = 0$ (i.e., no exogenous variable present). Then, however, nineteen more values were generated and the first ten discarded in forming the vector y, the first nine in forming the vector y_{-1}, and correspondingly the first ten values of x_{it} were also discarded in forming x.

The procedure described was repeated fifty times for each set of parameter values, α, β, ρ, and σ^2 chosen, giving for each repetition three vectors y, y_{-1}, and x, each 250×1.

b. Parameter Values

As indicated, in all experiments reported here, $T = 10$ and $N = 25$. The parameter α was taken to have values 0.10, 0.30, 0.50, 0.70, and 0.90. For each such value, three values of β were examined: $\beta = 0.0, 0.5$, and 1.0. For each of the fifteen combinations of α and β, the following values of ρ were investigated: $\rho = 0.00, 0.15, 0.30, 0.45, 0.60, 0.75, 0.90$, and 0.95. Throughout, σ^2 was set equal to 1. Although a constant term was estimated, the true constant was assumed to be zero. Thus, altogether 120 parameter combinations were examined in the experiments.

c. Methods of Estimation

For each of the 120 parameter combinations chosen, seven methods of estimation were considered.

(1) Generalized least-squares estimates employing the true value of ρ used in the generation of the observations. An estimate of the residual variance, $\hat{\sigma}^2$, was obtained by a slightly modified form of the standard formula for an unbiased estimator of σ^2.[13] The modification was simply not to make the usual adjustment for loss of degrees of freedom. This led to an estimate slightly (but very slightly, since $NT = 250$) biased downward, but comparable with the maximum-likelihood estimate of σ^2. Generalized least squares is, of course,

---

[13] See, for example, Goldberger, 1964, p. 234.

not a practical method of estimation since the true value of ρ is unknown; however, it provides a useful standard of comparison. We will refer to this method as GLS.

If we let the $NT \times 3$ matrix $[e_{NT}, y_{-1}, x] = Z$, where e_{NT} is an $NT \times 1$ vector consisting entirely of ones, the generalized least-squares estimates of the parameter vector $\delta' = (\gamma, \alpha, \beta)$ are given by

$$\hat{\delta} = [Z'\Omega^{-1}Z]^{-1}Z'\Omega^{-1}y. \tag{2.12}$$

Making use of our previous result on the diagonalization of Ω and partitioning the matrix Z as

$$Z = \begin{bmatrix} Z_1 \\ \vdots \\ Z_N \end{bmatrix},$$

where Z_i is the $T \times 3$ matrix of explanatory variables for the ith individual, and the vector y as

$$y = \begin{pmatrix} y_1 \\ \vdots \\ y_N \end{pmatrix},$$

we may write (2.12) as

$$\hat{\delta} = \left[\sum_{i=1}^{N} \frac{Z_i'(I_T - ee'/T)Z_i}{\eta} + \sum_{i=1}^{N} \frac{Z_i'ee'Z_i}{\xi} \right]^{-1} \cdot \left[\sum_{i=1}^{N} \frac{Z_i'(I_T - ee'/T)y_i}{\eta} \right.$$
$$\left. + \sum_{i=1}^{N} \frac{Z_i'ee'y_i}{\xi} \right]. \tag{2.13}$$

The first term in each of the squared brackets is a matrix or vector of sums of squares or cross products of the variables for each individual about the mean values of those variables for that individual; that is, essentially the moments we would use to calculate the estimates of γ, α, and β (but *not* the μ_i) were we to treat the random effects μ_i as constants to be estimated (but not actually estimate them). The second term in each of the square brackets is a matrix or vector of sums of squares or cross-products of the individual means, one with the other. Were we to use only this information to estimate δ, it would be as if we neglected all variation over time for each individual and looked only at the variation *across* individuals.

Clearly, both sorts of information – variation over time for different individuals and variation among individuals – should be utilized. The GLS estimates weight the first sort of information inversely to η and the second sort inversely to ξ. Using the definitions of ξ and η in terms of ρ, σ^2, and T in (2.7), we see that as $T \to \infty$, quite irrespective of the value of N, the GLS estimates of γ, α, and β tend to those we would obtain had we introduced separate constants for each individual. But, please note, such constants are not actually estimated.

The common sense of this result is essentially that when one has lots of information over time on each individual, individual variability tends to dominate the estimates; whereas, when there is little information on each individual, variation across individuals is much more important.

(2) Ordinary least-squares estimates of the relation (2.1) (i.e., not including individual constant terms). Again, σ^2 was estimated without adjustment for lost degrees of freedom. We will refer to this method as OLS. Note that $\hat{\delta}$, in (2.13), reduces to the OLS estimate when $\rho = 0$, for then $\xi = \eta$.

(3) Least-squares estimates of the parameters

$$y = \alpha y_{-1} + \beta x + \sum_{i=1}^{N} \mu_i \iota_i + v, \tag{2.14}$$

where the μ_i are N constants, ι_i is an $NT \times 1$ vector consisting entirely of zeros except for the ith individual and then of ones, and $v = (v_{11}, \dots, v_{1T}, \dots, v_{N1}, \dots, v_{NT})'$. An estimate of σ^2 was obtained from the usual estimate of the residual variance σ_v^2 in (2.14), unadjusted, however, for loss of degrees of freedom, and the estimates of the parameters μ_i, by

$$\hat{\sigma}^2 = \frac{\sum_i \left\{ \hat{\mu}_i - \sum_i \hat{\mu}_i / N \right\}^2}{N} + \hat{\sigma}_v^2. \tag{2.15}$$

An estimate of ρ was obtained as

$$r_c = \frac{\sum_i \left\{ \hat{\mu}_i - \sum_i \hat{\mu}_i / N \right\}^2}{N} \bigg/ \hat{\sigma}^2. \tag{2.16}$$

We will refer to this method as LSC.

(4) Instrumental-variable estimates using x_{it-1} as an instrument for y_{it-1}. The intraclass correlation coefficient was estimated from the calculated residuals, $\hat{\mu}_{it}$, by

$$r_i = \frac{\frac{1}{T} \sum_{i=1}^{N} \left(\sum_{t=1}^{T} \hat{u}_{it} \right)^2 - \frac{1}{NT} \sum_{i=1}^{N} \sum_{t=1}^{T} \hat{u}_{it}^2}{NT\hat{\sigma}^2}, \tag{2.17}$$

where

$$\hat{\sigma}^2 = \frac{\sum_{i=1}^{N} \sum_{t=1}^{T} \hat{u}_{it}^2}{NT}.^{14} \tag{2.18}$$

---

[14] Although (2.7) is a natural formula for estimating ρ from the calculated residuals, it differs from the maximum-likelihood estimate of ρ from *observed* $\hat{u}_{it}$, which is a common estimate in components of variance analysis. The maximum-likelihood estimate would be

$$\frac{\sum_{i=1}^{N} \left\{ \left[\sum_{t=1}^{T} \hat{u}_{it} \right]^2 - \sum_{t=1}^{T} \hat{u}_{it}^2 \right\}}{NT(T-1)\hat{\sigma}^2},$$

where $\hat{\sigma}^2$ is given by (2.18).

Standard errors of the estimated coefficients were computed from an estimate of the asymptotic variance-covariance matrix suggested by Sargan (1958, pp. 396–397). We will refer to this method as IV.

(5) "Two-round" estimates equivalent to generalized least squares using not the true value of ρ but the estimate r_c obtained in (3), a least-squares regression with individual constant terms. Standard errors for these estimates were not computed. We will refer to this method as 2RC.

(6) "Two-round" estimates similar to (5) but using r_i, an estimate of ρ based on the calculated residuals from the instrumental-variable estimate of equation (2.1) as given in (2.17). Standard errors for these estimates were not computed. We will refer to this method as 2RI.

(7) Maximum-likelihood estimates obtained by maximizing the logarithmic likelihood function.

$$L(\alpha, \beta, \gamma, \rho, \sigma^2) = -\frac{NT}{2}\log 2\pi - \frac{NT}{2}\log \sigma^2 - \frac{N}{2}\log[1 - \rho + T\rho]$$

$$-\frac{N(T-1)}{2}\log(1 - \rho) - \frac{1}{2\sigma^2}\sum_{i=1}^{N}\left\{\frac{1}{T[1 - \rho + T\rho]}\right.$$

$$\left.\times\left(\sum_{t=1}^{T}u_{it}\right)^2 - \frac{1}{T(1 - \rho)}\left(\sum_{t=1}^{T}u_{it}\right)^2 + \frac{1}{(1 - \rho)}\sum_{t=1}^{T}u_{it}^2\right\},$$

$$(2.19)$$

where $T = 10$, $N = 25$, and

$$u_{it} = y_{it} - \alpha y_{it-1} - \beta x_{it} - \gamma,$$

with respect to all the unknown parameters. Note that a nonzero constant term, γ, is allowed for.[15] Asymptotic standard errors were obtained from the

---

Except when ρ is very small or very large, the two estimates tend to be quite close. The maximum-likelihood estimate, however, does have one major defect for the use proposed: namely, it may be slightly negative, whereas r_i in (2.17) cannot be negative. It is proposed to use r_i in place of ρ in a "second-round" generalized least-squares estimation procedure. The possibility of a negative value has obvious disadvantages.

[15] Note that as $T \to \infty$, N fixed, the first term in curly brackets inside the summation over i becomes negligible and this term of the likelihood function becomes essentially the sum of squared deviations of the individual observations from the individual means. The terms

$$-\frac{N}{2}\log(1 - \rho + T\rho) - \frac{(NT - N)}{2}\log(1 - \rho) = \frac{N}{2}\log\frac{1 - \rho}{1 - \rho + T\rho} - \frac{NT}{2}\log(1 - \rho)$$

tend to $(-NT/2)\log(1 - \rho)$. In this form, however, it is clear that σ^2 and $1 - \rho$ enter the likelihood function only as the product $\sigma^2(1 - \rho)$ and cannot be separately identified.

standard result for the asymptotic variance-covariance matrix of maximum-likelihood estimates:

$$
-\begin{bmatrix}
\dfrac{\partial^2 L}{\partial \alpha^2} & \dfrac{\partial^2 L}{\partial \alpha \partial \beta} & \dfrac{\partial^2 L}{\partial \alpha \partial \gamma} & \dfrac{\partial^2 L}{\partial \alpha \partial \rho} & \dfrac{\partial^2 L}{\partial \alpha \partial \sigma^2} \\[2ex]
\dfrac{\partial^2 L}{\partial \alpha \partial \beta} & \dfrac{\partial^2 L}{\partial \beta^2} & \dfrac{\partial^2 L}{\partial \beta \partial \gamma} & \dfrac{\partial^2 L}{\partial \beta \partial \rho} & \dfrac{\partial^2 L}{\partial \beta \partial \sigma^2} \\[2ex]
\dfrac{\partial^2 L}{\partial \alpha \partial \gamma} & \dfrac{\partial^2 L}{\partial \beta \partial \gamma} & \dfrac{\partial^2 L}{\partial \gamma^2} & \dfrac{\partial^2 L}{\partial \gamma \partial \rho} & \dfrac{\partial^2 L}{\partial \gamma \partial \sigma^2} \\[2ex]
\dfrac{\partial^2 L}{\partial \alpha \partial \rho} & \dfrac{\partial^2 L}{\partial \beta \partial \rho} & \dfrac{\partial^2 L}{\partial \gamma \partial \rho} & \dfrac{\partial^2 L}{\partial \rho^2} & \dfrac{\partial^2 L}{\partial \rho \partial \sigma^2} \\[2ex]
\dfrac{\partial^2 L}{\partial \alpha \partial \sigma^2} & \dfrac{\partial^2 L}{\partial \beta \partial \sigma^2} & \dfrac{\partial^2 L}{\partial \gamma \partial \sigma^2} & \dfrac{\partial^2 L}{\partial \rho \partial \sigma^2} & \dfrac{\partial^2 L}{\partial (\sigma^2)^2}
\end{bmatrix}^{-1},
$$

where the partial derivatives of the logarithmic-likelihood function are evaluated at the maximum-likelihood estimates $\hat{\alpha}$, $\hat{\beta}$, $\hat{\gamma}$, $\hat{\rho}$, and $\hat{\sigma}^2$. The method used to obtain the maximum of the likelihood function was that suggested by Fletcher and Powell (1963) and programmed in ALGOL by Wells (1967) with the modification suggested by Box (1966) for incorporating the constraint that ρ lie in the interval (0, 1). To ensure that $\hat{\sigma}^2$ would be positive, the simple device of maximizing L with respect to σ instead of σ^2 was adopted. The method of bounding $\hat{\rho}$ was to maximize L with respect to $\theta = [\arcsin \sqrt{\rho}]$ or $\rho = \sin^2 \theta$.

Clearly, θ may range over the entire real line, whereas $\rho = \sin^2 \theta$ must lie between 0 and 1. The problem is that L will have multiple maxima (albeit widely separated) with respect to θ since $\sin \theta$ is a periodic function. The method of Fletcher and Powell, however, is a local procedure and the estimates were taken to be the first point at which a local maximum of L was obtained. As a starting point for the maximum-likelihood estimation procedure, the estimates of α, β, and γ from LSC and the estimate of σ^2, ρ, r_c, as in method (3) were used. We will refer to this method as ML.

When a boundary-point maximum of the likelihood function occurs, the usual formula for the asymptotic variance-covariance matrix given previously is no longer valid. Indeed, the matrix of second derivatives need not be negative definite at a boundary maximum. It is possible in such cases that the inverse of the information matrix has negative diagonal elements. Hence, in all cases (and there are a great many for $\rho = 0$) in which a boundary maximum (always $\hat{\rho} = 0$) occurred, the computation of asymptotic standard errors was omitted. To check many of the boundary maxima, a search procedure similar to that used in Nerlove (1967) was employed. The solution by the method of Fletcher and Powell was validated in every case checked by the search.

This remains true if N increases without bound; hence, ρ and σ^2 are not identifiable asymptotically.

3. COMPARATIVE PROPERTIES OF DIFFERENT
ESTIMATION PROCEDURES

For each of the methods of estimation described in the preceding subsection and for each choice of parameters, fifty sets of observations and estimates were generated in the manner described. To characterize the distributions of coefficient estimates, the mean, mean-square error, minimum, first quartile, median, third quartile, and maximum were computed. When estimated standard errors were computed, their distributions were characterized in the same way except that the variance of the distribution was computed rather than the mean-square error. The reason for computing the variance rather than mean-square error in these cases was simply that the "true" standard error was generally unknown.[16]

The results of the extensive calculations that were undertaken are summarized in detail in an appendix to this paper.[17] In the following pages, an attempt is made to describe the results qualitatively, emphasizing certain noteworthy features, and one "summary" table is presented.

To facilitate comparison of estimation procedures, the results are discussed under three headings: bias, relative mean-squares error, and characteristics of the maximum-likelihood estimates. The computed standard errors are discussed only tangentially and then with reference to how well they serve or do not serve to indicate the actual variability of the estimates.

a. Bias

Although small-sample bias is known to exist in all cases in which a lagged value of the dependent variables is one of the explanatory variables,[18] it is

---

[16] Except, of course, in the case of the generalized least-squares estimates.

[17] Previously available at the Cowles Foundation for Research in Economics, Box 2125, Yale Station, New Haven, Connecticut 06520 U.S.A. Copies now available on the internet at: http://www.arec. umd.edu/mnerlove/Tables1971.ZIP (23.1mb).

   The appendix tables consist of three sets referring to the values of β chosen: 0.0, 0.5, and 1.0. The case $\beta = 0.0$ is an especially interesting one inasmuch as the specification error involved, namely including a variable when it should be excluded, is one seldom analyzed. The first seven tables of each set present the means and mean-square errors of the estimates of $\alpha, \beta, \gamma, \sigma^2$ and, where appropriate, ρ, for various combinations of the true values of the parameters α and ρ. Each table covers a different estimation procedure: (1) generalized least-squares estimates (GLS); (2) ordinary least-squares estimates (OLS); (3) least-squares estimates with individual constant terms (LSC); (4) two-round estimates using $\hat{\rho}$ from LSC (2RC); (5) instrumental-variable estimates using x_{-1} as the instrument for y_{-1} (IV); (6) two-round estimates using $\hat{\rho}$ from IV (2RI); and (7) maximum-likelihood estimates (ML).

   The remaining five tables of each set give the means and variances of the computed standard errors of the estimates of α, β, and γ for the corresponding combinations of the true values of α and ρ. Standard errors were computed only for five of the seven types of estimates considered: GLS, OLS, LSC, IV, and ML. Maxima, minima, and quartiles of the distributions are not reported in the appendix although they were computed.

[18] See Hurwicz (1950).

apparent that such bias is very slight for the GLS estimates. The means of the GLS estimates of α are particularly close to the true values, irrespective of the value of β. The residual variance is also well estimated by GLS. β and γ are somewhat less well estimated, the bias in γ being slightly larger, the larger the true value of β. Perhaps the intuitive rationale of the virtually negligible small-sample bias is that when ρ is known, a cross section over time of the sort considered here in fact provides a large number of observations.

The picture is quite different when ordinary least-squares estimates are considered. Except when $\rho = 0$, in which case the GLS and OLS estimates coincide, the OLS estimate of α is severely biased upward. Indeed, for large values of ρ, the OLS estimate of α is a better estimate of ρ than it is of α. The coefficient of the exogenous variable, β, is strongly biased downward for large values of ρ except when the true value of β is zero; in this case, the bias is comparable to that of the GLS estimate and essentially negligible. The OLS estimate of σ^2 is strongly biased downward for large values of ρ and all values of β. When the estimated standard errors are examined, it is apparent that they are greatly affected by the under-estimation of the residual variance. The OLS estimate of the constant term is slightly but distinctly biased downward for $\beta = 0$, and greatly biased downward for large values of β and ρ.

As was the case in the experiments reported in Nerlove (1967), the introduction of individual constant terms in an attempt to remove the time-invariant individual effects produces estimates of α that are markedly too low. This is true regardless of the value of β or ρ, but the LSC estimates of α are noticeably less biased downward the higher the value of β and ρ; indeed, for $\beta = 1.0$ and $\rho = 0.9$, the bias in the LSC estimate of α is negligible when $\alpha = 0.9$ but increases as the true value of α falls. For small values of α, ρ, and β, the bias is fifty percent or more of the true parameter value. The LSC estimate of β is biased upward irrespective of the true value of β. The bias is greater the greater α, and less the greater ρ. When β is not zero and α is large, the LSC estimate of γ is biased upward, especially when the true value of ρ is small. The estimated value of ρ is biased upward, the more severely the lower the true value of ρ. On the other hand, the LSC estimate of σ^2, which depends on the "variance" of the constant terms as well as the estimate of the remaining residual variance, is biased upward but generally less so the lower the true value of ρ.

In Nerlove (1967, p. 46), the following argument was given for expecting the LSC estimate of α (and β) to be biased downward:

We are not, in fact, interested in the individual μ_is but rather only in ρ or σ_μ^2, i.e., the extent to which variation in the μ_is causes y_{it} to vary. By treating the μ_is as constants and estimating them, we must inevitably overestimate σ_μ^2 on account of errors of estimation of each individual μ_i. For T very large relative to N this effect should be very slight, but typically N will be substantially larger than T in applications of economic relevance. If such overestimation of σ_μ^2 does not result in a compensating underestimation of σ_ν^2, there is simply too little variation in y_{it} left over to be explained by variation in y_{it-1} and x_{it}. Thus, α and β should tend to be underestimated in value.

It was left, however, an open question as to why σ_ν^2 was not underestimated. It is clear that if x_{it} and y_{it-1} are positively correlated (which they are in the present case since x_{it} and y_{it} are positively correlated and $\alpha > 0$), then a *downward* bias in the estimate of α must be accompanied by an *upward* bias in the estimate of β. In general, then, it is not true that the bias in the estimates of both α and β will be in the same direction. It was noted previously that the LSC estimates of α and β ignore, in effect, the variation among the individual means and place too much weight (by comparison with GLS) on individual variation about their separate mean levels. In samples in which the number of individuals is large relative to the number of time periods for which each is observed and in which the variation among individuals is great, it is plausible that "effects" such as μ_i and βx_{it}, which do vary a great deal across individuals, should be given excessive weight by LSC. Consequently, the estimate of α might plausibly be expected to be biased downward by this same reasoning. Analytic results do not appear possible in this direction, however, and some further experimentation is necessary to establish the causes of the LSC bias.

Despite the upward bias in the LSC estimate of ρ (larger the smaller the true value of ρ), two-round estimates of α, β, γ, and σ^2 based on generalized least-squares estimates assuming the LSC $\hat{\rho}$ are not seriously biased in comparison with either the OLS or LSC estimates. Indeed, as we shall see, these two-round estimates appear to be superior over a wide range of true parameter values to all the other estimates considered. The 2RC estimate of α is biased downward, but this bias is greatly reduced as the true value of $\hat{\rho}$ rises (presumably because the LSC estimate $\hat{\rho}$ is less biased). The estimate of β is biased upward, but considerably less than the corresponding LSC estimate. Perhaps the principle source of difficulty is the distinct upward bias in the 2RC estimate of σ^2. Exceptionally erratic behavior was noted in Nerlove (1967) for a similar estimate. The presence of an exogenous variable appears greatly to mitigate this difficulty (when β, of course, is not equal to zero), but it does not remove it entirely.

The instrumental variable estimates illustrate clearly the implications of asymptotic efficiency and consistency for the behavior of estimates in small samples. It is often stated that large-sample properties are of no relevance to those who must of necessity be content with small samples; yet, such properties do serve as some guide to what we may expect in the finite case even if the sample is not really large. When the true value of β is zero, the IV estimates are inconsistent. In this case, we might expect highly erratic behavior as indeed occurs. Both the means and mean-square errors of all estimates very greatly and are often extremely large. When $\beta = 1.0$, on the other hand, the bias in the IV estimates of all the parameters is slight. The variances, however, of the distributions of the IV estimates are large, giving rise to fairly high mean-square errors despite the lack of bias. When $\beta = 0.5$, the IV estimates are considerably more erratic than for $\beta = 1.0$. To some extent, the increased variability affects the means of the distributions. (This is especially true for $\hat{\sigma}^2$.) Since the IV estimates are less efficient (asymptotically) the smaller β, but not inconsistent as long as β does not actually equal zero (or x_{it} and x_{it-1} are not perfectly correlated), we might expect little difference in the results for distributions of the estimates based on very large numbers of repetitions of each experiment. It is clear, however, that when only fifty repetitions of each experiment are performed, halving β greatly affects the results. It is also clear that this represents an important general implication both for Monte Carlo methods of investigation and for the reliability of results in actual estimation problems (where, in effect, only one repetition is performed). The *large-sample* property of inefficiency implies erratic *small-sample* behavior.

When $\beta = 0.0$, the two-round estimates that use the IV estimate of ρ to transform the data are greatly affected by the extreme variability of the estimates of ρ. Surprisingly, however, there seem to be certain systematic tendencies. The bias of $\hat{\alpha}$, for example, is negative for small values of ρ, but becomes large and positive as ρ increases. The bias of $\hat{\sigma}^2$ is erratic but does definitely appear to shift from positive to negative as ρ increases. When $\beta = 0.5$ or 1.0, the 2RI estimates are much better behaved. Only for $\rho = 0$, for example, do the biases of α appear non-negligible. The estimates of σ^2 show the greatest bias and behave somewhat erratically for $\beta = 0.5$.

Perhaps the most unexpected result of the present investigation was the exceedingly poor performance of the maximum-likelihood method under certain circumstances. This finding is so important that it is discussed separately in a later subsection. Here, however, we merely note that the biases in cases where a large number of boundary solutions (always $\hat{\rho} = 0$) did not occur are slight. A great many such solutions occurred for $\beta = 0.0$ and for $\alpha = 0.7$, even when $\beta = 0.5$ or 1.0. In these cases, the means of the distribution of the ML estimates were greatly affected.

On the whole, the 2RC estimates appear to have less bias over a wider range than do the other estimates examined.

b. Relative Mean-Square Errors

To compare the mean-square errors in a meaningful fashion, the ratios of the MSE for the OLS, LSC, 2RC, 2RI, and ML estimates of α, β, and γ to the corresponding mean-square error of the GLS estimate were formed.[19] In some sense, the GLS estimate represents an ideal and, because the different estimation techniques may be affected by the vicissitudes of the particular

---

[19] Tables giving these summary statistics are presented in the appendix to this paper.

experiments, examining their behavior relative to the GLS estimates may be helpful in avoiding the difficulties due to too small a number of repetitions.

When the true ρ is zero, ordinary least squares and generalized least squares coincide and the MSE is 1.00. Curiously, the OLS estimates of β and γ have smaller mean-square errors than the GLS estimates in certain cases. When $\beta = 0.0$, these are frequent, especially for small α and large ρ; this phenomenon occurs only for $\hat{\gamma}$ and not for $\hat{\beta}$ when $\beta = 1.0$ or 0.5. Needless to say, the GLS estimates are best only among unbiased linear estimates, and the phenomenon here observed is perfectly possible when comparison among biased estimates is made.

The instrumental variable estimates are terrible, as expected, when $\beta = 0.0$. The mean-square errors, however, fall markedly as β increases and are respectable, if not comparatively low, for $\beta = 1.0$.

Estimates of α or β based on least-squares regressions, including individual constant terms, are generally superior to OLS or IV estimates, except that in certain cases when ρ is small, their mean-square errors are greater than the OLS estimates. The LSC estimates of γ are frequently worse than the OLS estimates.

An unexpected result of the present investigation was the comparative behavior of the maximum-likelihood method and the two-round estimates using $\hat{\rho}$ from the LSC regressions. When $\hat{\rho}$ from an IV first round is used, we would expect the corresponding two-round estimates to be quite erratic when $\beta = 0.0$, simply because the underlying estimates of ρ are so poor. However, even when $\beta = 0.5$ or 1.0, the 2RC estimates have lower mean-square errors except when ρ is very small. Furthermore, the 2RC estimates, especially of α and β, very frequently have smaller relative mean-square errors than the ML estimates. One might have anticipated this in situations in which a large number of boundary solutions occur for values of ρ different from zero, but it also occurs even in situations in which the ML method might be expected to perform well.

On the basis of the criterion of minimum mean-square error, the 2RC estimates also compare favorably with all other estimates, including the ML, over a wide range of parameter values.

c. Characteristics of the Maximum-Likelihood Estimates

Table 1 shows, for each set of true parameter values, what percentage of the fifty repetitions converged and, for convergent cases, in what percentage boundary maxima were obtained. Since ρ and σ^2 were the only bounded parameters, only $\hat{\rho}$ and $\hat{\sigma}^2$ might be found at a boundary. In fact, all boundary points found were points for which $\hat{\rho} = 0$.

In only one case, out of the many thousands estimated, did convergence of the maximization procedure used fail to occur: one of the fifty repetitions for

Table 1. *Characteristics of Maximum-Likelihood Estimation Procedure for Various Parameter Values (All boundary points occur for $\hat{\rho} = 0$)*

		$\rho = 0.0$	$\rho = 0.15$	$\rho = 0.30$	$\rho = 0.45$	$\rho = 0.60$	$\rho = 0.75$	$\rho = 0.90$	$\rho = 0.95$
$\beta = 0.0$:									
% Boundary	$\alpha = 0.1$	64	4	0	0	‘0	0	0	0
% Converged		100	100	100	100	100	100	100	100
% Boundary	$\alpha = 0.3$	76	4	0	2	0	0	0	0
% Converged		100	100	100	100	100	100	100	100
% Boundary	$\alpha = 0.5$	60	8	16	38	34	34	42	46
% Converged		100	100	100	100	100	100	100	100
% Boundary	$\alpha = 0.7$	60	74	90	96	94	94	92	88
% Converged		100	100	100	100	100	100	100	100
% Boundary	$\alpha = 0.9$	66	88	100	98	94	98	92	86
% Converged		100	100	100	100	100	100	100	100
$\beta = 0.5$:									
% Boundary	$\alpha = 0.1$	66	0	0	0	0	0	0	0
% Converged		100	100	100	100	100	100	100	100
% Boundary	$\alpha = 0.3$	72	4	0	0	2	0	0	0
% Converged		100	100	100	100	100	100	100	100
% Boundary	$\alpha = 0.5$	70	14	14	18	18	16	4	0
% Converged		100	100	100	100	100	100	100	100
% Boundary	$\alpha = 0.7$	62	70	84	84	90	84	56	12
% Converged		100	100	100	100	100	100	100	100
% Boundary	$\alpha = 0.9$	66	74	58	58	42	18	0	0
% Converged		100	100	100	100	100	100	100	100
$\beta = 1.0$:									
% Boundary	$\alpha = 0.1$	60	2	0	0	0	0	0	0
% Converged		100	100	100	100	100	100	100	100
% Boundary	$\alpha = 0.3$	68	8	2	0	0	0	0	0
% Converged		100	100	100	100	100	100	100	100
% Boundary	$\alpha = 0.5$	70	8	0	0	2	0	0	0
% Converged		100	100	100	100	100	100	100	100
% Boundary	$\alpha = 0.7$	64	36	44	52	50	20	0	0
% Converged		100	100	100	100	100	100	100	100
% Boundary	$\alpha = 0.9$	74	8	4	0	0	0	0	0
% Converged		100	100	100	100	100	100	100	100

the parameter values $\alpha = 0.9$, $\beta = 1.0$, $\rho = 0.75$. Further investigation of this case suggested the presence of two local maxima very close together but, in view of the generally smooth behavior of the likelihood functions, this case requires still further study.

More disconcerting was the large number of boundary solutions obtained. Naturally, these are to be expected when the true value of ρ is zero or close to zero, but such solutions are far more widespread. They occur in great numbers for $\alpha = 0.7$ when $\beta = 0.0$ and $\beta = 1.0$, and when $\beta = 0.5$, such solutions occur for nearly all values of ρ and $\alpha = 0.5$, 0.7, or 0.9. The results do not appear to be due to the method of Fletcher and Powell, which was modified to permit bounding of $\hat{\rho}$. Because, in a large number of cases in which a boundary solution occurred, the maximum likelihood estimates were reestimated using the slower search procedure described in Nerlove (1967, pp. 54–55) with exactly the same results. Comparison of cases in which the method converged to interior solutions with those in which it converged to a boundary solution revealed that, despite a large true ρ, the likelihood function was extremely flat in the ρ direction. Small variations in the sample of random disturbances, thus, frequently produced a boundary solution. The present results strongly suggest that the serial properties of the exogenous variables interact in a significant way with the autoregressive structure under investigation to produce a boundary solution in situations in which one would not ordinarily expect one to occur. That a boundary solution can occur for the ML procedure under certain circumstances has been demonstrated in an unpublished paper by G. S. Maddala, but general conditions for the existence of a boundary solution have not been established.

4. CONCLUSIONS

While the results of the present investigation are not entirely unambiguous, the Dodo might well answer the question "But who has won?" by saying, "The 2RC method, of course!" Both in terms of relative bias and mean-square error, over a wide range of parameter values, the two-round procedure, using a value of $\hat{\rho}$ estimated from first-round regressions including individual constant terms, compares favorably with all the other estimation techniques investigated, including maximum likelihood, which has considerable intuitive appeal for most econometricians. All studies of this sort, however, have many dangling loose ends that require further investigation. Among those noted in preceding pages are the following: (1) the sensitivity of the various methods investigated to the presence of specification error, especially to the presence of serial correlation in the "remainder" effects v_{it} and/or the presence of an individual invariant, "period effect," λ_t; (2) the sensitivity of the various methods, particularly the maximum-likelihood method, to the choice of exogenous variables with different characteristics; (3) the question of whether the Monte Carlo results on bias and mean-square error can be well approximated by the so-called small σ asymptotics of J. Kadane, (i.e., approximations to finite sample moments obtained by letting the variance of the disturbance term tend to zero); (4) the reason or reasons why least squares with individual constant terms underestimates α and overestimates β and ρ; and (5) finally, the question of the shape of the likelihood function, particularly its flatness or peakedness in certain directions, and the possibility of more than one local maximum and the implications of this shape for the convergence of gradient maximization procedures.

References

Amemiya, T. (1967), "A Note on the Estimation of Balestra-Nerlove Models," Technical Report No. 4, Institute for Mathematical Studies in the Social Sciences, Stanford, CA, Stanford University, August 14.

Amemiya, T., and W. Fuller (1967), "A Comparative Study of Alternative Estimators in a Distributed Lag Model," *Econometrica, 35*: July–October, pp. 509–529.

Balestra, P., and M. Nerlove (1966), "Pooling Cross-Section and Time-Series Data in the Estimation of a Dynamic Model: The Demand for Natural Gas," Technical Report 8, Institute for Mathematical Studies in the Social Sciences, Stanford University, December 21, 1964; published in revised form in *Econometrica, 34*: July, pp. 585–612.

Box, M. J. (1966), "A Comparison of Several Current Optimization Methods, and the Use of Transformations in Constrained Problems," *Computer Journal, 9*: January, pp. 67–77.

Fisher, R. A. (1946), *Statistical Methods for Research Workers*, Edinburgh: Oliver and Boyd.

Fletcher, R., and M. J. D. Powel (1963), "A Rapidly Convergent Descent Method for Minimization," *Computer Journal, 6*: July, pp. 163–168.

Goldberger, A. S. (1964), *Econometric Theory*, New York: John Wiley.

Haavelmo, T. (1944), *The Probability Approach in Econometrics*, supplement to *Econometrica, 12*: July.

Hammersley, J. M., and D. C. Handscomb (1964), *Monte Carlo Methods*, London: Methuen.

Henderson, C. R. (1953), "Estimation of Variance and Covariance Components," *Biometrics, 9*: June, pp. 226–252.

Hildreth, C., and J. P. Hauck (1968), "Linear Models with Random Coefficients," *Journal of the American Statistical Association, 63*: June, pp. 584–595.

Hurwicz, L. (1950), "Least-Squares Bias in Times Series," in T. C. Koopmans, Ed., *Statistical Inference in Dynamic Economic Models*. New York: Wiley, pp. 365–383.

Hussain, A. (1966), "Combining Time-Series and Cross-Section Data in Simultaneous Linear Equations," unpublished doctoral dissertation, Department of Experimental Statistics, North Carolina State University at Raleigh.

Kadane, J. B. (1966), "Comparison of Estimators in Simultaneous Equations Econometric Models When the Residuals Are Small," unpublished doctoral dissertation, Stanford University.

Kuh, E. (1959), "The Validity of Cross Sectionally Estimated Behavior Equations in Time-Series Applications," *Econometrica, 27*: April, pp. 197–214.

Malinvaud, E. (1966), *Statistical Methods of Econometrics*. Chicago: Rand McNally and Co.

Nerlove, M. (1967), "Experimental Evidence on the Estimation of Dynamic Economic Relations from a Time Series of Cross Sections," *Economic Studies Quarterly, 18*: December, pp. 42–74.

Nerlove, M. (1971), "A Note on a Variance-Components Model Useful in the Study of Cross Sections Over Time," Cowles Foundation Discussion Paper No. 271 (April 9, 1969); revised version, *Econometrica, 39*: March, pp. 383–396.

Sargan, J. D. (1958), "The Estimation of Economic Relationships Using Instrumental Variables," *Econometrica, 26*: July, pp. 393–415.

Searle, S. R. (1968), "Another Look at Henderson's Methods of Estimating Variance Components," *Biometrics, 24*: December, pp. 749–778.

Theil, H., and L. B. M. Mennes (1959), "Conception Stochastique de Coefficients Multiplicateur dans l'Adjustment Linéaire des Séries Temporelles," *Publications de l'Institut Statistique de l'Université de Paris*, Vol. 8.

Wallace, T. D., and A. Hussain (1969), "The Use of Error Components Models in Combining Cross-Section with Time-Series Data," *Econometrica, 37*: January, pp. 55–72.

Wells, M. (1967), "Function Minimization," Algorithm 251, in *Collected Algorithms from CACM*. New York: Association for Computing Machinery.

FIVE

A Note on Error-Components Models[1]

Preface

The article reprinted here gives the detailed background to Appendix A of Chapter 1, "Decomposition of the Sum of Squares of a Variable Observed in a Two-Dimensional Panel." It also provides an equivalent analysis of the more complicated three-component error model. The important points to note are (1) the derivation of the characteristic roots of the two- and three-component error models without explicit evaluation of the characteristic vectors; and (2) representation of the transformation of the data that reduces the variance-covariance matrix of the stochastic disturbances to diagonality in terms of individual and time means and deviations therefrom without explicit evaluation of the characteristic vectors. This representation permits a clear interpretation of the information content of panel data observations.

In an earlier paper, Wallace and Hussain (1969) consider a model of fixed X regression in which the disturbances follow a three-component error formulation. They find, by trial and error, the inverse of the variance-covariance matrix of the disturbances for known error-component variances. Using this result, they establish the greater efficiency of the GLS estimates and the asymptotic equivalence of the two estimators when observations on the independent variables remain nonstochastic but increase nonrepetitively in number. A two-stage estimation procedure is suggested in which the error-component variances are estimated from a first-stage OLS regression. But they do not succeed in finding the appropriate transformation of the observations that makes these results simple to derive.

Back-to-back, in the same issue of *Econometrica* in which this chapter is published, Henderson (1971) complains that he solved the problem much earlier in Henderson (1953) of finding the inverse of the variance-covariance matrix, solved by Wallace and Hussain and which is essential to ML estimation. But this is not the same thing as finding the transformation that diagonalizes

---

[1] Reprinted with permission from *Econometrica, 39*: pp. 383–396, 1971.

this matrix; a method for transforming the original observations in order to diagonalize the variance-covariance matrix, it seems to me, is essential for applying maximum-likelihood methods to panels with a large cross-section dimension. This is done for the three-component model in the present chapter for the first time and much more generally in Searle and Henderson (1979), whose results are also reported in Searle, Casella, and McCullough (1992, pp. 144–146).[2]

References

Hemmerle, W. J., and H. O. Hartley (1973), "Computing Maximum-Likelihood Estimates for the Mixed AOV Model Using the W-Transformation," *Technometrics, 15*: pp. 819–831.

Henderson, C. R. (1953), "Estimation of Variance and Covariance Components," *Biometrics, 9*: pp. 226–252.

Henderson, C. R. (1971), "Comment on 'The Use of Error-Components Models in Combining Cross-Section with Time-Series Data'," *Econometrica, 39*: pp. 397–401.

Searle, S. R., and H. V. Henderson (1979), "Dispersion Matrices for Variance Components Models," *Journal of the American Statistical Association, 74*: pp. 465–470.

Searle, S. R., G. Casella, and C. E. McCullough (1992), *Variance Components*, New York: Wiley.

Wallace, T. D., and A. Hussain (1969), "The Use of Error-Components Models in Combining Cross-Section with Time-Series Data," *Econometrica, 37*: pp. 55–72.

[2] See also Hemmerle and Hartley (1973).

CHAPTER 5: ERRATA

The paper published in *Econometrica* was not the revision of December 1969 as stated there, but rather the unrevised version of July 1969. A number of important changes were made in the revision, as well as several minor alterations. An errata reporting these changes was later published in *Econometrica*, 40: 218, January 1972. Besides an acknowledgment to G. S. Maddala for his helpful comments, the important changes were as follows:

p. 232 eq. (4.6): Delete the term $\frac{NT}{\lambda_1}\bar{x}_{..}^2$ on the right-hand side and the term $\frac{NT}{\lambda_1}\bar{x}_{..}\bar{y}_{..}$ on the left-hand side.

After eq. (4.7), add the sentence; "Note that the terms involving λ_1 drop out entirely in this case."

p. 234, line 11, from the bottom: Delete the phrase, "the overall mean is weighted by NT."

line 10, from the bottom: Insert the phrase "is weighted" between "mean" and "by."

line 6, from bottom: Delete λ_1.

A Note on Error-Components Models

Marc Nerlove[1]

This note develops a slightly different formulation of one of the basic results presented in a paper by Wallace and Hussain (1969) on error-components models for disturbances in relationships designed to explain cross-sectional observations over time. In their discussion, Wallace and Hussain derive the inverse of the variance-covariance matrix of the disturbances by trial and error. Unfortunately, their formulation does not lead to a "natural" interpretation of the generalized least-squares estimates, or of the relationships of these estimates to other estimates in the same way diagonalization of the variance-covariance matrix by means of an appropriate orthogonal transformation does. The characteristic roots of the variance-covariance matrix for the disturbances in a three-component model that has been studied by Wallace and Hussain are derived here. It is shown how knowledge of these roots and the characteristic vectors associated with them leads to a form of the inverse matrix that may be more readily interpreted, as well as a number of other useful results, including an interpretation of the poor small-sample properties of estimates that incorporate dummy variables for each individual.

1. INTRODUCTION

In their paper, Wallace and Hussain (1969) explored the properties of a regression model having a disturbance made up of three unobserved error components. In the interpretation of this model applicable to the study of cross sections over time, these components may conveniently be characterized as an individual time-invariant effect, a period individual invariant effect, and a remainder. Wallace and Hussain analyze the asymptotic properties of various

[1] The research on which this note is based was supported by a grant from the National Science Foundation to the Cowles Foundation for Research in Economics at Yale University. I am indebted to David Grether and E. J. Hannan for extremely helpful discussions on the subject. They should not be held responsible for errors.

222

estimates when the independent variables of the analysis do not include any lagged values of the dependent variable. While this is an important case, it has been found that large-sample properties give little guide to the behavior of estimates of the coefficients of dynamic equations for samples of sizes relevant in many economic contexts (see Balestra and Nerlove, 1966; Nerlove, 1967; and Nerlove, 1971). The purpose of this note, however, is not to criticize the relevance of the findings of Wallace and Hussain, but rather to show that a slightly different formulation of one of their basic results may be more readily interpreted both in terms of nonstochastic and weakly nonstochastic independent variables with which they deal and in cases in which lagged values of the dependent variables are included among the explanatory variables.

In their discussion, Wallace and Hussain derive the inverse of the variance-covariance matrix of the disturbances by "trial, error, and generalization," (1969, p. 58). While there is nothing wrong with their result, it does not lead to a "natural" interpretation of the generalized least-squares estimates or of their relation to other estimates in the same way diagonalization of the variance-covariance matrix by means of an appropriate orthogonal transformation does. The purpose of this note is to exhibit the characteristic roots and vectors associated with the variance-covariance matrix for the disturbances in the three-component model analyzed by Wallace and Hussain and to show how knowledge of these roots and vectors leads to a form of the inverse matrix that may be more readily interpreted, as well as a number of other useful results. For this purpose, we adopt a more convenient notation, as follows.

Let there be $i = 1, \ldots, N$ individuals observed over $t = 1, \ldots, T$ time periods, and suppose that there exists a stochastic relationship connecting the observations on some dependent variable, y_{it}, with a number of independent variables, $x_{it}^{(1)}, \ldots, x_{it}^{(K)}$, and certain unobserved random variables u_{it}:

$$y_{it} = x_{it}^{(1)}\beta_1 + \cdots + x_{it}^{(K)}\beta_K + u_{it} \qquad (i = 1, \ldots, N; \, t = 1, \ldots, T). \quad (1.1)$$

If we array our observations first by individual and then by period, we may represent equations (1.1) by

$$y_i = X_i\beta + u_i \qquad (i = 1, \ldots, N), \quad (1.2)$$

where y_i is a $T \times 1$ vector, X_i is a $T \times K$ matrix, β is a $K \times 1$ vector, and u_i is a $T \times 1$ vector. We leave aside the question of whether there are any lagged values of y_{it} included among the columns of X_i. Letting

$$y = \begin{pmatrix} y_1 \\ \vdots \\ y_N \end{pmatrix}, \qquad X = \begin{bmatrix} X_1 \\ \vdots \\ X_N \end{bmatrix}, \qquad u = \begin{pmatrix} u_1 \\ \vdots \\ u_N \end{pmatrix}$$

be a $TN \times 1$ vector, a $TN \times K$ matrix, and a $TN \times 1$ vector, respectively, we have, finally,

$$y = X\beta + u, \quad (1.3)$$

which is the usual form of regression model. The special nature of the problem, however, is expressed in the assumptions we make about the variance-covariance matrix of the vector u, since we have assumed a homogeneous relation between dependent and independent variables over all time periods and all individuals.

Disturbances are generally supposed to represent the net effects of numerous individually unimportant but collectively significant variables that have been omitted from the analysis. Some of these, we may suppose, are specific to the individuals considered, some are specific to the time periods, and some are specific to both. We assume that u_{it} may be decomposed into the sum of three independent normal variables, each with zero mean,

$$u_{it} = \mu_i + \lambda_t + v_{it}, \tag{1.4}$$

such that

$$E\mu_i\mu_{i'} = \begin{cases} \sigma_\mu^2, & i = i', \\ 0, & i \neq i', \end{cases}$$

$$E\lambda_t\lambda_{t'} = \begin{cases} \sigma_\lambda^2, & t = t', \\ 0, & t \neq t', \end{cases} \tag{1.5}$$

$$Ev_{it}v_{i't'} = \begin{cases} \sigma_v^2, & i = i' \text{ and } t = t', \\ 0 & \text{otherwise}, \end{cases}$$

where μ_i represents the individual effects, λ_t the period effects, and v_{it}, the remainder. (For further justification, see Nerlove, 1971, pp. 360–62.) If we let

$$\sigma^2 = \sigma_\mu^2 + \sigma_\lambda^2 + \sigma_v^2,$$

$$\rho = \sigma_\mu^2/\sigma^2, \tag{1.6}$$

$$\omega = \sigma_\lambda^2/\sigma^2,$$

we may write the variance-covariance matrix associated with the vector u in simple form, which, however, makes use of the Kronecker product notation.

If A is a $p \times q$ matrix with typical element a_{ij}, and B is an $r \times s$ matrix, the Kronecker product of A and B, written $A \otimes B$, is defined as the $pr \times qs$ matrix

$$\begin{bmatrix} a_{11}B & \cdots & a_{1q}B \\ \vdots & & \vdots \\ q_{p1}B & \cdots & a_{pq}B \end{bmatrix}.$$

The following notation is also useful: I_{NT}, I_T, and I_N are identity matrices of orders $NT \times NT$, $T \times T$, and $N \times N$, respectively; e_{NT}, e_T, and e_N are vectors consisting entirely of ones of orders $NT \times 1$, $T \times 1$, and $N \times 1$, respectively.

Using this notation, we may write the variance-covariance matrix of u as

$$Euu' = \sigma^2 \Omega = \sigma^2 \{(1 - \rho - \omega)I_{NT} + \rho(I_N \otimes e_T e_T') + \omega(e_N e_N' \otimes I_T)\}. \quad (1.7)$$

Three problems are of interest: first, we need to obtain Ω^{-1}, or better still $\Omega^{-1/2}$, in order to generate the generalized least-squares estimate of β and/or the likelihood function. The generalized least-squares estimates are

$$\hat{\beta} = [X'\Omega^{-1}X]^{-1} X'\Omega^{-1}y \quad (1.8)$$

and may generally be found more simply computationally by first transforming X and y to

$$
\begin{aligned}
X^* &= \Omega^{-1/2} X, \\
Y^* &= \Omega^{1/2} y,
\end{aligned}
\quad (1.9)
$$

and then estimating β from the ordinary least-squares regression of y^* on X^*. The logarithmic-likelihood function, assuming μ_i, λ_t, and v_{it} are distributed independently and satisfy conditions (1.5), and assuming $\mu_i \sim n(0, \sigma_\mu^2)$, $\lambda_t \sim n(0, \sigma_\lambda^2)$, and $v_{it} \sim n(0, \sigma_v^2)$, is

$$
L(\beta, \rho, \omega, \sigma^2 \mid y, X) = -\frac{NT}{2} \log 2\pi + \frac{1}{2} \log |\Omega^{-1}|
$$
$$
-\frac{1}{2}(y - X\beta)'\Omega^{-1}(y - X\beta). \quad (1.10)
$$

The generalized least-squares estimates for known Ω amount, of course, to minimizing the last term in this expression and, thus, to neglecting the second term. Such neglect does not generally matter provided Ω is actually known, but loss of efficiency may result if Ω is first estimated in certain cases.

A second problem involves the derivation of $\Omega^{1/2}$. If one wishes to explore the properties of various sorts of estimation procedures by Monte Carlo experiments, a particularly useful approach when X involves lagged values of y, it is necessary to generate pseudorandom variables distributed normally with mean zero and variance-covariance matrix Ω. Since this must be done many times and for a variety of different values of the parameters ρ, ω, and σ^2, it is important to achieve computational efficiency. The optimal approach from this standpoint is to generate NT pseudorandom variables, w_{it}, which are $n(0, 1)$ and "independent," and then transform them by

$$u = \sigma \Omega^{1/2} w. \quad (1.11)$$

A third problem of considerable interest is the determination of the characteristic roots and vectors of Ω. As we shall see, knowledge of these roots and vectors leads to a form of Ω^{-1}, which admits of a particularly elegant interpretation. We shall first determine the characteristic roots and vectors of Ω, then obtain $\Omega^{1/2}$, and finally conclude with a discussion of Ω^{-1} and the generalized least-squares estimates and their properties.

2. THE CHARACTERISTIC ROOTS AND VECTORS OF Ω

The matrix Ω has three terms, one in I_{NT}, one in $I_N \otimes e_T e_T'$, and one in $e_N e_N' \otimes I_T$. It is, therefore, clear that any vector that annihilates both $I_N \otimes e_T e_T'$ and $e_N e_N' \otimes I_T$ must be a characteristic vector of Ω with associated root $1 - \rho - \omega$. Let φ_j, $j = 1, \ldots, N-1$, be $N-1$ vectors, each $N \times 1$, which are orthonormal and orthogonal to e_N:

$$e_N' \varphi_j = 0,$$

$$\varphi_j' \varphi_{j'} = \begin{cases} 1, & j = j', \\ 0, & j \neq j' \end{cases} \quad (j = 1, \ldots, N-1). \tag{2.1}$$

Let ψ_k, $k = 1, \ldots, T-1$, be $T-1$ vectors each $T \times 1$, which are orthonormal and each orthogonal to e_T:

$$e_T' \psi_k = 0,$$

$$\psi_k' \psi_{k'} = \begin{cases} 1, & k = k', \\ 0, & k \neq k' \end{cases} \quad (k = 1, \ldots, T-1). \tag{2.2}$$

Note that we can always find such sets of vectors. The $(N-1)(T-1)$ vectors $\varphi_j \otimes e_T e_T'$ are orthonormal and annihilate both $I_N \otimes e_T e_T'$ and $e_N e_N' \otimes I_T$, as may readily be verified. They are thus characteristic vectors of Ω associated with the characteristic root $1 - \rho - \omega$, which is of multiplicity $(N-1)(T-1)$.

Consider the Kronecker products $\varphi_j \otimes \xi_T$ and $\xi_N \otimes \psi_k$, where ξ_T and ξ_N are, respectively, any T and N dimensional vectors. Clearly, the vector $\varphi_j \otimes \xi_T$ annihilates the term containing $e_N e_N' \otimes I_T$ since the vectors φ_j are each orthogonal to the vector e_N. Similarly, $\xi_N \otimes \psi_k$ annihilates the term containing $I_N \otimes e_T e_T'$. It might thus be supposed that $N-1$ additional characteristic vectors of the form $\varphi_j \otimes \xi_T$ and $T-1$ of the form $\xi_N \otimes \psi_k$ may be found. To determine the form of ξ_T and ξ_N more specifically, observe that ξ_T and ψ_k must be orthogonal for $k = 1, \ldots, T-1$, and ξ_N and φ_j must also be for $j = 1, \ldots, N-1$, since the vectors $\varphi_j \otimes \psi_k$, $\varphi_{j'} \otimes \xi_T$, and $\xi_N \otimes \psi_{k'}$ must be orthogonal for any j, k, j', and k'. Thus, for example,

$$(\varphi_j \otimes \psi_k)'(\varphi_{j'} \otimes \xi_T) = \begin{cases} 0, & j \neq j', \\ \psi_k' \xi_T, & j = j', \end{cases}$$

which is necessarily zero only if $\psi_k' \xi_T = 0$. Similarly,

$$(\varphi_j \otimes \psi_k)'(\xi_N \otimes \psi_{k'}) = \begin{cases} 0, & k \neq k', \\ \varphi_j' \xi_N, & k = k', \end{cases}$$

which implies $\varphi_j' \xi_N$ must be zero for $j = 1, \ldots, N-1$. These conditions in turn imply that the vectors $\varphi_j \otimes \xi_T$ and $\xi_N \otimes \psi_k$ are all orthogonal. If they are to have unit length as well, $\xi_N' \xi_N = 1$ and $\xi_T' \xi_T = 1$. Now, by definition, the only vector orthogonal to and independent of ψ_k, $k = 1, \ldots, T-1$ is a scalar multiple of e_T; hence, the condition $\xi_T' \xi_T = 1$ implies

$$\xi_T = e_T/\sqrt{T}.$$

Similarly,

$$\xi_N = e_N/\sqrt{N}.$$

It follows then that the $N-1$ vectors $\varphi_j \otimes e_T/\sqrt{T}$, $j = 1, \ldots, N-1$ are also characteristic vectors of Ω, and it may be readily verified that the associated characteristic root of multiplicity $N-1$ is $1 - \rho - \omega + \rho T$. In the same way, it may be seen that the $T-1$ vectors $(e_N/\sqrt{N}) \otimes \psi_k$, $k = 1, \ldots, T-1$ are characteristic vectors of Ω associated with the root $1 - \rho - \omega + \omega N$, which is of multiplicity $T-1$.

The matrix Ω has altogether NT associated characteristic vectors; we have obtained $(N-1)(T-1) + (N-1) + (T-1) = NT - 1$, and only one further vector and root remain to be found. Consider the Kronecker product of the two vectors ξ_T and ξ_N determined previously: $(e_N/\sqrt{N}) \otimes (e_T/\sqrt{T})$. This vector is clearly orthogonal to all of the characteristic vectors of Ω previously determined, since the latter all contain either φ_j or ψ_k or both, one of which is orthogonal to one of the two terms in the Kronecker product $(e_N/\sqrt{N}) \otimes (e_T/\sqrt{T})$. It follows from the fact that the characteristic vectors span the space of column vectors of Ω that the remaining characteristic vectors must be simply a scalar multiple of $(e_N/\sqrt{N}) \otimes (e_T/\sqrt{T})$. Indeed, it is just that vector, and the associated characteristic root is $1 - \rho - \omega + \rho T + \omega N$, as may readily be verified by expanding $\Omega((e_N/\sqrt{N}) \otimes (e_T/\sqrt{T}))$.

We have proved the following theorem, originally suggested by E. J. Hannan:

Theorem: *Let* φ_j, $j = 1, \ldots, N-1$, ψ_k, $k = 1, \ldots, T-1$, e_N, *and* e_T *be the vectors defined in* (2.1) *and* (2.2), *and let* C *be the* $NT \times NT$ *matrix*

$$C = \begin{bmatrix} (e_N'/\sqrt{N}) \otimes (e_T'/\sqrt{T}) \\ (e_N'/\sqrt{N}) \otimes \psi_1' \\ \vdots \\ (e_N'/\sqrt{N}) \otimes \psi_{T-1}' \\ \varphi_1' \otimes (e_T'/\sqrt{T}) \\ \vdots \\ \varphi_{N-1}' \otimes (e_T'/\sqrt{T}) \\ \varphi_1' \otimes \psi_1' \\ \varphi_1' \otimes \psi_2' \\ \vdots \\ \varphi_{N-1}' \otimes \psi_{T-1}' \end{bmatrix}. \qquad (2.3)$$

Then, $C'C = I_{NT}$ and

$$C\Omega C' = C\{(1 - \rho - \omega)I_{NT} + \rho(I_N \otimes e_T e_T') + \omega(e_N e_N' \otimes I_T)\}C'$$

$$= \begin{bmatrix} \lambda_1 & 0 & 0 & 0 \\ 0 & \lambda_2 I_{T-1} & 0 & 0 \\ 0 & 0 & \lambda_3 I_{N-1} & 0 \\ 0 & 0 & 0 & \lambda_4 I_{(N-1)(T-1)} \end{bmatrix} = D_\lambda,$$

where $\lambda_1 = 1 - \rho - \omega + \omega N + \rho T$, $\lambda_2 = 1 - \rho - \omega + \omega N$, $\lambda_3 = 1 - \rho - \omega + \rho T$, and $\lambda_4 = 1 - \rho - \omega$ are the four distinct characteristic roots of Ω.

3. THE SQUARE ROOT OF Ω

The square root of Ω, $\Omega^{1/2}$, may be defined simply in terms of orthogonal matrix C and the matrix D_λ, defined in the theorem of the previous subsection:

$$\Omega^{1/2} = C' D_{\sqrt{\lambda}} C, \tag{3.1}$$

where

$$D_{\sqrt{\lambda}} = \begin{bmatrix} \sqrt{\lambda_1} & 0 & 0 & 0 \\ 0 & \sqrt{\lambda_2} I_{T-1} & 0 & 0 \\ 0 & 0 & \sqrt{\lambda_3} I_{N-1} & 0 \\ 0 & 0 & 0 & \sqrt{\lambda_4} I_{(N-1)(T-1)} \end{bmatrix}.$$

Let us partition C in (2.3) as

$$C = \begin{bmatrix} C_1' \\ C_2' \\ C_3' \\ C_4' \end{bmatrix}, \tag{3.2}$$

where

$$C_1 = (e_N/\sqrt{N}) \otimes (e_T/\sqrt{T}) = \frac{1}{\sqrt{NT}} e_{NT}, \qquad \text{an } NT \times 1 \text{ vector,}$$

$$C_2 = \frac{1}{\sqrt{N}} [e_N \otimes \psi_1, \dots, e_N \otimes \psi_{T-1}], \qquad \text{an } NT \times T - 1 \text{ matrix,}$$

$$C_3 = \frac{1}{\sqrt{T}} [\varphi_1 \otimes e_T, \dots, \varphi_{N-1} \otimes e_T], \qquad \text{an } NT \times N - 1 \text{ matrix,}$$

$$C_4 = [\varphi_1 \otimes \psi_1, \varphi_1 \otimes \psi_2, \dots, \varphi_{N-1} \otimes \psi_{T-1}],$$
$$\text{an } NT \times (T-1)(N-1) \text{ matrix.} \tag{3.3}$$

Thus,

$$\Omega^{1/2} = C' D_{\sqrt{\lambda}} C$$

$$= [C_1 C_2 C_3 C_4] \begin{bmatrix} \sqrt{\lambda_1} & 0 & 0 & 0 \\ 0 & \sqrt{\lambda_2} I_{T-1} & 0 & 0 \\ 0 & 0 & \sqrt{\lambda_3} I_{N-1} & 0 \\ 0 & 0 & 0 & \sqrt{\lambda_4} I_{(N-1)(T-1)} \end{bmatrix} \begin{bmatrix} C'_1 \\ C'_2 \\ C'_3 \\ C'_4 \end{bmatrix}$$

$$= \sqrt{\lambda_1} C_1 C'_1 + \sqrt{\lambda_2} C_2 C'_2 + \sqrt{\lambda_3} C_3 C'_3 + \sqrt{\lambda_4} C_4 C'_4. \tag{3.4}$$

Clearly,

$$C_1 C'_1 = \frac{1}{NT} e_{NT} e'_{NT}. \tag{3.5}$$

Consider the product

$$C'C = C_1 C'_1 + C_2 C'_2 + C_3 C'_3 + C_4 C'_4 = I_{NT}. \tag{3.6}$$

Premultiply (3.6) by $e_N e'_N \otimes I_T$. Since

$$(e_N e'_N \otimes I_T) C_1 C'_1 = N C_1 C'_1 = \frac{e_{NT} e'_{NT}}{T},$$

$$(e_N e'_N \otimes I_T) C_2 C'_2 = N C_2 C'_2,$$

$$(e_N e'_N \otimes I_T) C_3 C'_3 = [(e'_N \varphi_1) e_T / \sqrt{T}, \dots, (e'_N \varphi_{N-1}) e_T / \sqrt{T}] C'_3$$
$$= 0$$

(because $e'_N \varphi_k = 0$, for $k = 1, \dots, N-1$), and

$$(e_N e'_N \otimes I_T) C_4 C'_4 = [(e'_N \varphi_1) \psi_1, \dots, (e'_N \varphi_{N-1}) \psi_{T-1}]$$
$$= 0$$

(for the same reason), it follows that

$$C_2 C'_2 = \frac{e_N e'_N}{N} \otimes I_T - \frac{e_{NT} e'_{NT}}{NT}. \tag{3.7}$$

In the same manner, premultiplication of (3.6) by $I_N \otimes e_T e'_T$ shows that

$$C_3 C'_3 = I_N \otimes \frac{e_T e'_T}{T} - \frac{e_{NT} e'_{NT}}{NT}. \tag{3.8}$$

Combining (3.5), (3.6), (3.7), and (3.8), we obtain

$$C_4 C'_4 = I_{NT} - \frac{e_N e'_N}{N} \otimes I_T - I_N \otimes \frac{e_T e'_T}{T} + \frac{e_{NT} e'_{NT}}{NT}. \tag{3.9}$$

It follows that an explicit representation of $\Omega^{1/2}$ is

$$
\Omega^{1/2} = \sqrt{\lambda_1}\frac{e_{NT}e'_{NT}}{NT} + \sqrt{\lambda_2}\left\{\frac{e_N e'_N}{N}\otimes I_T - \frac{e_{NT}e'_{NT}}{NT}\right\}
$$
$$
+ \sqrt{\lambda_3}\left\{I_N \otimes \frac{e_T e'_T}{T} - \frac{e_{NT}e'_{NT}}{NT}\right\} \tag{3.10}
$$
$$
+ \sqrt{\lambda_4}\left\{I_{NT} - \frac{e_N e'_N}{N}\otimes I_T - I_N \otimes - \frac{e_T e'_T}{T} + \frac{e_{NT}e'_{NT}}{NT}\right\}.
$$

Let $w_{it}, i = 1, \ldots, N, t = 1, \ldots, T$, be NT independent, zero mean, unit variance, normal variables. Arrange these variables into an $NT \times 1$ vector $w' = (w_{11}, \ldots, w_{1T}, \ldots, w_{N1}, \ldots, w_{NT})$. The vector

$$
u = \sigma\Omega^{1/2}w = \sigma\sqrt{\lambda_1}\bar{w}_{..}e_{NT} + \sigma\sqrt{\lambda_2}\left\{e_N \otimes \begin{pmatrix}\bar{w}_{.1}\\ \vdots \\ \bar{w}_{.T}\end{pmatrix} - \bar{w}_{..}e_{NT}\right\}
$$
$$
+\sigma\sqrt{\lambda_3}\left\{\begin{pmatrix}\bar{w}_{1.}\\ \vdots \\ \bar{w}_{N.}\end{pmatrix}\otimes e_T - \bar{w}_{..}e_{NT}\right\}
$$
$$
+\sigma\sqrt{\lambda_4}\left\{w - e_N x\begin{pmatrix}\bar{w}_{.1}\\ \vdots \\ \bar{w}_{.T}\end{pmatrix} - \begin{pmatrix}\bar{w}_{1.}\\ \vdots \\ \bar{w}_{N.}\end{pmatrix}\otimes e_T + \bar{w}_{..}e_{NT}\right\} \tag{3.11}
$$

is distributed according to a multivariate normal distribution with mean zero and variance-covariance matrix $\sigma^2\Omega$. The barred expressions in (3.11) are defined as follows:

$$
\bar{w}_{..} = \frac{1}{NT}\sum_{i=1}^{N}\sum_{t=1}^{T}w_{it}, \quad \text{overall mean;}
$$
$$
\bar{w}_{.t} = \frac{1}{N}\sum_{i=1}^{N}w_{it}, \qquad t = 1, \ldots, T, \quad \text{period means; and} \tag{3.12}
$$
$$
\bar{w}_{i.} = \frac{1}{T}\sum_{t=1}^{T}w_{it}, \qquad i = 1, \ldots, N, \quad \text{individual means.}
$$

Thus, for a Monte Carlo experiment, we generate the numbers $u_{it}, i = 1, \ldots, N, t = 1, \ldots, T$, from NT "independent" pseudorandom numbers $w_{it} \sim n(0, 1)$

according to the formula:

$$u_{it} = \sigma \left(\frac{\sqrt{\lambda_1} - \sqrt{\lambda_2} - \sqrt{\lambda_3} + \sqrt{\lambda_4}}{NT} \right) \sum_{i=1}^{N} \sum_{t=1}^{T} w_{it}$$

$$+ \sigma \left(\frac{\sqrt{\lambda_2} - \sqrt{\lambda_4}}{N} \right) \sum_{i=1}^{N} w_{it} + \sigma \left(\frac{\sqrt{\lambda_3} - \sqrt{\lambda_4}}{T} \right) \sum_{t=1}^{T} w_{it} + \sigma \sqrt{\lambda_4} w_{it}.$$

$$(3.13)$$

4. THE INVERSE OF Ω AND THE GLS ESTIMATES OF β

Knowledge of the characteristic roots and vectors of Ω also permits an easy determination of Ω^{-1}. Since

$$\Omega = C' D_\lambda C, \tag{4.1}$$

$$\Omega^{-1} = C' D_{1/\lambda} C, \tag{4.2}$$

where

$$D_{1/\lambda} = \begin{bmatrix} 1/\lambda_1 & 0 & 0 & 0 \\ 0 & (1/\lambda_2) I_{T-1} & 0 & 0 \\ 0 & 0 & (1/\lambda_3) I_{N-1} & 0 \\ 0 & 0 & 0 & (1/\lambda_4) I_{(N-1)(T-1)} \end{bmatrix},$$

since $C^{-1} = C'$. By exactly the same reasoning as that used to deduce $\Omega^{1/2}$ in the previous subsection, we obtain

$$\Omega^{-1} = \frac{1}{\lambda_1} C_1 C_1' + \frac{1}{\lambda_2} C_2 C_2' + \frac{1}{\lambda_3} C_3 C_3' + \frac{1}{\lambda_4} C_4 C_4'$$

$$= \frac{1}{\lambda_1} \frac{e_{NT} e_{NT}'}{NT} + \frac{1}{\lambda_2} \left\{ \frac{e_N e_N'}{N} \otimes I_T - \frac{e_{NT} e_{NT}'}{NT} \right\}$$

$$+ \frac{1}{\lambda_3} \left\{ I_N \otimes \frac{e_T e_T'}{T} - \frac{e_{NT} e_{NT}'}{NT} \right\}$$

$$+ \frac{1}{\lambda_4} \left\{ I_{NT} - \frac{e_N e_N'}{N} \otimes I_T - I_N \otimes \frac{e_T e_T'}{T} + \frac{e_{NT} e_{NT}'}{NT} \right\}. \tag{4.3}$$

Using the vector y and the matrix X defined in Section 1, the generalized least-squares estimates of β are found by solving the normal equations

$$X' \Omega^{-1} X \hat{\beta} = X' \Omega^{-1} y, \tag{4.4}$$

or

$$\left\{ \frac{1}{\lambda_1} \frac{X'e_{NT}e'_{NT}X}{NT} + \frac{1}{\lambda_2}\left[X'\left(\frac{e_N e'_N}{N} \times I_T \right) X - \frac{X'e_{NT}e'_{NT}X}{NT} \right] \right.$$

$$+ \frac{1}{\lambda_3}\left[X'\left(I_N \otimes \frac{e_T e'_T}{T} \right) X - \frac{X'e_{NT}e'_{NT}X}{NT} \right]$$

$$\left. + \frac{1}{\lambda_4}\left[X'X - X'\left(\frac{e_N e'_N}{N} \otimes I_T \right) X - X'\left(I_N \otimes \frac{e_T e'_T}{T} \right) X + \frac{X'e_{NT}e'_{NT}X}{NT} \right] \right\} \hat{\beta}$$

$$= \left\{ \frac{1}{\lambda_1} \frac{X'e_{NT}e'_{NT}y}{NT} + \frac{1}{\lambda_2}\left[X'\left(\frac{e_N e'_N}{N} \otimes I_T \right) y - \frac{X'e_{NT}e'_{NT}y}{NT} \right] \right.$$

$$+ \frac{1}{\lambda_3}\left[X'\left(I_N \otimes \frac{e_T e'_T}{T} \right) y - \frac{Xe_{NT}e'_{NT}y}{NT} \right]$$

$$\left. + \frac{1}{\lambda_4}\left[X'y - X'\left(\frac{e_N e'_N}{N} \otimes I_T \right) y - X'\left(I_N \otimes \frac{e_T e'_T}{T} \right) y + \frac{X'e_{NT}e'_{NT}y}{NT} \right] \right\}.$$

$$(4.5)$$

Suppose that the relation (1.1) included only two independent variables $x_{it}^{(1)} = 1$, for all i and t, and $x_{it}^{(2)} = x_{it}$. β_1 may then be interpreted as the constant term; β_2 is the slope of the relation between y_{it} and x_{it}. If $\bar{x}..$ and $\bar{y}..$ denote the overall means of x_{it} and y_{it}, respectively, $\bar{x}_i.$ and $\bar{y}_i.$ the individual means, and $\bar{x}._t$ and $\bar{y}._t$ the period means, the normal equations reduce to a particularly suggestive form:

$$\left\{ \frac{NT}{\lambda_1}\bar{x}..^2 + \frac{N}{\lambda_2}\sum_{t=1}^{T}(\bar{x}._t - \bar{x}..)^2 + \frac{T}{\lambda_3}\sum_{i=1}^{N}(\bar{x}_i. - \bar{x}..)^2 \right.$$

$$\left. + \frac{1}{\lambda_4}\sum_{t=1}^{T}\sum_{i=1}^{N}(x_{it} - \bar{x}._t - \bar{x}_i. + \bar{x}..)^2 \right\} \hat{\beta}_2$$

$$= \left\{ \frac{NT}{\lambda_1}\bar{x}..\bar{y}.. + \frac{N}{\lambda_2}\sum_{t=1}^{T}(\bar{x}._t - \bar{x}..)(\bar{y}._t - \bar{y}..) + \frac{T}{\lambda_3}\sum_{i=1}^{N}(\bar{x}_i. - \bar{x}..)(\bar{y}_i. - \bar{y}..) \right.$$

$$\left. + \frac{1}{\lambda_4}\sum_{t=1}^{T}\sum_{i=1}^{N}(x_{it} - \bar{x}._t - \bar{x}_i. + \bar{x}..)(y_{it} - \bar{y}._t - \bar{y}_i. + \bar{y}..) \right\},$$

$$(4.6)$$

and

$$\hat{\beta}_1 + \bar{x}..\hat{\beta}_2 = \bar{y}... \qquad\qquad (4.7)$$

5. AN INTERPRETATION OF $\hat{\beta}$ AND ITS ASYMPTOTIC DISTRIBUTION[2]

The form of the normal equations in the simple case of one independent variable and a constant term, exhibited in the previous subsection, suggests an interesting interpretation of the generalized least-squares estimates. Let us write the relation to be estimated as

$$y_{it} = \beta_1 + \beta_2 x_{it} + \mu_i + \lambda_t + \nu_{it}. \tag{5.1}$$

Taking deviations from the overall mean annihilates β_1:

$$y_{it} - \bar{y}.. = \beta_2(x_{it} - \bar{x}..) + \mu_i + \lambda_t + \nu_{it} \qquad (i = 1, \ldots, N; \ t = 1, \ldots, T), \tag{5.2}$$

where we set $(1/N)\sum_{i=1}^{N} \mu_i = 0$, $(1/T)\sum_{t=1}^{T} \lambda_t = 0$, and $(1/NT)\sum_{i,t} \nu_{it} = 0$, their expected values. The ordinary least-squares estimates are given by solving the equation

$$\sum_{i,t}(y_{it} - \bar{y}..)(x_{it} - \bar{x}..) = b_2^{OLS} \sum_{i,t}(x_{it} - \bar{x}..)^2, \tag{5.3}$$

but, even in the case in which x_{it} is nonstochastic, this estimate is inefficient, although it is, in this case, unbiased.

To see how the inefficiency results, take means in Equation (5.2) over t and set $(1/T)\sum_t \lambda_t = 0$ and $(1/T)\sum_t \nu_{it} = 0$, their expected values:

$$\bar{y}_i. - \bar{y}.. = b_2(\bar{x}_i. - \bar{x}..) + \mu_i \qquad (i = 1, \ldots, N). \tag{5.4}$$

Equation (5.4) suggests that still another estimate of β_2 may be obtained by solving the normal equation

$$\sum_{i=1}^{N}(\bar{y}_i. - \bar{y}..)(\bar{x}_i. - \bar{x}..) = b_2^{(i)} \sum_{i=1}^{N}(\bar{x}_i. - \bar{x}..)^2. \tag{5.5}$$

This "regression" makes use of the variation in the sample across individuals, but not over time. Similarly, take means in Equation (5.2) over individuals and set $(1/N)\sum_i \mu_i = 0$ and $(1/N)\sum_i \nu_{it} = 0$, their expected values:

$$\bar{y}._t - \bar{y}.. = b_2(\bar{x}._t - \bar{x}..) + \lambda_t \qquad (t = 1, \ldots, T). \tag{5.6}$$

Equation (5.6) suggests that an additional estimate of β_2 may be obtained by

---

[2] This section was inspired by a similar treatment of the two-component model contained in an unpublished paper by G. S. Maddala.

solving the normal equations

$$\sum_{t=1}^{T}(\bar{y}_{\cdot t} - \bar{y}..)(\bar{x}_{\cdot t} - \bar{x}..) = b_2^{(t)} \sum_{t=1}^{T}(\bar{x}_{\cdot t} - \bar{x}..)^2. \qquad (5.7)$$

This "regression" makes use of the variation in the sample over time periods, but not across individuals. Finally, consider estimating both μ_i and λ_t as parameters in the relation (5.2). Doing so amounts to running a multiple regression involving both individual and period dummies. Alternatively, think of estimating μ_i from (5.4) by replacing b_2 by an estimate of β_2, and λ_t from (5.6) in the same way. Insert the resulting estimates of μ_i and λ_t in (5.2) and obtain

$$(y_{it} - \bar{y}_{i\cdot} - \bar{y}_{\cdot t} + \bar{y}..) = b_2(x_{it} - \bar{x}_{i\cdot} - \bar{x}_{\cdot t} + \bar{x}..) + v_{it}$$

$$(i = 1, \ldots, N; t = 1, \ldots, T). \quad (5.8)$$

Equation (5.8) suggests estimating β_2 from the normal equation

$$\sum_{i,t}(y_{it} - \bar{y}_{i\cdot} - \bar{y}_{\cdot t} + \bar{y}..)(x_{it} - \bar{x}_{i\cdot} - \bar{x}_{\cdot t} + \bar{x}..)$$

$$= b_2^{\mathrm{LSC}} \sum_{i,t}(x_{it} - \bar{x}_{i\cdot} - \bar{x}_{\cdot t} + \bar{x}..)^2. \qquad (5.9)$$

This estimate is denoted by superscribing LSC since it corresponds to the estimate obtained by treating μ_i and λ_t as constant parameters and estimating them as well as the slope and overall intercept of (5.1) by ordinary least squares. This "regression" makes use of the variation of the sample observations *about* their individual and period means, but not of the variation *among* individual means or period means. In addition, note that an estimate of β_2, of sorts, may be obtained from the ratio of the overall means of y_{it} and x_{it}.

Now consider the normal equation (4.6) of the preceding subsection. If we set $\rho = \omega = 0$, we find $\lambda_1 = \lambda_2 = \lambda_3 = \lambda_4 = 1$ and Equation (5.6) yields the ordinary least-squares estimate of β_2, b_2^{OLS}. In effect, the ordinary least-squares estimate weights the various bits of information contained in the sample about β_2 strictly in proportion to the number of observations used in constructing them; thus, the overall mean is weighted by NT, the sum of squared deviations of individual means about the overall mean by N, and so on. Common sense, however, would dictate weighting each bit in inverse proportion to the amount of misinformation or error about β_2 likely to be contained in that bit. This is, of course, just what the generalized least-squares estimates accomplish by weighting inversely to the characteristic roots $\lambda_1, \lambda_2, \lambda_3$ and λ_4. In a sense, this is the underlying rationale behind the greater efficiency of the generalized least-squares estimate of β_2 in comparison with the ordinary least-squares estimate.

By the same token, least-squares regressions introducing dummies for both period and individual are also inefficient, since such estimates give all the weight to the last term in the expressions occurring within both sets of curly brackets in (4.6). It is interesting, however, to note that when N and T are very large, as long as ρ and ω are not zero, this term does indeed dominate and the estimates $\hat{\beta}_2$ and b_2^{LSC} will be very close. The reason is easy to see from the expressions relating the characteristic roots of Ω to the parameters ρ and ω: $\lambda_1 = 1 - \rho - \omega + \omega N + \rho T$, $\lambda_2 = 1 - \rho - \omega + \omega N$, $\lambda_3 = 1 - \rho - \omega + \rho T$, and $\lambda_4 = 1 - \rho - \omega$. Only λ_4 does not depend on N or T, as long as $\omega \neq 0 \neq \rho$, and thus $1/\lambda_1$, $1/\lambda_2$, and $1/\lambda_3$ all tend to zero as both N and T increase, *irrespective of the manner in which they increase and irrespective of the value of ρ or of ω as long as neither is zero*, and provided $1/NT$ times each of the three terms on the left-hand side of (4.5) or (4.6) tends to a finite positive definite matrix or finite limit. Indeed, this is exactly what Wallace and Hussain prove for nonstochastic explanatory variables (1969, pp. 62–64) and is the essence of the theorem proved by Amemiya (1967) for the case in which a lagged value of the dependent variable is included as one of the explanatory variables.

A second advantage of expressing the generalized least-squares estimates of β in terms of the characteristic roots of Ω is that it gives some insight into the possible biases that may result if only the fourth term in (4.5) or (4.6) is considered in finite samples. Suppose that one has a sample in which the numbers of individuals is large relative to the number of time periods for which each individual is observed, and suppose for simplicity that period effects are absent. Including individual dummies is then equivalent to taking deviations from individual means in the estimation of β and to neglecting the variation of the individual means in the estimation of β. A variable that varies only across individuals, but not over time for the same individual, will receive a weight of zero in the explanation of the dependent variable. Similarly, a variable that varies mostly across individuals and only a little over time for the same individual will have its coefficient underestimated by any method that neglects variation across individuals among individual means.

Intuitively, it remains something of a puzzle as to why treating μ_i and λ_t as parameters, rather than as random variables, should become asymptotically unimportant. After all, as $N, T \to \infty$ there are an infinite number of such parameters; their numbers increase just as fast as the number of pieces of new information available as the sample size increases. The solution to the puzzle is simply that we are not, in fact, estimating them, but only β when we solve the normal equations

$$\left\{ X'X - X'\left(\frac{e_N e_N'}{N} \otimes I_T\right) X - X'\left(I_N \otimes \frac{e_T e_T'}{T}\right) X + \frac{X' e_{NT} e_{NT}' X}{NT} \right\} b^{\mathrm{LSC}}$$

$$= \left\{ X'y - X\left(\frac{e_N e_N'}{N} \otimes I_T\right) y - X'\left(I_N \otimes \frac{e_T e_T'}{T}\right) y + \frac{X' e_{NT} e_{NT}' y}{NT} \right\}, \quad (5.10)$$

which corresponds to the *relevant portion* of the normal equations obtained by treating μ_i and λ_t as constants to be estimated. Indeed, it is clear by examining the likelihood function (1.10) that ρ and ω are not identified asymptotically, although they are in finite samples. While the maximum-likelihood estimate of β does exist asymptotically, and does correspond asymptotically to b^{LSC}, maximum-likelihood estimates of ρ and ω do not exist asymptotically.

University of Chicago
Manuscript received July 1969; revision received December 1969.

References

Amemiya, T. (1967), "A Note on the Estimation of Balestra-Nerlove Models," Technical Report 4 (NSF-GS-1440), Institute for Mathematical Studies in the Social Sciences, Stanford University (August 14).

Balestra, P., and M. Nerlove (1966), "Pooling Cross-Section and Time-Series Data in the Estimation of a Dynamic Model: The Demand for Natural Gas," Technical Report 8 (NSF-GS-142), Institute for Mathematical Studies in the Social Sciences, Stanford University (December 21, 1964); published in revised form in *Econometrica, 34*: July, pp. 585–612.

Nerlove, M. (1967), "Experimental Evidence on the Estimation of Dynamic Economic Relations from a Time Series of Cross Sections," *Economic Studies Quarterly, 18*: December, pp. 42–74.

Nerlove, M. (1971), "Further Evidence on the Estimation of Dynamic Economic Relations from a Time Series of Cross Sections," *Econometrica, 39*: March, pp. 359–382.

Wallace, T. D., and A. Hussain (1969), "The Use of Error-Components Models in Combining Cross-Section with Time-Series Data," *Econometrica, 37*: January, pp. 55–72.

Growth-Rate Convergence, Fact or Artifact?

An Essay on Panel Data Econometrics[1]

Preface

Although the paper reprinted here was not published until 2000, it was actually written much earlier, around 1995, and grew out of the need to present a meaningful panel data problem to my first-year graduate class in applied econometrics. Such a problem arose in the debate on growth-rate convergence going on at the time.

Baumol's 1986 *AER* paper set off the debate on growth convergence. Baumol used Maddison's (1982) data on only a few countries for the period 1870–1970. A more extensive data-collection effort was, however, underway at the time: Kravis, Heston, and Summers (1978); Summers and Heston (1988); and Summers and Heston (1991). This effort, which resulted in the creation of the Penn World Tables (current version, Center for International Comparisons, 2001) set off an avalanche of studies based on analysis of the cross section of countries' time series on GDP per capita and other variables included or added to the table, beginning with Barro (1991) and Mankiw, Romer, and Weil (1992). Around this time, interest developed in exploiting the panel nature of the Penn World Table data. The paper by Islam (1995) shows the sensitivity of the estimates of the rate of growth convergence to the econometric method employed. My own work, reported in the paper reprinted here, suggests that the findings supporting convergence from estimates based on fixed-effects models of country-specific effects are an artifact of the method employed.

The paper begins by laying out the basic Solow/Swan framework in a manner simpler than Mankiw *et al.* (1992), then illustrates various estimates of the convergence rate for this model using quinquennial averages of the 1965–1985 data for a sample of ninety-four countries and a subsample of twenty-two countries. The results represent a striking confirmation of the sensitivity of convergence estimates to the econometric method employed. One method of maximum likelihood used in the comparisons corresponds to the original

[1] Reprinted with permission from J. Krishnakumar and E. Ronchetti, *Panel Data Econometrics: Future Directions*, Amsterdam: Elsevier, 2000, pp. 3–33.

238   *Essays in Panel Data Econometrics*

choice of Balestra and Nerlove (1966) by conditioning on the initial values considered as fixed. Alternative formulations of the likelihood function are explored in the papers reprinted in the next two chapters. The unconditional ML estimates presented here are not correct, as pointed out in the paper reprinted as Chapter 8 of this volume. One further important innovation is introduced in this paper; that is, the introduction of individual-specific linear trends. Such a modification in the specification complicates the estimation problem because it introduces first-order moving-average correlation in the transformed disturbances of the estimating equation, but the results are greatly improved, although still sensitive to variations in the econometric method employed.

References

Barro, R. J. (1991), "Economic growth in a Cross Section of Countries." *Quarterly Journal of Economics, 106*: pp. 407–443.

Baumol, W. J. (1986), "Productivity Growth, Convergence, and Welfare: What the Long-Run Data Show," *American Economic Review, 76*: pp. 1072–1085.

Center for International Comparisons (2001), *Penn World Table,* http//:www.pwt.econ.upenn.edu/.

Islam, N. (1995), "Growth Empirics: A Panel Data Approach." *Quarterly Journal of Economics, 110*: pp. 1127–1170.

Kravis, I. E., A. W. Heston, and R. Summers (1978), "Real GDP Per Capita for More Than One Hundred Countries," *Economic Journal, 88*: pp. 215–242.

Maddison, A. (1982), *Phases of Capitalist Development*, New York: Oxford University Press.

Mankiw, N. G., D. Romer, and D. N. Weil (1992), "A Contribution to the Empirics of Economic Growth." *Quarterly Journal of Economics, 108*: pp. 407–437.

Summers, R., and A. W. Heston (1988), "A New Set of International Comparisons of Real Product and Price Levels Estimates for 130 Countries, 1950–1985," *Review of Income and Wealth, 34*: pp. 1–25.

Summers, R., and A. W. Heston (1991), "The Penn World Table (Mark 5): An Expanded Set of International Comparisons, 1950–1988," *Quarterly Journal of Economics, 106*: pp. 327–368.

Growth-Rate Convergence, Fact or Artifact?

An Essay on Panel Data Econometrics*

Marc Nerlove

ABSTRACT

The sensitivity of the convergence rate, or the test for no convergence in the standard Barro-Baumol sense, to the econometric method employed is investigated. Two basic models are investigated: the first is the standard model with individual-specific effects for each country; the second is a model in which individual countries have different individual-specific trends in output per capita. All of the results reported support the growth-convergence hypothesis conditional on savings and population growth rates in the usual sense, but illustrate the rather different estimates of the rates of convergence obtained when different estimation techniques are used. In particular, I show that the use of fixed-effects panel models biases the results toward finding relatively rapid convergence and that when more appropriate maximum-likelihood estimates, unconditional on the initial observations, are employed, very slow convergence is implied (to within 90 percent of equilibrium only in excess of fifty years). Biases in the estimates of the coefficient of the "state" variable for all of the usual methods of panel data analysis imply biased estimates of

* This paper is based on an earlier paper of similar title presented at the Sixth Conference on Panel Data Econometrics, Amsterdam, 28–29 June 1996, and also presented as the 1998 Havlicek Lecture in Applied Econometrics at Ohio State University, April 16, 1998.

My interest in the question of how the econometric approach might have influenced recent findings with respect to the convergence hypothesis was stimulated by reading Islam (1995). But there is now a vast literature utilizing the data from the Penn World Tables, which I also use here. I do not attempt a comprehensive survey of this literature in this paper.

I thank Hashem Pesaran for helpful discussions, and Robert Barro, Michael Binder, William Greene, G. S. Maddala, and C. Spohr for useful comments. Special thanks are due to Anke Meyer, with whom I discussed every aspect of this work.

I am also indebted to Jinkyo Suh and Timothy Thomas for computational counsel and their assistance in straightening out the GAUSS programs that I wrote to obtain my earlier results. Suh also checked and double checked all derivations and verified that my programs accurately reflected the formulae derived.

the coefficients of any other variables included if these are correlated with the "state" variable, which is typically the case. Thus, the significance and possibly the sign of any other determinants of growth may be seriously affected. Alternative maximum-likelihood methods are developed that utilize the information contained in the initial observations for each country that reflect the operation of the growth process prior to the time at which we began to observe them.

1. INTRODUCTION

One of the most important implications of the classic papers of Solow (1956) and Swan (1956) is that the lower the starting level of real per capita GDP, relative to the long run or steady-state position, the faster is the growth rate. The Solow-Swan model assumes a constant-returns-to-scale production function with two inputs, capital and labor, and substitution between inputs, a constant savings rate, and constant rate of growth of population and neutral technical change, all exogenously given. Convergence of economies starting out at different levels of per capita income to the same steady-state rate of growth reflects the diminishing returns to capital implied by the production function assumed: economies starting out with lower levels of real per capita GDP relative to the long run or steady-state position have less capital per worker and, therefore, higher rates of return to capital. I will refer to this as the standard Barro-Baumol (BB) sense of the meaning of convergence.[1] Because the steady states of the Solow-Swan model depend on the savings rate, the rate of growth of population, and the rate of technical progress, some authors have argued that these factors need to be held constant in attempting to test the hypothesis of growth-rate convergence. Convergence is, in this sense, conditional. (When population growth is endogenously determined, this implication of the neoclassical model of economic growth does not necessarily follow; see Nerlove and Raut, 1996.)

The problem of BB-convergence in the standard neoclassical model is treated both theoretically and empirically in the recent text by Barro and Sala-i-Martin (1995) and empirically in a recent paper by Islam (1995). Bernard and Durlauf (1996) provide a useful framework for understanding the time-series and cross-sectional tests of the BB-convergence hypothesis and its relation to alternative definitions. Quah (1996) discusses the problem of convergence in more general form and distinguishes several different varieties. He argues

---

[1] There is a good deal of current discussion regarding the appropriate definition of "convergence." Bernard and Durlauf (1995) give a nice discussion emphasizing the restrictiveness of the approach adopted here (see also Quah, 1996), which is the most prevalent, going back to the earlier work of Barro (1991) and Baumol (1986). Since my main concern is to show that the econometrics matters, I will adopt the basic Solow/Swan model in what follows. However, the general point that inconsistency in the estimation of the coefficient of the state variable implies inconsistency in the estimation of the effects of other factors is valid in this context and in general.

that "Simply because panel data techniques happen to apply to data with extensive cross-section and time-series variation does not mean they are at once similarly appropriate for analyzing convergence." While I do not fault Quah's conclusion, current discussions do emphasize panel data and methods and derive strong conclusions regarding BB-convergence and the significance of other determinants of growth from such data. It is, therefore, appropriate to consider how these conclusions, within the context of BB-convergence, are affected by the econometric methods employed.

Perhaps even more important than the problem of convergence is the question of the determinants of growth. The World Bank Project on Economic Growth lists more than thirty published and working papers, almost all of which involve dynamic panel data analysis or cross-section analysis with a state variable or initial condition.[2] Although the focus of these papers is not convergence but the effects of the other variables included, if the coefficient of state variable in the statistical analysis is inconsistently estimated, in this sense "biased," then the coefficient of any variable correlated with the state variable will also be biased. Hence, quite misleading conclusions may be drawn concerning the significance, sign, and relative magnitude of other factors included in the analysis.

In Subsection 2, I derive a discrete form of the BB-convergence equation, also derived in a different way by Mankiw *et al.* (1992), and show that the usual equation for testing the convergence hypothesis can be obtained from it by a simple partial-adjustment model rather than the approximation about equilibrium usually employed. In general, no essential restrictions are neglected in this simpler derivation, although in certain contexts the specification may neglect certain cross-equation parameter restrictions. It is the classic Solow/Swan model that, for good or for ill, underlies all recent studies of the determinants of growth and provides the justification for including a lagged value of the dependent variable, initial condition, or other state variable.

Subsection 3 examines recent empirical investigations of BB-convergence and the rate of convergence, and argues that most are flawed by failure to allow for the inconsistencies of single cross-section or panel studies in a dynamic context.[3] In a dynamic context, a single cross section is best viewed as a panel with time dimension 1. I do not attempt here a general review of the effects of the methods used in more general studies of the determinants of growth, but I do examine the effects on the estimated coefficients of the savings rate and the rate of growth of population.

In this subsection, I look at the problem of implementing the convergence hypothesis in the context of cross-country data over time and, in particular,

---

[2] See http://www.worldbank.org/research/growth. The number has now grown to one hundred.
[3] A recent study by Lee, *et al.* (1996) arrives at similar conclusions but proposes a number of alternatives different from those investigated here. In particular, I do not agree that their formulation of the unconditional likelihood function is equivalent to the one I present.

whether the model ought to be recast so that individual countries are subject to individual specific trends.[4]

In Subsection 4, I discuss five existing methods of estimating the rate of convergence (and thus testing for convergence), show that four standard methods yield estimates that satisfy an inequality derived by Trognon and Sevestre (1996), and devise a new method of maximum-likelihood estimation based on the density of the observations *unconditional on the initial or starting values of the dependent variable*. I further show that under a mildly restrictive assumption, this unconditional maximum-likelihood method tends to maximum-likelihood conditional on the initial observations as the cross-section dimension of the panel increases. The "biases" in conventional panel methods are reflected in the estimates of the effects of other variables included in differing ways illustrated here.

Finally, in Subsection 5, I apply all six methods to several panel data sets drawn from the Penn World Tables. The results show clearly how misleading the standard estimates can be in assessing growth-rate convergence and in the estimation of the significance and magnitude of other variables included. The contrast between the conditional and the unconditional ML estimates for a small cross-section dimension and their similarity for a large cross-section dimension are illustrated. I argue that the usual procedures for doing feasible GLS or for obtaining starting values for ML are seriously flawed and likely to yield negative estimates of the random time-persistent cross-sectional effects. Results not presented here show that biases in the estimate of the coefficient of the lagged value of the dependent variable are transmitted to the estimates of other coefficients in the model such as the stock of human capital, making inferences about the determinants of growth problematic unless appropriate econometric methods are used.

Subsection 6 is the conclusion.

2. THE NEOCLASSICAL THEORY OF GROWTH CONVERGENCE

The Solow/Swan model of economic growth is the starting point for all recent empirical analyses of growth convergence and the determinants of growth. In

---

[4] Of course, the existence of conditioning country-specific trends is hardly convergence in any meaningful sense. No matter. My concern here and in Nerlove (1997) is to show the effect of the econometrics on the assessment of the effects of the initial conditions in the basic Solow/Swan model. Because the maximum-likelihood methods implemented in the paper require stationarity, I argue that the data should be differenced in order to implement this modification of the basic model. I refer to the two forms as the "levels" model and the "first-differenced" model, respectively. As it turns out, the results for the first-differenced model are a great deal more reasonable than those for the levels model. I suggest that this means that much of the recent convergence debate has focused on the wrong thing, namely convergence, rather than the effects of other factors on economic growth. Country-specific trends are a clear indication of important left-out variables.

this subsection, I review briefly the model and dynamize it in a particularly simple approximate way.

a. The Solow/Swan Model

Consider the standard Solow/Swan (Solow, 1956; Swan, 1956) model with exogenous population growth in discrete form: Let Y_t = output, K_t = capital stock, N_t = labor force assumed to be the same as population, S_t = savings, I_t = investment, s = the savings rate, δ = depreciation rate, and $\bar{n}$ = the exogenous rate of growth of population and labor force. Production can be represented by a constant returns to scale function:

$$Y_t = F(K_t, N_t), \tag{1}$$

or

$$y_t = f(k_t),$$

where $y_t = Y_t/N_t$, $k_t = K_t/N_t$, and $f(k) = F(k, 1)$. Solow/Swan assume that savings equals gross investment and is a constant fraction s of output:

$$I_t = S_t = sY_t. \tag{2}$$

The change in the capital stock equals gross investment minus depreciation:

$$K_{t+1} = (1 - \delta)K_t + I_t = sF(K_t, N_t) + (1 - \delta)K_t \tag{3}$$

Population grows exogenously at a rate:

$$N_{t+1} = (1 + \bar{n})N_t. \tag{4}$$

Thus,

$$k_{t+1} = sf(k_1) + (1 - \delta)k_t \bar{1} + n = g(k_t), \ k_0 \text{ given.} \tag{5}$$

The dynamics of the Solow/Swan model is entirely described by the path of k_t, the capital-labor ratio, since population grows exogenously, capital depreciates at a fixed rate, and gross investment is proportional to output.

The existence of stationary solutions to (5), i.e., k^* for which

$$k^* = g(k^*), \tag{6}$$

and the local stability of such solutions depends on the shape of the function g. The conditions that yield a non-negative globally stable steady-state solution are the following:

$$g'(0) > 1, g(0) = 0,$$

$$g'(k) < 1, \text{ for some } k > 0, \text{ and } g \text{ is concave.}$$

These properties follow if the production function satisfies:

$$f(0) = 0$$

$$f'(0) > \frac{\delta + \bar{n}}{s}$$

$$f'(k) < \frac{\delta + \bar{n}}{s},$$

and f is concave.

A stationary solution k^* is locally stable if $|g'(k^*)| < 1$. Clearly, $k^* = 0$ is unstable. Under concavity of f, whenever (6) holds for some $k^* > 0$, then there can be no other $k^* > 0$ for which (6) holds, and at that point $|g'(k^*)| < 1$, so the solution is necessarily unique.

b. Growth Convergence in the Neoclassical Model with Exogenous Population Growth and Savings

If $f(k_t)$ is Cobb-Douglas, we can solve explicitly for the time path of y_t: For $y_t = A_t k_t^a$, so that

$$k_t = \left(\frac{y_t}{A_t}\right)^{1/a} \tag{7}$$

and, hence, from (5)

$$y_t = \frac{n+1}{s} k_{t+1} - \frac{1-\delta}{s} k_t = \frac{n+1}{s}\left(\frac{y_{t+1}}{A_{t+1}}\right)^{1/\alpha} - \frac{1-\delta}{s}\left(\frac{y_t}{A_t}\right)^{1/\alpha} \tag{8}$$

α is the elasticity of output with respect to capital stock; if capital is fully employed and paid its marginal product, it is the implied share of capital in total output. A_t is any function of time that may affect the productivity of capital and labor; for example, neutral technical change or, more explicitly, investment in human capital or in infrastructure. In the "stationary state"

$$y_t^* = \left(\frac{n+\delta}{s}\right)^{-\alpha/(1-\alpha)} A_t^{1/(1-\alpha)}. \tag{9}$$

Taking logs

$$\log y_t^* = \frac{-\alpha}{1-\alpha} \log\left(\frac{n+\delta}{s}\right) + \frac{1}{1-\alpha} \log A_t. \tag{10}$$

Although (8) shows that the rate of convergence to equilibrium is not constant, an approximation is given by a partial adjustment model

$$\log y_t - \log y_{t-1} = (1 - \gamma)[\log y_t^* - \log y_{t-1}]. \qquad (11)$$

This yields the approximate relation to be estimated and the equation employed in recent studies:

$$\log y_t = \frac{\alpha(1 - \gamma)}{1 - \alpha}[\log s - \log(n + \delta)] + \frac{1 - \gamma}{1 - \alpha} \log A_t + \gamma \log y_{t-1}. \qquad (12)$$

The speed of convergence to equilibrium is inversely proportional to γ. With growth convergence, $0 < \gamma < 1$. In equilibrium, per capita GDP depends only on the parameters n, s, and the time path of A. In an empirical context, these differ from time to time and country to country. Clearly, the extent of convergence is conditional on s, n, δ and the time path of A_t. In empirical investigations, changing n and s and sometimes a measure of changing A have been introduced. In what follows, I take account of differing s and n over time and cross sectionally; in some additional analyses, I take account of other factors by including country-specific trends, but not other variables explicitly such as infrastructure investment, which might arguably affect A.[5] Including a simple linear trend, with coefficient τ, in place of the entire term $\frac{1-\gamma}{1-\alpha} \log A_t$ gives rise to quite a different model, particularly if one argues that the trends ought to be different for different countries.[6] I will refer to (12) where A may differ from country to country, but is assumed to be constant over time as the "levels" model. When the term $\frac{1-\gamma}{1-\alpha} \log A_t$ is replaced by a linear trend with slope that may differ from country to country but is assumed to be constant over time, (12) is replaced by

$$\Delta \log y_t = \frac{\alpha(1 - \gamma)}{1 - \alpha} \Delta[\log s - \log(n + \delta)] + v + \gamma \Delta \log y_{t-1}. \qquad (12')$$

where v is the slope of the trend and may differ from country to country. I refer

---

[5] As pointed out in a paper by Binder and Pesaran (1996), it makes a good deal of difference to the question of convergence at just what point one includes the stochastic disturbance. In this paper, I follow the usual practice of tacking it on the end of the equation to be estimated.

[6] In some further investigations not reported here, I have included A_t represented by the stock of human capital over time as measured by Barro and Lee (1993) raised to the power φ, $A_t = H_{it}^\varphi$, so that the coefficient of $\log H_{it}$ in the implied regression equation is $\frac{(1-\gamma)\varphi}{1-\alpha}$. The human capital variable constructed by Barro and Lee (1993) is available only for a subsample of countries by quinquennial for the period 1965–1985. Essentially, the stock of human capital in the population is measured by Barro and Lee as the average schooling in the population as a whole over twenty-five. In the results obtained, this variable is often the wrong sign and never significant.

to this model as the "first-difference" model.[7] This approach is implemented in Nerlove (1997) and the results obtained there are reported in Table 3 on page 262.

3. EMPIRICAL INVESTIGATIONS OF CONVERGENCE AND THE RATE OF CONVERGENCE

Equation (12) is widely used to examine the hypothesis of growth convergence (Mankiw *et al.*, 1992, p. 410; Barro and Sala-i-Martin, 1995, Chapter 12; Islam, 1995, p. 1133; Lee *et al.*, 1996). In empirical work, y_t is replaced by real per capita GDP; when varying s and n are taken into account, s is replaced by an average savings rate over the period $t - 1$ to t, and n is replaced by the growth rate of population over the period $t - 1$ to t. It is usual to use rates averaged over several years; following Islam (1995), I have used quinquennial averages. The restriction on the coefficients of $ln(s)$ and $ln(n + \delta)$, which arises from the constant-returns-to-scale assumption, implies that $ln(s)$ and $ln(n + \delta)$ can be collapsed into a single variable. Testing the growth-convergence hypothesis, in this context, revolves largely around the coefficient γ of the initial level of per capita real GDP. If this is positive but much less than one, the implication is that, on average, countries with low initial values are growing faster than those with high initial values and is therefore evidence of convergence. Whereas, if this coefficient is close to one, perhaps even slightly larger than one, the implication is that initial values have little or no effect or even a perverse one on subsequent growth; such a finding is therefore evidence against the neoclassical theory, which implies convergence. For example, if $\gamma = 0.9$, convergence to within 90 percent of final equilibrium occurs only in twenty-two periods, which, given quinquennial data, implies one hundred ten years! Similarly, 0.8 requires fifty-three years, 0.7 thirty-two years, while 0.2 requires only seven years and 0.1 is within 90 percent in five years.

The following estimates of γ using cross-country quinquennial data and based on the levels model are generally in excess of 0.7 no matter what econometric procedure is employed, but vary over a wide range depending on the method, 0.7 to 0.98. It is apparent that, for all practical purposes, coefficients in excess of 0.7 represent negligible convergence since, with unchanging s, n, and A, it would take more than a generation to achieve 90 percent of equilibrium real per capita GDP. Most recent work attempts to test whether $\gamma = 1$; however, this is a test for unit root in log y_{it}. Even under the best of circumstances, testing for a unit root is problematic (see Diebold and Nerlove, 1990). Here the problems are compounded by the short time dimension of the typical panel. Basing a test on the size of γ rather than equality with 1

---

[7] Differencing the model to achieve stationarity creates some interesting problems with respect to the disturbance term, which are discussed later. See especially Footnote 13.

finesses a host of problems of the sort discussed extensively in Diebold and Nerlove.[8]

Tests based on a single cross section (which can be viewed as a panel of time dimension 1) or on pooled cross-section time series (panel) data generally have yielded contradictory results: pooled panel data studies tend to reject the hypothesis of BB-convergence (relatively high $\gamma's$), even after controlling for population growth rates, savings rates, and other variables. Dynamic fixed-effects models are, of course, not possible for a single cross section, but recent work (Islam, 1995) using a dynamic fixed-effects panel model yields results supporting convergence. There are serious problems with tests such as these, which rely on the estimated coefficients of the initial or lagged value of the dependent variable in dynamic panel models, or in the special case of a single cross section, which arise from two sources of bias. In this paper, I show that these findings are probably statistical artifacts arising from biases in the econometric methods employed to test the growth convergence hypothesis in the BB sense. This does not mean that this sense is the correct one to employ in the more general context of convergence, as emphasized by Quah (1996), but demonstrates the sensitivity of the conclusions drawn about γ to the econometric method employed, irrespective of the validity of the relationship of such conclusions to more general notions of convergence.

The first source of bias is omitted variables, especially infrastructure and investments over time in infrastructure, and the natural resource base available to each country in cross-sectional or panel studies. Systematic differences in these across countries or regions will systematically bias the conclusions. To the extent that these effects are approximated by differing trends for each country, omitting such variables may account for the differences between the first-difference model and the levels model. Because such omitted variables are likely to be correlated with savings or investment rates in conventional or in human capital and with population growth rates, it is not altogether clear what the net effect of omitting them on the coefficient of the initial value will be in a single cross section. But in a pooled model, it is clear that, to the extent such differences are persistent, they will be highly correlated with the initial value and, therefore, omitting them will bias the coefficient of that variable

---

[8] Barnard and Durlauf (1995) use co-integration techniques on rather longer time series for fifteen OECD countries to test alternative time-series definitions of convergence and contrast the results with the standard BB-formulation. Using long annual time series (1865–1994) for sixteen OECD countries, Michelacci and Zaffaroni (1997) extend the Solow/Swan model to allow for cross-sectional heterogeneity in the pace of convergence and conclude that the uniform 2 percent rate of convergence found in much of the empirical literature is a consequence of fractionally integrated nonstationarity with underlying parameters strictly between 0.5 and 1.0. My first-difference formulation (1997) is equivalent to assuming a unit root, an hypothesis that is rejected by Michelacci and Zaffaroni.

upward toward one and thus toward rejecting convergence. This source of bias has been well known since the early paper by Balestra and Nerlove (1966) and is well supported by the Monte Carlo studies reported in Nerlove (1971). In this light, it is not surprising that pooled panel data, or single cross sections, which are a special case of panels with $T = 1$, even with inclusion of additional variables, often reject convergence.

Second, since there are likely to be many sources of cross-country or cross-region differences, many of which cannot be observed or directly accounted for, it is natural to try to represent these by fixed effects in a panel context. But, as is well known from the Monte Carlo investigations reported in Nerlove (1971) and demonstrated analytically by Nickell (1981), inclusion of fixed effects in a dynamic model biases the coefficient of the initial value of the dependent variable included as an explanatory variable downward, toward zero and, therefore, toward support for the convergence hypothesis. This may account for Islam's (1995) recent findings.

Alternative estimates based on more appropriate random-effects models, such as two-stage feasible generalized least squares or maximum-likelihood conditional on the initial observations are also biased in small samples and inconsistent in large, or in the case of instrumental-variable estimates, have poor sampling properties or are difficult to implement. Results for the alternative method of unconditional maximum likelihood suggested in Nerlove and Balestra (1996) are presented here.[9]

Even if one has little interest in the question of convergence, or its rate, *per se*, the question of whether the coefficient of the state variable, lagged dependent or initial value, is biased in the sense of being inconsistent is an important one since biases in this coefficient will affect the estimates of the coefficients of other variables correlated with it and their levels of significance. To the extent such estimates are important in the formulation of policies to promote growth, the matter is indeed a serious one.

In the remainder of this paper, I investigate the sensitivity of the convergence rate, or the test of no convergence, in the levels model to the econometric method employed, as well as the sensitivity of the estimates of the coefficients of other variables included. All of the results reported, except those for pooled panel data, support the growth convergence hypothesis conditional on savings and population growth rates, but illustrate the rather different estimates of the rates of convergence. In additional research not presented here, I also show that the coefficients of other explanatory variables vary considerably when different estimation techniques are used. In addition, a technique for examining

---

[9] See also Nerlove (1997). Lee *et al.* (1996) also estimate what they term is an unconditional likelihood function, but inasmuch as they do not transform to stationarity (their relationship includes both a constant and a linear trend), I do not think their formulation of the likelihood function based on what they refer to as the unconditional density of the dependent variable is equivalent to mine.

the shape of sections of a high dimensional likelihood function is developed that reveals interesting and somewhat unexpected relationships among the various estimates.

4. ALTERNATIVE METHODS FOR ESTIMATING RATES OF CONVERGENCE[10]

A good summary of the current state of knowledge about the properties of various estimators in dynamic panel models is contained is Sevestre and Trognon (1992, 2nd ed., 1996). Trognon (1978) was the first to show the inconsistency of maximum-likelihood conditional on the initial individual observations. Nickell (1981) shows the inconsistency of the estimates of the fixed-effects in a dynamic panel model. Kiviet (1995) derives exact results for the bias of leading estimators. In this subsection, following Sevestre and Trognon, I review the leading estimators and their properties for dynamic panel models.

For simplicity, in this subsection I restrict attention to the simple model containing one exogenous variable x_{it} and one lagged value of the dependent variable y_{it-1} as explanatory. Extension to the case in which more than one exogenous explanatory variable is included presents no serious difficulty.

$$y_{it} = \alpha + \beta x_{it} + \gamma y_{it-1} + \mu_i + \varepsilon_{it}, \quad i = 1, \ldots N, \quad t = 1, \ldots T. \quad (13)$$

Taking deviations from overall means eliminates the constant α. The usual assumptions are made about the properties of the μ_i and the ε_{it}:

(i) $E(\mu_i) = E(\varepsilon_{it}) = 0,$ all i and t,

(ii) $E(\mu_i \varepsilon_{jt}) = 0,$ all i, j, and t,

(iii) $E(\mu_i \mu_j) = \begin{cases} \sigma_\mu^2 & i = j \\ 0 & i \neq j, \end{cases}$

(iv) $E(\varepsilon_{it} \varepsilon_{js}) = \begin{cases} \sigma_\varepsilon^2 & t = s, \quad i = j \\ 0 & otherwise \end{cases}.$

Both μ_i and ε_{it} are assumed to be uncorrelated with x_{it} for all i and t. Clearly, however, y_{it-1} cannot be assumed to be uncorrelated with μ_i. It is clear, therefore, that OLS applied to (13) ignoring the component nature of the disturbances $v_{it} = \mu_i + \varepsilon_{it}$, which I call the *pooled regression*, will yield inconsistent estimates. In particular, if $\gamma > 0$, γ_{pooled} is "biased" upward. So, just as in the case of ordinary serial correlation, β_{pooled} is also "biased" and the OLS residuals understate the amount of serial correlation, which in this case is measured by the intraclass correlation coefficient ρ. This parameter measures

---

[10] I rely extensively in this section on the excellent discussion of Sevestre and Trognon, Chapter 7, in Mátyás and Sevestre (1996, pp. 120–144). Additional alternatives, more appropriate when longer time series are available, are treated by Lee *et al.* (1996), and are not discussed or implemented here.

the extent of unobserved or latent time-invariant, individual-specific variation relative to the total unobserved variation in the sample, $\frac{\sigma_\mu^2}{(\sigma_\mu^2+\sigma_\varepsilon^2)}$. It is extremely important in understanding the nature of the variation, both observed and unobserved, in the panel.

a. Inconsistency of the Pooled-Sample OLS Estimates of the Dynamic Error-Components Model

Since the panel has two dimensions, it is possible to consider asymptotic behavior as $N \to \infty$, $T \to \infty$, or both. Generally speaking, it is easier to increase the cross-section dimension of a panel, so the most relevant asymptotics are as $N \to \infty$. This is called *semi-asymptotics* in the panel data literature. It is not necessary to assume $|\gamma| < 1$ as long as T is fixed, but the way in which the initial values of the dependent variable, y_{i0}, are assumed to be generated is crucial. To see why, write (13) as

$$y_{it} = \gamma^t y_{i0} + \sum_{j=0}^{t-1} \gamma^j \beta x_{it-j} + \frac{1-\gamma^t}{1-\gamma}\mu_i + v_{it}, \quad \text{where } v_{it} = \sum_{j=0}^{t-1} \gamma^j \varepsilon_{it-j}. \quad (14)$$

Equation (14) expresses y_{it} as the sum of four terms: the first, $y^t y_{i0}$, depends on the initial values; the second on lagged values of the exogenous variable; the third on the individual, time-invariant component of residual variance; and the fourth on lagged values of the remaining component. This last term is an autoregressive process with initial values $v_{i0} = 0$ and $v_{it} = \gamma v_{it-1} + \varepsilon_{it}$. It need not be assumed to be stationary as long as T is fixed. It does not make sense in this context to assume that the y_{i0} are uncorrelated with either the μ_i or the lagged values of the x_{it}'s. On the other hand, ε_{i0} is a random variable with mean 0 and variance σ_ε^2 independently and identically distributed for all i. Thus, the initial observation can be written as a function of lagged xs, the μ_i and ε_{i0}:

$$y_{i0} = f(x_{i0}, x_{i-1}, \ldots, \mu_i, \varepsilon_{i0}). \quad (15)$$

Clearly, if the individual effects μ_i are assumed to be fixed and the lagged x's to be given, the y_{i0} are also fixed and uncorrelated with the disturbances in (15), $v_{it}, t = 1, \ldots, T$. But, if the individual effects are considered to be random, as Nerlove and Balestra (1996) have argued they should be, the initial observations are not exogenous since they are correlated with them, as they are part of the disturbance term, namely the third and fourth terms of (13).

It is common in the literature on panel data to assume that the y_{i0} are i.i.d. random variables that are characterized by their second moments and correlations with the individual effects, and not necessarily generated by the same process that generates the rest of the y_{it}s. The properties of various estimators depend on the process generating them. One possibility is to try to model and estimate this process together with the dynamic panel model (13).

b. Inconsistency of the OLS Estimators of the Dummy Variable or Fixed-Effects Model

The ordinary least-squares estimates of both the coefficient of the lagged dependent variable and the exogenous variable are inconsistent in the fixed-effects model. As is well known, the fixed-effects model is equivalent to taking deviations from individual (country) means and then estimating an ordinary OLS regression:

$$y_{it} - \bar{y}_i = \beta(x_{it} - \bar{x}_i) + \gamma(y_{it-1} - \bar{y}_{i-1}) + v_{it}, \quad \text{where}$$

$$v_{it} = \varepsilon_{it} - \bar{\varepsilon}_i. \tag{16}$$

Although $\sigma_{x\varepsilon}^2 = 0$,

$$\sigma_{y(-1)\varepsilon}^2 = \operatorname{plim} \frac{1}{T} \sum_t (y_{it-1} - \bar{y}_{i-1})(\varepsilon_{it} - \bar{\varepsilon}_{i-1})$$

$$= -\frac{1}{T^2} \frac{T - 1 - T\gamma + \gamma^T}{(1 - \gamma)^2} \sigma_\varepsilon^2 \neq 0. \tag{17}$$

Thus, the OLS estimates of both β and γ in the fixed-effects model are inconsistent, although as $T \to \infty$, the inconsistency disappears. But for finite, typically small T, it remains (see Nickell, 1981, p. 1424). For $T = 10$ and $\gamma = 0.5$, for example, the "bias" of the OLS estimate of γ, say c, is proportional to -0.16, the factor of proportionality being the OLS estimate of the variance of c from the within regression. It is always negative, implying that the bias of the OLS estimates of β, say b, is therefore upward. This conclusion holds regardless of whether one assumes the true model is fixed- or random-effects.

Although the inconsistency will be small when T is moderate to large, small values of T are typically the case. Nonetheless, Nerlove (1971) suggested using the fixed-effects model to estimate ρ for FGLS, in contrast to the earlier suggestion of Balestra and Nerlove (1966), hereinafter BN, of a consistent instrumental variable approach. BN also suggested but did not implement a method based on estimating ρ from the pooled and fixed-effects regressions. Rejection of instrumental variables by Nerlove (1971) was based on the instability of the results in Monte Carlo trials. Since the OLS estimates of the parameters from pooled or fixed-effects regressions are inconsistent, the estimates of ρ based on this regression will not be either; hence, the FGLS estimates computed using them will not generally be consistent. In the results reported here, an estimate of ρ is derived from the estimates of residual variance from both the fixed-effects and the pooled regressions, as suggested by *BN* (1966), and is not consistent.

c. Country Means Regression and the Estimation of ρ

Many authors (e.g., Greene, 1993, pp. 475–477; Judge *et al.*, 1988, pp. 484–488), hereinafter GJ, suggest basing an estimate of ρ on the cross-section regression of the overall means and either the pooled or fixed-effects regression. This suggestion, unfortunately, often leads to negative estimates of ρ and unwarranted rejection of the model. These estimates are also inconsistent. The GJ suggestion is, unfortunately, utilized in many computer packages for implementing FGLS for panel data or for obtaining starting values for ML, and often leads to the adoption of badly biased fixed-effects OLS when a negative estimate of ρ is obtained.

The GJ suggestion is to regress the group means of the independent variable on the group means of the dependent variables:

$$\bar{y}_i. = \alpha + \beta \bar{x}_i. + w_i, \quad \text{where } w_i = \mu_i + \bar{\varepsilon}_i. \tag{18}$$

The variance of w_i is $\sigma_\mu^2 + \frac{\sigma_\varepsilon^2}{T}$. The purely cross-sectional variation of the individual means gives us information on both the slope and the overall constant in the regression. This is often called the **between-groups** regression. In many panel data problems, purely cross-sectional variation may dominate, but this variation may not give us much information about the true value of the slope of the independent variable if the regression also contains a lagged value of the dependent variable. The residual SS/N = RSSB/N from this regression estimates $\sigma_\mu^2 + \frac{\sigma_\varepsilon^2}{T}$. But it will not be a very good estimate if the regression is estimated by OLS, since (18) will tend to fit too well if cross-section variation dominates the data.[11]

---

[11] For example, when a lagged value of the dependent variable is included as one of the explanatory variables, its mean may be very close to the mean of the unlagged variable; then the fit of (18) may be nearly perfect. The estimated residual variance may be close to zero in this case. In general, if there is a lot of associated cross-section variation, the residual of this relationship may be very small. If combined with the estimate of σ_ε^2 obtained from the within regression, the implied estimate of σ_μ^2 may well turn out to be negative (see Greene, pp. 474–476). But this does not imply that the model is misspecified. Balestra and Nerlove (1966, p. 607) suggest estimating σ_μ^2 from the fixed-effects model as the "variance" of the implied constant terms: $\sigma_\mu^2 = \frac{1}{N} \sum_i (\bar{y}_i. - \bar{y}.. - \hat{\beta}(\bar{x}_i. - \bar{x}..))^2$, where $\hat{\beta}$ is the OLS estimate of β in that regression. This suggestion is the one implemented in Nerlove (1971) and used to obtain FGL estimates below. Alternatively, if a regression with dummy variables for each individual, overall constant suppressed, has been estimated, it suffices to compute the variance, sum of squared deviations from the mean value divided by N, to estimate σ_μ^2.

In the following table, I present the three estimates of ρ discussed as possible candidates for the transformation involved in FGLS for the ninety-four-country sample and the model in levels. The Greene-Judge estimate is sharply biased downward and prone to be negative; similarly, the argument Nickell gives with reference to the downward bias in the coefficient of the lagged dependent variable in a fixed-effects regression suggests that the other coefficients will be biased upward, including the variance of the estimated fixed effects. Coupled with a downward bias in the estimate of the residual variance in the fixed-effects

σ_μ^2 is then estimated as $\sigma_w^2 - \frac{\sigma_\epsilon^2}{T}$, where an estimate of σ_ϵ^2 can be obtained from the fixed-effects regression. If T is large, the estimated value of σ_μ^2 is not likely to be negative no matter how well the between-groups regression fits. But if T is small, and particularly if the regression contains a lagged value of the dependent variable on the right-hand side, the chances of obtaining a negative, and therefore unacceptable, estimate of ρ are high irrespective of the validity of the model.

d. Generalized Least Squares and Feasible GLS

The means or between regression and the fixed-effects regression both contain information about the parameters of the model: the means regression reflects purely cross-sectional variation; whereas the fixed-effects regression reflects the individual variation over time. GLS combines these two types of information with weights that depend on the characteristic roots of $Euu' = \sigma^2\Omega$. The individual means themselves are weighted by the reciprocal of the square root of $\xi = 1 - \rho + T\rho$, while the deviations from these means are weighted by the reciprocal of the square root of $\eta = 1 - \rho$. A representative transformed observation is

$$y_{it}^* = \xi^{-1/2}\bar{y}_i. + \eta^{-1/2}(y_{it} - \bar{y}_i.), \quad i = 1, \ldots, N, \quad t = 1, \ldots, T.$$

Thus, y_{it}^* is a *weighted* combination (weighted by the reciprocals of the square roots of the characteristic roots of Ω) of individual means of the original observations $\bar{y}_i.$ and deviations from individual means $(y_{it} - \bar{y}_i.)$. The other variables are similarly transformed to x_{it}^* and y_{it-1}^*. GLS then amounts to running the OLS regression:

$$y_{it}^* = a + \beta x_{it}^* + \gamma y_{it-1}^* + v_{it}. \tag{19}$$

regression, this provides an explanation of the extremely high estimates obtained by the Nerlove (1971) method. It is interesting to note that the Balestra-Nerlove estimate, while substantially higher than the GJ estimate (it can never be negative) is, nonetheless, not too far out of line with the estimates of ρ obtained from the conditional likelihood function for the OECD countries and for both the conditional and unconditional likelihood functions for the ninety-four-country sample.

Alternative Estimates of ρ, Levels Model

Method	94 Countries	22 Countries
Balestra-Nerlove (1996)	0.2678	0.4027
Nerlove (1971)	0.7790	0.7038
G-J (1993/88)	0.0983	0.0804
Conditional ML	0.1133	0.4796
Unconditional ML	0.1288	0.7700

Let $\theta^2 = \eta/\xi = (\xi^{-1/2}/\eta^{-1/2})^2$ be the relative weight of the between variation to the within variation. Note that this weight tends to 0 from above as $T \to \infty$ (i.e., the within information dominates). For T small, $\theta^2 < 1$, so that the between variation is allowed to play a greater role. When the intraclass correlation, ρ, is close to one, the unobserved, residual cross-section variation is large relative to the unobserved individual variation. $\theta^2 = 1/(1 + T\frac{\rho}{1-\rho}) = 1/(1 + T\frac{\sigma_\mu^2}{\sigma_\varepsilon^2})$ is smaller for fixed T than when ρ is small. Between information gets a lower relative weight when ρ is large than when ρ is small, which corresponds to the usual weighting of data from sources with varying degrees of error.

To obtain an estimate of ρ for use in a feasible GLS, I prefer to obtain both an estimate of σ_ε^2 from a fixed-effects model and then an estimate of σ^2 from the pooled regression, as indicated previously. Although this estimate is not consistent, it is never negative and, empirically it gives at least the appearance of a tighter upper bound to the true value of γ than the pooled regression does and a closer approximation to the ML estimate.

e. Bounds for the Coefficient of the Lagged Dependent Variable

As Maddala (1971) has pointed out, the GLS estimates with $\lambda = 1/\theta^2$ can be considered members of a more general class of estimators obtained through different choices of λ. Let $\hat{\gamma}(\lambda)$ be the estimator of γ obtained by solving the GLS normal equations for an arbitrary value of λ. Sevestre and Trognon (1996, pp. 130–133) show that for the case in which $\beta = 0$, the purely autoregressive case, the following inequality holds:

$$\underset{\text{fixed-effects}}{\text{plim}\,\hat{\gamma}(0)} < \gamma < \underset{\text{GLS}}{\text{plim}\,\hat{\gamma}(\lambda)} < \underset{\text{OLS pooled}}{\text{plim}\,\hat{\gamma}(1)} < \underset{\text{means}}{\text{plim}\,\hat{\gamma}(\infty)}. \tag{20}$$

Remarkably, the GLS estimate is inconsistent even when a consistent estimate of ρ is used to compute FGLS estimates. The problem is that the lagged dependent variable is correlated even with the transformed disturbance.

Since plim $\hat{\gamma}(\lambda)$ is a continuous function of λ, there exists a value λ^* in the interval $[0, 1/\theta^2]$ for which $p \lim \hat{\gamma}(\lambda) = \gamma$. Sevestre and Trognon (1983) show that this value is

$$\lambda^* = K(1 - \rho) \Big/ \frac{(1 - \gamma^T)E(y_{i0}\mu_i)}{(1 - \gamma)\sigma^2} + K\xi, \tag{21}$$

where $K = \frac{T - 1 - T\gamma + \gamma^T}{T(1 - \gamma)^2}$, and ρ, ξ, and σ^2 are as before.

They also show that when $\beta \neq 0$, the estimate $\hat{\gamma}(\lambda)$ behaves almost the same as in the purely autoregressive case. Since the λ^* estimate is consistent when there are no exogenous variables, it remains so when there are. The trick is to obtain a consistent estimate of λ^* that can be accomplished by finding an appropriate instrumental variable for y_{-1}. Even in this case, the results depend heavily on the distribution of the estimate of λ^*.

In the dynamic error-components model, not only are the OLS pooled regression estimates, the fixed-effect or within estimates, and the between estimates inconsistent, but so are the GLS estimates using the true value of ρ. However, the method of instrumental variables may be used to obtain a feasible member of the λ-class of estimates that is consistent (see Sevestre and Trognon, 1996). Unfortunately, this estimate may have a very large variance, as demonstrated in Nerlove (1971).

Nonetheless, the fixed-effects and the pooled regressions may be used to bound the true value of γ even when exogenous regressors are also included. Empirically, I have found that FGLS appears to provide an even tighter bound, although since FGLS is also based on an inconsistent estimate of ρ, there is no guarantee that this is in fact an upper bound.

f. Maximum-Likelihood Conditional on the Initial Value of the Lagged Dependent Variable

When the likelihood function for the model (13) with $u_{it} = \mu_i \sim N(0, \sigma^2 \Omega)$ is derived in the usual way from the product of the densities of y_{it} conditional on x_{it} and y_{it-1}, the joint density is conditional on y_{i0}. This likelihood function can be written in terms of the earlier notation introduced as

$$\log L\left(\alpha, \beta, \gamma, \sigma_\mu^2, \sigma_\varepsilon^2 \mid y_{11}, \ldots, y_{NT}; x_{NT}; y_{10}, \ldots, y_{N0}\right)$$

$$= -\frac{NT}{2} \log 2\pi - \frac{NT}{2} \log \sigma^2 - \frac{N}{2} \log \xi - \frac{N(T-1)}{2} \log \eta$$

$$- \frac{1}{2\sigma^2} \sum_{i=1}^{N} \sum_{t=1}^{T} \left(y_{it}^* - \alpha \xi^{-1/2} - \beta x_{it}^* - \gamma y_{it-1}^*\right)^2, \tag{22}$$

where y^*, x^*, and y_{-1}^* are the transformed variables. Since $\xi = \frac{T}{1+\lambda(T-1)}$ and $\eta = \frac{\lambda T}{1+\lambda(T-1)}$, $\log L$ can be expressed as a function solely of $\lambda, \sigma^2, \alpha, \beta$, and γ. Trognon (1978) shows that, when the exogenous variable x is generated by a first-order autoregression with white noise input, $w \sim wn(0, \sigma_w^2 I)$, also assumed in the Monte Carlo experiments reported in Nerlove (1971),

$$x = \delta x_{-1} + w \tag{23}$$

maximization of the conditional-likelihood function (22) yields boundary solutions $\hat{\rho} = 0$, which, unlike interior maximum-likelihood solutions, are inconsistent, for a considerable and indeed likely range of parameter values. In particular, there is a value of γ in (13),

$$\gamma^* = \frac{(T-3)^2 - 8}{(T+1)^2},$$

such that when $\gamma < \gamma^*$, there exists an interior maximum of (22), which yields

consistent ML estimates, but that when $\gamma \geq \gamma^*$, there are values of ρ for which
the conditional-likelihood function (13) is maximized at the boundary $\rho = 0$
(i.e., for the OLS estimates of the pooled regression), which we know to be
inconsistent. The problem is that when T is small the permissible range of γ,
the coefficient of the lagged dependent variable, is implausible (e.g., negative
or very small). For example, for $T = 5, \gamma^* = -0.11$, while for $T = 10, \gamma^* =$
0.34. When $\gamma \geq \gamma^*$, whether or not an interior maximum with consistent ML
estimates occurs depends on the value of ρ: for $\rho < \rho^*$ boundary maxima
occur where

$$\rho^* = \left(\frac{T-1}{T+1}\right)^2 \frac{\beta^2 \sigma_w^2}{\sigma^2} \frac{1-\gamma}{(\gamma - \gamma^*)(1-\gamma\delta)^2}.$$

For example, when $T = 5, \beta = 1.0, \gamma = 0.75, \delta = 0.5$, and $\frac{\sigma^2}{\sigma^2} = 1.0, \gamma^* =$
-0.11 and the critical value of ρ is $\rho^* = 0.31$. That means that any true value of
the intraclass correlation less than 0.31 is liable to produce a boundary solution
to (22), $\rho = 0$, and inconsistent estimates of all the parameters. Using these
results, Trognon (1978) is able to replicate the Monte Carlo results reported
in Nerlove (1971).[12]

Even though ML may yield inconsistent estimates when the non-negligible
probability of a boundary solution is taken into account, it is nonetheless true
that the likelihood function summarizes the information contained in the data
about the parameters (Birnbaum, 1962; Barnard, Jenkins, and Winsten, 1962).
For this reason, sections of some of the multidimensional likelihood functions
are also presented in the next subsection. When first differences are taken to
eliminate a linear deterministic trend, the differenced model, the individual-
specific time-invariant effects become differences in the trend slopes. This
makes the interpretation of the model in first-difference form different than
that in levels. Moreover, the time- and individual-varying disturbance is now
likely to be serially correlated, a fact that needs to be taken into account in
the formulation of the unconditional-likelihood function.[13] The differenced
model is implemented in Nerlove (1997).

---

[12] Maddala (1971, pp. 346–347) gives a condition for the gradient of the concentrated-likelihood
function to be positive at a boundary $\rho = 0$ (OLS on the pooled data) for the conditional-
likelihood function. So if ρ is constrained to the interval $[0, 1]$, this implies a local maximum
at the boundary 0. Breusch (1987) shows that this condition can be easily checked at the
start of his iterative GLS procedure by beginning with the pooled OLS estimates and $\rho = 0$.
Unfortunately, these results apply only to the likelihood function when no lagged value of
the dependent variable is included or when those initial values are conditioned upon. I have
not been able to derive a similar result for the unconditional likelihood function below.

[13] Adding a trend, t, to (13)

$$y_{it} = \alpha + \beta x_{it} + \gamma y_{it-1} + \tau_i t + \mu_i + \varepsilon_{it}, \quad i = 1, \ldots N, \quad t = 1, \ldots, T, \tag{13'}$$

and differencing,

$$\Delta y_{it} = \beta \Delta x_{it} + \gamma \Delta y_{it-1} + \tau_i + \Delta \varepsilon_{it}, \quad i = 1, \ldots N, \quad t = 1, \ldots T, \tag{13''}$$

where Δ denotes the first-difference operator and τ_i is the individual-specific trend coefficient, assumed to have mean zero (enforced by eliminating any overall constant in the

g. Unconditional Maximum Likelihood

While it is not guaranteed that no boundary solution to the likelihood equations is obtained, yielding inconsistent estimates, it is apparent that in panels with a short time dimension the initial values provide important information about the parameters of the model, and to condition on them is to neglect this information.

It is not, in fact, difficult to obtain the unconditional-likelihood function once the marginal distribution of the initial values is specified. The problem is a correct specification of this distribution. If $|\gamma| \geq 1$ or the processes generating the x_{it} are not stationary, it will not, in general, be possible to specify the marginal distribution of the initial observations. I will assume that, possibly after some differencing, both the y_{it} and the x_{it} are stationary. The difficulties associated with the formulation of the unconditional-likelihood function in the case in which deterministic or stochastic trends are included are discussed in Footnote 13.

Under this assumption, the dynamic relationship to be estimated is stationary and $|\gamma| < 1$. Consider equation $(14)^{14}$ with the intercept eliminated, for y_{i0} and the infinite past:

$$y_{i0} = \sum_{j=1}^{\infty} \gamma^j \beta x_{i,-j} + \frac{1}{1-\gamma} \mu_i + v_{i0}, \quad \text{where } v_{it} = \gamma v_{it-1} + \varepsilon_{it}^{15}. \quad (23')$$

If $\beta = 0$, so that the relationship to be estimated is a pure autoregression for each y_{it}, the vector of initial values $y_0 = (y_{10}, \ldots y_{N0})'$ has a joint normal distribution with means 0 and variance-covariance matrix $\left(\frac{\sigma_\mu^2}{(1-\gamma)^2} + \sigma_v^2\right)$

differences by deducting the sample means). Thus, not only is the meaning of ρ altered, but if ε_{it} did not contain a unit root to start with, it will now; in particular, if ε_{it} is not serially correlated to start with, it will follow a first-order moving average process with unit root. The variance-covariance matrix of the new disturbances $\tau_i + \Delta\varepsilon_{it}$ is now block diagonal with blocks:

$$A = \sigma^2 \begin{bmatrix} 1 & a & b & \ldots b \\ a & 1 & a & b\ldots \\ b & a & 1 & a\ldots \\ \vdots & \vdots & \vdots & \ldots 1 \end{bmatrix}, \quad \text{where } \sigma^2 = \sigma_\tau^2 + \sigma_\varepsilon^2, \quad a = \frac{\sigma_\tau^2 - \sigma_\varepsilon^2}{\sigma^2}, \quad \text{and } b = \frac{\sigma_\tau^2}{\sigma^2}.$$

The characteristic roots of A give the necessary transform and Jacobian. This should be taken into account in the formulation of both the conditional- and the unconditional-likelihood functions. As indicated, however, differencing is unnecessary when the initial values are conditioning, but then a trend variable must be included as explanatory with as many different slopes as countries. See Nerlove (1997, Section 2.2) for an extended discussion of the transformation required to render the time-varying part of the disturbances serially uncorrelated.

[14] For a particular time period T and the infinite past $y_{iT} = \gamma^\infty y_{i-\infty} + \sum_{j=0}^{\infty} \gamma^j \beta x_{iT-j} + \frac{1-\gamma^\infty}{1-\gamma} \mu_i + v_{iT}$, where $v_{iT} = \sum_{j=0}^{\infty} \gamma^j \varepsilon_{iT-j}$ is the MA form of a first-order autoregression with white-noise input, equation (24) follows.

[15] If all variables are expressed as deviations from their overall means, there is no need to include an intercept; if not, μ_i should be replaced by $\alpha + \mu_i$.

$\times I_N = (\frac{\sigma_\mu^2}{(1-\gamma)^2} + \frac{\sigma_\varepsilon^2}{1-\gamma^2})I_N$. The unconditional likelihood is, therefore,

$$\log L\left(\gamma, \rho, \sigma_\mu^2, \sigma_\varepsilon^2 \mid y_{11}, \ldots, y_{NT}; \ldots; y_{10}, \ldots, y_{N0}\right)$$

$$= -\frac{NT}{2} \log 2\pi - \frac{NT}{2} \log \sigma^2 - \frac{N}{2} \log \xi - \frac{N(T-1)}{2} \log \eta$$

$$- \frac{1}{2\sigma^2} \sum_{i=1}^{N} \sum_{t=1}^{T} (y_{it}^* - \gamma y_{it-1}^*)^2$$

$$- \frac{N}{2} \log \left(\frac{\sigma_\mu^2}{(1-\gamma)^2} + \frac{\sigma_\varepsilon^2}{1-\gamma^2} \right) - \left[\frac{1}{2\left(\frac{\sigma_\mu^2}{(1-\gamma)^2} + \frac{\sigma_\varepsilon^2}{1-\gamma^2} \right)} \right] \sum_{i=1}^{N} y_{i0}^2. \quad (24)$$

This likelihood function can easily be concentrated: to maximize, express $\sigma_\mu^2, \sigma_\varepsilon^2, \xi$ and η in terms of ρ and γ. For given ρ and γ in the interval $[0, 1)$, concentrate the likelihood function with respect to σ^2. It follows that

$$\hat{\sigma}^2(\gamma, \rho) = \frac{RSS^*(\gamma, \rho)}{N(T+1)},$$

where $RSS^*(\gamma, \rho) = \sum_{i=1}^{N} \sum_{t=1}^{T} (y_{it}^* - \gamma y_{it-1}^*)^2 + \sum_{i=1}^{N} y_{i0}^2/[\frac{\rho}{(1-\gamma)^2} + \frac{1-\rho}{1-\gamma^2}]$.
Thus, the concentrated LF is

$$\log L^*(\gamma, \rho) = -\frac{N(T+1)}{2} \log 2\pi - \frac{N}{2} \log \xi - \frac{N(T-1)}{2} \log \nu$$

$$- \frac{N(T-1)}{2} \log \left\{ \frac{RSS^*(\gamma, \rho)}{N(T-1)} \right\} - \frac{N}{2} \left\{ \frac{\rho}{(1-\gamma)^2} + \frac{1-\rho}{1-\gamma^2} \right\}$$

$$- (1/2 RSS^*/N(T+1)) \sum_{i=1}^{N} \sum_{t=1}^{T} (y_{it}^* - \gamma y_{it-1}^*)^2$$

$$- \sum_{i=1}^{N} y_{i0}^2 \Big/ \left\{ (2/N(T+1)) \left[\frac{\rho}{(1-\gamma)^2} + \frac{1-\rho}{1-\gamma^2} \right] RSS^* \right\}.$$

This is quite a bit more complicated than the usual minimization of the sum of squares in the penultimate term, because RSS^*, in that term, depends on $\sum_{i=1}^{n} y_{i0}^2$, as well as on ρ and γ, which enter the final terms as well.

When $\beta \neq 0$, things are more complicated still. Various alternative specifications considered in the literature are reported and analyzed in Sevestre and Trognon (1996, pp. 136–138).[16] Considerable simplification, however, can be

---

[16] One interesting possibility discussed by Trognon and Sevestre (1996, pp. 136–138) is to choose y_{i0} a linear function of some *observed* individual-specific disturbances μ_i and a remainder. The first-order equations for maximizing the likelihood then take on a simple recursive form when $\beta = 0$, and permit other simplifications when $\beta \neq 0$. But if we knew some individual-specific time-invariant observed variables influenced behavior, why not incorporate them directly in (13), the equation to be estimated?

obtained if, following Nerlove (1971), we are willing to assume that x_{it} follows a well-specified common stationary time-series model for all individuals i. The first term in (23′) is $\varphi_{i0} = \beta \sum_{j=0}^{\infty} \gamma^j x_{i,-j}$. Hence, for any stationary process x_{it}, which may be serially correlated,

$$\frac{\varphi_{it}}{\beta} = \gamma \frac{\varphi_{it-1}}{\beta} + x_{it}$$

with variances

$$\sigma_{\varphi_i}^2 = \frac{\beta^2 \sigma_{x_i}^2}{1 - \gamma^2}. \tag{25}$$

If we suppose that the variance of the x_{it} is the same for all i, then the random variable

$$\phi_{it} = \sum_{j=0}^{\infty} \gamma^j \beta x_{it-j}$$

has a well-defined variance that is the same for all i and a function of β, γ, and σ_x^2. This then enters the final term in the unconditional likelihood (24), which now becomes:

$$\log L \left(\beta, \gamma, \sigma_\mu^2, \sigma_\varepsilon^2 \mid y_{11}, \ldots, y_{NT}; x_{11}, \ldots x_{NT}; y_{10}, \ldots, y_{N0} \right)$$

$$= -\frac{N(T+1)}{2} \log 2\pi - \frac{NT}{2} \log \sigma^2 - \frac{N}{2} \log \xi - \frac{N(T-1)}{2} \log \nu$$

$$- \frac{1}{2\sigma^2} \sum_{i=1}^{N} \sum_{t=1}^{T} (y_{it}^* - \beta x_{it}^* - \gamma y_{it-1}^*)^2$$

$$- \frac{N}{2} \log \left(\frac{\sigma_\mu^2}{(1-\gamma)^2} + \frac{\sigma_\varepsilon^2}{1-\gamma^2} \right) - \left[\frac{1}{2 \left(\frac{\sigma_\mu^2}{(1-\gamma)^2} + \frac{\sigma_\varepsilon^2}{1-\gamma^2} \right)} \right] \sum_{i=1}^{n} y_{i0}^2. \tag{26}$$

Concentrating the likelihood function to permit a one- or two-dimensional grid search is no longer possible. If gradient procedures yield an interior maximum, the ML estimates obtained are consistent as long as the random variables $\phi_{it} = \sum_{j=0}^{\infty} \gamma^j \beta x_{i,t-j}$ have well-defined variances and covariances, which they will if the x_{it} are generated by a stationary process. It doesn't really matter what this process is as long as it is stationary. Besides, since the x_{it} are assumed to be exogenous, we really have no basis on which to model their determination and are likely to misspecify this part of the model. In this sense, we ought to prefer this kind of "almost full-information" maximum likelihood. Still, we have to assume something about the variance of the x process in order to proceed. I suggest estimating σ_x^2 from the sample data.

To generalize these results to the case in which there are several explanatory variables in addition to the lagged value of the dependent variable, assume that X_{it} follows a stationary VAR process and replace βx_{it}^* by $X_{it}^* \beta$ and $\beta^2 \sigma_x^2$ by $\beta' \sum_{XX} \beta$ in the previous formula.

5. EMPIRICAL EVIDENCE ON GROWTH-RATE CONVERGENCE AND THE
COMPARATIVE PERFORMANCE OF DIFFERENT PANEL DATA METHODS

a. Numerical Results

To examine the effects of the econometric methods employed on the finding of growth-rate convergence or the lack of it, I initially used data on ninety-four countries for the period 1960–1985, and a subsample of twenty-two OECD countries, from the Penn World Tables 5.6, publicly available from the NBER website at ftp://nber.harvard.edu/pub/. The countries are listed in the appendix. Following Islam (1995), s and n were computed as quinquennial means over the preceding five-year span for the five years 1965, 1970, 1975, 1980, 1985; y was taken as the value reported in that year and in 1960 for the lagged value applicable to 1965. Characteristics of the sample are reported in Table 1. The results of the six methods applied to these data or to their first differences are reported in Tables 2 and 3. In the case of the latter, an appropriate transformation of the original data is made to eliminate the serial correlation introduced in the time-varying part of the disturbance by the first-difference transformation, as worked out in Nerlove (1997). I have listed the regression methods in the order in which the corresponding estimates of γ appear in the inequality of Trognon and Sevestre (Equation [20]). These estimates are followed by the maximum-likelihood estimates conditional on the initial values y_{i0} and the ML estimates unconditional on the initial values, assuming stationarity of both the processes generating the exogenous variable and real GDP per capita. In a substantive study of growth-rate convergence, it would clearly be important to include additional explanatory variables such as, for example, the stock of human capital, also available at the NBER Internet site,

Table 1. *Comparative Descriptive Statistics for the Two Samples*

Item	94-Country sample	22-Country sample	Ratio 22/94 values
Variance initial y	0.799	0.256	0.320
Variance final y	0.899	0.222	0.247
Correlation between y_0 and y_5	0.988	0.090	0.092
Variances about overall means:			
y	1.058	0.204	0.193
z	0.698	0.040	0.058
Pooled variances about country means:			
y	0.045	0.040	0.897
z	0.083	0.007	0.084

Table 2. *Parameter Estimates for the Model in Levels Alternative Econometric Analyses*

Method of analysis	94-Country sample	22-Country sample
1. Fixed-Effects OLS		
γ	0.7204 (0.0211)	0.7645 (0.0166)
β	0.1656 (0.0172)	0.1634 (0.0510)
Implied Capital Share	0.3719 (0.0278)	0.4096 (0.0783)
Residual Variance	0.0113	0.0020
2. Feasible GLS		
Estimate of ρ used*	0.2675	0.4027
γ	0.9130 (0.0119)	0.8282 (0.0156)
β	0.1520 (0.0135)	0.1913 (0.0422)
Implied Capital Share	0.6362 (0.0247)	0.5269 (0.0579)
Residual Variance	0.0213	0.0047
3. Pooled OLS		
γ	0.9487 (0.0090)	0.8857 (0.0125)
β	0.1244 (0.0108)	0.1764 (0.0308)
Implied Capital Share	0.7080 (0.0271)	0.6067 (0.0452)
Residual Variance	0.0193	0.0041
4. Country Means OLS		
γ	0.9817 (0.0112)	0.9320 (0.0148)
δ	0.0919 (0.0138)	0.1493 (0.0343)
Implied Capital Share	0.8339 (0.0704)	0.6870 (0.0593)
Residual Variance	0.0047	0.0580
5. Conditional ML		
ρ	0.1133 (0.0497)	0.4796 (0.1584)
γ	0.9339 (0.0122)	0.8189 (0.0245)
β	0.1370 (0.0131)	0.1908 (0.0438)
Implied Capital Share	0.6744 (0.0289)	0.5131 (0.0664)
Residual Variance	0.0194 (0.0013)	0.0052 (0.0012)
6. Unconditional ML		
Estimates of σ_x^2 used	0.0826	0.0069
ρ	0.1288 (0.0456)	0.7700 (0.0731)
γ	0.9385 (0.0105)	0.8085 (0.0228)
β	0.1334 (0.0124)	0.1815 (0.0521)
Implied Capital Share	0.6846 (0.0277)	0.4865 (0.0791)
Residual Variance	0.0197 (0.0013)	0.0113 (0.0028)

Figures in parentheses are standard errors.
*Estimated by the method suggested in Balestra and Nerlove (1966).

infrastructure investment, and so forth. However, for my purpose here, omission of relevant variables simply increases the unexplained disturbance variance and thus heightens the contrast among alternative estimators.

Turning now to the regression estimates presented in Tables 2 and 3:

Table 3. *Parameter Estimates for the Model in First Differences Alternative Econometric Analyses*

Method of analysis	94-Country sample	22-Country sample
1. Fixed Effects OLS		
γ	0.4007 (0.0375)	0.4544 (0.0611)
β	0.1199 (0.0187)	−0.0126 (0.0637)
Implied Capital Share	0.1667 (0.0246)	−0.0237 (0.1209)
Residual Variance	0.0077	0.0014
2. Feasible GLS		
Estimate of ρ used*	0.4866	0.3628
γ	0.4227 (0.0406)	0.5833 (0.0531)
β	0.1520 (0.0135)	0.1913 (0.0422)
Implied Capital Share	0.1864 (0.0259)	0.1322 (0.1218)
Residual Variance	0.0213	0.0047
3. Pooled OLS		
γ	0.7031 (0.0328)	0.6237 (0.0453)
β	0.1632 (0.0195)	0.0845 (0.0586)
Implied Capital Share	0.3548 (0.0373)	0.1834 (0.1121)
Residual Variance	0.0141	0.0022
4. Country Means OLS		
γ	0.9178 (0.0471)	0.7215 (0.0572)
β	0.1719 (0.0339)	0.1174 (0.0978)
Implied Capital Share	0.6763 (0.1263)	0.2965 (0.1873)
Residual Variance	0.0041	0.0005
5. Conditional ML		
ρ	0.2267 (0.0664)	0.0126 (0.0405)
γ	0.4540 (0.0651)	0.6187 (0.0490)
β	0.1368 (0.0208)	0.0815 (0.0601)
Implied Capital Share	0.2004 (0.0358)	0.1762 (0.1159)
Residual Variance	0.0122 (0.0009)	0.0021 (0.0003)
6. Unconditional ML		
Estimate of σ_x^2 used	0.0597	0.0058
ρ	0.2335 (0.0632)	0.0936 (0.0696)
γ	0.4364 (0.0578)	0.7254 (0.0512)
β	0.1340 (0.0201)	0.1478 (0.0727)
Implied Capital Share	0.1921 (0.0317)	0.3500 (0.1326)
Residual Variance	0.0120 (0.0008)	0.0027 (0.0004)

Figures in parentheses are standard errors.
*Estimated by the method suggested in Balestra and Nerlove (1966).

Consider the first four methods applied to the levels model. The estimates of γ for the ninety-four-country sample range from a low of 0.72 (fixed-effects regression) to a high of 0.98 (country-means regression), with pooled OLS and FGLS falling in between. For the OECD countries, the range is 0.76 to 0.93. The implied speed of convergence thus ranges from 90 percent in thirty-five years to 90 percent in 570 years. None could be characterized as evidence of reasonably rapid convergence. All of the estimates of γ satisfy the Trognon-Sevestre inequality, although the regressions contain an exogenous explanatory variable in contrast to the case considered by Trognon and Sevestre. Pooled OLS and FGLS also stand in the order predicted by the Trognon-Sevestre results. While it is tempting to infer that FGLS provides a tighter upper bound to the true value of γ than the pooled OLS regression estimate, the temptation should be resisted. The FGLS estimates are doubly inconsistent: they are based on an inconsistent estimate of ρ reflecting the inconsistency of the estimates of the residual variance and the fixed effects depending on which regressions they are derived from. Not only is the estimated value of β sensitive to the method of estimation, but also the estimate of the elasticity of output with respect to capital stock in the production function is extremely so, reflecting the dependence of the estimated value on the coefficient of the lagged dependent variable, γ. This parameter should estimate approximately (1-the share of labor in the real GDP). It is clear that all of the estimates of capital's share are wide of the mark. If, therefore, one were to infer policy implications from this parameter, it could be seriously misleading.

The most interesting estimates are those for conditional and unconditional maximum likelihood presented as Methods 5 and 6 in Table 2. In the case of the twenty-two-country OECD sample, these estimates differ quite a bit from one another, although unconditional ML is not far from the fixed-effects OLS regression, while conditional ML yields results close to FGLS using the Balestra-Nerlove (1966) first-round estimate of ρ. The contrast with the ninety-four-country sample is striking: the conditional and the unconditional ML estimates differ little from one another. They are close to the pooled OLS regression estimates (a consequence of the fact that the estimated value of ρ is small although significantly different from zero), but are both quite different than any of the inconsistent regression estimates. As found earlier, the estimates of β are quite insensitive to the method used, but the estimates of γ are not very different either; consequently, the implied estimates of capital's share are similar, albeit different for the two samples.[17]

---

[17] What accounts for these remarkable differences between the two samples and for the similarity of the unconditional and conditional ML estimates for the ninety-four-country sample? Consider the log of the ratio of the unconditional to the conditional likelihood (i.e., the marginal density of y_{i0}):

log{unconditional/conditional likelihood}

$$= -\frac{N}{2}\log 2\pi - \frac{N}{2}\log\left(\frac{\beta^2\sigma_x^2}{1-\gamma^2} + \frac{\rho\sigma^2}{(1-\gamma)^2} + \frac{(1-\rho)\sigma^2}{1-\gamma^2}\right)$$
$$- \left[\frac{1}{2\left(\frac{\beta^2\sigma_x^2}{1-\gamma^2} + \frac{\rho\sigma^2}{(1-\gamma)^2} + \frac{(1-\rho)\sigma^2}{1-\gamma^2}\right)}\right]\sum_{i=1}^{n}y_{i0}^2.$$

Turning now to parameter estimates for the first-difference model presented in Table 3:

The contrast with the levels model is remarkable; at least in terms of reasonableness, at last we seem to be in the right "ball park." Consider the first four methods applied to the levels model. The estimates of γ for the ninety-four-country sample range from a low of 0.40 (fixed-effects regression) to a high of 0.92 (country-means regression) with pooled OLS and FGLS falling in between. For the OECD countries, the range is 0.36 to 0.72. The implied speed of convergence is thus much more reasonable than obtained for the levels model, although none could be characterized as evidence of reasonably rapid convergence.[18] The estimates of γ still satisfy the Sevestre-Trognon inequality. As was the case for the levels model, the estimated value of β is sensitive to the method of estimation, although generally less so, and the estimate of the elasticity of output with respect to capital stock in the production function is more so, reflecting the dependence of the estimated value on the coefficient of the lagged dependent variable, γ. This parameter should estimate approximately (1-the share of labor in the real GDP). It is clear that these estimates bring us much closer to what could be considered a reasonable figure.

The most plausible estimates are those for conditional and unconditional maximum likelihood presented as Methods 5 and 6 in Table 3. In the case of the twenty-two-country OECD sample only, the estimates differ from one another.

Let the sample variance of y_{i0} be var y_0 and let

$$\varphi^2 = \left(\frac{\beta^2 \sigma_x^2}{1 - \gamma^2} + \frac{\rho \sigma^2}{(1 - \gamma)^2} + \frac{(1 - \rho)\sigma^2}{1 - \gamma^2} \right).$$

Then,

$$\log\{\text{unconditional/conditional likelihood}\} = -\frac{N}{2} \log 2\pi - \frac{N}{2} \log(\varphi^2) - \left[\frac{N \text{ var } y_0}{2\varphi^2} \right].$$

This function is clearly decreasing in N and var y_0. Its behavior with respect to φ^2 depends on the relation between var y_0 and φ^2. When var $y_0 > \varphi^2$, it is increasing; but when var $y_0 > \varphi^2$, it is decreasing. Thus, for a given var y_0, the log of the ratio of the unconditional to the conditional density tends to zero (i.e., the ratio tends to one, as N increases and as φ^2 increases). In other words, the unconditional becomes more and more like the conditional likelihood. For $\beta = 0.15$, $\gamma = 0.85$, $\sigma_x^2 = 0.08$, $\rho = 0.8$, and $\sigma^2 = 0.02$, $\varphi^2 = 0.73$. Table 1 presents some descriptive statistics for the two samples. Typically, var y_0 is much less than 0.73; for example, 0.256 for the twenty-two-country sample. On the other hand, it is about that value for the ninety-four-country sample. Thus, the principal explanation for the similarity of the conditional ML and the unconditional ML estimates for the ninety-four-country sample is the size of the cross-section dimension; similarly, the small sample in the OECD case accounts for the lack of similarity.

[18] See Footnote 4 concerning the issue of whether it is reasonable to characterize convergence conditional on country-specific trends as convergence at all.

Implied speeds of convergence are still, however, quite slow for the OECD countries, but much, much faster for the larger group of ninety-four-countries. Perhaps one can conclude that if differing country-specific trends are taken into account, so-called "beta convergence" obtains at a reasonable rapid rate for a group of diverse countries, but when the relatively homogeneous group of OECD countries is considered, convergence is much more problematic.

b. Graphical Results

Further insight into the support for the convergence hypothesis, as modified in this paper, which is given by the likelihood functions for the two samples, can be obtained graphically. Since the first-difference model gives by far the most plausible results, I present only graphs for this case. Bear in mind, however, that the convergence concept considered is "beta" convergence with a vengeance. Not only are the results conditioned on differing savings and population growth rates, but I am also allowing for differing linear trends among countries. The model is reduced to stationarity by first-differencing the quinquennial averages. The explanatory variables, in this case first differences of savings rates and population growth rates, are assumed to be exogenous and to be determined by some sort of stationary process. Having eliminated the constant term by taking deviations from the overall means of all variables, we are left with four parameters: ρ, γ, β, and σ^2. Although there are $\binom{4}{2} = 6$ possible pairs to consider, I focus on the crucial pairs: ρ *versus* γ and β *versus* σ^2. It is important that the likelihood functions as formulated reflect the operation of the process that generated the data before we began to observe them; the appearance of the unconditional likelihood functions is rather different even though the ML estimates are quite close to those given by the unconditional-likelihood functions.

Figures 1 and 2 give one-parameter slices and two-parameter 3-D plots of the likelihood for the pairs $\rho - \gamma$ and $\beta - \sigma^2$ for the ninety-four- and twenty-two-country samples, respectively. Each figure consists of eight plots each. The main finding is that the difference between the estimates for the two samples is not great except for a much slower speed of convergence (larger γ) for the more diverse ninety-four-country sample and is well supported by the shape of the likelihood functions in the two cases.

The likelihood reaches a unique maximum in every case. Except for σ^2, the functions are well behaved in the vicinity of the maximizing parameter values. Since the value of σ^2 is bounded from below by zero, the graph has the typical shape found in regression problems: a sharp rise from near zero followed by a long, slow decline. I find no evidence of double maxima or a boundary maximum of the likelihood function with respect to ρ. There is clearly considerable "trade-off" between ρ and γ for the ninety-four-country sample and to a lesser degree for the twenty-two-country sample.

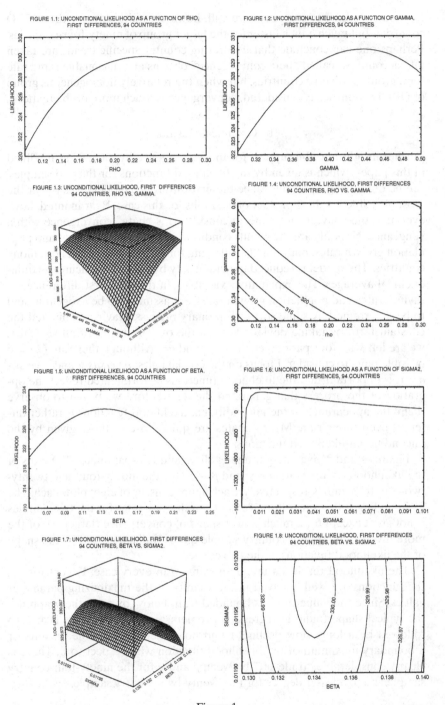

Figure 1.

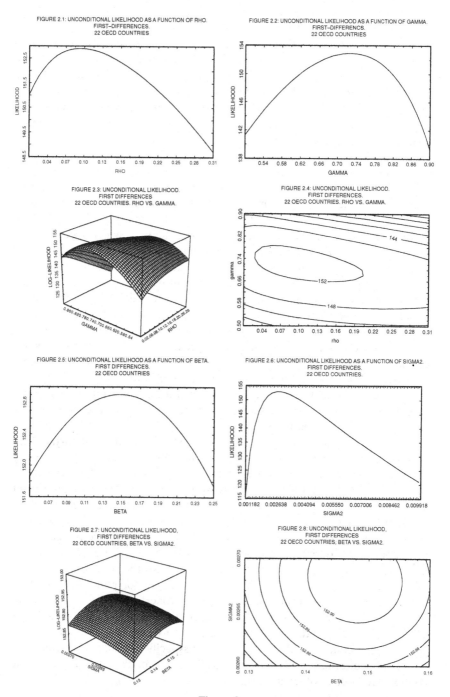

Figure 2.

6. CONCLUSIONS

The principal conclusion that can be drawn from this analysis is that, in panel data econometrics, method matters – a lot. Although, using a highly simplified Solow/Swan model without human capital stocks or infrastructure, I have found estimates of the adjustment parameter significantly different than one in every case, indicating convergence. All of the estimates based on analyses of levels, however, are so close to one, always greater than 0.7, that convergence to within 90 percent of equilibrium in less than one generation is effectively ruled out. This can hardly be called "convergence" in any relevant sense. Moreover, the estimates range from 0.72 to 0.98, suggesting a convergence range of from thirty-three to over five hundred years, with most clustering around 0.8, underscoring the importance of choice of econometric method. Much of the variation in estimates of the speed of convergence appears to be due to trade-offs between the crucial parameter ρ, which measures the importance of *unobserved* cross-sectional variation relative to total residual variation, and γ, which measures the speed of adjustment. For this reason, it is especially important to introduce other relevant variables, such as infrastructure investment and human capital stock, in order to reduce the importance of unobserved cross-sectional variation. When differing country-specific trends are take into account and when likelihood methods are employed that take into account the operation of the growth process prior to the point at which the data sample begins, however, the results are dramatically different: convergence to paths conditioned on differing savings and population growth rates and country-specific trends is quite rapid for the relatively homogeneous twenty-two-country sample, although it is still very slow for the more heterogeneous ninety-four-country sample.

A second important finding is that the Sevestre-Trognon inequality, proved only for the case $\beta = 0$, and then only asymptotically, holds for all the examples presented except for one reversal in the case of the first-difference model. Indeed, fixed-effects OLS always yields estimates of the adjustment parameter at the extreme low end of the range of estimates obtained. The "bias" of fixed-effects models in the estimation of dynamic panel models is apparent. In this context, the use of such methods biases a test for convergence or, more appropriately, rapid convergence, toward finding it. Fixed-effects models, however, are widely used, in part because they are the basis for two-round FGLS estimators, and because computer packages for panel data analysis incorporate an extremely misguided suggestion for estimating ρ, guaranteed to yield extremely low or even negative values of this parameter. These packages should be avoided and, if they are used and do yield a negative estimate, it should not be concluded that the model is misspecified or that fixed effects are a preferable alternative. Fixed-effects OLS remains badly biased in a dynamic context irrespective of whether the packaged routines fail.

I do find, however, that FGLS, using the Balestra-Nerlove (1966) estimate of ρ, which can never be negative, always lie between the fixed-effects OLS estimates and the pooled OLS estimates, which are known to yield upwardly biased estimates of γ. It is not appropriate to conclude that these FGLS estimates, however, represent a tighter upper bound to the true value of γ, since they are doubly inconsistent estimates and may lie below the true value. This is underscored by the finding that both conditional and unconditional ML yield different estimates of ρ and γ, sometimes higher and sometimes lower than FGLS. The interaction between ρ and γ is crucial in this regard.

Finally, maximum likelihood, unconditional on the initial observations, assuming them to be stationary and generated by the same dynamic process we are trying to estimate and assuming the exogenous variables also to be stationary, is feasible and indeed a viable alternative to conventional regression methods or conditional ML. Use of such methods will, however, generally involve removal of the overall means of all variables prior to analysis and omission of a constant term, and may also involve differencing to remove deterministic or stochastic trends. Formulation of the unconditional-likelihood function is somewhat more complicated in the case of differenced variables, but has been carried out here without significant trauma.

Appendix

Data on ninety-four Countries for the Period 1960–1985 from the Penn World Tables 5.6, Publicly Available from the NBER website at ftp://nber.harvard.edu/pub/.

22-Country sample	94-Country sample = 22-Country sample + the Following:		
Japan	Algeria	Mexico	Singapore
Austria	Botswana	Nicaragua	Sri Lanka
Belgium	Cameroon	Panama	Syria
Denmark	Ethiopia	Trinidad & Tobago	Thailand
Finland	Ivory Coast	Argentina	Angola
France	Kenya	Bolivia	Benin
Germany (FRG)	Madagascar	Brazil	Burundi
Greece	Malawi	Chile	Central African Republic
Ireland	Mali	Colombia	Chad
Italy	Morocco	Ecuador	Congo
Netherlands	Nigeria	Paraguay	Egypt
Norway	Senegal	Peru	Ghana
Portugal	South Africa	Uruguay	Liberia
Spain	Tanzania	Venezuela	Mauritania
Sweden	Tunisia	Bangladesh	Mauritius
Switzerland	Zambia	Hong Kong	Mozambique
Turkey	Zimbabwe	India	Niger
U.K.	Costa Rica	Israel	Rwanda
Canada	Dominican Rep.	Jordan	Somalia
U.S.	El Salvador	Korea	Togo
Australia	Guatemala	Malaysia	Uganda
New Zealand	Haiti	Burma	Zaire
	Honduras	Pakistan	Nepal
	Jamaica	Philippines	Papua New Guinea

References

Balestra, P., and M. Nerlove (1966), "Pooling Cross-Section and Time-Series Data in the Estimation of a Dynamic Economic Model: The Demand for Natural Gas," *Econometrica, 34*: pp. 585–612.

Barnard, G. A., G. M. Jenkins, and C. B. Winsten (1962), "Likelihood Inference and Time Series," (with discussion), *Journal of the Royal Statistical Society*, Series A, *125*: pp. 321–375.

Bernard, A. B., and S. N. Durlauf (1996), "Interpreting Tests of the Convergence Hypothesis," *Journal of Econometrics, 71*: pp. 161–173.

Bernard, A. B., and S. N. Durlauf (1995), "Convergence in International Output," *Journal of Applied Econometrics, 10*: pp. 97–108.

Barro, R. J. (1991), "Economic Growth in a Cross Section of Countries," *Quarterly Journal of Economics, 106*: pp. 407–443.

Barro, R. J., and Jong-Wha Lee (1993), "International Comparisons of Educational Attainment," NBER Working Paper No. 4349.

Barro, R. J., and X. Sala-I-Martin (1995), *Economic Growth*, New York: McGraw-Hill.

Baumol, W. (1986), "Productivity Growth, Convergence, and Welfare: What the Long-Run Data Show," *American Economic Review, 76*: pp. 1072–1085.

Binder, M., and M. H. Pesaran (1996), "Stochastic Growth," Working Paper No. 19-18, Department of Economics, University of Maryland.

Birnbaum, A. (1962), "On the Foundations of Statistical Inference," (with discussion) *Journal of the American Statistical Association, 57*: pp. 269–306.

Breusch, T. S. (1987), "Maximum Likelihood Estimation of Random-Effects Models," *Journal of Econometrics, 36*: pp. 383–389.

Diebold, F. X., and M. Nerlove (1990), "Unit Roots in Economic Time Series: A Selective Survey," in T. B. Fomby and G. F. Rhodes (Eds.), *Advances in Econometrics*, Vol. 8: *Co-Integration, Spurious Regressions, and Unit Roots*, Greenwich, CT: JAI Press, pp. 3–69.

Greene, W. (1993), *Econometric Analysis*, 2nd ed. New York: Macmillan Publishing.

Islam, N. (1995), "Growth Empirics: A Panel Data Approach," *Quarterly Journal of Economics, 110*: pp. 1127–1170.

Judge, G., R. C. Hill, W. Griffiths, H. Lütkepohl, and T-C. Lee (1988), *Introduction to the Theory and Practice of Econometrics*, 2nd ed. New York: Wiley.

Kiviet, Jan F. (1995), "On the Bias, Inconsistency, and Efficiency of Various Estimators in Dynamic Panel Models," *Journal of Econometrics, 68*: pp. 53–78.

Lee, K., M. H. Pesaran, and R. Smith (1996), "Growth and Convergence: A Multi-Country Empirical Analysis of the Solow Growth Model," unpublished.

Mankiw, N. G., D. Romer, and D. N. Weil (1992), "A Contribution to the Empirics of Economic Growth," *Quarterly Journal of Economics, 108*: pp. 407–437.

Mátyás, L., and P. Sevestre (1996), *The Econometrics of Panel Data: Handbook of Theory and Applications*, 2nd ed. Boston: Kluwer Academic Publishers.

Maddala, G. S. (1971), "The Use of Variance Components Models in Pooling Cross-Section and Time-Series Data," *Econometrica, 39*: pp. 341–358.

Michelacci, C., and P. Zaffaroni (1997), "Beta Convergence," unpublished working paper, EM/97/332, Suntory Center, London School of Economics and Political Science.

Mundlak, Y. (1978), "On the Pooling of Cross-Section and Time-Series Data," *Econometrica, 46*: pp. 69–86.

Nerlove, M. (1971), "Further Evidence on the Estimation of Dynamic Economic Relations from a Time Series of Cross Sections," *Econometrica, 39*: pp. 359–382.

Nerlove, M. (1994), "Reflections on Agricultural Development Population Growth and the Environment," presented at the Third Conference on Development Economics, Asian Development Bank, Manila, November 23–25. Published in M. G. Quibria and J. M. Dowling, *Current Issues in Economic Development*, New York: Oxford University Press, 1996, pp. 299–347.

Nerlove, M. (1997), "Likelihood Inference for Dynamic Panel Models," presented at the Seventh Conference on Panel Data Econometrics, 19–20 June 1997, Paris. *Annales d'Économie et de Statistique de l'INSEE 55–56*, 1999.

Nerlove, M. (1998), "Properties of Alternative Estimators of Dynamic Panel Models: An Empirical Analysis of Cross-Country Data for the Study of Economic Growth," forthcoming in *Analysis of Panels and Limited Dependent Variable Models*, C. Hsiao, K. Lahiri, L-F. Lee, and M. H. Pesaran (Eds.), Cambridge UK: Cambridge University Press, 1999.

Nerlove, M., and P. Balestra (1996), "Formulation and Estimation of Econometric Models for Panel Data," in L. Mátyás and P. Sevestre, op. cit., pp. 3–22.

Nerlove, M., and L. K. Raut (1997), "Growth Models with Endogenous Population: A General Framework," in *The Handbook of Family and Population Economics*, ed. by M. R. Rosenzweig and O. Stark, New York: Elsevier Scientific Publishers, pp. 1117–1175.

Nickell, S. (1981), "Biases in Dynamic Models with Fixed Effects," *Econometrica, 49*: pp. 1417–1426.

Quah, D. (1996), "Empirics for Economic Growth and Convergence," *European Economic Review, 40*: pp. 1353–1375.

Sevestre, P., and A. Trognon (1983), "Propriétés de grands échantillons d'une classe d'estimateurs des modèles autorégressifs à erreurs composées," *Annales de l'INSEE, 50*: pp. 25–49.

Sevestre, P., and A. Trognon (1996), "Linear Dynamic Models," in Mátyás and Sevestre, op. cit., pp. 120–144.

Solow, R. M. (1956), "A Contribution to the Theory of Economic Growth," *Quarterly Journal of Economics, 70*: pp. 65–94.

Swan, T. W. (1956), "Economic Growth and Capital Accumulation," *Economic Record, 32*: pp. 324–361.

Trognon, A. (1978), "Miscellaneous Asymptotic Properties of Ordinary Least-Squares and Maximum-Likelihood Methods in Dynamic Error Components Models," *Annales de l'INSEE, 30-31*: pp. 631–657.

SEVEN

Properties of Alternative Estimators of Dynamic Panel Models: An Empirical Analysis of Cross-Country Data for the Study of Economic Growth[1]

Preface

The paper reprinted here gives a more detailed analysis of the comparative properties of various estimates of the growth regressions using the Penn World Table panel. Models with individual-specific effects and with individual-specific trends are considered. The emphasis is on the correct formulation of the likelihood function, both conditional on the initial observations and unconditional, assuming that the initial observations on GDP per capita are generated by the same structural process as generates the observations in the within-sample period. The differences between the unconditional and conditional estimates are explored in detail.

The desirability of maximum-likelihood estimation is stressed in contrast to other approaches. Graphical methods are employed to study the likelihood functions of key parameters concentrated with respect to the other parameters of lesser interest. Likelihood methods are explored in greater generality in the next chapter.

---

[1] Reprinted with permission from C. Hsiao, K. Lahiri, L-F. Lee, and M. H. Pesaran, eds., *Analysis of Panels and Limited Dependent Variable Models*, New York, Cambridge University Press, 1999, pp. 136–170.

Properties of Alternative Estimators of Dynamic Panel Models: An Empirical Analysis of Cross-Country Data for the Study of Economic Growth

Marc Nerlove

1. INTRODUCTION

One of the most important implications of the classic papers of Solow (1956) and Swan (1956) is that the lower the starting level of real per capita GDP, relative to the long run of steady-state position, the faster is the growth rate. The Solow/Swan model assumes a constant-returns-to-scale production function with two inputs, capital and labor, and substitution between inputs, a constant savings rate, constant rate of growth of population, and neutral technical change, all exogenously given. Convergence of economies starting out at different levels of per capita income to the same steady-state rate of growth reflects the diminishing returns to capital implied by the production function assumed: economies starting out with lower levels of real per capita GDP relative to the long-run or steady-state position have less capital per worker and,

This chapter draws extensively from "Growth Rate Convergence, Fact or Artifact? An Essay in Panel Data Econometrics," prepared for the Sixth Conference on Panel Data Econometrics, Amsterdam, 28–29 June 1996. The research on which it is based was supported by the Maryland Agricultural Experiment Station, Project A-53.

My interest in the question of how the econometric approach might have influenced recent findings with respect to the convergence hypothesis was stimulated by reading Islam (1995a). Although I wound up going directly to the Penn World Tables for the data underlying the analyses presented here. I began by working with the series Islam was kind enough to supply and for which I am greatly indebted to him.

I thank Hashem Pesaran for helpful discussions, and Robert Barro, Michael Binder, William Greene, Kajal Lahiri, G. S. Maddala, and C. Spohr for useful comments. Pietro Balestra suggested the method used to obtain the likelihood function for the differenced model. Special thanks are due to Anke Meyer, with whom I discussed every aspect of this work.

I am also indebted to Jinkyo Suh and Timothy Thomas for computational counsel and their assistance in straightening out the GAUSS programs that I wrote to obtain the results reported here. Suh also checked and double-checked all derivations and verified that my programs accurately reflected the formulae derived, and carried out further analyses for this revision in connection with the differenced model.

This chapter is dedicated to my long-time friend and one-time colleague, G. S. Maddala.

therefore, higher rates of return to capital. I will refer to this as the standard Barro-Baumol (BB) sense of the meaning of convergence. There is a good deal of current discussion regarding the appropriate definition of "convergence."[1] My purpose here is not to question this notion of convergence, but rather to show that estimates of the coefficient of the lagged dependent variable in a dynamic panel model that has been used to study this phenomenon are extremely sensitive to the method of estimation employed. Because the steady state of the Solow-Swan model depends on the savings rate, the rate of growth of the population, and the rate of technical progress, many have argued that these factors need to be held constant in attempting to test the hypothesis of growth-rate convergence. Convergence is, in this case, conditional. Convergence may also be conditional on other factors such as the accumulation of human capital or investment in infrastructure or, indeed, other unobserved factors that are trending at different rates in different countries or regions.[2]

The problem of BB-convergence in the standard neoclassical model is treated both theoretically and empirically in the text by Barro and Sala-i-Martin (1995) and empirically in a paper by Islam (1995a). Bernard and Durlauf (1996) provide a useful framework for understanding the time-series and cross-sectional tests of the BB-convergence hypothesis and its relation to alternative definitions. Quah (1996) discusses the problem of convergence in more general form and distinguishes several different varieties. He argues that "Simply because panel data techniques happen to apply to data with extensive cross-section and time-series variation does not mean they are at once similarly appropriate for analyzing convergence." While I do not fault Quah's conclusion, current discussions do emphasize panel data and methods, and derive strong conclusions regarding BB-convergence and the significance of other determinants of growth from such data. It is, therefore, appropriate to consider how these conclusions, *within the context of BB-convergence*, are affected by the econometric methods employed.

Perhaps even more important than the problem of convergence is the question of the determinants of growth. The World Bank Project on Economic Growth lists fifteen published papers and fifteen working papers, almost all of which involve dynamic panel data analysis or cross-section analysis with a state variable or initial condition.[3] Although the focus of these papers is not convergence but rather the effects of the other variables included, if the

---

[1] Bernard and Durlauf (1995) give a nice discussion emphasizing the restrictiveness of the approach, going back to the earlier work of Barro (1991) and Baumol (1986), on which my analysis of econometric methods is based (see also Quah, 1996), and which is the most prevalent. Other recent contributions include Islam (1995b); Caselli, Esquivel, and Lefort (1996); and the fine survey by de la Fuente (1997).

[2] When population growth is endogenously determined, this implication of convergence, conditional or otherwise, of the neoclassical model of economic growth does not necessarily follow: see Nerlove and Raut (1997).

[3] See http//www.worldbank.org/html/research/growth.

coefficient of the state variable in the statistical analysis is inconsistently estimated, in this sense "biased," then the coefficient of any variable correlated
with the state variable will also be biased. Hence, quite misleading conclusions may be drawn concerning the significance, sign, and relative magnitude
of other factors included in the analysis, conclusions that may significantly
affect the policy implications of the analysis.

Subsection 2 examines recent empirical investigations of BB-convergence
and the rate of convergence, and argues that most are flawed by failure to allow
for the inconsistencies of single cross-section or panel studies in a dynamic
context.[4] In a dynamic context, a single cross section is best viewed as a panel
with time dimension 1. I do not attempt here a general review of the effects
of the methods used in more general studies of the determinants of growth,
but elsewhere I have examined the effects on the estimated coefficients of the
Barro and Lee (1993) estimates of the stock of human capital.[5]

In Subsection 3, I discuss four common methods of estimating the coefficient
of the "state" variable interpreted in terms of the rate of convergence (and thus
testing for convergence), and show that these four methods yield estimates that
satisfy an inequality derived by Sevestre and Trognon (1996). One broad class
of estimates with which I do not deal here are those based on the generalized
method of moments and the so-called matrix method due to Chamberlain
(1984), or derived from his work (Holtz-Eakin, Newey, and Rosen [1988] and
Arellano and Bond [1991]).[6] These methods are not only somewhat difficult
to implement, but also the resulting estimates are, by construction, insensitive
to the way in which initial values of the "state" variable have presumably been
generated. I argue that, if the process generating the data in the sample period
is stationary, or can be made so by suitable transformation of the data, the

---

[4] This point is also made by Caselli *et al.* (1996) in a study that came to my attention after
Nerlove (1996) was written. A recent study by Lee *et al.* (1996) arrives at similar conclusions
but proposes a number of alternatives different from those investigated here. In particular,
I believe that their formulation of what they call the unconditional-likelihood function is
quite different from that proposed here because they include deterministic trends in their
model and cannot, therefore, directly formulate the likelihood *unconditional on the initial
observations* (see Footnote 11).

[5] See the appendix to Nerlove (1996).

[6] For an extensive exposition of these methods and a very general formulation, see Crépon and
Mairesse (1996). The method is based on a series of transformations of the basic equation
(1); the resulting equation is then estimated as a cross-section regression on the original
explanatory variables in all periods. Caselli *et al.* (1996) use a variant that is an application of
the GMM method applied to the first differences of the series. They then use the stock or state
variables as instruments. This implies that they are predetermined and, therefore, conditions
on their values. If indeed the process, originally or in first-difference form, is stationary,
the procedure does discard the information in the initial observations, which is just what
unconditional ML seeks to avoid. Since conditional ML should give estimates with the same
desirable properties as GMM and is very easy to compute under these circumstances, it is not
clear to me why Caselli *et al.*, and others have avoided its use.

initial values of the state variable convey a great deal of information about that process since they reflect how it has operated in the past. Thus, conditioning on those initial conditions is clearly an undesirable feature, especially when the time dimension of the panel is short.

In Subsection 3.f, I present a new method of maximum-likelihood estimation based on the density of the observations *unconditional on the initial or starting values of the dependent variable*. I argue more generally for methods of inference that look at more than just the maximum of the likelihood function, on the basis of the *likelihood principle* of Fisher (1922, 1925). This approach fully takes into account what information the initial conditions contain about how the process has operated in the past and is thus of special relevance to short time-dimension ("shallow") panels. I extend this method to the case of country-specific trends. These make the underlying processes being investigated nonstationary, but simple forms of nonstationarity can be removed by differencing the data.

Finally, in Subsection 4, I apply all six methods to two panel data sets drawn from the Penn World Tables, for both a model with country-specific intercept effects and one with country-specific trends. The results show clearly how misleading the standard estimates can be in assessing growth-rate convergence and in the estimation of the significance and magnitude of other variables included. The contrast between the conditional and the unconditional ML estimates for a small cross-section dimension and their similarity for a large cross-section dimension is illustrated, as is the importance of looking at the likelihood function itself more broadly. I also show that the usual procedures for doing feasible GLS or for obtaining starting values for ML are seriously flawed and likely to yield negative estimates of the random time-persistent cross-sectional effects. The results also show that biases in the estimate of the coefficient of the lagged value of the dependent variable are transmitted to the estimates of other coefficients in the model, making inferences about the determinants of growth problematic unless appropriate econometric methods are used.

Subsection 5 is the conclusion.

2. RECENT EMPIRICAL INVESTIGATIONS OF CONVERGENCE AND THE RATE OF CONVERGENCE

Let y_t = per capita output, k_t = the capital–labor ratio, s = the savings rate, δ = the depreciation rate of capital, and n = the exogenous rate of population growth and labor force. All of these variables may differ over times as indicated by their subscript t, but also, in a cross-country context, they are certain to differ from one country to another in a fashion that persists over time. An additional subscript is introduced in the sections that follow this one to indicate that fact. If the production function is Cobb-Douglas, $y_t = A_t k_t^a$, where A_t reflects other than conventional factors of production affecting growth and where α, the elasticity of per capita output with respect to the capital–labor ratio, is often interpreted in terms of capital's share as implied by payment of capital as its marginal product. Under these circumstances, it can easily be shown using a simple partial-adjustment model that

$$\log y_t = \frac{\alpha(1-\gamma)}{1-\alpha}[\log s - \log(n+\delta)] + \frac{1-\gamma}{1-\alpha}\log A_t + \gamma \log y_{t-1}. \quad (1)$$

The speed of convergence to equilibrium is inversely proportional to γ, with growth convergence $0 < \gamma < 1$. In equilibrium, per capita GDP depends only on the parameters n and s, and on the time path of A_t. In an empirical context, these differ from time to time and country to country. Clearly, the extent of convergence is conditional on s, n, δ, and the time path of A_t. In empirical investigations, changing n and s and sometimes a measure of changing A_t have been introduced. I examine models in which A_t is assumed to be constant although differing from one country to another and an alternative formulation in which A_t can be represented by a simple linear trend that plausibly also differs from country to country.

Equation (1) has been widely used to examine the hypothesis of growth convergence (Mankiw *et al.* [1992, p. 410], Barro and Sala-i-Martin [1995, Chapter 12], Islam [1995a, p. 1133], Lee *et al.* [1996], Caseli, *et al.* [1996]). In empirical work, y_t is replaced by real per capita GDP; when varying s and n are taken into account, s is replaced by an average savings rate over the period $t-1$ to t, and n is replaced by the growth rate of population over the period $t-1$ to t. It is usual to use rates averaged over several years; following Islam (1995a), I have used quinquennial averages. The restriction on the coefficients of $\ln(s)$ and $\ln(n+\delta)$, which arises from the constant-returns-to-scale assumption, implies that $\ln(s)$ and $\ln(n+\delta)$ can be collapsed into a single variable. Testing the growth-convergence hypothesis, in this context, resolves largely around the coefficient γ of the lagged level of per capita real GDP. If this is positive but much less than one, the implication is that, on average, countries with low initial values are growing faster than those with high initial values and is, therefore, evidence of convergence. Whereas, if this coefficient is close to one, perhaps even slightly larger than one, the implication is that initial values have little or no effect or even a perverse one on subsequent growth: such a finding is, therefore, evidence against the neoclassical theory that implies convergence. For example, if $\gamma = 0.9$, convergence to within 90 percent of final equilibrium occurs only in twenty-two periods, which, given quinquennial data, implies 110 years! Similarly, 0.8 requires fifty-three years, 0.7 requires thirty-two years, while 0.2 requires only seven years, and 0.1 is within 90 percent in five years.[7]

---

[7] Derivation of the model and the calculations behind this statement are given in Nerlove (1996, pp. 5–8 and Appendix Table 2).

The estimates of γ for the levels model presented using cross-country quinquennial data are generally in excess of 0.7 no matter what econometric procedure is employed, but vary over a wide range depending on the method, 0.7 to 0.98. But for the differenced model, many estimates of γ are much smaller, in the vicinity of 0.5.[8] It is apparent that, for all practical purposes, coefficients in excess of 0.7 represent negligible convergence, since, with unchanging s, n, and A, it would take more than a generation to achieve 90 percent of equilibrium real per capita GDP. Most recent studies attempt to test whether $\gamma = 1$; however, this is a test for a unit root in log y_{it}. Even under the best of circumstances, testing for a unit root is problematic (see Diebold and Nerlove, 1990). Here the problems are compounded by the short time dimension of the typical panel. Basing a test on the size of γ rather than equality with 1 finesses a host of problems of the sort discussed extensively in Diebold and Nerlove (1990).[9]

Tests based on a single cross section (Which can be viewed as a panel of time dimension 1) or on pooled cross-section time series (panel) data generally have yielded contradictory results: pooled panel data studies tend to reject the hypothesis of BB-convergence (relatively high γs), even after controlling for population growth rates, savings rates, and other variables. Dynamic fixed-effects models are, of course, not possible for a single cross section, but recent work (Islam, 1995a) using a dynamic fixed-effects panel model yields results supporting convergence. There are serious problems with tests, such as those that rely on the estimated coefficients of the lagged, or initial value, of the dependent variable in dynamic panel models or in the special case of a single cross section, which arise from two sources of bias. In this paper, I show some of these findings are probably artifacts arising from biases in the econometric methods employed. This demonstrates the sensitivity of the conclusions drawn about γ to the econometric method employed, irrespective of the validity of the relationship estimated.

The first source of bias is omitted variables, especially infrastructure and investments over time in infrastructure, and the natural resource base available to each country, in cross-sectional or panel studies. Systematic differences across countries or regions will systematically bias the conclusions. Because such variables are likely to be correlated with savings or investment rates in conventional or in human capital, and with population growth rates,

---

[8] Using a GMM estimator, Caselli *et al.* obtained an estimate of about 0.51–0.53; that is, much more rapid convergence and close to the estimates obtained for the ninty-four-country sample using either conditional or unconditional ML. My estimates for the twenty-two-country sample are much higher, however.

[9] Barnard and Durlauf (1995) use co-integration techniques on rather longer time series for fifteen OECD countries to test alternative time-series definitions of convergence and contrast the results with the standard BB-formulation.

it is not altogether clear what the net effect of omitting them on the coefficient of the initial value will be in a single cross section. But in a pooled model, it is clear that, to the extent such differences are persistent, they will be highly correlated with the initial value and, therefore, omitting them will bias the coefficient of that variable upward toward one and thus toward rejecting convergence. This source of bias has been well known since the early paper by Balestra and Nerlove (1966) and is well supported by the Monte Carlo studies reported in Nerlove (1971). In this light, it is not surprising that pooled panel data, or single cross sections, which are a special case of panels with $T = 1$, even with inclusion of additional variables, often reject convergence.

Second, since there are likely to be many sources of cross-country or cross-region differences, many of which cannot be observed or directly accounted for, it is natural to try to represent these by fixed effects in a panel context. But, as is well known from the Monte Carlo investigations reported in Nerlove (1971) and demonstrated analytically by Nickell (1981), inclusion of fixed effects in a dynamic model biases the coefficient of the initial value of the dependent variable included as an explanatory variable downward, toward zero and, therefore, toward support for the convergence hypothesis. This may account for Islam's (1995a) findings.

Alternative estimates based on more appropriate random-effects models, such as two-stage feasible generalized least squares or maximum-likelihood conditional on the initial observations are also biased in small samples and inconsistent in large, or, in the case of instrumental variable estimates, have poor sampling properties or are difficult to implement. For example, the papers by Knight, Loayza, and Villaneuva (1993); Loayza (1994); and Islam (1995a) employ a method, among others, proposed by Chamberlain (1984), generally referred to as the Π-matrix approach.[10] The alternative of unconditional maximum likelihood suggested in Nerlove and Balestra (1996) is implemented for the first time in this paper.[11]

Even if one has little interest in the question of convergence, or its rate, per se, the question of whether the coefficient of the state variable, lagged dependent or initial value, is biased in the sense of being inconsistent is an important one since biases in this coefficient will affect the estimates of the

[10] See also Crépon and Mairesse (1996).

[11] Lee *et al.* (1997) also estimate from what they maintain is an unconditional-likelihood function, but inasmuch as they do not transform to stationarity (their relationship includes both a constant and a linear trend), I do not think their formulation of the likelihood function is based on the unconditional density of the dependent variable as proposed here. In fact, they estimate from a likelihood based on the *conditional* density of the dependent variable given the initial value. The relation between conditional and unconditional likelihood is discussed at length in Nerlove (1997).

coefficients of other variables correlated with it and their levels of significance. To the extent such estimates are important in the formulation of policies to promote growth, the matter is indeed a serious one.[12]

In the remainder of this paper, I investigate the sensitivity of the coefficient of the lagged dependent or state variable to the econometric method employed, as well as the sensitivity of the estimates of the coefficients for other variables included. All of the results reported, except those for pooled panel data, support the growth convergence hypothesis conditional on savings and population growth rates, but illustrate the rather different estimates of the rates of convergence, and of the coefficients of other explanatory variables, obtained when different estimation techniques are used. In addition, a technique for examining the shape of sections of a high-dimensional likelihood function is developed that reveals interesting and somewhat unexpected relationships among the various estimates.

3. ALTERNATIVE METHODS FOR ESTIMATION[13]

A good summary of the current state of knowledge about the properties of various estimators in dynamic panel models is contained in Sevestre and Trognon (1996). Trognon (1978) was the first to show the possible inconsistency of maximum likelihood conditional on the initial individual observations. Nickell (1981) shows the inconsistency of the estimates of the fixed effects in a dynamic panel model. Kiviet (1995) derives exact results for the bias of leading estimators. In this subsection, following Sevestre and Trognon, I review the leading estimators and their properties for dynamic panel models. I will assume a random-effects model for the disturbance for the reasons set forth in Nerlove and Balestra (1996) and because fixed effects can be viewed as a special case from the standpoint of estimation.

For simplicity, in this subsection I restrict attention to the simple model containing one exogenous variable x_{it} and one lagged value of the dependent variable y_{it-1} as explanatory. Extension to the case in which more than one exogenous explanatory variable is included presents no serious difficulty.

$$y_{it} = \alpha + \beta x_{it} + \gamma y_{it-1} + \mu_i + \varepsilon_{it}, \quad i = 1, \ldots, N, \quad t = 1, \ldots, T. \quad (2)$$

Taking deviations from overall means eliminates the constant α. The usual

---

[12] For example, in (1) the parameter α could be derived from the coefficient of the variable log $s - \log(n + \delta)$ as coefficient/(coefficient $+ 1 - \gamma$), so there is a double source of bias. Indeed, a number of authors accept or reject statistical formulations based on the estimated value of α, which should approximate capital's share.

[13] I rely extensively in this subsection on the excellent discussion of Sevestre and Trognon, Chapter 7 in Mátyás and Sevestre (1996, pp. 120–144). Additional alternatives, more appropriate when longer time series are available, are treated by Lee *et al.* (1997) and are not discussed or implemented here.

assumptions are made about the properties of the μ_i and the ε_{it}.

(i) $E(\mu_i) = E(\varepsilon_{it}) = 0, \quad$ all i and t,

(ii) $E(\mu_i\varepsilon_{it}) = 0, \quad$ all i and t,

(iii) $E(\mu_i\mu_j) = \begin{cases} \sigma_\mu^2 & i = j \\ 0 & i \neq j, \end{cases}$

(iv) $E(\varepsilon_{it}\varepsilon_{js}) = \begin{cases} \sigma_\varepsilon^2 & t = s, \quad i = j \\ 0 & otherwise. \end{cases}$

Both μ_i and ε_{it} are assumed to be uncorrelated with x_{it} for all i and t. While this assumption is far from innocuous, for example, if savings rates or population growth are not independent of per capita income or unobserved factors that affect it, I adopt it here, not only because it is conventional, but also because one has to cut off somewhere. Clearly, however, y_{it-1} cannot be assumed to be uncorrelated with μ_i. It is clear, therefore, that OLS applied to (2) ignoring the component nature of the disturbances $\mu_{it} = \mu_i + \varepsilon_{it}$, which I call the *pooled regression*, will yield inconsistent estimates. In particular, if $\gamma > 0$, γ_{pooled} is "biased" upward. So, just as in the case of ordinary serial correlation β_{pooled} is also "biased" and the OLS residuals understate the amount of serial correlation, which in this case is measured by the intraclass correlation coefficient ρ. This parameter measures the extent of unobserved or latent time-invariant, individual-specific, variation relative to the total unobserved variation in the sample, $\sigma_\mu^2/(\sigma_\mu^2 + \sigma_\varepsilon^2)$. It is extremely important in understanding the nature of the variation, both observed and unobserved, in the panel.

a. Inconsistency of the Pooled-Sample OLS Estimates of the Dynamic Error-Components Model

Since the panel has two dimensions, it is possible to consider asymptotic behavior as $N \to \infty$, $T \to \infty$, or both. Generally speaking, it is easier to increase the cross-section dimension of a panel, so the most relevant asymptotics are as $N \to \infty$. This is called *semi-asymptotics* in the panel data literature. It is not necessary to assume $|\gamma| < 1$ as long as T is fixed, but the way in which the initial values of the dependent variable, y_{i0}, are assumed to be generated is crucial. To see why, write (2) as

$$y_{it} = \gamma^t y_{i0} + \sum_{j=0}^{t-1} \gamma^j \beta x_{it-j} + \frac{1-\gamma^t}{1-\gamma} v_i + v_{it}, \quad \text{where } \mu_{it} = \sum_{j=0}^{t-1} \gamma^j \varepsilon_{it-j}. \quad (3)$$

Equation (3) expresses y_{it} as the sum of four terms: the first, $\gamma^t y_{i0}$, depends on the initial values; the second on lagged values of the exogenous variable; the third on the individual, time-invariant, component of residual variance; and the fourth on lagged values of the remaining component. This last term is an autoregressive process with initial values $v_{i0} = 0$ and $v_{it} = \gamma v_{it-1} + \varepsilon_{it}$. It need not be assumed to be stationary as long as T is fixed. It does not make sense in this context to assume that the y_{i0} are uncorrelated with either the μ_i or the lagged values of x_{it}. On the other hand, ε_{i0} is a random variable with mean 0 and variance σ_ε^2 independently and identically distributed for all i. Thus, the initial observation can be written as a function of lagged xs, the μ_i and ε_{i0}:

$$y_{i0} = f(x_{i0}, x_{i-1}, \ldots, \mu_i, \varepsilon_{i0}). \tag{4}$$

Clearly, if the individual effects μ_i are assumed to be fixed and the lagged xs to be given, the y_{i0} are also fixed and uncorrelated with the disturbances in (3), $v_{it}, t = 1, \ldots, T$. But if the individual effects are considered to be random, as Nerlove and Balestra (1996) have argued they should be, the initial observations are not exogenous since they are correlated with them, as they are part of the disturbance term, namely the third and fourth terms of (3).

It is common in the literature on panel data to assume that the y_{i0} are i.i.d. random variables that are characterized by their second moments and correlations with the individual effects, and not necessarily generated by the same process that generates the rest of the y_{it}. The properties of various estimators depend on the process generating them. One possibility is to try to model and estimate this process together with the dynamic panel model (2).

b. Inconsistency of the OLS Estimators of the Dummy Variable or Fixed-Effects Model

The ordinary least-squares estimates of both the coefficient of the lagged dependent variable and the exogenous variable are inconsistent in the fixed-effects model. As is well known, the fixed-effects model is equivalent to taking deviations from individual (country) means and then estimating an ordinary OLS regression

$$y_{it} - \bar{y}_i = \beta(x_{it} - \bar{x}_i) + \gamma(y_{i,t-1} - \bar{y}_{i,t-1}) + v_{it}, \quad \text{where } v_{it} = \varepsilon_{it} - \bar{\varepsilon}_i. \tag{5}$$

Although $\sigma_{x\varepsilon} = 0$,

$$\sigma_{y(-1)\varepsilon}^2 = \rho N \overset{\lim}{\longrightarrow} \infty \frac{1}{T} \sum_t (y_{i,t-1} - \bar{y}_{i,-1})(\varepsilon_{it} - \bar{\varepsilon}_{i,-1})$$

$$= -\frac{1}{T^2} \frac{T - 1 - T\gamma + \gamma^T}{(1-\gamma)^2} \sigma_\varepsilon^2 \neq 0. \tag{6}$$

Thus, the OLS estimates of both β and γ in the fixed-effects model are inconsistent, although as $T \to \infty$, the inconsistency disappears. But for finite, typically small T, it remains (see Nickell, 1981, p. 1424). For $T = 10$ and $\gamma = 0.5$, for example, the "bias" of the OLS estimate of γ, say c, is proportional to -0.16, the factor of proportionality being the OLS estimate of the variance of c from the within regression. It is always negative, implying that the bias of the OLS estimate of β, say b, is therefore upward. This conclusion holds regardless of whether one assumes the true model is fixed or random effects.

Although the inconsistency will be small when T is moderate to large, small values of T are typically the case. Nonetheless, Nerlove (1971) suggested using the fixed-effects model to estimate ρ for FGLS, in contrast to the earlier suggestion of Balestra and Nerlove (1966), hereinafter BN, of a consistent instrumental variable approach. BN also suggested but did not implement a method based on estimating ρ from the pooled and fixed-effects regressions. Rejection of instrumental variables by Nerlove (1971) was based on the instability of the results in Monte Carlo trials. Since the OLS estimates of the parameters from pooled or fixed-effects regressions are inconsistent, the estimates of ρ based on this regression will also be; hence, the FGLS estimates computed using them will not generally be consistent. In the results reported here, an estimate of ρ is derived from the estimate of residual variance from both the fixed-effects and the pooled regressions, as suggested by BN (1966), and is not consistent.

Many authors (e.g., Greene, 1993, pp. 475–477; Judge *et al.*, 1988, pp. 484–488, hereinafter GJ) suggest basing an estimate of ρ on the cross-section regression of the overall means and either the pooled or fixed-effects regression. This suggestion, unfortunately, often leads to negative estimates of ρ and unwarranted rejection of the model. These estimates are also inconsistent. The GJ suggestion is, unfortunately, utilized in most computer packages for implementing FGLS for panel data or obtaining starting values for ML, and often leads to the adoption of badly biased fixed-effects OLS when a negative estimate of ρ is obtained.

The GJ suggestion is to regress the group means of the independent variable on the group means of the dependent variables

$$\bar{y}_i = \alpha + \beta \bar{x}_i + w_i, \quad \text{where } w_i = \mu_i + \bar{\varepsilon}_i. \tag{7}$$

The variance of w_i is $\sigma_\mu^2 + \frac{\sigma_\varepsilon^2}{T}$. The purely cross-sectional variation of the individual means gives us information on both the slope and the overall constant in the regression. This is often called the *between-groups* regression. In many panel data problems, purely cross-sectional variation may dominate, but this variation may not give us much information about the true value of the slope of the independent variable if the regression also contains a lagged value of the dependent variable. The residual SNN = RSSB/N from this regression estimates $\sigma_\mu^2 + \frac{\sigma_\varepsilon^2}{T}$. But it will not be a very good estimate if the regression is estimated by OLS, since (7) will tend to fit too well if cross-section variation dominates the data.[14] σ_μ^2 is then estimated as $\sigma_w^2 - \frac{\sigma_\varepsilon^2}{T}$, where an estimate of σ_μ^2

---

[14] For example, when a lagged value of the dependent variable is included as one of the explanatory variables, its mean may be very close to the mean of the unlagged variable; then the fit of (7) may be nearly perfect. The estimated residual variance may be close to zero in this case. In general, if there is a lot of associated cross-sectional variation, the residual of this relationship may be very small. If combined with the estimate of σ_ε^2 obtained from the within regression, the implied estimate of σ_μ^2 may well turn out to be negative (see Greene, 1993, pp. 474–476). But this does not imply that the model is misspecified. Balestra and Nerlove

can be obtained from the fixed-effects regression. If T is large, the estimated value of σ_μ^2 is not likely to be negative, no matter how well the between-groups regression fits. But if T is small, and particularly if the regression contains a lagged value of the dependent variable on the right-hand side, the chances of obtaining negative and, therefore, unacceptable estimates of ρ are high irrespective of the validity of the model.[15]

c. Generalized Least Squares and Feasible GLS

The means or between regression and the fixed-effects regression both contain information about the parameters of the model: the means regression reflects purely cross-sectional variation, whereas the fixed-effects regression reflects the individual variation over time. GLS combines these two types of information with weights that depend on the characteristic roots of $Euu' = \sigma^2\Omega$. The individual means themselves are weighted by the reciprocal of the square root of $\xi = 1 - \rho + T\rho$, while the deviations from these means are weighted by the reciprocal of the square root of $\eta = 1 - \rho$. A representative transformed observation is

$$y_{it}^* = \xi^{-1/2}\bar{y}_{i.} + \eta^{-1/2}(y_{it} - \bar{y}_i), \quad i = 1, \ldots, N, \quad t = 1, \ldots, T.$$

Thus, y_{it}^* is a *weighted* combination (weighted by the reciprocals of the square roots of the characteristic roots of Ω) of individual means of the original observations $\bar{y}_i$, and the deviations from individual means $(y_{it} - \bar{y}_{i.})$. The other variables are similarly transformed to x_{it}^* and y_{it-1}^*. GLS amounts to running the OLS regression:

$$y_{it}^* = \alpha^* + \beta x_{it}^* + \gamma y_{it-1}^* + v_{it}. \tag{8}$$

(1966, p. 607) suggest estimating σ_μ^2 from the fixed-effects model as the "variance" of the implied constant terms:

$$\sigma_\mu^2 = \frac{1}{N}\sum_i (\bar{y}_i - \bar{y} - \hat{\beta} - \bar{x})^2,$$

where $\hat{\beta}$ is the OLS estimate of β in that regression. This suggestion is the one implemented in Nerlove (1971). Alternatively, if a regression with dummy variables for each individual, overall constant suppressed, has been estimated, it suffices to compute the variance, sum of squared deviations from the mean value divided by N, to estimate σ_μ^2.

[15] In Footnote 21, I compare three different estimates of ρ based on the OLS regressions: (1) the original suggestion of Balestra and Nerlove (1966); (2) an estimate based only on the fixed-effects regression (Nerlove, 1971); and (3) the suggestion of Judge *et al.* (1988) and Greene (1993), which is the basis for most computer packages doing panel econometrics. The first and earliest suggestion generally yields results closer to the maximum-likelihood estimates than the others. The second yields estimates that are generally considerably higher. The last yields results that are far too low and often found to be negative, although not in the results reported here. I have presented estimates of ρ obtained by all three methods and compared them with estimates of ρ obtained from conditional and from unconditional maximum likelihood in the table in Footnote 22.

v_{it} is the transformed disturbance. Note that the constant has a different interpretation.

Let $\theta^2 = \eta/\xi = (\xi^{-1/2}/\eta^{-1/2})^2$ be the relative weight of the between variation to the within variation. Note that this weight tends to 0 from above as $T \to \infty$ (i.e., the within information dominates). For T small, $\theta^2 < 1$, so that the between variation is allowed to play a greater role. When the intraclass correlation, ρ, is close to one, the unobserved, residual cross-section variation is large relative to the unobserved individual variation.

$$\theta^2 = \frac{1}{1 + T\frac{\rho}{1-\rho}} = \frac{1}{1 + T\frac{\sigma_\mu^2}{\sigma_\varepsilon^2}}$$

is smaller for fixed T than when ρ is small.

Between information gets a lower relative weight when ρ is large than when ρ is small, which corresponds to the usual weighting of data from sources with varying degrees of error.

To obtain an estimate of ρ for use in a feasible GLS, I prefer to obtain both an estimate of σ^2 from the pooled regression, as indicated previously. Although this estimate is not consistent, it is never negative and empirically it gives at least the appearance of a tighter upper bound to the true value of γ than the pooled regression does and a closer approximation to the ML estimate.

d. Bounds for the Coefficient of the Lagged Dependent Variable

As Maddala (1971) pointed out, the GLS estimates with $\lambda = 1/\theta^2$ can be considered members of a more general class of estimators obtained through different choices of λ. Let $\hat{\gamma}(\lambda)$ be the estimator of γ obtained by solving the GLS normal equations for an arbitrary value of λ. Sevestre and Trognon (1996, pp. 130–133) show that for the case in which $\beta = 0$, the purely autoregressive case, the following inequality holds:

$$\rho \lim \hat{\gamma}(0) < \gamma < \rho \lim \hat{\gamma}(\lambda) < \rho \lim \hat{\gamma}(1) < \rho \lim \hat{\gamma}(\infty)$$
$$\text{fixed-effects} \qquad \text{GLS} \qquad \text{OLS pooled} \qquad \text{means} \tag{9}$$

Remarkably, the GLS estimate is inconsistent even when a consistent estimate of ρ is used to compute FGLS estimates. The problem is that the lagged dependent variable is correlated even with the transformed disturbance.

Since $\rho \lim \hat{\gamma}(\lambda)$ is a continuous function of λ, there exists a value λ^* in the interval $[0, 1/\theta^2]$ for which $\rho \lim \hat{\gamma}(\lambda) = \gamma$. Sevestre and Trognon (1983) show that this value is

$$\lambda^* = K(1 - \rho) \Big/ \left\{ \frac{(1 - \gamma^T)E(y_{i0}\mu_i)}{(1 - \gamma)\sigma^2} + K\xi \right\}, \tag{10}$$

where $K = \frac{T - 1 - T\gamma + \gamma^T}{T(1-\gamma)^2}$, and ρ, ξ, and σ^2 are as before.

They also show that when $\beta \neq 0$, the estimate $\hat{\gamma}(\lambda)$ behaves almost the same as in the purely autoregressive case. Since the λ^* estimate is consistent when there are no exogenous variables, it remains so when there are. The trick is to obtain a consistent estimate of λ^*, which can be accomplished by finding an appropriate instrumental variable for y_{-1}. Even in this case, the results depend heavily on the distribution of the estimate of λ^*.

In the dynamic error-components model, not only are the OLS pooled-regression estimates, the fixed-effect or within estimates, and the between estimates inconsistent, but so are the GLS estimates using the true value of ρ. However, the method of instrumental variables may be used to obtain a feasible member of the λ-class of estimates that is consistent (see Sevestre and Trognon, 1996). Unfortunately, this estimate may have a very large variance, as demonstrated in Nerlove (1971).

Nonetheless, the fixed-effects and the pooled regression may be used to bound the true value of γ even when exogenous regressors are also included. Empirically, I have found that FGLS appears to provide an even tighter bound, although since FGLS is also based on an inconsistent estimate of ρ, there is no guarantee that this is, in fact, an upper bound.

e. Maximum Likelihood Conditional on the Initial Value of the Lagged Dependent Variable

When the likelihood function for the model (2) with $u_{it} = \mu_i + \varepsilon_{it} \sim N(0, \sigma^2 \Omega)$ is derived in the usual way from the product of the densities of y_{it} conditional on x_{it} and y_{it-1}, the joint density is conditional on y_{i0}. This likelihood function can be written in terms of the earlier notation introduced as,

$$\log L\left(\alpha, \beta, \gamma, \sigma_\mu^2, \sigma_\varepsilon^2 \big| y_{11}, \ldots, y_{NT}; x_{11}, \ldots, x_{NT}; y_{10}, \ldots, y_{N0}\right)$$

$$= -\frac{NT}{2} \log 2\pi - \frac{NT}{2} \log \sigma^2 - \frac{N}{2} \log \xi - \frac{N(T-1)}{2} \log \eta$$

$$- \frac{1}{2\sigma^2} \sum_{i=1}^{N} \sum_{t=1}^{T} \left(y_{it}^* - \alpha \xi^{-1/2} - \beta x_{it}^* - \gamma y_{it-1}^*\right)^2, \tag{11}$$

where y^*, x^*, y_{-1}^* are the transformed variables. Since

$$\xi = \frac{\lambda}{1 - (\lambda - 1)/T} \quad \text{and} \quad \eta = \frac{1}{1 - (\lambda - 1)/T},$$

$\log L$ can be expressed as a function solely of $\lambda, \sigma^2, \alpha, \beta$, and γ. Trognon (1978) shows that, when the exogenous variable x is generated by a first-order autoregression with white-noise input, $w \sim wn(0, \sigma_w^2 I)$, also assumed in the Monte Carlo experiments reported in Nerlove (1971),

$$x = \delta x_{-1} + w, \tag{12}$$

then maximization of the conditional likelihood function (12) yields boundary solutions $\hat{\rho} = 0$, which, unlike interior maximum-likelihood solutions, are inconsistent, for a considerable and, indeed, likely range of parameter values. In particular, there is a value of γ in (2)

$$\gamma^* = \frac{(T-3)^2 - 8}{(T+1)^2},$$

such that when $\gamma < \gamma^*$, there exists an interior maximum of (11) that yields consistent ML estimates, but that when $\gamma \geq \gamma^*$, there are values of ρ for which the conditional likelihood function (2) is maximized at the boundary $\rho = 0$ (i.e., for the OLS estimates of the pooled regression, which we know to be inconsistent). The problem is that when T is small, the permissible range of γ, the coefficient of the lagged dependent variable, is implausible (e.g., negative or very small). For example, for $T = 5$, $\gamma^* = -0.11$, while for $T = 10$, $\gamma^* = 0.34$. When $\gamma \geq \gamma^*$, whether or not an interior maximum with consistent ML estimates occurs depends on the value of ρ. For $\rho < \rho^*$, boundary maxima occur where

$$\rho^* = \left(\frac{T-1}{T+1}\right)^2 \frac{\beta^2 \sigma_w^2}{\sigma^2} \frac{1-\gamma}{(\gamma - \gamma^*)(1 - \gamma\delta)^2}.$$

For example, when $T = 5$, $\beta = 1.0$, $\gamma = 0.75$, $\delta = 0.5$, and $\frac{\sigma_w^2}{\sigma^2} = 1.0$, $\gamma^* = -0.11$ and the critical value of ρ is $\rho^* = 0.31$. That means that any true value of the intraclass correlation less than 0.31 is liable to produce a boundary solution to (11) $\rho = 0$ and inconsistent estimates of all the parameters. Using these results, Trognon (1978) is able to replicate the Monte Carlo results reported in Nerlove (1971).

Even though ML may yield inconsistent estimates when the non-negligible probability of a boundary solution is taken into account, it is nonetheless true that the likelihood function summarizes the information contained in the data about the parameters.[16] From a conventional, Neyman-Pearson point of view, what matters about the likelihood function is only its maximum and curvature in the neighborhood of the maximum, and all the desirable properties and the assessment of the reliability of the maximum-likelihood estimates are only asymptotic. It is perhaps not surprising that only the maximum and the Hessian at the maximum are all that matters from a conventional point of view, in view of the fact that for the mean of a normal distribution, the quadratic approximation is exact and, because of the central limit theorem in its many

---

[16] Although clearly implied in what Fisher wrote in the 1920s (Fisher, 1922, 1925), the likelihood principle, which essentially holds that the likelihood function is the sole basis for inference, did not come into prominence until the 1950s, and 1960s, principally through the work of Barnard, Birnbaum, and Edwards (see the references cited) written largely in reaction to both the classical Neyman-Pearson (frequentist) and the Bayesian approaches to inference. A good discussion is Lindsey (1996).

forms, many estimators, including ML estimators in regular cases, tend to normality in distribution. So the problem of possible inconsistency of the ML estimates should not concern us unduly from the standpoint of likelihood inference. It is the whole shape of the likelihood function, which expresses what the data have to say about the model and its parameters, that matters.[17] For this reason, sections of some of the multidimensional likelihood functions are also presented in the next subsection. When first differences are taken to eliminate a linear deterministic trend, the individual-specific time-invariant effects become differences in the trend slopes. This makes the interpretation of the model in first-difference form different than that in levels. Moreover, the time- and individual-varying disturbance is now likely to be serially correlated, a fact that needs to be taken into account in the formulation of the unconditional-likelihood function. A parallel set of results for the country-specific trends model is presented in the next subsection.

f. Unconditional Likelihood and Unconditional Maximum Likelihood

While it is not guaranteed that a boundary solution to the likelihood equations is obtained, which would yield ML estimates that are inconsistent, it is apparent, as suggested previously, that in panels with a short time dimension the initial values provide important information about the parameters of the model, and to condition on them is to neglect this information.

It is not, in fact, difficult to obtain the unconditional-likelihood function once the marginal distribution of the initial values is specified. The problem is a correct specification of this distribution. If $|\gamma| \geq 1$ or the processes generating the x_{it} are not stationary, it will not, in general, be possible to specify the marginal distribution of the initial observations. I will assume that, possibly after some differencing, both the y_{it} and the x_{it} are stationary. The derivation of the unconditional-likelihood function in the case in which deterministic or stochastic trends are included is contained in Nerlove (1997).[18]

---

[17] The principle of likelihood inference and its application to dynamic panel models is elaborated in Nerlove (1997). A maximum at the boundary conveys perfectly valid information about the parameter in question, as does a near-plateau solution at which the asymptotic standard errors derived from the information matrix are huge. More importantly, the existence of two or more local maxima at not very different likelihood values but widely separated values of the parameters, such as I have obtained in the case of regional Indonesian data, is even more revealing.

[18] Adding trend, t, to (2)

$$y_{it} = \alpha + \beta x_{it} + \gamma y_{it-1} + \tau_i t + \mu_i + \varepsilon_{it}, \quad i = 1, \ldots, N, \quad t = 1, \ldots, T, \tag{2'}$$

and differencing,

$$\Delta y_{it} = \beta \Delta x_{it} + \gamma \Delta y_{it-1} + \tau_i + \Delta \varepsilon_{it}, \quad i = 1, \ldots, N, \quad t = 1, \ldots, T, \tag{2''}$$

where Δ denotes the first-difference operator and τ_i is the individual-specific trend coefficient, assumed to have mean zero (enforced by eliminating any overall constant in the differences by deducting the sample mean). Thus, not only is the meaning of ρ altered, but

Under this assumption, the dynamic relationship to be estimated is stationary and $|\gamma| < 1$. Consider equation (3)[19] with the intercept eliminated, for y_{i0} and the infinite past

$$y_{i0} = \sum_{j=1}^{\infty} \gamma^j \beta x_{i,-j} + \frac{1}{1-\gamma}\mu_t + v_{i0}, \quad \text{where } v_{it-1} = \gamma v_{it} + \varepsilon_{it}.[20] \tag{13}$$

If $\beta = 0$, so that the relationship to be estimated is a pure autoregression for each y_{it}, the vector of initial values $y_0 = (y_{10}, \ldots, y_{N0})$, has a joint-normal distribution with means 0 and variance–covariance matrix

$$\left[\frac{\sigma_\mu^2}{(1-\gamma)^2} + \sigma_v^2\right] I_N = \left(\frac{\sigma_\mu^2}{(1-\gamma)^2} + \frac{\sigma_\varepsilon^2}{1-\gamma^2}\right) I_N.$$

The unconditional likelihood is, therefore,

$$\log L\left(\gamma, \rho, \sigma_\mu^2, \sigma_\varepsilon^2 | y_{11}, \ldots, y_{NT}; \ldots; y_{10}, \ldots, y_{N0}\right)$$
$$= -\frac{NT}{2}\log 2\pi - \frac{NT}{2}\log\sigma^2 - \frac{N}{2}\log\xi - \frac{N(T-1)}{2}\log\eta$$
$$- \frac{1}{2\sigma^2}\sum_{i=1}^{N}\sum_{t=1}^{T}(y_{it}^* - \gamma y_{it-1}^*)^2$$
$$- \frac{N}{2}\log\left(\frac{\sigma_\mu^2}{(1-\gamma)^2} + \frac{\sigma_\varepsilon^2}{1-\gamma^2}\right) - \left[\frac{1}{2\left(\frac{\sigma_\mu^2}{(1-\gamma)^2} + \frac{\sigma_\varepsilon^2}{1-\gamma^2}\right)}\right]\sum_{i=1}^{N}y_{i0}^2. \tag{14}$$

Also if ε_{it} did not contain a unit root to start with, it will now; in particular, if ε_{it} is not serially correlated to start with, it will follow a first-order moving average process with unit root. The variance-covariance matrix of the new disturbances $\tau_i + \Delta\varepsilon_{it}$ is now block diagonal with blocks

$$A = \sigma^2 \begin{bmatrix} 1 & a & b & \ldots b \\ a & 1 & a & b.. \\ b & a & 1 & a\ldots \\ \vdots & \vdots & \vdots & \ldots 1 \end{bmatrix},$$

where $\sigma^2 = \sigma_\tau^2 + \sigma_\varepsilon^2$, $a = \frac{\sigma_\tau^2 - \sigma_\varepsilon^2}{\sigma^2}$, and $b = \frac{\sigma_\tau^2}{\sigma^2}$.

The characteristic roots of A give the necessary transform and Jacobian. This is taken into account in the formulation of both the conditional- and the unconditional-likelihood functions. As indicated, however, differencing is unnecessary when the initial values are conditioning.

[19] For a particular time period T and the infinite past

$$y_{iT} = \gamma^x y_{i-x} + \sum_{j=0}^{x}\gamma^j\beta x_{i-j} + \frac{1-\gamma^x}{1-\gamma}\mu_i + v_{iT}, \quad \text{where } v_{iT} = \sum_{j=0}^{x}\gamma^j\varepsilon_{iT-j}.$$

Since $1 \geq |\gamma|$ and $v_{iT} = \sum_{j=0}^{x}\gamma^j\varepsilon_{iT-j}$ is the MA form a first-order autoregression with white-noise input, equation (13) follows.

[20] If all variables are expressed as deviations from their overall means, there is no need to include an intercept; if not, μ_i should be replaced by $\alpha + \mu_i$.

This likelihood function can easily be concentrated: to maximize, express $\sigma_\mu^2, \sigma_\varepsilon^2, \xi$, and η in terms of ρ and γ. For given ρ and γ in the interval $[0, 1)$, concentrate the likelihood function with respect to σ^2. It follows that

$$\hat{\sigma}^2(\gamma, \rho) = \frac{\text{RSS}^*(\gamma, \rho)}{N(T+1)},$$

where

$$\text{RSS}^*(\gamma, \rho) = \sum_{i=1}^{N}\sum_{t=1}^{T}(y_{it}^* - \gamma y_{it-1}^*)^2 + \left(\sum_{i=1}^{N} y_{i0}^2 \Bigg/ \left[\frac{\rho}{(1-\gamma)^2} + \frac{1-\rho}{1-\gamma^2}\right]\right).$$

Thus, the concentrated LF is

$$\log L^*(\gamma, \rho) = -\frac{N(T+1)}{2}\log 2\pi - \frac{N}{2}\log \xi - \frac{N(T-1)}{2}\log \eta$$

$$-\frac{N(T-1)}{2}\log\left\{\frac{\text{RSS}^*(\gamma, \rho)}{N(T-1)}\right\} - \frac{N}{2}\left\{\frac{\rho}{(1-\gamma)^2} + \frac{1-\rho}{1-\gamma^2}\right\}$$

$$-\left(\tfrac{1}{2}\text{RSS}^*/N(T+1)\right)\sum_{i=1}^{N}\sum_{t=1}^{T}(y_{it}^* - \gamma y_{it-1}^*)^2$$

$$-\sum_{i=1}^{N} y_{i0}^2 \Bigg/ \left\{(2/N(T+1))\left[\frac{\rho}{(1-\gamma)^2} + \frac{1-\rho}{1-\gamma^2}\right]\text{RSS}^*\right\}.$$

Maximizing L^* is quite a bit more complicated than the usual minimization of the sum of squares in the penultimate term because RSS^*, in that term, depends on $\sum_{i=1}^{N} y_{i0}^2$, as well as on ρ and γ, which enter the final terms as well. When $\beta \neq 0$, things are more complicated still. But more important than finding the maximum of L^* is its shape above the γ–ρ plane. It is apparent from the following results that there may be significant trade-offs between γ and ρ without large effects on the value of the likelihood.

Various alternative specifications of the likelihood function considered in the literature are reported and analyzed in Sevestre and Trognon (1996, pp. 136–138).[21] Considerable simplification, however, can be obtained if, following Nerlove (1971), we are willing to assume that x_{it} follows a well-specified common stationary time-series model for all individuals i. The first term in (13) is $\varphi_{i0} = \beta \sum_{j=0}^{\infty} \gamma^j x_{i,-j}$. Hence, for any stationary processes x_{it}, which may be

---

[21] One interesting possibility discussed by Sevestre and Trognon (1996, pp. 136–138) is to choose y_{i0} a linear function of some *observed* individual-specific time-invariant exogenous variables and a disturbance that is decomposed as the sum of the individual-specific disturbances u_i and a remainder. The first-order equations for maximizing the likelihood then take on a simple recursive form when $\beta = 0$, and permit other simplifications when $\beta \neq 0$. But if we knew that some individual-specific time-invariant observed variables influenced behavior, why not incorporate them directly in (2), the equation to be estimated?

serially correlated,

$$\frac{\varphi_{it}}{\beta} = \gamma \frac{\varphi_{it-1}}{\beta} + x_{it}$$

with variances

$$\sigma_{\varphi_i}^2 = \frac{\beta^2 \sigma_{x_i}^2}{1 - \gamma^2}. \tag{15}$$

If we suppose that the variance of the x_{it} is the same for all i, then the random variable

$$\phi_{it} = \sum_{j=0}^{\infty} \gamma^j \beta x_{it-j}$$

has a well-defined variance that is the same for all i and a function of β, γ, and σ_x^2. This then enters the final term in the unconditional likelihood (14), which now becomes

$$
\begin{aligned}
&\log L\big(\beta, \gamma, \sigma_\mu^2, \sigma_\varepsilon^2 \big| y_{11}, \ldots, y_{NT}; x_{11}, \ldots x_{NT}; y_{10}, \ldots, y_{N0}\big) \\
&= -\frac{N(T+1)}{2} \log 2\pi - \frac{NT}{2} \log \sigma^2 - \frac{N}{2} \log \xi - \frac{N(T-1)}{2} \log \eta \\
&\quad - \frac{1}{2\sigma^2} \sum_{i=1}^{N} \sum_{t=1}^{T} (y_{it}^* - \beta x_{it}^* - \gamma y_{it-1}^*)^2 \\
&\quad - \frac{N}{2} \log \left(\frac{\beta^2 \sigma_x^2}{1 - \gamma^2} + \frac{\sigma_\mu^2}{(1-\gamma)^2} + \frac{\sigma_\varepsilon^2}{1 - \gamma^2} \right) \\
&\quad - \left[\frac{1}{2 \left(\frac{\beta^2 \sigma_x^2}{1-\gamma^2} + \frac{\sigma_\mu^2}{(1-\gamma)^2} + \frac{\sigma_\varepsilon^2}{1-\gamma^2} \right)} \right] \sum_{i=1}^{N} y_{i0}^2.
\end{aligned}
\tag{16}
$$

Concentrating the likelihood function to permit a one- or two-dimensional grid search is no longer possible. Nor is it possible to graph the likelihood surface with respect to variations in all of the parameters; although "slicing" the likelihood function along any hyperplane in the parameter space can reveal the trade-offs between any pair of parameters. If gradient or search procedures yield an interior maximum, the ML estimates obtained are consistent as long as the random variables $\phi_{it} = \sum_{j=0}^{\infty} \gamma^j \beta x_{i,t-j}$ have well-defined variances and covariances, which they will if the x_{it} are generated by a stationary process. It does not really matter what this process is as long as it is stationary. Besides, since the x_{it} are assumed to be exogenous, we really have no basis on which to model their determination and are likely to misspecify this part of the model. In this case, we ought to prefer this kind of "almost full-information" maximum likelihood. Still, we have to assume something about the variance of the x process in order to proceed. I suggest estimating σ_x^2 from the sample data.

To generalize these results to the case in which there are several explanatory variables in addition to the lagged value of the dependent variable, assume that X_{it} follows a stationary VAR process and replace βx_{it}^* by $X_{it}^* \beta$ and $\beta^2 \sigma_x^2$ by $\beta' \Sigma_{xx} \beta$ in the preceding formula.

4. EMPIRICAL EVIDENCE ON THE COMPARATIVE PERFORMANCE OF DIFFERENT PANEL DATA METHODS

To examine the effects of the econometric methods employed on the finding of growth-rate convergence or the lack of it, I initially used data on ninety-four countries for the period 1960–1985, and a subsample of twenty-two OECD countries, from the Penn World Tables 5.6, publicly available from the NBER website at ftp://nber.harvard.edu/pub/. This is the same data set that has been used in dozens of previous studies. Following Islam (1995), s and n were computed as quinquennial means over the preceding five-year span for the years 1965, 1970, 1975, 1980, and 1985; y was taken as the value reported in that year and in 1960 for the lagged value applicable to 1965. The results of the six methods applied to these data are reported in Table 7.1 for the usual undifferenced model. Table 7.2 reports the results for the country-specific trends model that requires differencing to reduce the process to stationarity. In this case, the conditional- and unconditional-likelihood functions are defined for the first difference of the original data.

I have listed the regression methods in the order in which the corresponding estimates of γ appear in the inequality of Sevestre and Trognon (1996) (Equation 9). These estimates are followed by the maximum-likelihood estimates conditional on the initial values y_{i0} or Δy_{i0} and the ML estimates unconditional on the initial values, assuming stationarity of both the processes generating the exogenous variable and real GDP per capita. In a substantive study of growth-rate convergence, it would clearly be important to include additional explanatory variables such as, for example, the stock of human capital, as available at the NBER Internet site, infrastructure investment, and so forth. However, my focus here is on properties of alternative estimators and for this purpose, omission of relevant variables simply increases the unexplained disturbance variance and thus heightens the contrast among alternative estimators.

Turning now to the regression estimates presented in Table 7.1, consider the first four methods. The estimates of γ for the ninety-four-country sample range from a low of 0.72 (fixed-effects regression) to a high of 0.98 (country-means regression) with pooled OLS and FGLS falling in between.[22] For the

---

[22] In the following table, I present the three estimates of ρ discussed as possible candidates for the transformation involved in FGLS for the ninety-four-country sample and the model in levels. It is argued that the Greene-Judge estimate is sharply biased downward and prone to be negative; similarly, the argument Nickell gives with reference to the downward bias in the coefficient of the lagged dependent variable in a fixed-effects regression suggests that the

OECD countries, the range is 0.76 to 0.93. The implied speed of convergence thus ranges from 90 percent in thirty-five years to 90 percent in 570 years. None could be characterized as evidence of reasonably rapid convergence. All of the estimates γ satisfy the Sevestre–Trognon inequality, although the regressions contain an exogenous explanatory variable in contrast to the case considered by Sevestre and Trognon. Pooled OLS and FGLS also stand in the order predicted by the Sevestre-Trognon results. While it is tempting to infer that FGLS provides a tighter upper bound to the true value of γ than the pooled OLS regression estimate, the temptation should be resisted. The FGLS estimates are doubly inconsistent: they are based on an inconsistent estimate of ρ reflecting the inconsistency of the estimates of the residual variance and the fixed effects depending on the regressions from which they are derived. Not only is the estimated value of β sensitive to the method of estimation, but also the estimate of α, the elasticity of output with respect to capital stock in the production function, is extremely so, reflecting the dependence of the estimated value on the coefficient of the lagged dependent variable, γ. This parameter should estimate approximately (1 – the share of labor in the real GDP). It is clear that all of the estimates of α are wide of the mark. If, therefore, one were to infer policy implications from this parameter, it could be seriously misleading.

The most interesting estimates are those for conditional and unconditional maximum likelihood presented as Methods 5 and 6 in Tables 7.1 and 7.2 for the level model and the first-difference model, respectively. For the model in levels and the twenty-two-country OECD sample, these estimates differ quite a bit from one another, although unconditional ML is not far from the fixed-effects OLS regression, while conditional ML yields results close to FGLS using the Balestra-Nerlove (1966) first-round estimate of ρ. For the ninety-four-country

---

other coefficients will be biased upward including the variance of the estimated fixed effects. Coupled with a downward bias in the estimate of the residual variance in the fixed-effects regression, this provides an explanation of the extremely high estimates obtained by the Nerlove (1971) method. It is interesting to note that the Balestra-Nerlove estimate, while substantially higher than the GJ estimate (it can never be negative), is nonetheless not too far out of line with the estimate of ρ obtained from the conditional-likelihood function for the OECD countries and for both the conditional and unconditional likelihood for the ninety-four–country sample.

Alternative Estimates of ρ

Method	94 Countries	22 Countries
Balestra-Nerlove (1966)	0.2678	0.4027
Nerlove (1971)	0.7790	0.7038
G-J (1993/88)	0.0983	0.0804
Conditional ML	0.1133	0.4796
Unconditional ML	0.1288	0.7700

Table 7.1. *Parameter Estimates for the Model in Levels Alternative Econometric Analyses*

Method of Analysis	94-Country Sample	22-Country Sample
1 Fixed-Effects OLS		
γ	0.7204 (0.0211)	0.7645 (0.0166)
β	0.1656 (0.0172)	0.1634 (0.0510)
Implied α	0.3719 (0.0278)	0.4096 (0.0783)
Residual Variance	0.0113	0.0020
2 Feasible GLS		
Estimate of ρ used*	0.2675	0.4027
γ	0.9130 (0.0119)	0.8282 (0.0156)
β	0.1520 (0.0135)	0.1913 (0.0422)
Implied α	0.6362 (0.0247)	0.5269 (0.0579)
Residual Variance	0.0213	0.0047
3 Pooled OLS		
γ	0.9487 (0.0090)	0.8857 (0.0125)
β	0.1244 (0.0108)	0.1764 (0.0308)
Implied α	0.7080 (0.0271)	0.6067 (0.0452)
Residual Variance	0.0193	0.0041
4 Country Means OLS		
γ	0.9817 (0.0112)	0.9320 (0.0148)
β	0.0919 (0.0138)	0.1493 (0.0343)
Implied α	0.8339 (0.0704)	0.6870 (0.0593)
Residual Variance	0.0047	0.0580
5 Conditional ML		
ρ	0.1133 (0.0497)	0.4796 (0.1584)
γ	0.9339 (0.0122)	0.8189 (0.0245)
β	0.1370 (0.0131)	0.1908 (0.0438)
Implied α	0.6744 (0.0289)	0.5131 (0.0664)
Residual Variance	0.0194 (0.0013)	0.0052 (0.0012)
6 Unconditional ML		
Estimates of σ_x^2 used	0.0826	0.0069
ρ	0.1288 (0.0456)	0.7700 (0.0731)
γ	0.9385 (0.0105)	0.8085 (0.0228)
β	0.1334 (0.0124)	0.1815 (0.0521)
Implied α	0.6846 (0.0277)	0.4865 (0.0791)
Residual Variance	0.0197 (0.0013)	0.0113 (0.0028)

Notes: Figures in parentheses are standard errors.
*Estimated by the method suggested in Balestra and Nerlove (1966).

sample, the conditional and the unconditional ML estimates differ little from one another. They are close to the pooled OLS regression estimates (a consequence of the fact that the estimated value of ρ is small although significantly different from zero), but are both quite different than any of the inconsistent

Table 7.2. *Parameter Estimates for the Model in First Differences Alternative Econometric Analyses*

Method of Analysis	94-Country Sample	22-Country Sample
1 Fixed-Effects OLS		
γ	0.4007 (0.0375)	0.4544 (0.0611)
β	0.1199 (0.0187)	−0.0126 (0.0637)
Implied α	0.1667 (0.0246)	−0.0237 (0.1209)
Residual Variance	0.0077	0.0014
2 Feasible GLS		
Estimate of ρ used*	0.4866	0.3628
γ	0.4227 (0.0406)	0.5833 (0.0531)
β	0.1520 (0.0135)	0.1913 (0.0422)
Implied α	0.1864 (0.0259)	0.1322 (0.1218)
Residual Variance	0.0213	0.0047
3 Pooled OLS		
γ	0.7031 (0.0328)	0.6237 (0.0453)
β	0.1632 (0.0195)	0.0845 (0.0586)
Implied α	0.3548 (0.0373)	0.1834 (0.1121)
Residual Variance	0.0141	0.0022
4 Country Means OLS		
γ	0.9178 (0.0471)	0.7215 (0.0572)
β	0.1719 (0.0339)	0.1174 (0.0978)
Implied α	0.6763 (0.1263)	0.2965 (0.1873)
Residual Variance	0.0041	0.0005
5 Conditional ML		
ρ	0.2267 (0.0664)	0.0126 (0.0405)
γ	0.4540 (0.0651)	0.6187 (0.0490)
β	0.1368 (0.0208)	0.0815 (0.0601)
Implied α	0.2004 (0.0358)	0.1762 (0.1159)
Residual Variance	0.0122 (0.0009)	0.0021 (0.0003)
6 Unconditional ML		
Estimates of σ_x^2 used	0.0597	0.0058
ρ	0.2335 (0.0632)	0.0936 (0.0696)
γ	0.4364 (0.0578)	0.7254 (0.0512)
β	0.1340 (0.0201)	0.1478 (0.0727)
Implied α	0.1921 (0.0317)	0.3500 (0.1326)
Residual Variance	0.0120 (0.0008)	0.0027 (0.0004)

Notes: Figures in parentheses are standard errors.
*Estimated by the method suggested in Balestra and Nerlove (1966).

regression estimates. The estimates of β are quite insensitive to the method used, presumably because the estimates of γ are not very different; consequently, the implied estimates of α are similar, albeit different for the two samples. While the results for the first-difference model are quite different from those for the levels model, the same pattern of relation between conditional and unconditional estimates emerges.

To understand better the relation between the conditional and the unconditional ML estimates, consider the log of the ratio of the unconditional to the conditional likelihood; that is, the marginal density of y_{i0}:

log{unconditional/conditional likelihood}

$$= -\frac{N}{2}\log 2\pi - \frac{N}{2}\log\left(\frac{\beta^2\sigma_x^2}{1-\gamma^2} + \frac{\rho\sigma^2}{(1-\gamma)^2} + \frac{(1-\rho)\sigma^2}{1-\gamma^2}\right)$$

$$- \left[\frac{1}{2\left(\frac{\beta^2\sigma_x^2}{1-\gamma^2} + \frac{\rho\sigma^2}{(1-\gamma)^2} + \frac{(1-\rho)\sigma^2}{1-\gamma^2}\right)}\right]\sum_{i=1}^{N} y_{i0}^2.$$

Let the sample variance of y_{i0} be var y_0 and let

$$\varphi^2 = \left(\frac{\beta^2\sigma_x^2}{1-\gamma^2} + \frac{\rho\sigma^2}{(1-\gamma)^2} + \frac{(1-\rho)\sigma^2}{1-\gamma^2}\right).$$

Then,

log{unconditional/conditional likelihood} $= f(\varphi^2)$

$$= -\frac{N}{2}\log 2\pi - \frac{N}{2}\log(\varphi^2) - \left[\frac{N\,\text{var}\,y_0}{2\varphi^2}\right].$$

The maxima of the two likelihood functions will occur at about the same values of the parameters on which φ depends when $df(\varphi^2)$ is close to zero, which occurs at $\varphi^2 = \text{var}\,y_0$. At the unconditional ML estimates for the levels model, for example, for the ninety-four-country sample, $\varphi^2 = 0.91$ and var $y_0 = 0.80$, while, for the twenty-two-country sample, $\varphi^2 = 0.25$ and var $y_0 = 0.26$.

Table 7.2 presents parallel results for the first-difference model. Once again, the first four estimates of γ fall in the order to be expected from the Sevestre–Trognon inequality, although they are all lower than for the levels model, in the first three cases much lower, implying much more rapid convergence to equilibrium. The estimates of all the parameters are much different for the twenty-two-country sample and quite variable. Perhaps the most interesting findings, however, are for the conditional and unconditional ML estimates. The estimates of ρ for the ninety-four-country sample are quite close to one another and those for the twenty-two-country sample far apart, but now there is a remarkable reversal of the magnitudes of ρ and γ as between the ninety-four and the twenty-two-country samples: for the former, ρ is about one-half of the estimated value for γ, but in the last case of the twenty-two-country sample, ρ is only a small fraction of the estimated value of γ.

Further insight into the conditional and unconditional likelihood functions for the two samples can be obtained graphically. Having eliminated the constant term by taking deviations from the overall means of all variables, we are

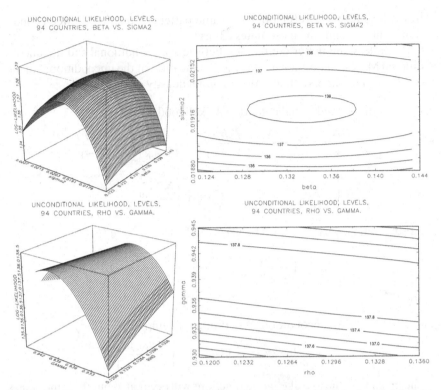

Figure 7.1. Unconditional Likelihood, Ninety-Four-Country Sample, Levels Model. Estimated Values: $\rho = 0.130(0.0417)$; $\gamma = 0.938(0.0105)$; $\beta = 0.134(0.124)$; $\sigma^2 = 0.0197(0.0013)$.

left with four parameters: ρ, γ, β, and σ^2. Figure 7.1 plots the unconditional likelihood function for the ninety-four-country sample, levels model. Figure 7.2 plots the likelihood function for the twenty-two-country sample, levels model. Likelihood functions are plotted in Figures 7.3 and 7.4 for the first-difference model, respectively, for the ninety-four- and twenty-two-country samples. I have plotted both three-dimensional likelihood surfaces for pairs of variables and two-dimensional contours. "Slices" are taken at the likelihood-maximizing values for the parameters not plotted. These plots clearly reveal the implications of the data for the "interactions" between pairs of parameters. Although there are $\binom{5}{2} = 10$ possible pairs to consider, I focus on the crucial pairs: ρ versus γ and β versus σ^2.

Although the likelihood reaches a unique maximum in every case, which is quite well defined, it is clear that there are significant trade-offs between each pair of parameters. In the case of the twenty-two OECD countries, the unconditional ML estimates are precisely determined. As suggested previously, this is because for small N, the weight of the initial observations and the parameters determining them is more substantial than for large cross-sectional

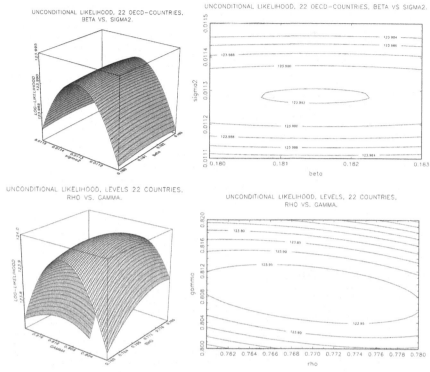

Figure 7.2. Unconditional Likelihood, Twenty-Two-Country Sample, Levels Model. Estimated Values: $\rho = 0.770(0.0731)$; $\gamma = 0.809(0.0228)$; $\beta = 0.182(0.0521)$; $\sigma^2 = 0.0113(0.0028)$.

samples. As indicated the likelihood function is sufficient for the parameters of the model and provides useful insight into what the data tell us about these parameters quite apart from the values that maximize it.

5. CONCLUSIONS

The principal conclusion that can be drawn from this analysis is that, in panel data econometrics, method matters–a lot. Although using a highly simplified Solow (1956) and Swan (1956) model without human capital stocks or infrastructure, I have found estimates of the adjustment parameter significantly different than one in every case, indicating convergence. All of the estimates for the model in levels, however, are so close to one, always greater than 0.7, that convergence to within 90 percent of equilibrium in less than one generation is effectively ruled out. This can hardly be called "convergence" in any relevant sense. Moreover, the estimates range from 0.72 to 0.98, suggesting a convergence range of from thirty-three to over five hundred years, with most clustering around 0.8, underscoring the importance of choice of econometric

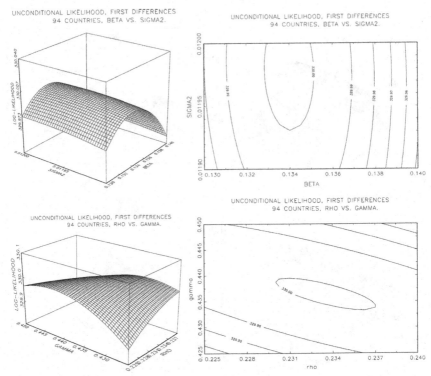

Figure 7.3. Unconditional Likelihood, Ninety-Four-Country Sample, First-Difference Model. Estimated Values: $\rho = 0.234(0.0632)$; $\gamma = 0.436(0.0578)$; $\beta = 0.134(0.0201)$; $\sigma^2 = 0.0120(0.0008)$.

method. When the model is estimated in first-difference form, the estimates of γ are much lower, indicating rapid convergence in the case of the ninety-four-country sample. The method of choice, unconditional ML, yields well-defined and reasonable estimates in every case. Much of the variation in estimates of the speed of convergence appears to be due to trade-offs between the crucial parameter ρ, which measures the importance of unobserved cross-sectional variation relative to total residual variation, and γ, which measures the speed of adjustment. For this reason, it is especially important to introduce other relevant variables, such as infrastructure investment and human capital stock, in order to reduce the importance of *unobserved* cross-sectional variation.

A second important finding is that the Sevestre-Trognon inequality, proved only for the case $\beta = 0$, and then only asymptotically, holds for all the examples presented. Indeed, fixed-effects OLS always yields estimates of the adjustment parameter at the extreme low end of the range of estimates obtained. The "bias" of fixed-effects models in the estimation of dynamic panel models is apparent. In this context, the use of such methods biases a test for convergence

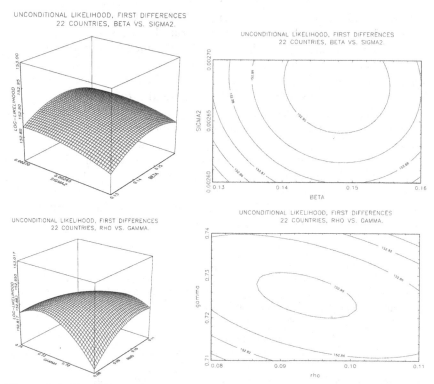

Figure 7.4. Unconditional Likelihood, Twenty-Two-Country Sample, First-Difference Model. Estimated Values: $\rho = 0.094(0.0696)$; $\gamma = 0.725(0.0512)$; $\beta = 0.148(0.0727)$; $\sigma^2 = 0.0027(0.0004)$.

or, more appropriately, rapid convergence, toward finding it. Fixed-effects models, however, are widely used, in part because they are the basis for two-round FGLS estimators, and because computer packages for panel data analysis incorporate an extremely misguided suggestion for estimating ρ, guaranteed to yield extremely low or even negative values of this parameter. These packages should be avoided, and, if they are used and do yield a negative estimate, it should not be concluded that the model is misspecified or that fixed effects are a preferable alternative. Fixed-effects OLS remains badly biased in a dynamic context irrespective of whether the packaged routines fail.

I do find, however, that FGLS, using the Balestra-Nerlove (1966) estimates of ρ, which can never be negative, always lie between the fixed-effects OLS estimates and the pooled OLS estimates, which are known to yield upwardly biased estimates of γ. It is not appropriate to conclude that these FGLS estimates, however, represent a tighter upper bound to the true value of γ, since they are doubly inconsistent estimates and may lie below the true value. This is underscored by the finding that both conditional and unconditional ML yield different estimates of ρ and γ, sometimes higher and sometimes lower than FGLS. The interaction between ρ and γ is crucial in this regard.

Finally, maximum likelihood, unconditional on the initial observations, assuming them to be stationary and generated by the same dynamic process we are trying to estimate and assuming the exogenous variables also to be stationary, is feasible and indeed a viable alternative to conventional regression methods or conditional ML. Use of such methods will, however, generally involve removal of the overall means of all variables prior to analysis and omission of a constant term and may also involve differencing to remove deterministic or stochastic trends. Formulation of the unconditional-likelihood function is somewhat more complicated in the case of differenced variables but, as demonstrated, quite feasible nonetheless. The unconditional and simpler conditional ML method may yield similar results under certain circumstances, but cannot generally be expected to do so.

References

Arellano, M., and S. Bond (1991), "Some Tests of Specification for Panel Data: Monte Carlo Evidence and an Application to Employment Equations," *Review of Economic Studies, 58*: pp. 277–297.

Balestra, P., and M. Nerlove (1966), "Pooling Cross-Section and Time-Series Data in the Estimation of a Dynamic Economic Model: The Demand for Natural Gas," *Econometrica, 34*: pp. 585–612.

Barnard, G. A. (1949), "Statistical Inference," *Journal of the Royal Statistical Society, Series B, 11*: pp. 115–149.

———— (1951), "The Theory of Information," *Journal of the Royal Statistical Society, Series B, 13*: pp. 46–64.

———— (1966); "The Use of the Likelihood Function in Statistical Practice," *Proceedings of the Fifth Berkeley Symposium on Mathematical Statistics and Probability, 1*: pp. 27–40.

———— (1967), "The Bayesian Controversy in Statistical Inference," *Journal of the Institute of Actuaries, 93*: pp. 229–69.

Barnard, G. A., G. M. Jenkins, and C. B. Winsten (1962), "Likelihood Inference and Time Series," (with discussion), *Journal of the Royal Statistical Society, Series A, 125*: pp. 321–375.

Barro, R. J. (1991), "Economic Growth in a Cross-Section of Countries," *Quarterly Journal of Economics, 106*: pp. 407–443.

Barro, R. J., and Jong-Wha Lee (1993), "International Comparisons of Educational Attainment," NBER Working Paper No. 4349.

Barro, R. J., and X. Sala-i-Martin (1995), *Economic Growth*, New York: McGraw-Hill.

Baumol, W. (1986), "Productivity Growth, Convergence, and Welfare: What the Long-Run Data Show," *American Economic Review, 76*: pp. 1072–1085.

Bernard, A. B., and S. N. Durlauf (1995), "Convergence in International Output," *Journal of Applied Econometrics, 10*: pp. 97–108.

——— (1996), "Interpreting Tests of the Convergence Hypothesis," *Journal of Econometrics, 71*: pp. 161–173.

Binder, M., and M. H. Pesaran (1996), "Stochastic Growth," Working Paper No. 19–18, Department of Economics, University of Maryland.

Birnbaum, A. (1962), "On the Foundations of Statistical Inference," (with discussion), *Journal of the American Statistical Association, 57*: pp. 269–306.

Caselli, F., G. Esquivel, and F. Lefort (1996), "Reopening the Convergence Debate: A New Look at Cross-Country Growth Empirics," *Journal of Economic Growth, 1*: pp. 363–389.

Chamberlain, G. (1984), "Panel Data," in Z. Griliches and M. Intriligator (eds.), *Handbook of Econometrics, II*, Amsterdam: Elsevier, pp. 1247–1313.

Crépon, B., and J. Mairesse (1996), "The Chamberlain Approach," in L. Mátyás and P. Sevestre, *The Econometrics of Panel Data: Handbook of Theory and Applications*, 2nd ed., Boston: Kluwer, pp. 323–391.

de la Fuente, A. (1997), "The Empirics of Growth and Convergence: A Selective Review," *Journal of Economic Dynamics and Control, 21*: pp. 23–73.

Diebold, F. X., and M. Nerlove (1990), "Unit Roots in Economic Time Series: A Selective Survey," in T. B. Fomby and G. F. Rhodes (Eds.), *Advances in Econometrics, Vol. VIII: Co-integration, Spurious Regressions, and Unit Roots*, Greenwich, CT: JAI Press.

Edwards, A. W. F. (1972) *Likelihood*, New york, Cambridge University Press.

Fisher, R. A. (1922), "On the Mathematical Foundations of Theoretical Statistics," *Philosophical Transactions of the Royal Society of London, Series A, 222*: 309–368.

——— (1925), "Theory of Statistical Estimation," *Proceedings of the Cambridge Philosophical Society*, pp. 700–725.

Greene, W. (1993), *Econometric Analysis*, 2nd ed., New York: Macmillan.

Holtz-Eakin, D., W. Newey, and H. Rosen (1988), "Estimating Vector Autoregressions with Panel Data," *Econometrica, 56*: pp. 1371–1395.

Islam, N. (1995a), "Growth Empires: A Panel Data Approach," *Quarterly Journal of Economics, 110*: pp. 1127–1170.

——— (1995b), "Convergence: Variations in Concept and Results," Unpublished, International Institute for Advanced Studies, Cambridge, MA.

Judge, G., R. C. Hill, W. Griffiths, H. Lütkepohl, and T-C. Lee (1988), *Introduction to the Theory and Practice of Econometrics*, 2nd ed., New York: Wiley.

Kiviet, Jan F. (1995), "On the Bias, Inconsistency, and Efficiency of Various Estimators in Dynamic Panel Models," *Journal of Econometrics, 68*: pp. 53–78.

Knight, M., N. Loazya, and D. Villaneuva (1993), "Testing the Neoclassical Growth Model," *IMF Staff Papers, 40*: pp. 512–541.

Lee, K., M. H. Pesaran, and R. Smith (1997), "Growth and Convergence in a Multi-Country Empirical Stochastic Solow Model," *Journal of Applied Econometrics, 12*: pp. 357–392.

Lindsey, J. K. (1996), *Parametric Statistical Inference*, Oxford: Clarendon Press.

Loayza, N. (1994), "A Test of the International Convergence Hypothesis Using Panel Data," Policy Research Working Paper No. 1333, The World Bank.

Maddala, G. S. (1971), "The Use of Variance Component Models in Pooling Cross-Section and Time-Series Data," *Econometrica, 39*: pp. 341–358.

Mankiw, N. G., D. Romer, and D. N. Weil (1992), "A Contribution to the Empirics of Economic Growth," *Quarterly Journal of Economics, 108*: pp. 407–437.

Mátyás, L., and P. Sevestre (1996), *The Econometrics of Panel Data: Handbook of Theory and Applications*, 2nd ed., Boston: Kluwer Academic Publishers.

Mundlak, Y. (1978), "On the Pooling of Cross-Section and Time-Series Data," *Econometrica, 46*: pp. 69–86.

Nerlove, M. (1971), "Further Evidence on the Estimation of Dynamic Economic Relations from a Time Series of Cross Sections," *Econometrica, 39*: pp. 359–382.

—— (1996), "Growth-Rate Convergence, Fact or Artifact? An Essay in Panel Data Econometrics," Paper presented to the Sixth Conference on Panel Data Econometrics, Amsterdam, June 28–29.

—— (1997), "Likelihood Inference for Dynamic Panel Models." *L'Annales d'Economie et de Statistique de l'INSEE* (forthcoming).

Nerlove, M., and P. Balestra (1996), "Formulation and Estimation of Econometric Models for Panel Data," in L. Mátyás and P. Sevestre (1996).

Nerlove, M., and L. K. Raut (1997), "Growth Models with Endogenous Population: A General Framework," in M. R. Rosenzweig and O. Stark (Eds.), *The Handbook of Family and Population Economics*, pp. 1117–1174. New York: Elsevier Scientific Publishers.

Nickell, S. (1981), "Biases in Dynamic Models with Fixed Effects," *Econometrica, 49*: pp. 1417–1426.

Quah, D. (1996), "Empirics for Economic Growth and Convergence," *European Economic Review, 40*: 1353–1375.

Sevestre, P., and A. Trognon (1983), "Propiétés de grands échantillons d'une classe d'estimateurs des modéles autoregréssives à erreurs compossées," *Annales de l'INSEE, 50*: pp. 25–49.

—— (1996), "Linear Dynamic Models," in Mátyás and Sevestre (1996), pp. 126–144.

Solow, R. M. (1956), "A Contribution to the Theory of Economic Growth," *Quarterly Journal of Economics, 70*: pp. 65–94.

Swan, T. W. (1956), "Economic Growth and Capital Accumulation," *Economic Record, 32*: pp. 324–361.

Trognon, Alain (1978), "Miscellaneous Asymptotic Properties of Ordinary Least-Squares and Maximum-Likelihood Methods in Dynamic Error-Components Models," *Annales de l'INSEE, 30–31*: pp. 631–657.

EIGHT

Likelihood Inference for Dynamic Panel Models[1]

Preface

It is, I think, important to emphasize the relevance of the likelihood approach in *applied* econometrics. Every real-world problem is, to a greater or lesser extent, unique. The likelihood method is a general-purpose tool, but one of great flexibility and adaptability to the kinds of specific problems universally encountered in serious empirical econometrics. Moreover, it leads the user naturally to focus on the economics of the data-generation process and, in some respects more importantly, on how the data have been collected and processed before the econometrician has access to them.

The likelihood principle essentially holds that the likelihood function is the sole basis for inference. The principle is very closely associated with the problem of parametric inference. Indeed, one hardly finds any discussion of it outside of the context of traditional parametric statistical models and their use, and I would be hard put even to give a clear definition of the concept in a general nonparametric context. It is also closely associated with the method of maximum-likelihood estimation, both historically and conceptually, and, while the maximum or maxima of the likelihood function are, in some sense, its most interesting or significant point(s), it or they are not the only point(s). Taken seriously, the likelihood principle suggests that one might want to consider other points, for example, in the vicinity of a maximum particularly with respect to curvature, but farther away as well. The implications of the likelihood principle for the estimation of dynamic panel models are explored in this chapter. Correct formulation of the likelihood unconditional on the initial observations and graphical methods are emphasized. Perhaps the greatest benefit of looking at the likelihood function at points in the parameter space away from the likelihood-maximizing values is to reveal the fragility of inferences based on the ML and other estimates that may superficially appear to be rather precise.

[1] Reprinted with permission from *Annales d'Économie et de Statistique, 55–56*: pp. 370–410, 1999.

The *likelihood principle* is applied to the problem of inference in dynamic panel models. The principle states that the likelihood function contains "... *all* the information which the data provide concerning the relative merits of ..." alternative parametric hypotheses. The usual asymptotic theory of maximum likelihood is based on a quadratic approximation to the likelihood function in the nearby neighborhood of a local maximum of the function. One needs to look at the entire function more broadly in order to ascertain the true significance of the data for the hypotheses under consideration, not only because of the possibilities of multiple local maxima and boundary solutions, but also because the data are typically differentially informative with respect to different regions of the parameter space. In order to handle cases in which the likelihood function depends on more than two parameters, the devices of "concentrating" and of "slicing" or sectioning the function in the direction of a hyperplane or surface reflecting the variation of all but two of the parameters are introduced. The likelihood functions for two basic dynamic panel models: (1) a model involving individual-specific effects which reflect the influence of latent time-persistent variables; (2) a model involving individual-specific time trends which reflect the nonstationarity introduced by trending latent variables, are derived. The methods are applied to the analysis of cross-country economic growth. The findings demonstrate the power and feasibility of general methods of likelihood inference, especially to reveal problems of inference and areas of ignorance.

Likelihood Inference for Dynamic Panel Models

Marc Nerlove*

What has now appeared is that the mathematical concept of probability is ... inadequate to express our mental confidence or diffidence in making ... inferences, and that the mathematical quantity which usually appears to be appropriate for measuring our order of preference among different possible populations does not in fact obey the laws of probability. To distinguish it from probability, I have used the term "Likelihood" to designate this quantity; since both the words "Likelihood" and "probability" are loosely used in common speech to cover both kinds of relationship.

R. A. Fisher,
Statistical Methods for Research Workers, 1925.

Within the framework of a statistical model, all the information which the data provide concerning the relative merits of two hypotheses is contained in the likelihood ratio of those hypotheses on the data. ... For a continuum of hypotheses, this principle asserts that the likelihood function contains all the necessary information.

A. W. F. Edwards,
Likelihood, 1972.

You are living on a Plane. What you style Flatland is the vast level surface of what I may call a fluid, or in, the top of which you and your countrymen move about, without rising above or falling below it.

* M. Nerlove: University of Maryland.
This paper was prepared for the Seventh Conference on Panel Data Econometrics, 19–20 June 1997, Paris. The research on which it is based was supported by the Maryland Agricultural Experiment Station.

I am indebted to G. S. Maddala for his comments, to two anonymous referees for theirs, and to A. Meyer for numerous helpful suggestions and for her wise expository counsel. J. Suh provided able computational assistance in connection with earlier drafts. I am especially indebted to P. Sevestre, A. Trognon and an anonymous referee for pointing out an error in my original formulation of the likelihood function and suggesting appropriate revision.

I am not a plane Figure, but a Solid. You call me a Circle; but in reality I am not a Circle, but an infinite number of Circles, of size varying from a Point to a Circle of thirteen inches in diameter, one placed on the top of the other. When I cut through your plane as I am now doing, I make in your plane a section which you, very rightly, call a Circle. For even a Sphere – which is my proper name in my own country – if he manifest himself at all to an inhabitant of Flatland – must needs manifest himself as a Circle.

E.A. Abbott,
Flatland, 1884.

It was six men of Indostan
To learning much inclined,
Who went to see the Elephant
(Though all of them were blind),
That each by observation
Might satisfy his mind.
The First approached the Elephant,
And happening to fall
Against his broad and sturdy side,
At once began to bawl:
"God bless me! but the Elephant
Is very like a wall!"
The Second, feeling of the tusk,
Cried, "Ho! what have we here
So very round and smooth and sharp?
To me 'tis mighty clear
This wonder of an Elephant
Is very like a spear!"

The Third approached the animal,
And happening to take
The squirming trunk within his hands,
Thus boldly up and spake:
"I see," quoth he, "the Elephant
Is very like a snake!"
The Fourth reached out an eager hand,
And felt about the knee.
"What most this wondrous beast is like
Is mighty plain, "quoth he;
"Tis clear enough the Elephant
Is very like a tree!"
The Fifth, who chanced to touch the ear.
Said: "E'en the blindest man
Can tell what this resembles most;
Deny the fact who can
This marvel of an Elephant
Is very like a fan!"

The Sixth no sooner had begun
About the beast to grope,
Than, seizing on the swinging tail
That fell within his scope,
"I see," quoth he, "the Elephant
Is very like a rope!"
And so these men of Indostan
Disputed loud and long.
Each in his own opinion
Exceeding stiff and strong,
Though each was partly in the right,
And all were in the wrong!
Moral: So oft in theologic wars.
The disputants, I ween,
Rail on in utter ignorance
Of what each other mean,
And prate about an Elephant
Not one of them has seen!

John Godfrey Saxe,
"The Blind Men and the Elephant: A Hindoo Tale," 1880.

1. INTRODUCTION

This paper applies the likelihood principle of Fisher (1921, 1922, 1925, and 1932), Barnard (1949, 1951, 1966, and 1967), Barnard, Jenkins, and Winsten (1962), and Birnbaum (1962) to the problem of inference in dynamic panel models.[1] Beginning with Chamberlain (1984), an extensive literature on non-likelihood methods for estimation and inference about dynamic panel models has emerged; much of it is surveyed in Sevestre and Trognon (1996) and by Baltagi (1995, Chapter 8, pp. 125–148). I do not propose to survey this literature here or to compare the alternative estimates suggested with the results of likelihood inference, although such comparison would no doubt be highly

---

[1] Although *likelihood* and inference from likelihood resembles Laplace's method of *inverse probability* (Laplace, 1774–1814), which provides the principal basis for the Bayesian approach to inference, Fisher (1932) was at great pains to distinguish the two, and, indeed, was sharply critical of the use of prior distributions, especially of the use of "*noninformative*" priors to represent ignorance.

useful. Much of what I have to say represents an application of the ideas contained in Bhargava and Sargan (1983), which have been unfortunately neglected in recent discussions of estimating dynamic panel models.

In Subsection 1, I develop the principle that the likelihood function contains "... *all* the information which the data provide concerning the relative merits of ..." alternative parametric hypotheses. The usual asymptotic theory of maximum likelihood is shown to be based on a quadratic approximation to the likelihood function in the nearby neighborhood of a local maximum of the function. I argue that one needs to look at the entire function more broadly in order to ascertain the true significance of the data for the hypotheses under consideration, not only because of the possibilities of multiple local maxima and boundary solutions, but also because the data are typically differentially informative with respect to different regions of the parameter space. In order to handle cases in which the likelihood function depends on more than two parameters, I introduce the devices of "*concentrating*" and of "*slicing*," or sectioning the function in the direction of a hyperplane or surface reflecting the variation of all but two of the parameters.

In Subsection 2, I derive the likelihood functions for two basic dynamic panel models: (1) a model involving individual-specific effects that reflect the influence of latent time-persistent variables; and (2) a model involving individual-specific time trends that reflect the nonstationarity introduced by trending latent variables. In developing the likelihood functions for these two leading cases, I argue for reduction of models of type (2) to stationary models of type (1) by differencing. In this case, however, it is necessary to modify the likelihood functions to reflect the effects of differencing on the unobserved residual variation. The differenced model now has a different interpretation from the original models of type (1) in that the individual-specific effects now represent individual-specific trend slopes. I further argue that in stationary cases, which include both levels models and differenced models, the initial observations of the dependent variables contain useful information on the process that must have generated those observations in the past, before the panel was observed, and that this information depends positively on their variance and on the number of individuals in the panel, and is thus of particular importance for "*shallow*" panels.[2] A distinction is made between treating the initial observations on the dependent variable in a dynamic panel model as

---

[2] Maddala (1971) discusses a similar problem, pooling cross-section and time-series data, from a Bayesian point of view. The analysis with diffuse priors is similar in a number of respects to that presented here based on the likelihood principle. Some of Maddala's results are discussed later. As is the case with much of the literature in this area, however, those about likelihood or maximum likelihood are based on a likelihood function that fixes the initial observations. Breusch's (1987) remarkable result, for example, about the convergence of iterated generalized least squares to the ML estimates holds only for the case in which the likelihood function is formulated holding the initial observations fixed in the dynamic case.

fixed (*i.e.*, as exogenously given) and conditioning on them, assuming, as suggested in Bhargava and Sargan (1983), that their values are generated by the same data-generating process (DGP) as we are attempting to estimate from the observed panel data sample.

Finally, in Subsection 3, to assess the feasibility and power of likelihood methods for inference about dynamic panel models, I use data on ninety-four countries for the period 1960–1985, and a subsample of twenty-two OECD countries, from the Penn World Tables 5.6. The twenty-two-country sample consists of primarily European countries, all highly developed and tied together by a network of trading relations; the ninety-four-country sample is much more heterogeneous, consisting of the aforementioned twenty-two plus seventy-two additional countries ranging from Mozambique and Haiti to the former "*Asian Tigers*." This is the same data set that has been used in dozens of previous studies.

In a previous paper (Nerlove, 1996), I compared some commonly used methods of estimation in dynamic panel models with one another. I showed that many of the earlier findings are probably statistical artifacts arising from biases in the econometric methods employed. Here, I focus especially on the need to take advantage of the relatively large amount of information contained in the initial observations and the desirability of exploring the possibility of differing country-specific trends. Using a simple variant of the Solow-Swan growth model widely used in recent studies of the convergence process, I demonstrate here that likelihood methods that take account of individual-specific trends and of the information present in the initial observations, whether in levels or in first-differenced form, lead to similar results regarding the convergence hypothesis, but rather different conclusions with respect to the amount of unobserved individual specific variability relative to the overall residual variance from the growth relationships. The results suggest that, in the case of the individual-specific trend model, provided one takes account of the way in which initial observations are generated, the data may simply be pooled without changing the inference about the rate of convergence. But the results support the contention that fixed-effects models should be avoided because their use amounts to throwing away important information contained in the cross-sectional variation of the exogenous explanatory variables and of the initial values of the dependent variable. The analysis demonstrates the power and feasibility of general methods of likelihood inference, especially to reveal problems of inference and areas of ignorance.

2. THE LIKELIHOOD PRINCIPLE

Although clearly implied in what Fisher wrote in the 1920s (1922, 1925), the likelihood principle, which essentially holds that the likelihood function is the sole basis for inference, did not come into prominence until the 1950s and 1960s, principally through the work of Barnard, Birnbaum, and Edwards (see the references cited later; Barndorff-Nielsen (1988) and Lindsey (1996), written largely in reaction to both the classical Neyman-Pearson (frequentist) and the Bayesian approaches to inference [Jeffereys, 1934, 1961; see also Press, 1989]).

A statistical model consists of a random vector $x \in X$ of observations having a joint distribution function $F(x; \theta)$, with corresponding density $f(x; \theta)$, depending on the unknown parameters $\theta \in \Theta$. It is assumed that F is known. The *likelihood function* determined by any given outcome x is defined as the function on Θ equal to $cf(x; \theta)$, where c is an arbitrary positive constant that may depend on x but does not depend on θ. Two likelihood functions defined on the same parameter space Θ, whether arising from the same "experiment" or from different "experiments," E_1 and E_2, are *equivalent* if their ratio is positive and independent of Θ for all $\theta \in \Theta$ except possibly at points at which both functions are zero (so that the ratio is undefined).

The *likelihood principle* asserts that for a given experiment E, the evidential meaning of any outcome x, for inference regarding θ is contained entirely in the likelihood function determined by x. All other aspects of how the data may have been generated are irrelevant (*e.g.*, the sample space), provided, of course, that the sample space itself doesn't depend on θ. It follows that if two "experiments," E_1, and E_2, have pdf's $f(x, \theta)$ and $g(y, \theta)$, respectively, and if for some particular outcomes, x^* of E_1 and y^* of E_2,

$$f(x^*, \theta) = h(x^*, y^*)g(y^*, \theta), h(x^*, y^*) > 0, \quad \text{for all } \theta \in \Theta,$$

then these outcomes must result in the same inference about θ.

Birnbaum (1962) derives the likelihood principle from the sufficiency principle and a still more basic assumption, the so-called *conditionality principle*. This principle states that if an "experiment" involving θ is chosen from a collection of possible experiments, *independently of* θ, then any experiment not chosen is irrelevant to the statistical analysis. The conditionality principle makes clear the implication of the likelihood principle that any inference should depend only on the outcome observed and not on any other outcome we might have observed and, thus, sharply contrasts the method of likelihood inference from the Neyman-Pearson, or frequentist, approach, in which inference does depend crucially on a hypothetical sequence of experiments, the outcome of but one of which is observed. In particular, questions of unbiasedness, minimum variance, consistency, and the like, and the whole apparatus of confidence intervals, significance levels, and power of tests, are ruled out of bounds. While maximum-likelihood estimation does satisfy the likelihood principle (and thus sufficiency and conditionality), the frequentist assessment in terms of asymptotic properties is irrelevant. In this paper, I apply the likelihood principle to the problem of inference about the parameters of dynamic panel models and try to make clear the role of the maximum of the likelihood function and its Hessian evaluated at the maximum in approximating the whole of the likelihood function for purposes of inference.

The likelihood principle is clearly incomplete from the standpoint of inference since it nowhere states how the evidential meaning of the likelihood function is to be determined. To the principle, therefore, "likelihoodists" generally append the *method of support* (a term coined by Jeffereys, 1934). The *support function* is defined as the natural logarithm of the likelihood function. Since the likelihood function incorporates an arbitrary constant, the support function is defined only up to the addition of an arbitrary constant. Conventionally, this constant is often taken to be the value that makes support at the maximum equal zero. In multiplicative terms, this is equivalent to normalizing the likelihood function by dividing it by its value at the maximum. Only relative support for a particular parameter value over another can be interpreted in any case, so the constant disappears when looking at the difference between support values of different parameter values. The *method of maximum support* is the *method of maximum likelihood*. But the interpretation of the parameter value that yields this maximum and of the inverse of the negative of the Hessian at the point of maximum is different than in the frequentist interpretation in terms of asymptotic properties. The likelihoodist interpretation of these magnitudes is in terms of a quadratic approximation to the support function in the neighborhood of its maximum.

It is clear that the difference in the value of the support function at two different values of a parameter has the significance that the value for which support is greater is more consistent with the observed data than the value of lesser support. What we have is essentially a likelihood ratio test without the frequentist apparatus of asymptotic chi-square. It is also clear that the values of parameters for which maximum support is obtained (i.e., the maximum-likelihood estimates), especially if the maximum is unique, have a special significance in relation to other possible values. Moreover, how sharply defined such a maximum of the likelihood function is, if a unique maximum exists, is also clearly relevant to any inference we may wish to draw. On the negative side, a poorly behaved likelihood function (e.g., one having ridges of equal likelihood, many local maxima, or a maximum on the boundary of an *a priori* admissible region of the parameter space) is generally indicative of an incompletely or ill-formulated underlying statistical model.

From a frequentist point of view, what matters about the likelihood function is only its maximum and curvature in the neighborhood of the maximum, and all the desirable properties and the assessment of the reliability of the maximum-likelihood estimates are only asymptotic. Greene (1993, pp. 111–116) gives a very brief discussion of these matters; Davidson and MacKinnon (1993, Chapter 8, pp. 243–287) give a more complete and rigorous discussion; a more intuitive discussion with many econometric examples is given by Cramer (1986). That only the maximum and the Hessian at the maximum are all that matters from a frequentist point of view is perhaps not surprising in view of the fact that for the mean of a normal distribution, the quadratic approximation is exact (see the following discussion) and because of the central limit theorem in its many forms many estimators, including ML estimators in regular cases, tend to normality in distribution.

When we are dealing with only one or two parameters, looking at the whole of the likelihood or support function is feasible, although some summary measures may be helpful. For three or more parameters, however, it is no longer possible to examine the whole of the support function. In this case, concentrating the likelihood function and corresponding support function may be helpful, and looking at a quadratic approximation to the support function in the neighborhood of the maximum may be revealing.

First, we can section or slice the support function along the plane of all but one or two of the parameters; in the case in which all but one of the parameters has been eliminated in this way, we are back to a two-dimensional plot. When we have done this for all but two parameters, we can plot a three-dimensional surface and associated contours of equal support. The latter is particularly useful if we want to examine how two of the parameters interact with one another. It would be natural to choose the values of all but one or two of the parameters equal to the maximizing values. Proceeding in this way amounts to looking at the *concentrated likelihood function* and associated *concentrated support function*.

A second but not mutually exclusive alternative is to follow the lead of those frequentists who maximize likelihood functions and characterize the entire likelihood function by the point in the parameter space at which the maximum is attained and a quadratic approximation to the entire function at that point. The point of maximum support, particularly if unique, obviously has considerable intuitive appeal. A quadratic approximation at that point is likely to be pretty good if we want to consider only points quite nearby, and has the added advantage of being directly interpretable from a frequentist point of view in terms of the information matrix of asymptotic maximum-likelihood theory. The disadvantage is that except for cases, such as the mean or regression function associated with a normal distribution, for which the quadratic approximation is exact, the approximating function may be quite wide of the mark. Moreover, when the likelihood function has two or more local maxima, which may be far apart, the inferential significance of this fact may be lost if one focuses exclusively on the behavior of the function in the vicinity of the highest maximum. Boundary maxima, which are of frequent occurrence in dynamic panel problems, also present a special problem from a frequentist point of view since the asymptotic theory is no longer applicable. But from the standpoint of likelihood inference, there is nothing that stops us from comparing the value of support at the boundary values of the parameters with other values in the interior of the permissible region.

What I am suggesting for viewing the support function in a multiparameter case is essentially what one typically does in viewing a three-dimensional surface when we look at a contour map: we take a slice through the surface in the direction parallel to the plane of the two arguments. A slice can, of course, be thought of more generally as any lower dimensional hyperplane, whether parallel to the plane defined by the axes of a subset of arguments or in some other direction. In four dimensions, a slice in any two-dimensional plane, which eliminates all the arguments but two, yields a surface of the functional values in three dimensions. Fixing, or conditioning on, the values of any subset of parameters is obviously a way of defining a particular hyperplane corresponding to the remaining parameters; in this instance, those values that maximize support, given the values corresponding to a point chosen on the hyperplane, on which we want to view the support, assume a special significance. In discussions of maximum likelihood, *concentration of the likelihood function* with respect to a subset of parameters corresponds to selecting a hyperplane for the remaining parameters in just this way. Sometimes we say that we are "maximizing out" the deselected parameters. In the method of maximum likelihood, for example, it frequently turns out that, given the values of one or two of the parameters, it is very easy to maximize with respect to the remaining ones.

3. LIKELIHOOD FUNCTIONS FOR TWO BASIC DYNAMIC PANEL MODELS

In this subsection, I present a method of maximum-likelihood estimation based on the density of the observations *unconditional on the initial or starting values of the dependent variable, in which the same process as that under investigation is assumed to generate the data prior to the point at which we begin to observe them.*[3] I argue more generally for methods of inference that look at more than

---

[3] Anderson and Hsiao (1981, 1982) have also considered unconditional ML and its relation to conditional ML for a number of different cases. See also Hsiao (1986). In Anderson and Hsiao (1981), they study a simple autoregressive process with additive term specific to the unit under the following alternative assumptions about the initial conditions: (a) initial state fixed; (b) initial state random; (c) the unobserved individual effect independent of the unobserved dynamic process with the initial value fixed; and (d) the unobserved individual effect independent of the unobserved dynamic process with the initial value random. The problem is greatly complicated by the presence of exogenous regressors and is studied in Anderson and Hsiao (1982) for panel data both with and without lagged dependent variables. The same four cases are studied as for the simple autoregression considered in the 1981 paper, but a number of different assumptions are made about the exogenous explanatory variable. The key distinction is between time-varying and time invariant exogenous variables. Clearly, to examine asymptotic properties, some assumptions have to be made about the behavior of the exogenous variables, which is a tricky matter since, being exogenous, we effectively deny knowledge of how they might be generated; however, see my solution later. The important point is that none of the four alternative assumptions about the initial state of the system being observed presupposes that it must have been in operation prior to the initial observation. Bhargava and Sargan (1983) suggest essentially the same approach as that developed here. Because, however, they focus on the maximum of the likelihood function and do not compare their approach with those that were then and are still now more standard, their work has not had the recognition it deserves. Such a reconsideration and extension is, I hope, the contribution of this paper.

just the maximum of the likelihood function, on the basis of the *likelihood principle* of Fisher (1922, 1925). This approach fully takes into account what information the initial conditions contain about how the process has operated in the past and is thus of special relevance to short time-dimension ("shallow") panels. I extend this method to the case of country-specific trends. These make the underlying processes being investigated nonstationary, but with simple forms of nonstationarity that can be removed by differencing the data.

A good summary of the current state of knowledge about the properties of various estimators in dynamic panel models is contained in Sevestre and Trognon (1992, 2nd ed., 1996). Trognon (1978) was the first to show the possible inconsistency of maximum likelihood holding the initial observations fixed. Nickel (1981) shows the inconsistency of the estimates of the fixed-effects in a dynamic panel model. Kiviet (1995) derives exact results for the bias of leading estimators. I will assume a random-effects model for the disturbance for the reasons set forth in Nerlove and Balestra (1996) and because fixed effects can be viewed as a special case from the standpoint of estimation.

Even though ML may yield inconsistent estimates when the non-negligible probability of a boundary solution is taken into account, it is nonetheless true that the likelihood function summarizes the information contained in the data about the parameters. Indeed, from a likelihood point of view, a boundary maximum is especially informative with respect to what the data reveal about the model assumed. From a conventional Neyman-Pearson point of view, what matters about the likelihood function is only its maximum and curvature in the neighborhood of the maximum, and all the desirable properties and the assessment of the reliability of the maximum-likelihood estimates are only asymptotic. From this standpoint, boundary solutions are much more than inconvenient. That only the maximum and the Hessian at the maximum are all that matters from a conventional point of view is perhaps not surprising in view of the fact that for the mean of a normal distribution, the quadratic approximation is exact and, because of the central limit theorem in its many forms, many estimators, including ML estimators in regular cases, tend to normality in distribution. So the problem of possible inconsistency of the ML estimates should not concern us unduly from the standpoint of likelihood inference. It is the whole shape of the likelihood function that expresses what the data have to say about the model and its parameters that matters.[4] For this reason, "slices" or sections of the multidimensional likelihood functions are

---

[4] Maddala (1971, p. 346) shows that the likelihood function may have at most two local maxima. In work not reported here, I have obtained likelihood functions with two local maxima, one for large values of ρ and small γ, the other for large γ and ρ close to 0. When these yield a similar value of the likelihood function, I would argue that the data are telling us that it's difficult to distinguish. A method that does must, therefore, be misleading. For the cross-country data considered in this paper, I do not find evidence of two local maxima, but rather that the likelihood function is rather flat in the ρ direction, which leads to the conclusion that the data are relatively noninformative with respect to ρ.

also presented in the empirical example of the next subsection. In Subsection 2.b, I consider a model in which first differences are taken to eliminate a linear deterministic trend; in this case, the individual-specific time invariant effects become differences in the trend slopes. This makes the interpretation of the model in first-difference form different from that in levels. Moreover, the time- and individual-varying disturbance is now likely to be serially correlated (indeed, to follow a first order MA process with unit root), a fact that needs to be taken into account in the formulation of the unconditional-likelihood function. A parallel set of results for the individual-specific trends model is presented in Subsection 2.b.

a. The Model in Levels

For simplicity, I restrict attention to the simple model containing one exogenous variable x_{it} and one lagged value of the dependent variable y_{it-1} as explanatory. Extension to the case in which more than one exogenous explanatory variable is included presents no serious difficulty.

$$Y_{it} = \alpha + \beta x_{it} + \gamma y_{it-1} + \mu_i + \varepsilon_{it}, i = 1, \ldots N, t = 1, \ldots T. \qquad (1)$$

Taking deviations from overall means eliminates the constant α. The usual assumptions are made about the properties of the μ_i and the ε_{it}:

(i) $E(\mu_i) = E(\varepsilon_{it}) = 0$, all i and t,

(ii) $E(\mu_i \varepsilon_{jt}) = 0$, all i, j and t,

(iii) $E(\mu_i \mu_j) = \begin{cases} \sigma_\mu^2 & i = j \\ 0 & i \neq j, \end{cases}$

(iv) $E(\varepsilon_{it} \varepsilon_{js}) = \begin{cases} \sigma_\varepsilon^2 & t = s, i = j \\ 0 & \text{otherwise.} \end{cases}$

Both μ_i and ε_{it} are assumed to be uncorrelated with x_{it} for all i and t. While this assumption is far from innocuous, for example, if the independent variable x_{it} is not independent of the dependent variable y_{it} or unobserved factors that affect it, I adopt it here, not only because it is conventional, but also because one has to cut off somewhere. Clearly, however, y_{it-1} cannot be assumed to be uncorrelated with μ_i.

(1) Specification of the Joint Distribution of the Observations, Both Conditional and Unconditional on the Initial Observations. The intraclass correlation coefficient ρ is defined as $\sigma_\mu^2/(\sigma_\mu^2 + \sigma_\varepsilon^2)$. This parameter measures the extent of unobserved or latent time-invariant, individual-specific, variation relative to the total unobserved variation in the sample. It is extremely important in understanding the nature of the variation, both observed and unobserved,

in the panel. Also useful are the characteristic roots of Ω = the variance-covariance matrix of the disturbances $u_{it} = \mu_i + \varepsilon_{it} : \xi = 1 - \rho + T\rho$ and $\eta = 1 - \rho$.[5] $\lambda = 1 + T\rho/(1 - \rho)$ measures the *relative* information contributed over time by the individual specific unobserved effects μ for each individual.

If $|\gamma| \leq 1$ or the processes generating the x_{it} are not stationary, it will not make sense to assume that the process generating the y_{it} is the same prior to the period of observation as for $t = 1, \ldots T$. I will assume that, possibly after some differencing, both the y_{it} and the x_{it} are stationary. In this case, the initial observations are determined by

$$y_{i0} = \sum_{j=0}^{\infty} \gamma^j \beta x_{i,-j} + \frac{1}{1-\gamma} \mu_i + v_{i0}, \quad \text{where } v_{it} = \gamma v_{it-1} + \varepsilon_{it}.^{6,7} \quad (2)$$

The joint distribution of $y_{iT}, \ldots, y_{i1}, y_{i0}$ depends on the distribution of μ_i, ε_{it}, and x_{it}. If y_{i0} is literally taken as fixed, which is to deny the plausible assumption that it is generated by the same process as generates the y_{it} that are observed, the conditional likelihood function for the model (1) with $u_{it} = \mu_i + \varepsilon_{it} \sim N(0, \sigma^2 \Omega)$ is derived in the usual way from the product of the densities of y_{it} conditional on x_{it} and y_{it-1}, the joint density is conditional on y_{i0}.[8]

---

[5] The GLS estimates for a regression based on the variance-covariance matrix of the disturbances in (1) has a ready interpretaion in terms of these roots. A regression of the means for each cross-sectional observation over time and a pooled regression of the individual observations taken as deviations from these means both contain information about the parameters of the model. The means regression reflects purely cross-sectional variation; whereas, the fixed-effects regression reflects the individual variation over time. GLS combines these two types of information with weights that depend on the characteristic roots of $Euu' = \sigma^2 \Omega$. The individual means themselves are weighted by the reciprocal of the square root of $\xi = 1 - \rho + T\rho$, while the deviations from these means are weighted by the reciprocal of the square root of $\eta = 1 - \rho$. A representative transformed observation is

$$y_{it}^* = \xi^{-1/2} \bar{y}_{i\cdot} + \eta^{-1/2}(y_{it} - \bar{y}_{i\cdot}), \quad i = 1, \ldots, N, \quad t = 1, \ldots, T.$$

The GLS estimates are just the OLS estimates using the transformed observations. The GLS estimates are appropriate when the model is not dynamic (*i.e.*, $\gamma = 0$), or when the initial values y_{i0} are literally assumed to be fixed. It is not, as we shall see, appropriate when the same data-generating process assumed to generate the observations is also assumed to generate the values of the dependent variable prior to the period of observation.

[6] For a particular time period T and the infinite past

$$y_{iT} = \gamma^{\infty} y_{i-\infty} + \sum_{j=0}^{\infty} \gamma^j \beta x_{T-j} + \frac{1-\gamma^{\infty}}{1-\gamma} \mu_i + v_{iT}, \quad \text{where } v_{iT} = \sum_{j=0}^{\infty} \gamma^j \varepsilon_{iT-j}.$$

Since $1 \geq |\gamma|$, and $v_{iT} = \sum_{j=0}^{\infty} \gamma^j \varepsilon_{iT-j}$ is the MA form of a first-order autoregression with white-noise input, equation (2) follows.

[7] If all variables are expressed as deviations from their overall means, there is no need to include an intercept; if not, μ_i should be replaced by $\alpha + \mu_i$.

[8] By repeated application of the definition of the *joint distribution* in terms of the product of the conditional and the marginal, it can easily be seen that the joint distribution is the product of the conditional distributions $f(y_{iT} \mid y_{iT-1}) \ldots f(y_{i1} \mid y_{i0})$, for fixed y_{i0}. Unfortunately, when

This likelihood function can be written in terms of the notation introduced previously as

$$\log L\left(\alpha, \beta, \gamma, \sigma_\mu^2, \sigma_\varepsilon^2 | y_{11}, \ldots, y_{NT}; x_{11}, \ldots x_{NT}; y_{10}, \ldots, y_{N0}\right)$$

$$= -\frac{NT}{2}\log 2\pi - \frac{NT}{2}\log\sigma^2 - \frac{N}{2}\log\xi - \frac{N(t-1)}{2}\log\eta$$

$$- \frac{1}{2\sigma^2}\sum_{i=1}^{N}\sum_{t=1}^{T}(y_{it}^* - \beta x_{it}^* - \gamma y_{it-1}^*)^2, \tag{3}$$

where y^*, x^*, and y_{-1}^* are the transformed variables and the overall constant has been eliminated by expressing all observations as deviations from their overall means.[9] Since

$$\xi = \frac{T}{1 + \lambda(T-1)} \quad \text{and} \quad \eta = \frac{\lambda T}{1 + \lambda(T-1)},$$

$\log L$ can be expressed as a function solely of $\lambda, \sigma^2, \alpha, \beta,$ and γ. λ is defined previously. Trognon (1978) shows that, when the exogenous variable x is generated by a first-order autoregression with white-noise input,

$$x = \delta x_{-1} + w, \tag{4}$$

$w \sim wn(0, \sigma_w^2 I)$, also assumed in the Monte Carlo experiments reported in Nerlove (1971), maximization of the conditional-likelihood function (3) yields boundary solutions $\hat{\rho} = 0$, which, unlike interior maximum-likelihood solutions, are inconsistent, for a considerable and, indeed, likely range of parameter values. In particular, there is a value of γ in (1),

$$\gamma^* = \frac{(T-3)^2 - 8}{(T+1)^2},$$

such that when $\gamma < \gamma^*$, there exists an interior maximum of (3) that yields consistent ML estimates, but that when $\gamma \geq \gamma^*$, there are values of ρ for which the likelihood function (3) is maximized at the boundary $\rho = 0$ (*i.e.*, for the OLS estimates of the pooled regression of untransformed observations, which we know to be inconsistent). The problem is that when T is small, the permissible range of γ, the coefficient of the lagged dependent variable, is implausible (*e.g.*, negative or very small). For example, for $T = 5$, we get $\gamma^* = -0.11$, while for $T = 10$, we get $\gamma^* = 0.34$. When $\gamma \geq \gamma^*$, whether or not an interior maximum with consistent ML estimates occurs depends on the value of ρ. For $\rho < \rho^{**}$,

---

the y_{i0} are generated by the same process that generates the observed values of $y_{it}, t = 1\ldots T$, this convenient "Markov" property no longer holds. This unfortunate fact seems first to have been pointed out by Blundell and Smith (1991). I am indebted to P. Sevestre, A. Trognon, and an anonymous referee for pointing out the error in my original formulation and the reference to Blundell and Smith's paper.

[9] See the explanation of this transformation in Footnote 5.

boundary maxima occur where

$$\rho^{**} = \left(\frac{T-1}{T+1}\right)^2 \frac{\beta^2 \sigma_w^2}{\sigma^2} \frac{1-\gamma}{(\gamma - \gamma^*)(1 - \gamma\delta)^2}.$$

For example, when $T = 5$, $\beta = 1.0$, $\gamma = 0.75$, $\delta = 0.5$, $\gamma^* = -0.11$, and the critical value of ρ is $\rho^{**} = 0.31$. That means that any true value of the intraclass correlation less than 0.31 is liable to produce a boundary solution to (2) $\rho = 0$ and inconsistent estimates of all the parameters. Using these results, Trognon (1978) is able to replicate the Monte Carlo results reported in Nerlove (1971).[10]

Because the likelihood function (3), which assumes the initial observations to be given exogenously, has generally been the basis for inference about dynamic panel models, I compare the results obtained therefrom with alternative estimates based on the assumption that the initial ys are generated by the same DGP as generated by the within-sample observations in Subsection 3.

To proceed in a manner consistent with the hypothesis that the presample values are generated by the same process as the within-sample observations, we need to derive the joint distribution of $y_{iT}, \ldots, y_{i1}, y_{i0}$ from (1) and (2). Since ε_{it} and μ_i are assumed to be independently normally distributed with mean zero and variances σ_ε^2 and σ_μ^2 respectively, matters depend on what is assumed about how the x_{it} are generated in the presample period even though we may propose to condition on the observed values within the sample period. Consider a single individual i of the N observed. Various alternative specifications considered in the literature are reported and analyzed in Sevestre and Trognon (1996, pp. 136–138).[11] Considerable simplification, however, can be obtained if, following Nerlove (1971), we are willing to assume that x_{it} follows a well-specified common stationary time-series model for all individuals i. The first term in (2) is

$$\varphi_{i0} = \beta \sum_{j=0}^{\infty} \gamma^j x_{i,-j}.$$

[10] Maddala (1971, pp. 346–347) gives a condition for the gradient of the concentrated likelihood function to be positive at a boundary $\rho = 0$ (OLS on the pooled data) for the conditional likelihood function. So if ρ is constrained to the interval $[0, 1)$, this implies a local maximum at the boundary 0. Breusch (1987) shows that this condition can be easily checked at the start of his iterative GLS procedure by beginning with the pooled OLS estimates and $\rho = 0$. Unfortunately, these results apply only to the likelihood function when no lagged value of the dependent variable is included or when those initial values are assumed fixed. I have not been able to derive a similar result for the unconditional-likelihood function.

[11] One interesting possibility discussed by Sevestre and Trognon (1996, p. 136–138) is to choose y_{i0} a linear function of some *observed* individual-specific time-invariant exogenous variables and a disturbance that is decomposed as the sum of the individual-specific disturbances μ_i and a remainder. The first-order equations for maximizing the likelihood then take on a simple recursive form when $\beta = 0$, and permit other simplification when $\beta \neq 0$. But if we knew some individual-specific time-invariant observed variables influenced behavior, why not incorporate them directly in (2), the equation to be estimated?

Hence, for any stationary processes x_{it} which may be serially correlated

$$\frac{\varphi_{it}}{\beta} = \gamma \frac{\sigma_{it-1}}{\beta} + x_{it}$$

with variances that depend on the serial autocovariances of the exogenous variable in the presample period, say $\Gamma_i(j) = \text{cov}(x_{it}, x_{it-j})$,

$$\sigma_{\varphi_i}^2 = \frac{\beta^2 \sigma_{x_i}^2 + 2\gamma \sum_{j=0}^{\infty} \gamma^j \Gamma_i(j+1)}{1 - \gamma^2}. \tag{5}$$

If we suppose that each x_{it} follows a first-order autoregressive process common for all i,

$$x_{it} = \delta x_{it-1} + \omega_{it}, \quad \omega_{it} \text{ iid} \sim (0, \sigma_\omega^2),$$

then the random variable

$$\phi_{it} = \sum_{j=0}^{\infty} \gamma^j \beta x_{it-j}$$

has a well-defined variance, which is the same for all i and a function of β, γ, and σ_x^2,

$$\sigma_0^2 = \frac{\beta^2 \sigma_x^2 (1 + \gamma\delta)}{(1 - \gamma^2)(1 - \gamma\delta)}. \quad ^{12}$$

The joint distribution of

$$\begin{bmatrix} \mu_i + \varepsilon_{iT} \\ \vdots \\ \mu_i + \varepsilon_{i1} \\ y_{i0} \end{bmatrix} \text{ is } N(0, \Sigma),$$

where

$$\Sigma = \begin{bmatrix} \sigma_\varepsilon^2 I_T + \sigma_\mu^2 e_T e_T' & d^* e_T \\ d^* e_T' & \sigma_0^2 \end{bmatrix}, e_T = \begin{bmatrix} 1 \\ \vdots \\ 1 \end{bmatrix},$$

---

[12] I am indebted to A. Trognon for pointing this out to me. When the x_{it} are serially correlated more generally, the result is much more complicated. See Bhargava and Sargan (1983). In Subsection 3, I assume that the xs are generated in the presample period by first-order autoregressions common to all individuals and estimate both the common variance and common serial correlation from the pooled within-sample variation of the xs. With only four or five time points, little else seems feasible. The first-order serial correlations are indeed rather small so that this correction makes hardly any difference to the results as compared with those assuming the xs are random.

with

$$\sigma_0^2 = \frac{\beta^2 \sigma_x^2 (1 + \gamma\delta)}{(1 - \gamma^2)(1 - \gamma\delta)} + \frac{\sigma_\mu^2}{(1 - \gamma)^2} + \frac{\sigma_\varepsilon^2}{1 - \gamma^2} \quad \text{and} \quad d^* = \frac{\sigma_\mu^2}{1 - \gamma}.$$

The joint density of $y_{iT}, \ldots, y_{i1}, y_{i0}$ given the within-sample observations on $x_{iT}, \ldots, x_{i1}$, JPDF, may be factored into the product of the joint conditional on y_{i0}, CPDF, and the marginal of y_{i0}, MPDF.

$$\text{MPDF} = \frac{1}{\sqrt{2\pi\sigma_0^2}} \exp\left\{ -\frac{1}{2\sigma_0^2} y_{i0}^2 \right\}, \qquad (6)$$

and

$$\text{CPDF} = \frac{1}{(2\pi)^{\frac{T}{2}}} |S|^{-\frac{1}{2}} \exp\left\{ -\frac{1}{2} v' S^{-1} v \right\}, \qquad (7)$$

where

$$v = \begin{bmatrix} y_{iT} - \beta x_{iT} - \gamma y_{iT-1} - \dfrac{c}{\sigma_0^2} y_{i0} \\ \vdots \\ y_{i1} - \beta x_{i1} - \gamma y_{i0} - \dfrac{c}{\sigma_0^2} y_{i0} \end{bmatrix}, \qquad (8)$$

with $c = \dfrac{\sigma_\mu^2}{1 - \gamma}$, and where

$$S = \sigma_\varepsilon^2 I_T + \zeta^2 e_T e_T', \qquad (9)$$

with $\zeta^2 = \sigma_\mu^2 - \dfrac{c^2}{\sigma_0^2}$.

Note that while c cannot be negative as long as $|\gamma| < 1$, ζ^2 could be if the variance σ_0^2 were small enough, but this is unlikely for plausible values of the parameters β, γ, σ^2, and ρ.

(2) The Joint Likelihood Conditional on the Initial Observations and the Exogenous Variables. The conditional likelihood, CLF, for the parameters β, γ, σ^2, and ρ is the log of the product of the CPDFs in (7) over individuals. Note that the problem has been reparameterized in terms of c, σ_0^2, ζ^2, and S, but these are all functions of the original four parameters and the observations withinsample of the dependent and explanatory variables; once the parameters β, γ, σ^2, and ρ are given, so are c, σ_0^2, ζ^2, and S, and the value of the CLF for the sample data. But the CLF is not so easy to calculate, since S, albeit block diagonal, is rather large and must be inverted. The usual trick in such cases is to diagonalize S using an orthogonal transformation; provided we introduce two additional reparameterizations, we can cast the problem into

the form used to formulate the GLS estiamtors. Let

$$q^2 = \sigma_\varepsilon^2 + \zeta^2 \quad \text{and} \quad \rho^* = \frac{\zeta^2}{q^2}, \text{ so that } 1 - \rho^* = \frac{\sigma_\varepsilon^2}{q^2}.$$

S is then diagonalized with the characteristic roots

$$\xi^* = 1 - \rho^* + \rho^* T,$$
$$\eta^* = 1 - \rho^*,$$

along the diagonal by the transform

$$v_i^* = (\xi^*)^{-\frac{1}{2}}\left(\frac{1}{T}\right)e_T e_T' v_i + (\eta^*)^{-\frac{1}{2}}\left(I_T - \frac{1}{T}e_T e_T'\right)v_i.$$

The joint conditional likelihood, CLF, can now be written:

$$\log L(\beta, \gamma, \rho, \sigma^2 \mid y_{11}, \ldots, y_{NT}; x_{11}, \ldots x_{NT}; y_{10}, \ldots, y_{N0})$$
$$= -\frac{NT}{2}\log 2\pi - \frac{NT}{2}\log q^2 - \frac{N}{2}\log \xi^* - \frac{N(T-1)}{2}\log \eta^*$$
$$- \frac{1}{2q^2}\sum_{i=1}^{N}\sum_{t=1}^{T}(v_{it}^*)^2. \tag{10}$$

(10) is the same form as (3), but ξ, η, and q^2, as well as v^*, are complex transforms of β, γ, σ^2, and ρ and the observations.

(3) The Joint Likelihood Unconditional on the Initial Observations. To obtain the joint unconditional likelihood, we may simply take the log of the product of the joint marginal PDFs of the initial observations and add it to the CLF in (10); thus,

$$\log L(\beta, \gamma, \rho, \sigma^2 \mid y_{11}, \ldots, y_{NT}; x_{11}, \ldots x_{NT}; y_{10}, \ldots, y_{N0})$$
$$= -\frac{NT}{2}\log 2\pi - \frac{NT}{2}\log q^2 - \frac{N}{2}\log \xi^* - \frac{N(T-1)}{2}\log \eta^*$$
$$- \frac{1}{2q^2}\sum_{i=1}^{N}\sum_{t=1}^{T}(v_{it}^*)^2$$
$$- \frac{N}{2}\log(\sigma_0^2) - \left[\frac{1}{2\sigma_0^2}\right]\sum_{i=1}^{N}y_{i0}^2. \tag{11}$$

Concentrating the likelihood function to permit a one- or two-dimensional grid search is not possible. Nor is it possible to graph the likelihood surface with respect to variations in all of the parameters. However, "slicing" the likelihood function along any hyperplane in the parameter space can reveal the trade-offs between any pair of parameters. If gradient or search procedures yield an interior maximum, the ML estimates obtained are consistent as long as the random variables $\phi_{it} = \sum_{j=0}^{\infty}\gamma^j\beta x_{i,t-j}$ have well-defined variances and covariances, which they will if the x_{it} are generated by a stationary process. It doesn't really matter what this process is as long as it is stationary. Besides, since the x_{it} are assumed to be exogenous, we really have no basis on which to model their determination and are likely to misspecify this part of the model. In this sense, we ought to prefer this kind of "almost full-information" maximum likelihood. Still, we have to assume something about the variance of the x process in order to proceed. I suggest estimating σ_x^2 from the sample data.

To generalize these results to the case in which there are several explanatory variables in addition to the lagged value of the dependent variable, assume that X_{it} follows a stationary VAR process and replace βx_{it}^*, by $X_{it}^* \beta$ and $\beta^2 \sigma_x^2$ by $\beta' \Sigma_{XX} \beta$ in the previous formula.

The expression

$$\varphi^2 = \frac{\beta^2 \sigma_x^2 (1 + \gamma \delta)}{(1 - \gamma^2)(1 - \gamma \delta)} + \frac{\sigma_\mu^2}{(1 - \gamma)^2} + \frac{\sigma_\varepsilon^2}{1 - \gamma^2}$$

is the unconditional variance of the initial observations y_{i0}. The absolute value of the difference between the log of the unconditional-likelihood function and the log of the conditional-likelihood function is

$$f(\varphi^2) = \frac{N}{2} \left[\log 2\pi + \log \varphi^2 + \frac{\operatorname{var} y_0}{\varphi^2} \right]. \tag{12}$$

$f(\varphi^2)$ is an increasing function of N and var y_0, but given N and var y_0, reaches a minimum for $\varphi^2 = \operatorname{var}(y_0)$ (*i.e.*, when the sample value is close to the true value of the unconditional variance of the initial observations). So the larger the number of cross-section observations and the larger the sample variance of the initial observations, the greater the information contained in them about the prior operation of the process that generated the data. But the closer are φ^2 and var y_0, the less informative are the initial observations on the dependent variable.

b. The Model in First Differences[13]

Adding an individual-specific trend, t, to (1)

$$y_{it} = \alpha + \beta x_{it} + \gamma y_{it-1} + \tau_i t + \mu_i + \varepsilon_{it}, i = 1, \ldots N, t = 1, \ldots T, \tag{13}$$

and differencing,

$$\Delta y_{it} = \beta \Delta x_{it} + \gamma \Delta y_{it-1} + \tau_i + \omega_{it}, \omega_{it} = \Delta \varepsilon_{it}, i = 1, \ldots N, t = 1, \ldots T, \tag{14}$$

---

[13] I am indebted to P. Balestra for his suggestions on how to work out the likelihood functions in the first-difference case. The transformation is a special case of that given in Balestra (1980), special because the parameter of the MA process in the disturbances is *a priori* known to be 1. Baltagi and Li (1994), in a paper that later came to my attention, also give a transformation that would permit the same derivation.

where Δ denotes the first-difference operator and τ_i is the individual-specific trend coefficient, assumed to have mean zero (enforced by eliminating any overall constant in the differences by deducting the sample means). Thus, not only is the meaning of ρ altered, but also if ε_{it} did not contain a unit root to start with, ω_{it} will now; in particular, if ε_{it} is not serially correlated to start with, ω_{it} will follow a first-order moving average process with unit root. The variance-covariance matrix of the new disturbances $w_{it} = \tau_i + \Delta\varepsilon_{it}$ is now block diagonal with blocks:

$$A = \tilde{\sigma}^2 \begin{bmatrix} 1 & a & b & \dots b \\ a & 1 & a & b .. \\ b & a & 1 & a \dots \\ \vdots & \vdots & \vdots & \dots 1 \end{bmatrix},$$

where $\tilde{\sigma}^2 = \sigma_\tau^2 + 2\sigma_\varepsilon^2$, $a = \dfrac{\sigma_\tau^2 - \sigma_\varepsilon^2}{\sigma^2}$, and $b = \dfrac{\sigma_\tau^2}{\tilde{\sigma}^2}$.

Let $z_{it} = [\Delta y_{i,t-1} \Delta x_{it}]$ and $\delta = [\gamma \beta]'$, $w_{i,t} = \tau_i + \omega_{i,t}$, $\omega_{i,t} = \Delta\varepsilon_{i,t}$. Assume

(i) $E(\tau_i) = E(\omega_{i,t}) = 0, \quad \forall i, t$

(ii) $E(\tau_i \omega_{j,t}) = 0, \quad \forall i, j, t.$

Stacking observations over time, we can write the model (15) as:

$$\Delta y_{it} = z_{it}\delta + w_{it}, i = 1, 2, \dots, N, t = 2, \dots, T, \text{ or} \tag{15}$$

$$\Delta y_i = z_i\delta + w_i = z_i\delta + (\tau_i e_{T-1} + \omega_i), \quad i = 1, 2, \dots, N, \tag{16}$$

where e_{T-1} is $(T-1) \times 1$ column vector of ones. Now, consider mean vector and the variance-covariance matrix of w_i:

$$E(w_i) = E(\tau_i e_{T-1} + \omega_i) = E(\tau_i)e_{T-1} + E(\omega_i) = 0, \quad \text{by assumption (i).}$$

$$E(w_i w_i') = E[(\tau_i e_{T-1} + \omega_i)(\tau_i e_{T-1} + \omega_i)']$$

$$= E(\tau_i^2)e_{T-1}e_{T-1}' + E(\omega_i \omega_i')$$

$$= \sigma_\tau^2 e_{T-1}e_{T-1}' + \sigma_\varepsilon^2 B, \qquad \text{by assumption (ii),}$$

where B is the $(T-1) \times (T-1)$ variance-covariance matrix of ω_i.

B is a tridiagonal matrix having 2 on the main diagonal and (-1) on the adjacent diagonals.

We can transform the first-differenced data so as to reduce the model in first differences to the previous case, with exactly the same likelihood functions in the differenced and transformed data and one less time observation per individual.

Since matrix B is positive definite and symmetric, there exits a nonsingular matrix, P, such that $PBP' = I_{T-1}$ or $PP' = B^{-1}$. Premultiplying (16) by P

yields

$$P\Delta y_i = Pz_i\delta + Pw_i = Pz_i\delta + P(\tau_i e_{T-1} + \omega_i), \quad \text{or} \qquad (17)$$
$$Y_i = Z_i\delta + W_i,$$

where

$$Y_i = P\Delta y_i, \; Z_i = Pz_i, \quad \text{and} \quad W_i = Pw_i. \qquad (18)$$

Then, $E(W_i) = E(Pw_i) = PE(w_i) = 0$, and

$$\begin{aligned} E(W_i W_i') &= E[(Pw_i)(Pw_i)'] = PE(w_i w_i')P' \\ &= P[\sigma_\tau^2 e_{t-1} e_{T-1}' + \sigma_\varepsilon^2 B]P', \\ &= \sigma_\tau^2(Pe_{T-1})(Pe_{T-1})' + \sigma_\varepsilon^2 PBP' \\ &= \sigma^2 - \tau l_T l_T' + \sigma_\varepsilon^2 I_{T-1}, \end{aligned} \qquad (19)$$

where $l_T = Pe_{T-1}$. (19) is almost the same as the usual error-component structure assumed in the previous case.

We proceed as follows to determine the matrix P and the vector l_T explicitly in order to obtain the required transformation of the data:

Since l_{T-1} is defined as $l_{T-1} = Pe_{T-1}$, we have only to know the structure of the transformation matrix P. Here, we know the variance-covariance matrix B and so the transformation matrix P is easily obtained from the following formula (Balestra, 1980):

$$P = DL, \text{ where } D = diag[\{t(t+1)\}^{-1/2}], \quad \text{and} \qquad (20)$$

$$L = \begin{bmatrix} 1 & 0 & 0 & 0 \\ 1 & 2 & 0 & 0 \\ \cdots & \cdots & \cdots & 0 \\ 1 & 2 & \cdots & (T-1) \end{bmatrix}.$$

Then,

$$l_{T-1} = Pe_{T-1} = \frac{1}{2}\begin{bmatrix} (1 \times 2)^{1/2} \\ (2 \times 3)^{1/2} \\ [(T-1) \times T]^{1/2} \end{bmatrix}, \quad \text{and} \qquad (21)$$

$$l_{T-1}' l_{T-1} = \frac{(T-1)T(T+1)}{12}.$$

Note the difference between this and the previous case, which involves only e_{T-1}.

To obtain the results for the conditional- and the unconditional-likelihood functions that parallel (10) and (11), simply replace Δy_{it}, $\Delta y_{i,t-1}$, and Δz_{it} by the transformed values, Y_{it}, $Y_{i,t-1}$, and Z_{it}, σ_μ^2 by σ_τ^2, and note $\xi^* = 1 - \rho^* + (l_T' l_T)\rho^*$, and $\eta^* = 1 - \rho^*$.

4. AN EMPIRICAL EXAMPLE: A STUDY OF CROSS-COUNTRY ECONOMIC GROWTH USING PANEL DATA

To assess the feasibility and power of likelihood methods for inference about dynamic panel models, I used data on ninety-four countries for the period 1960–1985, and a subsample of twenty-two OECD countries, from the Penn World Tables 5.6, to estimate growth equations based on the Solow-Swan model.

The Solow-Swan model is the basis for almost all previous investigations and for mine as well. Let y_t = per capita output, k_t = the capital-output ratio, s = the savings rate, δ = the depreciation rate of capital, and n = the exogenous rate of population growth and labor force. All of these variables may differ over time as indicated by their subscript t, but also, in a cross-country context, they are certain to differ from one country to another in a fashion that persists over time. An additional subscript is introduced in the subsections that follow this one to indicate that fact. If the production function is Cobb-Douglas, $y_t = A_t k_t^\alpha$, where A_t reflects other than conventional factors of production affecting growth and where α, the elasticity of per capita output with respect to the capital-labor ratio, is often interpreted in terms of capital's share as implied by payment of capital at its marginal product. Under these circumstances, it can easily be shown, using a simple partial-adjustment model, that

$$\log y_t = \frac{\alpha(1-\gamma)}{1-\alpha}[\log s - \log(n+\delta)] + \frac{1-\gamma}{1-\alpha}\log A_t + \gamma \log y_{t-1}. \qquad (22)$$

The speed of convergence to equilibrium is inversely proportional to γ. With growth convergence, $0 < \gamma < 1$. In equilibrium, per capita GDP depends only on the parameters n, s, and the time path of A. In an empirical context, these differ from time to time and country to country. Clearly, the extent of convergence is conditional on s, n, δ and the time path of A_t. In empirical investigations, changing n and s and sometimes a measure of changing A have been introduced. I will examine both models in which A is assumed to be constant, although differing from one country to another, and models in which A_t can be represented by a simple linear trend that plausibly also differs from country to country.

The twenty-two-country sample consists of primarily European countries, all highly developed and tied together by a network of trading relations; the ninety-four-country sample is much more heterogeneous, consisting of the aforementioned twenty-two plus seventy-two additional countries, ranging from Mozambique and Haiti to the former "*Asian Tigers*." This is the same data set that has been used in dozens of previous studies. Following Islam (1995), s and n were computed as quinquennial means over the preceding five-year span for the five years 1965, 1970, 1975, 1980, and 1985; y was taken as the value reported in that year and in 1960 for the lagged value applicable to 1965. In Table 1, the results are presented for the levels model, in which country-specific effects affect the intercepts of the growth equation

Table 1. *Estimates for Levels Model: Initial Values Fixed, Conditional on Initial Values, and Unconditional on Initial Values*

Parameter and Asymptotic SE	Initial Values Fixed	Conditional on Initial Values	Unconditional on Initial Values
	22-Country Sample*		
ρ	0.479556	0.031697	0.160681
	(0.159799)	(0.031697)	(0.0990826)
β	0.190831	0.184085	0.182334
	(0.0437728)	(0.0308587)	(0.0446144)
γ	0.818900	0.847753	0.924592
	(0.0247031)	(0.0177327)	(0.0205759)
σ^2	0.0051711	0.00382173	0.0070908
	(0.00125519)	(0.000516093)	(0.00113581)
Value of the log likelihood at the maximum	150.428	150.555	125.534
	94-Country Sample**		
ρ	0.11335	0.083019	0.237873
	(0.0498337)	(0.0409863)	(0.0998864)
β	0.13698	0.134063	0.107422
	(0.0131633)	(0.0115891)	(0.00946837)
γ	0.933858	0.884125	0.905776
	(0.0122516)	(0.0224599)	(0.0225057)
σ^2	0.0193751	0.019816	0.0249423
	(0.00130877)	(0.0014518)	(0.00322775)
Value of the log likelihood at the maximum	264.927	266.379	219.119

*Pooled variance of z used = 0.00685407;
  first-order auto correlation of exogenous variable = 0.221664 (0.0947161).
**Pooled variance of z used = 0.0825989;
  first-order autocorrelation of exogenous variable = 0.0492158 (0.0461772).

and, in Table 2, for the country-specific trends model, which requires differencing to reduce the process to stationarity. In this case, what I call the first-difference model, the conditional- and unconditional-likelihood functions are defined for the first differences of the original data and the likelihood functions modified from those for the levels model, as described in the preceding subsection.

a. Recent Empirical Investigations

Equation (22) has been widely used to examine the hypothesis of growth convergence (Mankiw *et al.*, 1992, p. 410; Barro and Sala-i-Martin, 1995,

328 *Essays in Panel Data Econometrics*

Table 2. *Estimates for First-Difference Model: Initial Values Fixed, Conditional*
on Initial Values, and Unconditional on Initial Values

Parameter and Asymptotic SE	Initial Values Fixed	Conditional on Initial Values	Unconditional on Initial Values
22-Country Sample*			
ρ	0.0579534	0^a	0.081813
	(0.109428)	boundary solution	(0.0622182)
β	0.0774602	0.0850119	0.166463
	(0.0607837)	(0.0588837)	(0.0645896)
γ	0.609856	0.625553	0.717044
	(0.0535543)	(0.0498566)	(0.0S0307)
σ^2	0.00217154	0.00216912	0.00251659
	(0.000329513)	(0.000327028)	(0.000330903)
Value of the log likelihood at the maximum	145.162	145.006	217.455
94-Country Sample**			
ρ	0.23146	0^b	0^c
	(0.0682271)	boundary solution	boundary solution
β	0.151188	0.16218	0.157364
	(0.0198895)	(0.0194522)	(0.0185484)
γ	0.603417	0.722558	0.709571
	(0.0434691)	(0.0444235)	(0.04253)
σ^2	0.0144502	0.0141222	0.0134793
	(0.00117773)	(0.0010374)	(0.000931503)
Value of the log likelihood at the maximum	275.38	268.000	403.267

*Pooled variance of z used = 0.00576147;
  first-order autocorrelation of exogenous variable = -0.0741272 (0.107713).
**Pooled variance of z used = 0.0597062;
  first-order autocorrelation of exogenous variable = -0.171714 (0.0509342).
[a] Actual value obtained from unrestricted maximization -0.00233507 (0.0264442).
[b] Actual value obtained from unrestricted maximization -0.0181188 (0.0248979).
[c] Actual value obtained from unrestricted maximization -0.0273869 (0.019909).

Chapter 12; Islam, 1995, p. 1133; Lee *et al.*, 1996; and Casseli *et al.*, 1996).
In empirical work, y_t, is replaced by real per capita GDP; when varying s and
n are taken into account, s is replaced by an average savings rate over the
period $t - 1$ to t, and n is replaced by the growth rate of population over the
period $t - 1$ to t. It is usual to use rates averaged over several years; following
Islam (1995) and others, I have used quinquennial averages. The restriction on
the coefficients of $\ln(s)$ and $\ln(n + \delta)$, which arises from the constant-returns-
to-scale assumption, implies that $\ln(s)$ and $\ln(n + \delta)$ can be collapsed into a

single variable. Testing the growth-convergence hypothesis, in this context, revolves largely around the coefficient γ of the initial level of per capita real GDP. If this is positive but much less than one, the implication is that, on average, countries with low initial values are growing faster than those with high initial values and is, therefore, evidence of convergence. Whereas, if this coefficient is close to one, perhaps even slightly larger than one, the implication is that initial values have little or no effect or even a perverse one on subsequent growth; such a finding is, therefore, evidence against the neoclassical theory that implies convergence. For example, if $\gamma = 0.9$, convergence to within 90 percent of final equilibrium occurs only in twenty-two periods, which, given quinquennial data, implies one hundred-ten years! Similarly, 0.8 requires fifty-three years, 0.7 requires thirty-two years, while 0.2 requires only seven years and 0.1 is within 90 perecent in five years. In the likelihood analyses reported later, the maximum occurs for the levels model at between 0.85 and 0.93 for both the twenty-two and the ninety-four-country samples; but for the differenced model, the estimates are much lower, 0.6 to 0.7, implying more rapid convergence (to trend, which is hardly "convergence" in any intuitive meaning of that term).

The estimates of γ obtained heretofore using cross-country quinquennial data are generally in excess of 0.7 no matter what econometric procedure is employed, but vary over a wide range, depending on the method, 0.7 to 0.98. But for the differenced model, many estimates of γ are much smaller, in the vicinity of 0.6–0.7.[14] (See Nerlove (1996) for a summary and comparison of many of the standard methods of analysis with one another and with the likelihood methods proposed here.) It is apparent that, for all practical purposes, coefficients in excess of 0.7 represent negligible convergence since, with unchanging s, n, and A, it would take more than a generation to achieve 90 percent of equilibrium real per capita GDP. Most recent work attempts to test whether $\gamma = 1$; however, this is a test for unit root in log y_{it}. Even under the best of circumstances, testing for a unit root is problematic.[15]

Tests based on a single cross-section (which can be viewed as a panel of time dimension 1) or on pooled cross-section time-series (panel) data generally

---

[14] Using a GMM estimator derived from a modified Chamberlain approach (Chamberlain, 1984; Crépon and Mairesse, 1996) Caselli *et al.* (1996) obtain an estimate of about 0.51–0.53, *i.e.*, much more rapid convergence, but still not close to the estimates obtained for the ninety-four-country sample using either conditional or unconditional ML, even for the first-differenced data.

It is interesting to note that these methods are basically instrumental variable methods that use lagged values of the explanatory variables as instruments, an approach that was employed in Balestra and Nerlove (1966) to obtain initial consistent estimates of the residual variance-covariance matrix on which to base feasible GLS.

[15] Bernard and Durlauf (1995) use co-integration techniques on rather longer time-series for fifteen OECD countries to test alternative time-series definitions of convergence and contrast the results with the standard formulation.

have yielded contradictory results: pooled panel data studies tend to reject the hypothesis of convergence (relatively high γs), even after controlling for population growth rates, savings rates, and other variables. Dynamic fixed-effects models are, of course, not possible for a single cross-section, but recent work (Islam, 1995) using a dynamic fixed-effects panel model yields results supporting convergence. There are serious problems with tests such as these, which rely on the estimated coefficients of the initial, or lagged value, of the dependent variable in dynamic panel models, or in the special case of a single cross-section, which arise from two sources of bias. In this paper, I contrast these findings with results obtained from likelihood methods that take account of the information contained in the initial observations about the process that must have generated those observations in the presample period. In Nerlove (1996), I showed that many of the earlier findings are probably statistical artifacts arising from biases in the econometric methods employed and now here, especially failure to take advantage of the relatively large amount of information contained in the initial observations and failure to take account of differing country-specific trends. This demonstrates the sensitivity of the conclusions drawn about γ to the econometric method employed, irrespective of the validity of the relationship estimated.

The first source of bias is omitted variables, especially infrastructure and investments over time in infrastructure, and the natural-resource base available to each country in cross-sectional or panel studies. Systematic differences in these across countries or regions will systematically bias the conclusions. Because such variables are likely to be correlated with savings or investment rates in conventional or in human capital and with population growth rates, it is not altogether clear what the net effect of omitting them on the coefficient of the initial value will be in a single cross section.[16] But in a pooled model, it is clear that, to the extent such differences are persistent, they will be highly correlated with the initial value and, therefore, omitting them will bias the coefficient of that variable upward toward one and thus toward rejecting convergence. This source of bias has been well known since the early paper by Balestra and Nerlove (1966) and is well supported by the Monte Carlo studies reported in Nerlove (1971). In this light, it is not surprising that pooled panel data, or single cross sections, which are a special case of panels with $T = 1$, even with inclusion of additional variables, often reject meaningful convergence.

Second, since there are likely to be many sources of cross-country or cross-region differences, many of which cannot be observed or directly accounted for, it is natural to try to represent these by fixed effects in a panel context. But, as is well known from the Monte Carlo investigations reported in Nerlove (1971) and demonstrated analytically by Nickell (1981), inclusion of fixed effects in a dynamic model biases the coefficient of the initial value of the

---

[16] Caselli *et al.* (1996) attempt to control for the endogeneity of these explanatory variables.

dependent variable included as an explanatory variable downward, toward zero and, therefore, toward support for the convergence hypothesis. This may account for Islam's (1995a) recent findings.[17]

Alternative estimates based on more appropriate random-effects models, such as two-stage feasible generalized least squares or maximum-likelihood conditional on the initial observations are also biased in small samples and inconsistent in large, or in the case of instrumental variable estimates have poor sampling properties or are difficult to implement. For example, the papers by Knight, Loayza, and Villanueva (1993); Loayza (1994); and Islam (1995a) employ a method, among others, proposed by Chamberlain (1984), generally referred to as the Π-matrix approach.[18] The alternative of unconditional maximum likelihood suggested in Nerlove and Balestra (1996) is implemented here. In the case of country-specific trends, this method requires differencing the data in order to achieve stationarity, which, in turn, requires a transformation of the differenced data to eliminate first-order MA effects in the disturbances for both the conditional and the unconditional likelihood functions.[19]

Even if one has little interest in the question of convergence or its rate, per se, the question of whether the coefficient of the state variable, lagged dependent or initial value, is biased in the sense of being inconsistent is an important one since biases in this coefficient will affect the estimates of the coefficients of other variables correlated with it and their levels of significance. To the extent such estimates are important in the formulation of policies to promote growth, the matter is indeed a serious one.[20]

b. New Estimates Based on Maximizing the Conditional and Unconditional Likelihood Functions

Tables 1 and 2 present the maximum-likelihood estimates for the levels and for the first-difference model, respectively, for the twenty-two-country and

[17] As pointed out to me by H. Pesaran, these country-specific effects may also be trends, since many of the latent variables specific to each individual in the cross section may themselves be trending. Taking such country-specific trends into account has been one of the great challenges of doing this paper.

[18] See also Crépon and Mairesse (1996).

[19] Lee *et al.* (1996) also estimate from what they maintain is an unconditional-likelihood function, but inasmuch as they do not transform to stationarity (their relationship includes both a constant and a linear trend), I do not think their formulation of the likelihood function based on the unconditional density of the dependent variable is correct. They use annual observations to obtain sufficient degrees of freedom to estimate individual country-specific trends, but I think they are only fooling themselves if they think that much of the information contained in the annual observations is real, as opposed to interpolated.

[20] For example in (13), the parameter α could be derived from the coefficient of the variable $\log s - \log(n + \delta)$ as coefficient/(coefficient $+ 1 - \gamma$), so there is a double source of bias. Indeed, a number of authors accept or reject statistical formulations based on the estimated value of α, which should approximate capital's share.

for the ninety-four country samples (Tables 1 and 2 appear on pages 327–328 above). I give the estimates of ρ, β, the coefficient of the difference $[\log s - \log(n + \delta)]$, γ, the coefficient of the lagged dependent variable, and σ^2, for three methods of estimation: (1) the standard formulation that treats the initial values of the dependent variable as exogenously fixed; (2) ML estimates based on a likelihood function that, although it conditions on the initial values, treats them as having been generated by the same dynamic process that generates the within sample values; and (3) the ML estimates from the unconditional LF under the same assumptions. Presumably, except for computational difficulty, Method (3) should be the method of choice. In Figures 1 through 12, I present slices through the likelihood function in the direction of each of the four parameters at the maximizing values of the other three.

Consider first the levels model: The estimates of ρ, the ratio of the unobserved country-specific variation relative to the total unobserved residual variation, are rather different for the three approaches: for the twenty-two-country sample, these range from 0.48 for the method that assumes the initial values to be given exogenously, to 0.03, effectively 0, for ML conditional on the initial values, to 0.16, also close to zero for ML unconditional on the initial values. For the ninety-four-country sample, the corresponding results are 0.11, 0.08, and 0.23. The estimate value of ρ, even for the method that takes the initial values as exogenously given, is close to zero.

For the first-difference model, the estimates of ρ are not merely close to zero; in several of the ML analyses, boundary solutions with $\rho = 0$ occur: in both cases for conditional ML and for the ninety-four-country sample for unconditional ML.

The values of γ are quite high for all methods of estimation, on the order of 0.9, implying extremely slow convergence, in the levels model, and between 0.6 and just over 0.7 in the case of the differenced model, implying converge to trend at a moderate rate.

The estimates of β are quite similar for each method (except unconditional ML) for given sample and model: 0.18 to 0.19 for the levels model for twenty-two countries and 0.10 to 0.14 for the ninety-four-country sample; 0.08 to 0.16 for twenty-two country and the first-difference model; and about 0.15 for all methods and the ninety-four-country sample.[21] The estimates of σ^2 are also similar for different methods of estimation, but differ across sample and model.

Thus, the parameter whose estimates show the greatest variability both across method and across model and sample is ρ. Since ρ has a different interpretation in the levels than in the differenced model, this is perhaps not

---

[21] From (22), β has the interpretation $\frac{\alpha(1-\gamma)}{1-\alpha}$, so that for $\gamma = 0.8$ and $\beta = 0.15$, α, which estimates capital's share of GDP, is over 40 percent, unreasonably high for most of the countries in the sample.

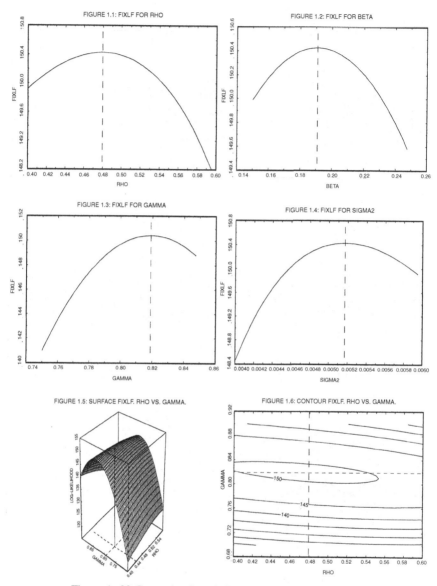

Figure 1. 22 Countries, Levels Model, Fixed Initial Values

too surprising. But ρ is also unreliably determined by the data, as revealed in the likelihood slices, particularly in the three-dimensional slices for ρ and γ holding β and σ^2 at their maximizing values. In interpreting the two-dimensional ρ slices, it is important to pay attention to the scale of variation of the ρ and the corresponding variation in the likelihood; I have graphed the likelihood for a very narrow range of ρ so that the maximum would stand

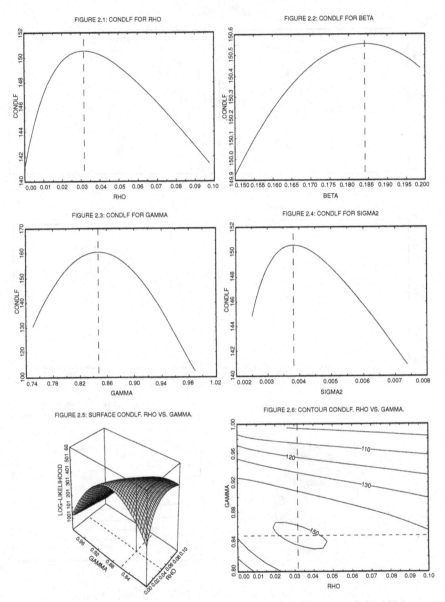

Figure 2. 22 Countries, Levels Model, Likelihood Conditional on Initial Values

out. A more panoramic view would reveal how flat the function really is. This is much better suggested by the three-dimensional slices with ρ and γ varying.

These slices, ρ *versus* γ, suggest that the conventional asymptotic standard errors, which are a reflection of the quadratic approximation to the likelihood

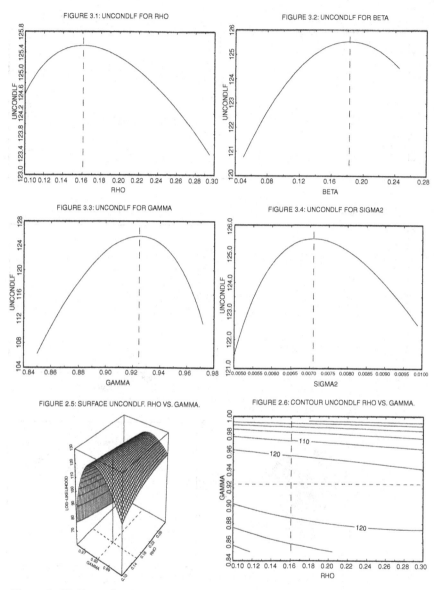

Figure 3. 22 Countries, Levels Model, Likelihood Unconditional on Initial Values

around its maximum, are of some help but not a sure guide to assessing support for the possible values of the parameters. While γ is well determined in most instances, ρ is not. Although the algorithms for maximizing the likelihood functions converged without difficulties in every case, it is clear, especially from more panoramic views than those presented here, that the likelihood

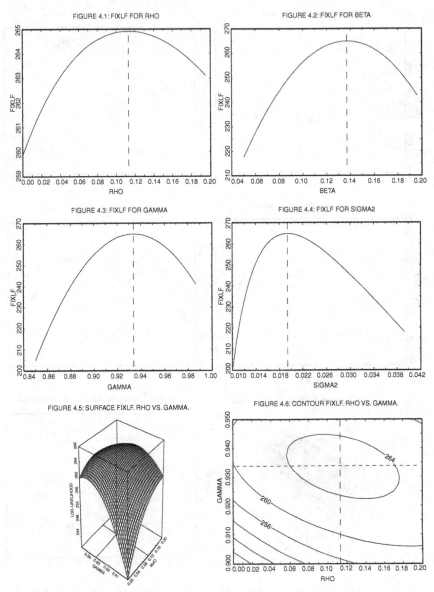

Figure 4. 94 Countries, Levels Model, Fixed Initial Values

functions of the $\rho - \gamma$ "slices" are rather flat over considerable ranges in the ρ direction. Rather than offering much support for the ML estimates, these partial views suggest rather clearly what is *not* supported by the data. A value of ρ much different from zero is not strongly supported by either the conditional- or the unconditional-likelihood functions. However, even for

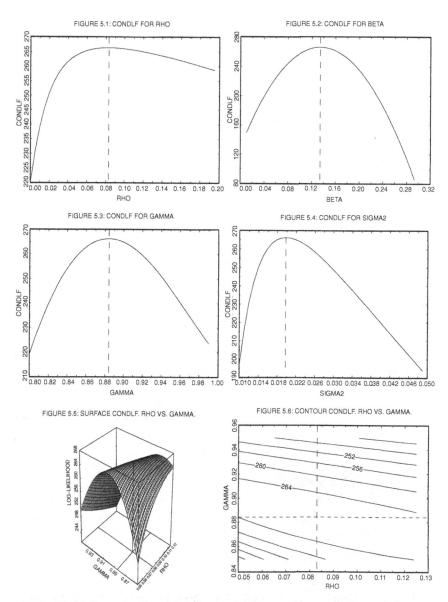

Figure 5. 94 Countries, Levels Model, Likelihood Conditional on Initial Values

values of ρ considerably different from zero, the other parameters are not greatly affected. In particular, estimates of γ about 0.7 in the differenced case and 0.9 in levels case are consistent with the observations.

Apparently, treating the initial values of the dependent variable as determined by the same DGP as assumed to be in operation during the sample

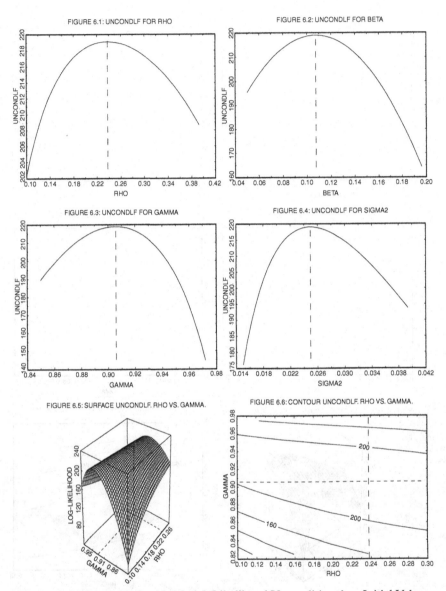

Figure 6. 94 Countries, Levels Model, Likelihood Unconditional on Initial Values

period reduces greatly the effects of unobserved individual-specific time-invariant variability. It is interesting to note that, in the case in which the initial observations are exogenously given, a value of $\rho = 0$ implies that the ML estimates are the OLS estimates obtained from the pooled sample, which we have reason to believe are badly biased (Nerlove, 1971). Yet, remarkably, these estimates, while different from ML assuming the initial values

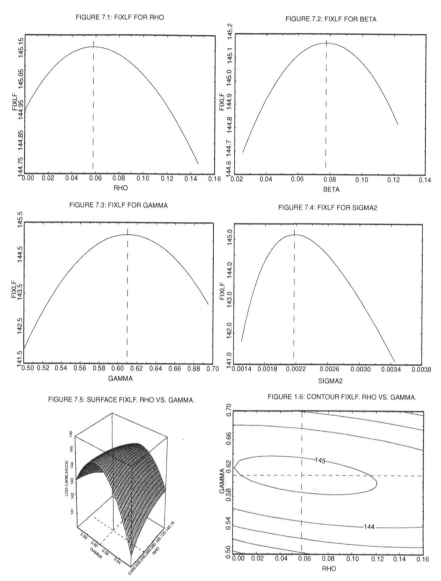

Figure 7. 22 Countries, First-Difference Model, Fixed Initial Values

exogenously given, are not greatly different from those obtained by conditional or unconditional ML. They are reported in Table 3.

It would certainly simplify matters if this finding were the norm in panel data econometrics. Unfortunately, there is little reason to believe that is the case. The results from conditional or unconditional ML are different, and we may not always find ρ close to zero.

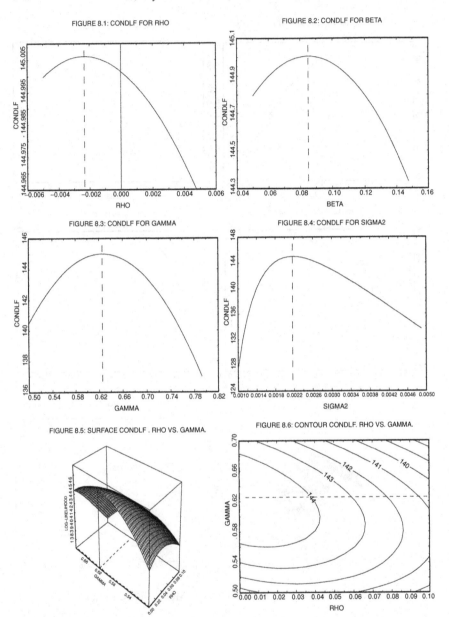

Figure 8. 22 Countries, First-Difference Model, Likelihood Conditional on Initial Values

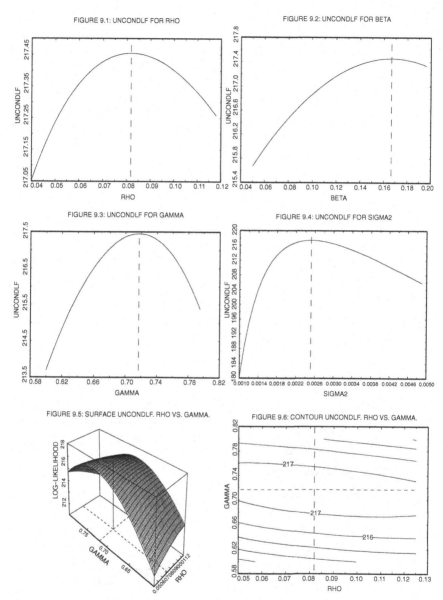

Figure 9. 22 Countries, First-Difference Model, Likelihood Unconditional on Initial Values

Perhaps the greatest benefit of looking at the likelihood function at points in the parameter space away from the likelihood maximizing values is to reveal the fragility of inferences based on the ML and other estimates that may appear to be rather precise.

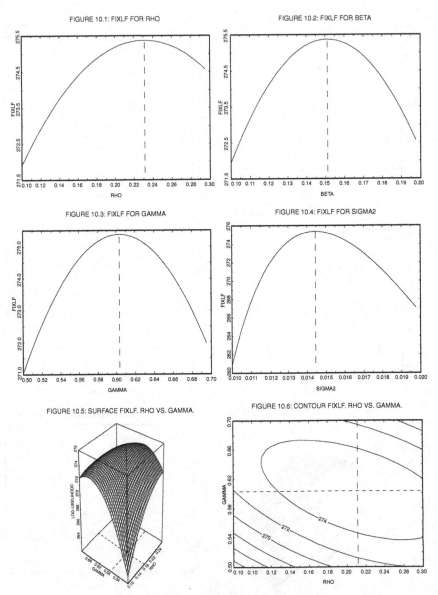

Figure 10. 94 Countries, First-Difference Model, Fixed Initial Values

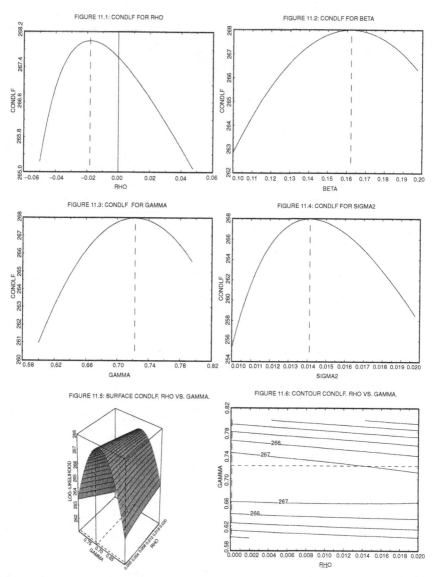

Figure 11. 94 Countries, First-Difference Model, Likelihood Conditional on Initial Values

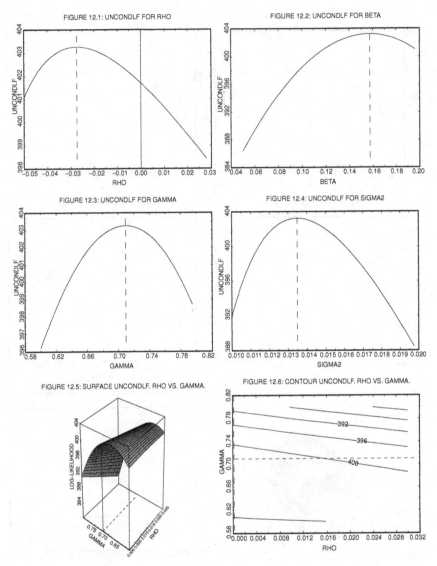

Figure 12. 94 Countries, First-Difference Model, Likelihood Unconditional on Initial Values

Notes to the Tables. *Data on 94 Countries for the Period 1960–1985 from the Penn World Tables 5.6, at http://datacentre.epas.utoronto.ca:5680/pwt/pwt.html.*

22-Country Sample:	94-Country Sample = 22-Country	Sample + the Following:
Japan	Algeria	Uruguay
Austria	Botswana	Venezuela
Belgium	Cameroon	Bangladesh
Denmark	Ethiopia	Hong Kong
Finland	Ivory Coast	India
France	Kenya	Israel
Germany (FRG)	Madagascar	Jordan
Greece	Malawi	Korea
Ireland	Mali	Malaysia
Italy	Morocco	Burma
Netherlands	Nigeria	Pakistan
Norway	Senegal	Philippines
Portugal	South Africa	Singapore
Spain	Tanzania	Sri Lanka
Sweden	Tunisia	Syria
Switzerland	Zambia	Thailand
Turkey	Zimbabwe	Angola
United Kingdom	Costa Rica	Benin
Canada	Dominican Republic	Burundi
United States	El Salvador	Central African Republic
Australia	Guatemala	Chad
New Zealand	Haiti	Congo
	Honduras	Egypt
	Jamaica	Ghana
	Mexico	Liberia
	Nicaragua	Mauritania
	Panama	Mauritius
	Trinidad & Tobago	Mozambique
	Argentina	Niger
	Bolivia	Rwanda
	Brazil	Somalia
	Chile	Togo
	Colombia	Uganda
	Ecuador	Zaire
	Paraguay	Nepal
	Peru	Papua New Guinea

Table 3. *OLS Estimates for the Pooled Sample (Assuming $\rho = 0$)*

Sample/Model	Constant	β	γ	R^2
22 Countries,	−9.97768e-016	0.176383	0.885673	0.979902
Levels	(0.00621794)	(0.0314036)	(0.0127242)	
94 Countries,	−3.93308e-015	0.124376	0.94871	0.981786
Levels	(0.00642963)	(0.0108054)	(0.00908077)	
22 Countries,	8.61813e-017	0.0845224	0.623732	0.701965
First Differences*	(0.00508174)	(0.0600006)	(0.0464055)	
94 Countries,	7.30839e-017	0.163245	0.703141	0.584696
First Differences*	(0.00615419)	(0.0196173)	(0.0329342)	

Note: Regressions based on deviations from overall means: intercept should be zero.
*Data are transformed to eliminate first-order residual MA process.

References

Abbott, E. A. (1884), *Flatland*, New York: Dover, reprinted 1946.

Anderson, T. W., and C. Hsiao (1981), "Estimation of Dynamic Models with Error Components," *Journal of the American Statistical Association*, 76, pp. 598–606.

Anderson, T. W., and C. Hsiao (1982), "Formulation and Estimation of Dynamic Models Using Panel Data," *Journal of Econometrics*, *18*: pp. 47–82.

Balestra, P. (1980), "A Note on the Exact Transformation Associated with the First-Order Moving Average Process," *Journal of Econometrics*, *14*: pp. 381–394.

Balestra, P., and M. Nerlove (1966), "Pooling Cross-Section and Time-Series Data in the Estimation of a Dynamic Economic Model: The Demand for Natural Gas," *Econometrica*, *34*: pp. 585–612.

Baltagi, B. H. (1995), *Econometric Analysis of Panel Data*, New York: Wiley.

Baltagi, B. H., and Q. Li (1994), "Estimating Error-Component Models with General MA(q) Disturbances," *Econometric Theory*, *10*: pp. 396–408.

Barnard, G. A. (1949), "Statistical Inference," *Journal of Royal Statistical Society*, Ser. B11, pp. 115–149.

Barnard, G. A. (1951), "The Theory of Information," *Journal of Royal Statistical Society*, Ser. B13, pp. 46–64.

Barnard, G. A. (1966), "The Use of the Likelihood Function in Statistical Practice," *Proceedings of the Fifth Berkeley Symposium on Mathematical Statistics and Probability*, *1*: pp. 27–40.

Barnard, G. A. (1967), "The Bayesian Controversy in Statistical Inference," *Journal of the Institute of Actuaries*, *93*: pp. 229–269.

Barnard, G. A., Jenkins G. M., and C. B. Winsten (1962), "Likelihood Inference and Time Series," *Journal of Royal Statistical Society*, Ser. A125, pp. 321–372.

Barndorff-Nielsen, O. E. (1988), *Parametric Statistical Models and Likelihood*, Lecture Notes in Statistics, No. 50 Berlin: Springer-Verlag.

Barro, R. J., and X. Sala-I-Martin (1995), *Economic Growth*, New York: McGraw-Hill.

Baumol, W. (1986), "Productivity Growth, Convergence, and Welfare: What the Long-Run Data Show," *American Economic Review*, *76*: pp. 1072–1085.

Bernard, A. B., and S. N. Durlauf (1995), "Convergence in International Output," *Journal of Applied Econometrics*, *10*: pp. 97–108.

Bhargava, A., and J. D. Sargan (1983), "Estimating Dynamic Random-Effects Models from Panel Data Covering Short Time Periods," *Econometrica*, *51*: pp. 1635–1659.

Birnbaum, A. (1962), "On the Foundations of Statistical Inference," *Journal of American Statistical Association*, *57*: pp. 269–306.

Blundell, R., and R. J. Smith (1991), "Conditions initiales et estimation efficace dans les modèles dynamiques sur données de panel," *Annales d'Économie et de Statistique*, *20/21*: pp. 109–124.

Breusch, T. S. (1987), "Maximum-Likelihood Estimation of Random-Effects Models," *Journal of Econometrics*, *36*: pp. 383–389.

Caselli, F., Esquivel, G., and F. Lefort (1996), "Reopening the Convergence Debate: A New Look at Cross-Country Growth Empirics," *Journal of Economic Growth*, *1*: pp. 363–389.

Chamberlain, G. (1984), "Panel Data," pp. 1247–1313 in Z. Griliches and M. Intriligator, eds., *Handbook of Econometrics*, II. Amsterdam: Elsevier.

Cramer, J. S. (1986), *Econometric Applications of Maximum-Likelihood Methods*, Cambridge, UK: Cambridge University Press.

Crépon, B., and J. Mairesse (1996), "The Chamberlain Approach," pp. 323–391 in L. *Mátyás* and P. Sevestre, *op. cit.*

Davidson R., and J. G. MacKinnon (1993), *Estimation and Inference in Econometrics*, New York: Oxford University Press.

De la Fuente, A. (1997), "The Empirics of Growth and Convergence: A Selective Review," *Journal of Economic Dynamics and Control, 21*: pp. 23–73.

Edwards A. W. F. (1972), Likelihood. Cambridge: University Press.

Fisher R. A. (1921), "On the Probable Error of a Coefficient of Correlation Deduced from a Small-Sample Mean," *Metron*, 1(4), pp. 3–32.

Fisher R. A. (1922), "On the Mathematical Foundations of Theoretical Statistics," *Philosophical Transactions of the Royal Society of London*, Series A. 222, pp. 309–368.

Fisher R. A. (1925), "Theory of Statistical Estimation," *Proceedings of the Cambridge Philosophical Society, 22*: pp. 700–725.

Fisher R. A. (1932), "Inverse Probability and the Use of Likelihood," *Proceedings of the Cambridge Philosophical Society, 28*: pp. 257–261.

Fisher R. A. (1990), *Statistical Methods, Experimental Design, and Scientific Inference, Being a Reprint of Statistical Methods for Research Workers* (1925), *The Design of Experiments* (1935), and *Statistical Methods and Scientific Inference* (1956). Oxford: University Press.

Greene W. H. (1993), *"Econometric Analysis, 2nd Edition*, New York: Macmillan.

Hsiao C. (1986), *Analysis of Panel Data*, Cambridge, UK: Cambridge University Press.

Islam N. (1995), "Growth Empirics: A Panel Data Approch," *Quarterly Journal of Economics, 110*: pp. 1127–1170.

Jeffereys H. (1934), "Probability and Scientific Method," *Proceedings of the Royal Society*, Ser. A, *146*: pp. 9–16.

Jeffereys H. (1961), *Theory of Probability*. Oxford: University Press.

Kiviet J. F. (1995), "On the Bias, Inconsistency and Efficiency of Various Estimators in Dynamic Panel Models," *Journal of Econometrics, 68*: pp. 53–78.

Knight M., Loayze N., and D. Villanueva (1993), "Testing the Neoclassical Growth Model," *IMF Staff Papers, 40*: pp. 512–541.

Laplace P. S. 1774–1814, especially *Théorie analytique des probabilités*, 1812. Cited in Stephen M. Stigler, *The History of Statistics*, Chapter 3, "Inverse Probability," pp. 99–138. Cambridge, MA: Harvard University Press, 1986.

Lee K., Pesaran M. H., and R. Smith (1996), "Growth and Convergence: A Multicountry Empirical Analysis of the Solow Growth Model," *unpublished.*

Lindsey J. K. (1996), *Parametric Statistical Inference*. Oxford: Clarendon Press.

Loayza N. (1994), "A Test of the International Convergence Hypothesis Using Panel Data," *Policy Research Working Paper* No. 1333. The World Bank.

Maddala G. S. (1971), "The Use of Variance Components Models in Pooling Cross-Section and Time-Series Data," *Econometrica, 39*: pp. 341–358.

Maddala G. S. (1971), "The Likelihood Approach to Pooling Cross-Section and Time-Series Data," *Econometrica, 39*: pp. 939–953.

Mankiw N. G., Romer D., and D. N. Weil (1992), "A Contribution to the Empirics of Economic Growth," *Quarterly Journal of Economics, 108*: pp. 407–437.

Mátyás L., and P. Sevestre (1996), *"The Econometrics of Panel Data: Handbook of Theory and Applications*. 2nd ed. 1996. Boston: Kluwer Academic Publishers, 1992.

Mundlak Y. (1978), "On the Pooling of Cross-Section and Time-Series Data," *Econometrica, 46*: pp. 69–86.

Nerlove M. (1971), "Further Evidence on the Estimation of Dynamic Economic Relations from a Time-Series of Cross-Sections," *Econometrica, 39*: pp. 359–382.

Nerlove M. (1996), "Growth Rate Convergence, Fact or Artifact? An Essay in Panel Data Econometrics," *paper presented to the Sixth Conference on Panel Data Econometrics*, Amsterdam, 28–29 June.

Nerlove M., and P. Balestra (1996), "Formulation and Estimation of Econometric Models for Panel Data," pp. 3–22 in L. Mátyás and P. Sevestre, *op. cit.*

Nickell S. (1981), "Biases in Dynamic Models with Fixed Effects," *Econometrica, 49*: pp. 1417–1426.

Press S. J. (1989), *Bayesian Statistics: Principles, Models, and Applications*. New York: Wiley.

Saxe J. G. (1880). *The Poems: Complete Edition*, Boston: Houghton, Mifflin & Co.

Sevestre P., A. Trognon (1983). "Propriétés de grands échantillons d'une classe d'estimateurs des modèles autorégressives à erreurs composées," *Annales de l'INSEE, 50*: pp. 25–49.

Sevestre P., and A. Trognon (1996), "Dynamic Linear Models," pp. 120–144 in Mátyás and Sevestre, *op. cit.*

Trognon A. (1978). "Miscellaneous Asymptotic Properties of Ordinary Least-Squares and Maximum-Likelihood Methods in Dynamic Error-Components Models," *Annales de l'INSEE, 30–31*: pp. 631–657.

Name Index

Subject Index

354